Music from a Speeding Train

STANFORD STUDIES IN JEWISH HISTORY AND CULTURE

EDITED BY *Aron Rodrigue and Steven J. Zipperstein*

Music from a Speeding Train
Jewish Literature in Post-Revolution Russia

Harriet Murav

STANFORD UNIVERSITY PRESS

STANFORD, CALIFORNIA

Stanford University Press
Stanford, California

©2011 by the Board of Trustees of the Leland Stanford Junior University. All rights reserved.

This book has been published with the assistance of the Program in Jewish Culture and Society at the University of Illinois.

No part of this book may be reproduced or transmitted in any form or by any means, electronic or mechanical, including photocopying and recording, or in any information storage or retrieval system without the prior written permission of Stanford University Press.

Printed in the United States of America on acid-free, archival-quality paper

Library of Congress Cataloging-in-Publication Data

Murav, Harriet, 1955- author.

    Music from a speeding train : Jewish literature in post-revolution Russia / Harriet Murav.

        pages cm.–(Stanford studies in Jewish history and culture)
Includes bibliographical references and index.
ISBN 978-0-8047-7443-7 (cloth : alk. paper)
   1. Russian literature–Jewish authors–History and criticism. 2. Russian literature–20th century–History and criticism. 3. Yiddish literature–Soviet Union–History and criticism. 4. Yiddish literature–20th century–History and criticism. I. Title. II. Series: Stanford studies in Jewish history and culture.
   PG2998.J4M87 2011
   891.709'892400904–dc22   2011011024

Typeset by Bruce Lundquist in 10.5/14 Galliard

For Bruce

Contents

	Acknowledgments	ix
	Note on Transliteration and Translation	xi
	Introduction	1

Part I: From the Revolution Through the Second World War

1.	The Stillbirth of Revolution	21
2.	Socialist Construction, the *Luftmentsh*, and the New Jew	66
3.	Fighting the Great Patriotic War	111
4.	In Mourning: Responding to the Destruction of the Jews	150

Part II: Postwar Reconstructions

	Introduction	199
5.	*Yeder zeyger a yortsayt*: The Past as Memory in Postwar Literature	209
6.	Jewish Spaces and Retro-Shtetls	245
7.	Translating Empire	285
8.	Afterwards	319
	Notes	347
	Works Cited	371
	Index	395

Acknowledgments

I am grateful to the University of Illinois at Urbana-Champaign for awarding me a Mellon Fellowship for this project in 2004, and to the John Simon Guggenheim Foundation for a fellowship awarded in 2006–2007. The Research Board at the University of Illinois at Urbana-Champaign provided additional generous funding. My colleagues in the Program in Jewish Culture and Society, directed by Matti Bunzl, read and critiqued many chapters, as did graduate students and colleagues in the Russian Reading Circle. The Slavic Reference Service, headed by Helen Sullivan, solved numerous research problems quickly and with a sense of humor, and in so doing showed me new avenues of inquiry. The enormous Slavic collection at the University of Illinois library made fortuitous research accidents possible. Nadja Berkovich and Faith Stein provided invaluable research assistance, going well beyond the call of duty.

I would like to thank Valery Dymshits in St. Petersburg, Inna and Arnol'd Lesovoi in Kiev, and Olga Martynova and Oleg Iur'ev in Frankfurt for hosting me and spending hours talking to me about Russian literature and Jews. I am grateful to Viktor Kel'ner of the Russian National Library in St. Petersburg for his help with David Vygodskii's archive, and for all the conversations we have had about Jewish book production in Russia. Gennady Estraikh and Mikhail Krutikov answered every tedious question I asked them, and generously shared their vast knowledge of Russian and Yiddish literature with me. Eugene Avrutin was consistently supportive. The late Joseph Sherman helped me understand Perets Markish's difficult Yiddish poetry. David Shneer read early versions of the manuscript and provided enthusiastic criticism. Olga Litvak responded promptly and informatively to many random inquiries. Thanks also go to John Garrard for many exchanges about Vasilii Grossman, to Sasha Senderovich for exchanges about Semen Gekht and other writers, and to Marat Grinberg for discussions of Boris Slutskii. Stephanie Sandler's comments and engaged reading of an earlier version of the manuscript led to important revisions. This was not an easy book to write; the emotional weight was overwhelming at times. Steve Zipperstein was amazingly encouraging at precisely the right moments. He understood what I meant immediately, and in more ways than one I could not have finished the project without his support.

Parts of the Introduction and Chapter Seven originally appeared as "Memory and Monument in Baym Dnyeper" in *David Bergelson: From Modernism to Socialist Realism*, edited by Joseph Sherman and Gennady Estraikh (Oxford: Legenda, 2007), reprinted here with the permission of the publisher. A part of Chapter One was published earlier as "Carnival and Catastrophe" in *Word, Music, History: A Festschrift for Caryl Emerson*, edited by Lazar Fleishman and Gabriella Safran (Berkeley, CA: Berkeley Slavic Specialties, 2005), Volume 2. Sections of Chapters Three and Four were first published as "Violating the Canon: Reading Der Nister with Vasilii Grossman" in *Slavic Review*, 67(3), Fall 2008, published by the American Association for the Advancement of Slavic Studies and reprinted here with the permission of the publisher. A portion of Chapter Seven appeared earlier as "The Jew as Translator in Soviet Russia," 26 *Cardozo Law Review* 2401 (2005), and is reprinted here with the permission of the publisher. A section of Chapter Eight was published as "Red Zion" in *Post-Communist Nostalgia*, edited by Maria Todorova and Zsuzsa Gille (New York: Berghahn Books, 2010).

My children, Sam, David, Penelope, and Sissela, supported the work that went into this project, sharing my ups and downs. Bruce Rosenstock lived with the whole thing and read in and around my work, listening to what I had to say. He was unstintingly generous with every discovery I thought I made, and every problem I encountered. He—and his knowledge of philosophy, history, literary criticism, Bible, Talmud, Hebrew, and computers—was always right there, waiting for me.

Note on Transliteration and Translation

In transliterating Russian, I have used the Library of Congress system, and in transliterating Yiddish, I followed the YIVO guidelines, with the exception, for the most part, of words and names commonly appearing in English. Consistency has proved difficult. I use "David" and not "Dovid" and "Moshe" and not "Moyshe." I use "Peretz" in reference to the Yiddish author Yitskhok Leybush, who died in 1915, but "Perets Markish" for the Yiddish author who died in 1952. I use "luftmentsh" and not the more familiar "luftmensch." In transliterating the names of authors who originally wrote in Yiddish and were translated into Russian, I use the Yiddish and not the Russian spelling of the name; for example, "Altman" and not "Al'tman." Transliterating Hebrew words that entered Yiddish and indicating their difference from Hebrew phrases quoted in Yiddish has been especially challenging. I have followed the Soviet Yiddish orthography used by the authors I discuss; for example, I transliterate "yizkor" as "yisker." In transliterating Yiddish appearing in a Russian text, I followed YIVO transliteration rules but also tried to preserve the author's spelling and style, including inaccuracies. Russian appearing in Yiddish received Yiddish transliteration. Unless otherwise noted, all translations are my own.

Music from a Speeding Train

Introduction

> This is how one pictures the angel of history. His face is turned toward the past. Where we perceive a chain of events, he sees one single catastrophe which keeps piling wreckage upon wreckage and hurls it in front of his feet. The angel would like to stay, awaken the dead, and make whole what has been smashed. But a storm is blowing from Paradise; it has caught his wings with such force that the angel can no longer close them. This storm irresistibly propels him into the future to which his back is turned, while the pile of debris before him grows skyward. This storm is what we call progress.
>
> Benjamin 1969, 258

The storm of progress propels Walter Benjamin's "angel of history" into the future, but at the same time, the ongoing catastrophe of history accumulates rubble at his feet. The storm of progress, the pile of debris, and the angel's unfulfilled wish to redeem what has been destroyed shape the landscape of Russian-Jewish and Soviet Yiddish literature of the twentieth century, a century that saw massive dislocation and death, and yet also the creation of an extraordinary literature in both Russian and Yiddish.[1] In a speech given in Warsaw in 1930, the Yiddish writer David Bergelson said that literature from the Soviet Union was like a symphony orchestra playing on an express train. Those standing on the platform hear the "interrupted, incomplete sounds" as the train passes and want to catch it (1930, 439). The train was commonly used as a symbol of progress at this time, but splitting the perspective between those on it and those not was unique to Bergelson. He framed the question of the Jewish reader's response to Soviet literature as a physics problem, the difference between the source and the observer and the effect of relative motion on sound (the Doppler effect). In so doing, Bergelson suggests the fundamental paradox underlining Soviet culture: its actors are always too early or too late for their bright future. It continually eludes them. For those left behind on the platform, the train of progress only piles up disaster. Jewish literature in Russian and Yiddish from the Soviet century is in both places at once—on the rushing express train and on the platform, contemplating the bodies that lie in its wake.

The story of Russian-Jewish and Soviet Yiddish literature in the twentieth century remains largely untold. Most versions end the story in the late 1930s, or in 1952, when leading Yiddish authors were shot. Many critics insist that what was published after the 1920s was the result of force. The story does not end at midcentury, however, but continues into the 1960s and 1970s, when Yiddish and Russian translations of Yiddish resumed publication; and extends through the turn of the twenty-first century, as Russian-Jewish authors craft new works.

Studies by Jeffrey Veidlinger, David Shneer, Gennady Estraikh, Mikhail Krutikov, and Anna Shternshis have demonstrated the importance of Soviet Yiddish institutions and writers, established a model of cultural production in which the categories "Jewish" and "Soviet" could coexist, and argued for the rich cross-fertilization of Yiddish and Russian literature.[2] Other scholars have discussed Russian-Jewish authors such as Isaac Babel, but no full-scale literary study combining Russian and Yiddish is available.[3] The wall that has been erected in the critical literature separating Yiddish from Russian obscures the rich interplay between the two languages and literary traditions. Although some critics, especially Efraim Sicher, have noted that Babel's artistic and political concerns were similar to those of the Yiddish writers of the same period, few discussions include both literatures.[4] It is as if Babel, Perets Markish, and Bergelson lived on different planets, as if Babel did not translate from Yiddish (in addition to editing the translation of Sholem Aleichem, Babel translated Bergelson's story "Dzhiro dzhiro," about a little girl in a New York tenement), and as if he and Bergelson did not speak at the same inaugural conference of the Soviet Writer's Union in 1934. That was when Babel said he had become a "master of the genre of silence." While the critical literature has neglected the literary interactions of Babel, Markish, and Bergelson, the writers themselves were familiar with each other's work. Shimon Markish, the son of the Yiddish writer and an important critical voice in Russian-Jewish literature, has written that both his father and Bergelson were "entranced" by Babel's work.[5] The Russian-language poet Osip Mandelshtam was similarly entranced by the performance of the Yiddish actor Solomon Mikhoels.[6]

This study is a work of restoration, an attempt to recover Jewish literature and culture from the Soviet Union, in order to tell a story long overshadowed by the teleology of "hope to ashes." The recovery does not depend on a trip to archives closed until 1991, when the Soviet Union collapsed. The recovery depends rather on the act of reading. My readings situate Isaac Babel, David Bergelson, Mandelshtam, Perets Markish, Leyb Kvitko, Der Nister, Semen Gekht, Itsik Kipnis, Il'ia Erenburg, Emmanuel Kazakevich, Vasilii Grossman, Semen Lipkin, Il'ia Sel'vinskii, Fridrikh Gorenshtein, Shire Gorshman, Dina Kalinovskaia, Dina Rubina, Alexander Melikhov, Inna Lesovaia, and other authors in the same literary universe in which modernism and socialist realism, revolution and catastrophe, as well as traditional Jewish writings, including the Hebrew Bible, liturgy, and classic rabbinic texts provide the framework for creativity.

Traditional Jews saw ongoing reality in light of biblical precedent, according to a paradigm that linked each successive event to "the continuum of Jewish sacred history" (Miron 2000, 40).[7] Before the 1917 revolutions and outside any ideological commitment to socialism, Yiddish authors pushed their readers to abandon this biblical lens, and offered in its place the conventions of literary realism, which emphasizes the here and now and the ordinariness of daily life. Later, in the 1930s, official cultural doctrine in the Soviet Union stressed the role of the arts in creating a path toward the future, subordinating the present and the past to its purposes.[8]

Nonetheless, the Jewish historiographical habit of seeing the present in light of the past persisted. The Soviet century, for all its emphasis on construction and mobilization, also gave rise to the reinvention of a backward-glancing Jewish temporality. During his interrogation Bergelson described the power of biblical images, especially the destructions of the Temple, commemorated on the Ninth of Av (Rubenstein and Naumov 2001, 150–51). Mandelshtam's writing reveals a secular but nonetheless Jewish temporal orientation: his exploration of the fractured chronology of his epoch, his repulsion from and subsequent attraction to the Jewish past, and his renunciation of contemporaneity put him in the same orbit of thought as authors who knew classic Yiddish literature and whose religious upbringing enabled them to see the destruction of their own era in light of ancient Jewish history.[9] Writing in the early Soviet era, Mandelshtam came to see his own present moment as an aftereffect of catastrophe. Both Benjamin's angel of history and Mandelshtam's terrible century look backward, only Mandelshtam's century, like a wounded beast, looks back at "the traces left by its own paws" (*na sledy svoikh zhe lap*) (Mandelshtam 1991, 103).

Zvi Gitelman and Anna Shternshis have established that religious observance and knowledge were not significant factors in Soviet Jewish identity.[10] Soviet Jews shared a secular and ethnic form of Jewish identification rather than an attachment to the Jewish calendar or the Jewish textual tradition. Soviet nationality policy in the 1930s, urbanization, and the devastation of the Second World War, taken together, resulted in what Gitelman calls a "thin culture," devoid of external manifestations of Jewishness (Gitelman 2003, 49). My readings, especially of postwar Jewish literature, suggest that this culture was not necessarily so thin; my focus, however, is not on personal identity but rather on artistic compositions, primarily prose and poetry, and also journalism and films—in other words, cultural artifacts whose formal patterns can be traced, analyzed, and put in dialogue with other works.[11] The literary methodology that I use includes close reading, the examination of poetics, and the exploration of intertextuality. Rhythm and sound can enhance the experience of temporal disjuncture that many of these works sought to create; hidden quotation can reanimate silenced voices. My formalism is a defensive reaction against the ways that most of the works I discuss have been previously received; it is a way of recovering the pleasure of reading a body of literature that has been made invisible as literature.[12] After the catastrophic violence of the twentieth century and the hope and delusion of the Soviet project, what still remains is the trace left by the text, which must be considered in its historical context but cannot be reduced to a mere reflection of it, or to a repository of identity markers, the author's biography, or the reigning political doctrine of the time (which the author may support or oppose). These things must be taken into account, but the text has to be understood in its own terms, according to its own internal logic.

Most of the authors I discuss, with the exception of Babel, Mandelshtam, and Grossman, are unknown to the English-language audience.

New translations from Yiddish and new anthologies of Russian-Jewish literature in English have changed the picture somewhat.[13] Nonetheless, the undeserved obscurity of many of the writers in this study stems not only from linguistic obstacles. The long-term consequences of the Cold War have led many scholars to accept the lachrymose view of Soviet Jewry, and its corollary in the oft-quoted line, "Hitler killed the readers and Stalin killed the writers."[14] According to this view, there was little Jewish culture in the Soviet Union after the 1920s until the so-called Jewish national revival after the Arab-Israeli Six-Day War. The chapters that follow provide more detailed historical background, but a few general remarks challenging this view must be made at the outset. Jews and secular Jewish culture in Yiddish and Russian were not the particular target of negative government campaigns in the 1920s; Jews lost their lives in the purges of the 1930s but were not uniquely singled out as Jews, although Jewish cultural institutions, like those of other nationalities, were targeted.[15] Yiddish and Jewish-oriented literature flourished during the war against Hitler. Stalin murdered Mandelshtam and Babel, the Yiddish actors Solomon Mikhoels and Veniamin Zuskin, and the Yiddish writers Bergelson, Der Nister, Leyb Kvitko, David Hofshteyn, Markish, Shmuel Persov, and Itsik Fefer, but many other Yiddish writers of note survived Hitler and Stalin and saw their work published after the Second World War (I discuss Shmuel Halkin, Shire Gorshman, Moshe Altman, and Itsik Kipnis, for example).[16] Jewish literary and visual artists were prominent figures in Soviet life; Yuri Slezkine, among others, has amply documented their success as professionals and members of the elite.[17]

A central misapprehension about literature from the Soviet Union, whether authored by Jews or not, is that it lacks artistic interest. There is no point in reading anything written in Soviet Yiddish or in Russian after the 1920s, because from 1934 on, socialist realism was the only officially tolerated doctrine in all the arts. Many critics repeat Stalin's dictum about Soviet "national cultures as being 'national in form, socialist in content'" (Martin 2001, 182).[18] The forced marriage of national form and socialist content produced a wide range of results, including some that subverted the socialist project. The only works that that were strictly "socialist in content and national in form" were birthday greetings to Stalin, translations of Marx and Lenin into Yiddish, and so on.

Entering the world of Jewish literature from the Soviet Union, readers may expect to find themselves in a remote backwater, in an ancient grandmotherly apartment infused with the smell of mothballs; decorated with sofas draped in plastic slipcovers, busts of Lenin, and dishes of hard candies so old that their flavors would be indistinguishable; and enveloped by the "gentle aroma of decay," as in Gedali's shop. What I discovered, in contrast, was an intensely vibrant literature, violent and erotic, earthy and prophetic, expressing searing pain, savage irony, and bitter humor, and in active dialogue with its time and place. These works are not merely vessels of an obsolete ideology, of value only as historical documents. On the contrary, they are hauntingly beautiful, emotionally compelling, and philosophically engaged, "good to think with" in relation to current critical issues, including the questions of how the state inscribes itself on the bodies of its citizens, how gender relates to narratives of foundation, and how literature testifies to atrocity. These works disturb our ideas about the Jewish past; reading them attentively expands and unsettles our model of the Jewish literary imagination, particularly in relation to Yiddish.

How I found Jewish literature from the Soviet Union is another story. In the bibliographic sources published during the Soviet times, there was no entry labeled "Jewish works"; even when the term *evreiskii* appeared, it meant literature written in Yiddish, and not all Yiddish literature found its way into Soviet reference books. This is where conversation proved more helpful than bibliography. Many of the works I discuss were recommended to me by other knowledgeable scholars, including Ol'ga Boravaia, Valerii Dymshits, Gennady Estraikh, Leonid Katsis, Viktor Kel'ner, and Mikhail Krutikov. Every time I traveled to the former Soviet Union, I asked people what they read when they were growing up, what books were on their parents' bookshelves, how they found out about the Holocaust, what literature from the Soviet Union they considered Jewish, and why.

A brief introduction to Yiddish literature, a clarification of the term "Soviet Yiddish," and a preliminary discussion of socialist realism will help set the stage for the chapters that follow. Modern secular Yiddish literature emerged in the 1860s, with the work of Sh. Y. Abramovitsh (Mendele Moykher Sforim, the Book Seller), Y. L. Peretz, and Sholem

Rabinovitsh (Sholem Aleichem).[19] These canonical authors created prose works that were often harshly critical of traditional Jewish life in the small market towns of the Pale of Settlement. Satire, an orientation to the forms of oral speech, and a verbose, folksy narrator are the hallmarks of the best-known Yiddish classics, although Peretz's prose and drama do not conform to this model. There is a direct continuity between the didactic social criticism characteristic of nineteenth-century Yiddish and works from the early Soviet period, which also attacked the shtetl, depicting its way of life as moribund. Yiddish writers in the Soviet Union in the postwar period continued to respond to the legacy of the classics; Moshe Altman, for example, references Freud, Bergson, and Sholem Aleichem, and Kanovich similarly engages Peretz.

The rise of secular Yiddish culture coincided with the development of modern Hebrew literature; Abramovitsh, for example, wrote in both languages. By the end of the nineteenth and the beginning of the twentieth century, Jews had also created a Russian-language literature aimed at Jews; among the prominent authors were the poet Semen Frug and the prose author Semen Iushkevich. The journal *Razsvet* (Dawn), which later became *Evreiskaia zhizn'* (Jewish life), played a major role.[20] In 1908 Kornei Chukovsky, who would become one of the Soviet Union's preeminent theoreticians of translation, wrote a provocative article on the contribution of Jews to Russian literature.[21] Appealing to the secular, Russian-speaking Jewish intelligentsia, S. An-sky sought to renew Jewish art and literature with the objects, photographs, music, stories, and folklore that he had gathered during his ethnographic expeditions in the Pale of Settlement before the First World War.[22] He used Russian and Yiddish for his fiction, drama, and polemical writings. In 1918 the critic Abram Efros predicted a "renaissance" for Jewish culture on the basis of An-sky's discoveries (Efros 2001).

In the same period, a new type of Yiddish literature began to appear. Formal experimentation, new developments in poetry, and an orientation away from the shtetl and toward European, universal, and humanist ideals were the watchwords of this new departure. A variety of literary movements emerged in Kiev, New York, and elsewhere that focused on the emotional experience of individuals free from the burden of heritage and community. The early lyric poetry of Perets Markish and David

Hofshteyn celebrates the beauty and pleasure of subjective experience in the moment of its unfolding.[23] In the ironically titled "Ikh gleyb s'iz mir bashert" (I believe I am fated), Hofshteyn renounces fate, burdens, and debts, and enjoys the light, like "mother-of-pearl," that plays on his eyelids, reflected from the parchment walls of his room (Hofshteyn 1987). What later became formalized as the "Kiev group" included I. J. Singer, Kadia Molodovsky, the theoretician Moshe Litvakov, in addition to Bergelson, Markish, Osher Shvartsman, and Der Nister.[24] A Jewish cultural movement that emphasized high art in both Hebrew and Yiddish briefly flowered in the period 1917–19 (Moss 2009). The Kiev Kultur-Lige, one of the central institutions of this movement, oversaw the production of remarkable works of visual and literary art.[25]

Jewish cultural activists had long debated whether Hebrew or Yiddish should be the language of the Jewish people, but by 1920–21, the Jewish sections of the Communist Party closed Hebrew down, and in 1921 Yiddish became the official language of the Jewish people in the Soviet Union, a government-sponsored language of an ethnic minority.[26] Hebrew may have been shut down, but it was not forgotten. For example, Itsik Kipnis's postwar autobiographical fiction "Fun mayne togbikher" (From my diaries), published in the Soviet Yiddish journal *Sovetish heymland* (Soviet homeland) in 1965, pays homage to Chaim Nachman Bialik, the Hebrew national poet. Like other languages of the new Soviet state, including Russian, Yiddish underwent a process of reform, centered mostly on the phonetic spelling of its Hebrew words.[27] Other ethnic minority languages were subject to transformations with far greater long-range consequences; for example, changing from Arabic to Latin alphabets.[28] "Soviet Yiddish" in a technical sense refers to works that used Soviet Yiddish orthography; in terms of themes, Soviet Yiddish writers produced works promoting pig-farming, intermarriage, and other changes that would undermine traditional Jewish practice.[29]

But they also created a form of Jewish literature within the Soviet framework. Choosing Yiddish as the language of literary creativity was a profoundly *Jewish* choice, as Bergelson argued in the communist Yiddish journal *In shpan* (In harness), which he helped to create. In "Dray tsentern" (Three centers), an article published in 1926, Bergelson said that Yiddish was going to survive best in Moscow. Economically successful American Jews were making the "old Jewish mistake" of pursuing assimilation. Bergelson explicitly used the language of religious conversion ("*optsushmadn*") to critique American Jews, who used English to enter the mainstream. The propertied classes feel that "if baptismal water (*shmad-vaser*) converts only the body, language converts also the soul" (1926, 84). In contrast, the "conscious Jewish worker" has no desire to lose Yiddish, because to do so would be to risk becoming an "impotent and sterile stammerer" (*a shafungslozer impotenter kvatpe*) (85). Losing Yiddish threatens creativity, rendered in the masculinist terms of impotence; indeed its loss threatens the very capacity to speak.

So much for Yiddish as mere form. Bergelson's polemically bleak assessment of the possibilities of Jewish expression in languages other than Yiddish, however, ought to be taken with a grain of salt, given that his audience was Moscow. A few remarks about the issue he raises—Jewish literature in non-Jewish languages—are nonetheless in order. By 1926 outstanding examples had already appeared, including, in Russian, the work of Babel and Mandelshtam, and in German, Kafka.[30] Soviet officials may not have recognized the fluidity of language and the hybridity of artistic utterance, but writers in the Soviet Union both theorized and expressed themselves creatively by using this open-ended model (see Chapter Seven).[31] Jewish authors working in Russian looked over their shoulder at Yiddish (for example, Babel, Gekht, Sel'vinskii, and Karabchievskii), and writers working in Yiddish and Russian looked back to the scenes and cadences of the Hebrew Bible (Bergelson, Der Nister, Markish, Altman, Gorshman, Slutskii, Lipkin, and Grossman).

In using the terms "Russian-Jewish literature" and "Jewish literature in Russian" I mean Russian-language work with Jewish themes written by Jews. Since this study is concerned with cultural production in Soviet Russia generally, I will also discuss works written by Jews without any ostensible Jewish content. I intend to push on the question of what constitutes Jewish literature. A body of critical work engages this issue; however, one of the most provocative discussions is not focused specifically on Jews but rather on the broad question of ethnicity and literature.[32] Werner Sollors explains:

> Especially since Herder and the Grimms, the notion has gained dominance that a 'people' is held together by a subliminal culture of fairy

tales, songs, and folk beliefs—the original ethnic ('völkisch') subsoil of the common people's art forms that may culminate in the highest artistic achievements. As a result of this legacy "ethnicity" as a term for literary study largely evokes the accumulation of cultural bits that demonstrate the original creativity, emotive cohesion, and temporal depth of a particular collectivity, especially in a situation of emergence—be it from obscurity, suppression, embattlement, dependence, diaspora, or previous membership in a larger grouping. (Sollors 1995, 290)

Authors producing literature with a high quotient of "cultural bits" in order to demonstrate the cohesion of a particular people are often doing so under the glare of the colonial spotlight, under the watchful eyes of an external power that denies them status, rights, and acceptance. Sollors's argument sheds light on the pitfalls of defining ethnic literature. Literary scholars tracking down "cultural bits" run the risk of ignoring how external constraints shape what they look like. Scholarship preoccupied with defining and policing the borders of ethnic identity in order to demarcate the field of ethnic literature can end up miming the oppressive surveillance of a state or colonial apparatus. The critic who dismisses a Soviet era literary work in Yiddish or Russian because it is not Jewish enough (because it lacks "Jewish cultural bits") resembles Soviet era critics (in the case of Yiddish works, these would have been Jews) who dismissed a work because it was too "nationalist" and not sufficiently Soviet. In 1929 the Yiddish critic Moshe Litvakov attacked the Yiddish poet Perets Markish on the grounds that his civil war epic *Brider* (Brothers) was too Jewish, even though he did not use these words (Litvakov 1929). In 1937 Moshe Litvakov was shot.[33] The Soviet bureaucrats who closed down Yiddish journals and publication houses in 1949 amassed evidence of Jewish nationalism in the works of prominent Yiddish writers of the time in order to justify their attempt to destroy Yiddish culture in the Soviet Union. Their reading practices ought not to provide a model for our own.

"Cultural bits" can be important when examined in dynamic interaction with other literary factors, but an exclusive focus on their accumulation is not productive, because it reduces both Jewish identity and Jewish literature to static monoliths. A literary work that features a higher number of Jewish characters with dark, mournful eyes, side curls, dreaminess, or disabilities in horsemanship and other athletic or martial skills is no more Jewish than a text lacking protagonists with such alleged Jewish characteristics. Framing the question of Soviet Jewish studies with a fixed template of what Jews and Jewishness are precludes the discovery of anything new. This includes even some recent definitions of the Jew, such as Yuri Slezkine's model of Jews as "Mercurians," service nomads, whose mobility, intellect, and adaptability make them well-suited to be moderns (2004). Assumptions about Jewishness must be suspended in order to discover the meanings and associations of this term in Russia and elsewhere in the twentieth and early twenty-first century. To explore the specificity of Russian-Jewish cultural production in both Russian and Yiddish, it is necessary to trace the absences, and incongruities, noticing what has been *re-marked* in a second, translated, or sometimes encoded language, instead of looking for the authentic essence of Jewish identity. Doing so, I hope, provides an escape from the "matrix of continuity" and makes more concrete the concept of "contiguity, the state of being a borderline," which Dan Miron argues is necessary for a "new Jewish literary thinking" (2010, 305–7). Literary texts are produced by a structure of differences; they are not transparent vessels of "identity." Literary authors—as Sollors and Bakhtin before him point out—speak in multivocal, heteroglot languages. The chapters that follow attempt to make visible the space in between, where Russian and Jewish and Yiddish writing touch one another.

 The theme of continuity nonetheless has a place in my argument. Work produced by Jews in Russia in the twentieth and early twenty-first centuries comprises a unique Jewish cultural entity, informed both by Soviet civilization, which they helped to build, and by the heritage of the past. Whether they purport to "overcome" and remake Jewish life in the former Pale of Settlement, as in the 1920s and 1930s, whether they merely revisit this legacy, or what is more often the case, it visits and haunts them, as in the postwar and post-Soviet periods, the culture created by Jews in both Russian and Yiddish has a deep attachment to Jewish life of the past.

 The preoccupation with the past challenges the prime directive of the Soviet aesthetic system known as "socialist realism." Invented in 1932, socialist realism was officially promulgated at the First Congress of the Soviet Writer's Union in 1934, when it was declared to be "the basic method of Soviet literature and literary criticism. It demands of the artist the truthful, historically concrete representation of reality in its revolutionary development. Moreover, the truthfulness and historical concreteness of the artistic representation must be linked with the task of ideological transformation and education of workers in the spirit of socialism."[34] There is an obvious disparity between the truthful representation of reality and its representation in an idealized form, or "in its revolutionary development." Meir Viner, a well-known critic of both Yiddish and Russian literature, explained in 1935 that "to see and recognize authentic reality means to see and recognize the inevitable future in its more or less developed embryo."[35] Socialist realist literature glossed over reality, as Soviet critics themselves pointed out in the 1950s. The template for socialist realist literature shifted over the course of Soviet history, but generally artistic works had to show their "ideological commitment" (*ideinost'*), party-mindedness (*partiinost'*), national/popular spirit (*narodnost'*), and "contemporaneity" (*sovremennost'*).[36] Another requirement concerned the representation and self-representation of the "national minorities," which necessarily included the stereotype of the Russian friend and comrade teaching the minority individual, under the policy known as the "friendship of nations" (discussed in Chapters Two and Seven).

Some aspects of socialist realism are alien to Western culture. The didactic goal of educating workers in the spirit of socialism contradicts the American promise about the individual's right to pursue happiness. On closer inspection, however, there are parallels to be drawn.[37] The purpose of the transformation of individuals under socialism, as Maxim Gorkii said at the 1934 Congress of Soviet Writers, was for the sake of their happiness. Capitalism and socialism competed over which system could best secure personal happiness and the happiness of minority groups. Socialist realist art and literature from the Soviet Union, not unlike Norman Rockwell paintings, Disneyland, and "I'm Dreaming of a White Christmas" and other artifacts of American culture, provided the reassuring vision of age-old dreams fulfilled in the here and now, as in the popular Soviet song of the 1930s "The March of the Aviator," the first line of which reads, "We were born to make fairy tales come true."[38]

Jews contributed to the sound of that quintessentially American holiday, Christmas (it may be unnecessary to point out that Irving Berlin wrote "White Christmas"), just as they contributed to the sound, look, and narrative of Soviet life ("Aviator" was composed by two Jews).

Katerina Clark's classic work on socialist realism shows that the art produced under its aegis sought to transform the time of daily life, *chronos*, into sacred time, *kairos*.[39] Personal happiness under socialism exceeded the lives of mere individuals to achieve transcendent historical significance: the triumph of socialism and the end of time; eternity now. Evgenii Dobrenko emphasizes Clark's key point about time: the socialist realist "dream factory . . . represented the future as the present . . . everything produced by Socialist Realism already existed, had already come to pass" (Dobrenko 2004, 700). Socialist realism transformed everyday life into an airbrushed, pumped-up monument to the everyday life that socialism was to have achieved—hence novels about heroic nighttime factory construction and ergonomic work methods (for example, Markish's *Eyns af eyns* [One by one], discussed in Chapter Two). If eternity is now, then the merely mundane, inconvenient, and unpleasant dimensions of ordinary life simply do not exist. Socialist realism, as Dobrenko puts it, "de-realized everydayness."

The second volume of Bergelson's novel *At the Dnieper*, published in 1940, shows how socialist realism substitutes the future for the present. In one scene, a worker in the revolutionary underground confronts the death of his colleague, Matosov:

> Looking at this fallen body, he felt only dimly that he was looking at something important, as if Matosov were already shielded from his view by a gravestone inscribed with the epitaph: "Here lies a man who in descending to work here in the pit, had paid up his account in the book of the present, unworthy time, and had paid in advance his account in the book of the time to come, the pure, worthy future." (Bergelson 1940, 297)

Matosov paid for his leap into the future with his life, but the language of the epitaph obscures the loss. The imaginary gravestone, with its heroic rhetoric of self-sacrifice, shields the corpse from view, leaving only the problem of how to get rid of it. Instead of preserving memory, the memorial inscription impedes memory.

The socialist realist manipulation of time, narrative, and memory is central to this study. As a number of scholars have observed, the revolutionary period and the avant-garde movements of the time, in which Jews fully participated, aimed at a radical shift with regard to the past. Revolutionary culture did not acknowledge the value of memory. However, beginning in the 1930s, and especially during the Second World War, the past began to have value. Bergelson's *At the Dnieper*, for example, published in 1940 and set in the period leading up to the 1905 revolution, looks back to the bright future, anticipating the triumph of the revolution, the end of anti-Semitism, and the birth of a new form of Jewish culture. As Vladimir Papernyi argues in *Kul'tura dva* (Culture two), Soviet culture's tolerance for a certain triumphant version of the past coexisted with revolutionary disdain for anything other than the future (2006).

The teleological, instrumental, and linear narrative characteristic of socialist realism leaves little space for loss. Soviet Jewish literature in Yiddish and Russian, in contrast, used a variety of artistic means to acknowledge loss—sometimes in expressionist images of wounded bodies, sometimes through a poetics of silence, and sometimes in references to the Hebrew Bible and other traditional Jewish texts and rituals. The penultimate scene of Bergelson's *At the Dnieper*, for example, is a *yisker* (memorial) service. As Bergelson describes the service, the congregation mourns their losses both as individuals and as members of the Jewish people as a whole: "everyone remembered the great anguish and immense desolation of the people, to whom they, gathered here, belong" (534). This passage alone challenges the view that socialist realist literature is only about collective farms and cement factories. Bergelson's description of a synagogue memorial service should, furthermore, put to rest the formula that Soviet Yiddish was national merely in form. Other works, of course, also challenge this established wisdom.[40]

I am not claiming that remembrance, mourning, and the backward glance are the unique province of Jewish authors, or that all Jewish authors wrote about these themes. In Il'ia Erenburg's *Julio Jurenito* and *The Life and Death of Nikolai Kurbov*, mourning is absent, even though *Jurenito* imagines the future annihilation of all the Jews of Europe. Scholars of Silver Age Russian literature identify an all-pervasive sense of catastrophe in works that predate the revolution.[41] Biblical motifs are not unique to Jewish authors. In "Lot's Wife" (Lotova zhena, 1924) Anna Akhmatova inverts the biblical story to privilege the backward glance at the destruction of a world. The poet will "never forget" the woman "who gave her life for a single glance" (568). Nearly seventy years later Russian journalists used the creation story from Genesis to describe the utterly new beginning of Russian history following the August 1991 putsch and subsequent collapse of the Soviet Union (see Chapter Eight).

Without arguing for uniqueness, then, I contend that the traditional emphasis on remembrance lends a distinctive color to the work produced by Jewish artists working in both Russian and Yiddish in the 1920s, and even in the 1950s and 1960s when Jewish cultural production had come to a virtual standstill in Russia and beyond, through the beginning of the twenty-first century. For Markish, Bergelson, Babel, Gekht, Grossman, Gorshman, and others the obligation and the pain of remembering came together with the desire for a socialist future and the obligation and pain of building it. My interest in this fractured temporality—the literary Doppler effect—has motivated my choice of authors and texts. I focus mostly on prose, because prose accommodates the explorations of time, narrative, and memory that are my particular concern. The poetry that I discuss, including works by Markish, Mandelshtam, Slutskii, Lipkin, and Sel'vinskii, shares the multiplicity of perspective and the doubled temporality of prose. I address works that were censored and banned, but I center on what was published, what was considered sufficiently "Soviet," because my claim is about the Jewish presence in Soviet mainstream culture. I discuss the image of the Jew as outsider, other, and pariah in Chapter Seven; my primary goal, however, is to show what Jews as insiders created within the framework of Soviet culture.

The first part of the book is framed chronologically. Chapter One, "The Stillbirth of Revolution," explores the trauma of the civil war years by focusing on Markish, Babel, Gekht, Bergelson, and Mandelshtam. In Markish's *Brider* (Brothers) (1929) the creation of the new type of Jewish Bolshevik partisan unfolds against the backdrop of the dissolution of the social order. Markish's officially praised civil war epic, however, contains a subtle form of lament over the destruction of the shtetl: he quotes his own earlier pogrom poem of 1921 "Di kupe" (The mound). In both works, the lament appears indirectly in the image of the body exceeding its limits. This imagery resembles the world of Babel's *Red Cavalry* with its graphic depictions of death, rot, and decay. In Bergelson's cycle of civil war stories, especially "Birgerkrig" (Civil war), authority breaks down and violence erupts in a decentered narrative, whose focus constantly shifts and changes. Gekht's stories from the 1920s reveal a similarly abject landscape. Iurii Libedinskii's novella "Commissars" and Fadeev's "The Rout" provide a contrast. Libedinskii, who was Jewish, and Fadeev, who was not, both portray Jews in the new, stronger, Soviet world unmarred by remnants of the past.

Chapter Two, "Socialist Construction, the *Luftmentsh*, and the New Jew," uses the concept of gender, masculinity, and the body to explore the Jewish literary imagination of a new Soviet political order. Soviet Yiddish and Russian novels, journalism, and film associated with the vast socialist construction projects of the 1930s explicitly link the reconstruction of the Jewish male body with socialist construction and national belonging. Markish and Bergelson rework the biblical trope of the covenant in their literary imagining of the new Soviet promised land. Babel's story "Karl-Yankel" (1931, published in Russian and translated into Yiddish) provides a grotesquely comical fiction of circumcision on trial. In Yiddish works of the 1930s, gaining a place in the new Soviet community is uncertain; the promise remains unfulfilled; and the doomed shtetl Jew never leaves the scene. In films from the 1930s ostensibly designed to tout the Soviet transformation of the Jew (*The Return of Neitan Bekker* and *Seekers of Happiness*), it is the shtetl Jew who steals the show. The emblematic figure of the past haunts the project of the future. Writing by women Yiddish authors in the 1930s, however, takes a different tack. Shire Gorshman's stories of her experience on a Jewish agricultural commune in Crimea reject the biblically inflected Soviet narrative of foundation developed by Markish, Bergelson, and others.

Chapter Three, "Fighting the Great Patriotic War," and Chapter Four, "In Mourning: Responding to the Destruction of the Jews," explore Russian and Yiddish fiction and reportage from the 1940s, focusing on the Jewish participation in the Soviet war effort and the Jewish response to what was not called the Holocaust. Writers such as Emmanuel Kazakevich (who switched from Yiddish to Russian at this time), Vasilii Grossman, Il'ia Erenburg, Der Nister, Bergelson, and the poets Il'ia Sel'vinskii and Boris Slutskii negotiated a difficult position both as Soviets and as Jews. In Grossman's "Staryi uchitel'" (The old teacher), for example, the title character locates the Nazi murder of Jews within a universalizing framework of the Nazi war against all the nationalities of Europe. In "An eydes" (A witness) Bergelson makes a case for the continued existence of Yiddish literature as a literature of testimony even as he tells the story (in Yiddish) of the translation of Yiddish testimony into Russian. Bergelson's story "Geven iz nakht un gevorn iz tog" (It was night and became day, 1943) explores the question of what the Jew's proper response to the German ought to be. In his poem "Kandava" (1947), Sel'vinskii describes himself both as a Jewish victim of the Nazi genocide and also as a triumphant Soviet and Jewish army officer accepting the German surrender at Kandava (Sel'vinskii in fact participated in the ceremony in May 1945 as a Soviet officer). The poem, remarkably, frames its account of military triumph with the Jewish nightmare of the death camp. The double position as Soviet and as Jew—victor and victim—had implications for the problem of representing, remembering, mourning, and testifying to what took place on the battlefields and killing fields. In contrast to the dominant scholarship that claims there was little artistic representation of the Nazi genocide in the Soviet Union, I demonstrate the scope and power of the Soviet Jewish response to the killings that took place under German occupation, focusing in particular on work published in Russian and Yiddish in the 1940s.

Whereas the first part of this study focuses on events—the revolution, the civil war, the five-year plans, the "Great Patriotic War," and the Nazi genocide—the second part moves beyond a chronological framework in order to avoid the well-worn narrative of Soviet Jewish oppression, national reawakening, and redemption via immigration. The introduction to Part II takes up the problem of postwar continuity in the face of catastrophe: Boris Slutskii's poem about the death of Yiddish, "Ia osvobozhdal Ukrainu" (I liberated Ukraine), provides the key to the problem. Cold War politics have influenced the reception of postwar Jewish literature from the Soviet Union; competing Western and Soviet narratives, as I show in Part II, have made Soviet Jewish writers nearly invisible as anything other than mouthpieces of Soviet propaganda. The concluding chapter discusses the collapse of the Soviet Union. The hero of Alexandr Melikhov's 1993 novel *The Confession of a Jew*, like Benjamin's angel, finds himself at a trash heap, surrounded by the flattened tin cans of Soviet civilization.

Part I *From the Revolution Through the Second World War*

One   The Stillbirth of Revolution

> Let us reject the old world
> Shake its dust from our feet!
> Workers' Marseillaise[1]
>
> I don't want anything to do with the comfort-givers
> Those that dwell upon the earth between other worlds!
> The size of my human loneliness,
> The scale of my mourning—
> That is my comfort,
> My certainty
> And my strength . . .
>
> Hofshteyn 1922, 19

In the years following the 1917 revolution Jewish and non-Jewish authors in the new land of the Soviets celebrated the overcoming of all boundaries. The lines dividing class, nationality, language, gender, genres, the self from the world, the proper from the improper, the sacred from the profane, the literary from the nonliterary, and art from life, were to be no more. A certain wariness, however, accompanied the celebration. In David Bergelson's ironic short story "A zeltener sof" (A rare ending), a writer witnesses a scene at a party. Plates and glasses break when a drunken guest knocks over a bottle of wine: "Together with the glasses and the plates the entire sense of respectability among people, the whole responsibility for maintaining order in life, were also shattered, and therefore one was supposed to be joyful [*darf men zayn freylekh*]" (1930b, 238). The new obligation to be joyful jars against the liberation from all obligations. The story ends with a police raid and multiple arrests.

In Andrei Sobol's one-act play, significantly titled "Pereryv" (Intermission), identities are in flux and the past changes its meaning. An international theater troupe performs a lighthearted version of the ritual murder trial of Mendel Beilis. The Jewish national trauma, the centuries-old "blood libel," is nothing more than a bit of theater. The event no longer defines the essence of Jewish experience. In the play, the Jewish actor playing the Catholic priest who accused Beilis of ritual murder is also something of an actor in real life, whose roles include a Bolshevik in Russia and a vendor of pornography in Constantinople. Sobol', who was born in 1888, and committed suicide in 1926, was a member of a Zionist-socialist group in his early years, served time in tsarist prisons, and became a commissar on the Northern Front after the February revolution. He served with Isaac Babel, Eduard Bagritskii, and others on the editorial board of the literary journal *Moriak* (The sailor). A year before his suicide, he wrote to a friend, a former revolutionary terrorist living in Palestine, that even though without Russia he was "dead" as a writer, he was desperate to get away from Russia and live at least temporarily in Palestine.[2]

Sobol's "Intermission" and Bergelson's "A Rare Ending" emphasize the ephemeral nature of events. Nothing is permanent. The suspension of all boundaries could mean that the Jews were at home everywhere in "whole round earth," as the ending of Perets Markish's 1929 *Brider* (Brothers) proclaims, or it could signal the beginning of universal homelessness. In Lev Lunts' short story "Native Land" (Rodina) the revolution fails to resolve the problem of national identification:

> In Petersburg on a summer evening my friend and I go out to look for alcohol. In the next room, my father, an old Polish Jew, bald, with a gray beard and side curls prays facing east, but his soul weeps because his only son, the last scion of an ancient family, drinks rotgut on Sabbath eve. And the old Jew sees the blue sky of Palestine, where he never was, but which he saw, and sees, and will see. And I, an unbeliever, also cry, because I want to and cannot see far away Jordan and the blue sky, because I love the city of my birth, and my native language, which is an alien language. (Lunts 1981, 14)

In this fantastical story the two friends find themselves transported to ancient Babylon, where one becomes a prophet and the other, a slave. In Lunts's picture of the Jew, the native and the alien uneasily cohabit the same body. Lunts (1901–24), a playwright and short story writer, studied Hebrew and was invited by the Hebrew theater group Habima to develop materials for their productions. In a letter to his parents, Lunts expressed his unease as a Russian-Jewish writer, finding a contradiction between his Jewishness, in which he "rejoiced," and the demands of being a Russian-language writer (1981, 318).

The 1920s was a decade of great artistic experimentation in all areas of the arts, and Jews occupied prominent roles across the new movements in literature, the visual arts, film, and criticism. Lunts was a founding member of the Serapion Brothers, a group that included Veniamin Kaverin (pseudonym of Zil'ber) and advocated the importance of intriguing plots, with Western literature as a key model. Kaverin's portrait of a Jewish gangster, a former rabbinical student, in "Konets khazy" (The end of the gang, 1925) includes biblical references and Yiddish expressions. Il'ia Sel'vinskii and Eduard Bagritskii were on the other side of the artistic spectrum. They helped to found the Literary Center for Constructivism, which rejected literary models of the past in favor of an emphasis on new forms of literary production more closely tied to the laboratory and the factory. Iurii Libedinskii, on the other hand, was associated with the proletarian writers' movement. In the same time period, Yiddish culture underwent a similar ferment of artistic and political movements and allegiances. Experimentation in the literary and visual arts combined to produce a print culture of remarkable artistic quality.[3] David Hofshteyn's poem cycle *Troyer* (Mourning), the source of the second epigraph to this chapter, was published in Kiev in 1922, with illustrations by Marc Chagall. There is no single form of Jewish expression in the 1920s.

As Lunts's story "Native Land" and Sobol's letter both reveal, the opening of new possibilities both in art and in life did not necessarily reconcile the contradictions of the past. For some writers, working in both Russian and Yiddish, the free-floating carnival of revolution came together with a heightened sense of ongoing catastrophe, produced by the First World War and the devastation of the Russian Civil War, during which many thousands of Jewish lives were lost. The two events were related: when the newly formed Soviet Union signed the Treaty of Brest-Litovsk in 1918, it lost territories that the imperial Russian government had once controlled, including Poland, Lithuania, and Ukraine, thereby making possible the series of national conflicts that followed in those regions. The Pale of Settlement, where most of imperial Russia's Jews lived, comprised precisely this area. Peter Holquist speaks of a "continuum of crisis" in the period 1914–21 (2002). The anti-Jewish policies of the Imperial Russian Army during the First World War, including the classification of Jews as enemies and the massive deportations based on this assumption, fed directly into the "deterioration of basic legal and social norms," with disastrous consequences for Jews (Lohr 2001). The anti-Jewish violence of the civil war period, however, was distinctive in its duration, scope, and scale: a given locale could be in pogrom mode for "weeks or months on end" (Miliakova 2007, vii). Whites, Reds, the Polish Army, the army of the Ukrainian National Republic, and numerous roaming military bands all perpetrated the killings, rapes, and mutilations, and the destruction of Jewish property. There is general agreement that the lower limit of Jewish deaths in the period 1918–22 in Ukraine, Belorussia, and the European part of Russia (the former Pale of Settlement) was fifty thousand and the upper limit, two hundred thousand.[4]

Hofshteyn's response to these events expresses two conflicting impulses: he mourns and, in mourning, revels in his autonomy. The poet rejects all authorities ("the comfort-givers"), taking refuge and strength in the superman scale of his own human mourning. This and other Yiddish poetry of the 1920s and early 1930s, and Perets Markish's *Brothers*, Isaac Babel's *Red Cavalry*, Semen Gekht's work, and Bergelson's civil war stories, are haunted by a particular sense of loss over "the pillage and murder of the Jewish shtetls in Ukraine."[5] These texts construct the present as an "intermission," an uncertain moment between epochs.

Mikhail Bakhtin developed his theory of the body and popular culture in the mid-1930s, not long after Markish, Bergelson, Babel, and Gekht produced their civil war literature. In his book on Rabelais, Bakhtin described the realm of carnival as the creation of a new, collective body in which individuals lose their individuality while the "people," the mass body, gains immortality. The open orifices of the grotesque body, according to Bakhtin, indicate openness to the world and an unchanging cycle of birth and death. The overflowing mass body is pregnant with new life.[6] In Markish, Kvitko, Babel, Gekht, and Bergelson, in contrast, birth is precarious, and the body—displaced, fragmented, and swollen in illness—is paradoxically full of loss. These authors represent the outcome of the revolution as stillbirth.

Nicholas Abraham and Maria Torok's theory of psychic incorporation provides a better analytic model of Markish, Babel, and Bergelson than Bakhtin's carnival. Abraham and Torok describe incorporation as an alternative to mourning. Instead of acknowledging loss, subjects narcissistically take lost objects into themselves, thereby threatening, even as they try to preserve, the boundaries of their own identities. A loss that "cannot be acknowledged" results in the creation "of a secret tomb inside the subject" (Abraham and Torok 1994, 131). Incorporation is a regressive process, in which the desires of the past come back to haunt the present.

A New Masculine Order

In the mid-1920s, emerging literary templates for the depiction of the civil war emphasized order, unity, and discipline. For example, Iurii Libedinskii's novella *Komissary* (Commissars), published in 1925, describes the reeducation of a group of civil war heroes. In the novella, the military commander says that in 1918 "we built a disciplined army and cauterized anarchy with red-hot iron" (96). Libedinskii's medicalizing language compares political disorder to a festering wound, suggesting by contrast a closed-off, integral, and masculine body as the image of a healthy body politic.[7] In Aleksandr Fadeev's *Razgrom* (The rout) the partisan detachment finds itself trapped in a wood with the enemy on one side and a swamp on the other. The mass of overwhelmed and frightened men, who have been reduced to a "heap," ready to cry and despair, "were suddenly transformed into an inhumanly quick, obedient, fierce movement" (1947, 150). It is none other than the Jewish commander Levinson who brings about the transformation. In spite of his physical weakness, small stature, and unimposing appearance (he has a wedge-shaped red beard that makes him resemble a gnome), Levinson, who has few compunctions about violence and no interest in the past, exerts an overwhelming, compelling force over his men.[8]

In 1929 the Soviet and Jewish literary critic Abram Lezhnev described a demand for literary work that captured the dynamism and rapid tempo of change that was unfolding in daily life. The great novel of life, the five-year plan, was already written, and literature had to catch up. One of the most important changes had to do with human nature itself. The new emphasis on the remaking of the self, or "reforging" (*perekovka*), was not compatible with a preoccupation with loss. As Lezhnev explained, the proponents of proletarian literature saw "psychologicalism" as a retreat into the self and an attraction to psychopathology, both of which bordered on the decadent modernist style of the 1890s, and the neurasthenic self-analysis characteristic of that era (1929, 34).[9]

Markish's *Brothers*, Babel's *Red Cavalry*, and Bergelson's "Civil War" challenge these models of the revolution. None of these works shows how "authentic communists forged an army with proletarian discipline."[10] The image of forging as a tool of self-creation reflects the masculine ethos of the time, the hallmarks of which Eliot Borenstein in *Men Without Women* characterizes as "production rather than reproduction, participation in the historic process rather than domestic ahistoricity, heavy industry, construction, and, of course, 'the struggle'" (2000, 3). In contrast to this ethos, in Markish, Babel, Gekht, and Bergelson the opposition between the domestic and the political, the Jewish and the non-Jewish space, and the closed and the open body become blurred. In their works, the trope of the festering wound, the open, flowing body, and the "mound" overwhelm all boundaries to become dominant elements of the artistic text. It is not only the destruction of the past that they lament but, in addition, the failure of the revolution to give birth to something new.

Markish's *Brothers*

Born in 1895 (a year after Babel) in Volynia, Ukraine, Markish attended heder, and was apprenticed to a cantor for a brief period. He was wounded on the front in the First World War. In his early lyrical works, reminiscent of Walt Whitman and Vladimir Maiakovskii, Markish celebrates his absolute freedom from the past and the future; he proclaims that he belongs to "the now that belongs to no one" (*nishtiker atsind*); he is undefined, unfettered, unlimited.[11] He was one of the most prolific authors in the Soviet Yiddish canon. *Brider* (Brothers) was published in 1929, and Russian translations of the Yiddish appeared in 1935 and 1969.[12] The 1969 Russian translation of *Brothers* was included in a volume of his selected poetic works in the prestigious series the *Poet's Library*, originally edited by Maxim Gorkii. The introduction praises Markish as a "leading Soviet Jewish poet," whose work "objectively reflects" the history of the Jews in the twentieth century, beginning with the revolution and concluding with the "Soviet triumph over the fascist enemy." In 1938 the *Great Soviet Encyclopedia* praised the work as "one of the most important in the literature of the peoples of the USSR," and the 1969 volume states that the original publication of the Yiddish work was "a significant event for all Soviet literature" (25). Very little of Markish has been translated into English.

Brider, at first glance, satisfies the new demand for a new type of Jewish literature and a new type of Jewish hero, who embodies change. On closer inspection, however, it reveals a continuity with his pogrom poem of 1921, "Di kupe" (The mound). The two "brothers," Shloyme-Ber and Azril, wield bayonets, commandeer horses, shoot Jewish speculators, join with other nationalities in the "holy struggle," and die heroically for the revolution. Markish represents Shloyme-Ber's transformation into a Bolshevik using the imagery of forging typical of proletarian poetry of the 1920s:

> In the fire is thirst, and in the fire is pain
> And in the fire Shloyme-Ber forges himself and glows
>
> *Un in sreyfe iz—dorsht, un in sreyfe iz—payn,*
> *Un in sreyfe zikh shmidt un zikh glit Shloyme-Ber!*
>
> (Markish 1929, 32)
>
> His hands are iron hard and strong,
> The words he speaks, like bullets.
>
> *Un hent—azoyne ayzerne un shtarke*
> *Un—koyln zaynen verter, vos er redt.*
>
> (78)

In a review of the Russian translation of *Brothers*, Shmuel Levman wrote that it was "precisely the two brothers, who plunge into the revolution as it were their natural element, who resolve the thousand year problem of the fate of the Jewish people" (1936). The two brothers "traverse the fiery path of the revolution as full members of the great international family of the revolutionary and victorious proletariat." Yuri Slezkine similarly argues that Shloyme-Ber exemplifies a new "breed of saber-wielding Jewish horseman and partisans [who] become familiar heroes of Soviet folklore, fiction, and recollection" (2004, 191).

Markish rewrites the shtetl Jew as a Bolshevik internationalist. In a battle scene at the end of the poem, Shloyme-Ber is the last man standing on the Bolshevik side. A White Cossack asks him, "So tell me, commissar, are you a Jew or not?" (*Nu, zog, komisar, du—a yid bist tsi neyn?*) (1929, 260). Shloyme-Ber's answer contains the new Soviet solution to the old Jewish question:

> I am a glassworker from the glass factory,
> And from my life-experience I am a Bolshevik,
> And I am for the Soviet worker and peasant
> And will fight until my last bit of strength and breath
>
> *Kh'bin a hutnik aleyn—fun der hutner fabrik,*
> *Un fun lebns-farshtand bin ikh a Bolshevik,*
> *Un ikh gey far sovetn fun arbeter, poyer—*
> *Un vel geyn biz mayn letstn otem un koyekh*
>
> (260)

Shloyme-Ber's solution to the "thousand year problem of the fate of the Jewish people" denies the Cossack's definition of the Jew. For the Cossack, the terms "Jew" and "commissar" are virtually synonymous. In Shloyme-Ber's answer, Markish constructs the Jew's new role as a worker and a fighter, united with other Soviets. The passage attempts to replace the image of the Jew as the embodiment of the "age-old" Jewish question—that is, as weak, clannish, particularistic, and marginal—with an image of the Jew as a full-fledged participant in the new order.

Markish describes the successful integration of Jews into the new Soviet universal collective by depicting Jews as one national group among others. In a set of passages emphasizing the size of the Soviet land and the diversity of its regions and peoples, who haul barges on the Volga, pasture their flocks on the tundra, mine coal underground, and forge themselves in smelting fires, Markish explicitly names characteristically Jewish places and occupations. He includes in his panoramic view the individual "Who has dealt in raisins and almonds,/Raised pigeons in a shtetl,/Who sang his heart out playing his fiddle,/Who patched and sewed (*Ver es hot gehandlt rozhinkes mit mandlen,/Ver es hot dort toybn in shtetelekh gehodevet,/Ver es hot dos harts gezegn af a fidl,/Ver es hot gelatet, ver es hot genodlt*) (1929, 172–73). The 1969 Russian translation of the work omits these references. For the barge-haulers and the pigeon-fanciers and the tailors—for Jew and non-Jew alike—Soviet power is on the march, and now is the time to rise up, "to dare." Markish's reiteration of Soviet universalist discourse emphasizes that differences in region, religion, language, and occupation make no difference.

Part of the successful transformation of the shtetl Jew is a rejection of the past, which is dying. Markish stresses the decrepitude of the shtetl and its inhabitants, and contrasts it to the dynamism and joy of the young heroes. For example, "the houses in the shtetl sit in mourning; the rooftops rattle and are choked with fear" (1929, 63). In another chapter, he writes, "the houses lie on the ground like old empty suitcases waiting for someone to take them away" (91).

The poem also reveals, however, a more subtle form of lament over the destruction of the shtetl, expressed indirectly in the image of the body exceeding its limits. This imagery resembles the graphic depictions of death, rot, and decay in Babel's *Red Cavalry*. For example, in "Crossing the Zbrucz," the first story in the cycle, Liutov finds "torn pieces of women's fur coats and human excrement" on the floor, along with the corpse of an old man, whose daughter, with her "swollen belly," declares irreplaceable. "I want to know where in the world will you find a father like my father," she says, ending the story (Babel 1990, 2:7).

The Undead

In *Brothers* the creation of the new type of Jewish Bolshevik unfolds against the backdrop of the destruction of previous boundaries. The ending of the poem proclaims, "Now our fatherland is the whole round earth." The triumph over all limits, however, is not a movement forward but a retreat back to a presocial, embodied, undifferentiated, feminized realm, in which all distinctions are set aside, including the distinction between the inside and the outside of the body. In Markish's *Brider* the dead refuse to stay dead, and come back to haunt the living.

Jewish towns take on a life of their own from beyond the grave. Markish imagines scenes of devastation from the civil war as a floating shtetl of corpses on the waves of the Dnieper: "Jews float on it, like planks of wood" (*shvimen af im yidn, yidn vi gehiltsn*) (1929, 72). The waves of the river are "clothed" in the hats and coats of the Jews, and the river "breathes with difficulty, choked in blood." The river carries the stock figures of the shtetl—"the grocers, merchants, the tavern keepers, the saints and sinners . . . all with their beards and side curls, all unburied." The macabre scene comes to life as the corpses continue to conduct their affairs as if they were still alive, including a bride who swims off to the side, ashamed to be with all the others, and also an innkeeper who

sleeps on the waves, still holding his goblet,
For whom should he pour a drink? He mumbles and shakes his head. . . .
The Jews greet each other as if meeting again at a fair:
Tired out, they swim along the waves, as if on wagons,
They swim as if they are coming from a great fair . . .
One comes up, swimming along, asking another: "From where?"
"Thank God, from there, thank God, from there!" . . .

Shloft shinkar af khvalyes, shloft mit kelishokl,
Vemen zol er ongisn?—Bleblt er un shoklt . . .
Shvimt men af di khvalyes, vi af vogns,—mide,
Shvimt men, vi fun groyse yerlekhe yaridn . . .
Kumt men on antkegn, shvimendik:—funvanen?
—Danken Got, fun dortn, danken Got, fundanen! . . .

(Markish 1929, 73)

This image and others like it in *Brothers* recall a passage from Markish's own earlier work "The Mound," where the poet describes the Dnieper as "a river of purification" (*taykh fun tare*) in which dead Jews, the victims of the pogrom, "swim unaccompanied," denied the rites of burial and abandoned like so much refuse. The poet offers the dead bodies of the Jews—nothing more than a waste product of the river—as a "dowry" to the local "Ukrainian daughters" (1921, 21).

Brider: Style as Symptom

The poetic feature that makes the poem unique, its excess, indicates a terrible ambivalence at its core: the tension between celebration of the revolution and pain over the destruction of the Jewish community. The hyperbole, repetition, and the sheer wordiness of the poem are symptomatic of the inability to acknowledge catastrophe fully. Emerging literary norms, as we have seen, prescribed an affect of joy and a muscular, masculine body. In an essay of 1928, Voronskii even used this image to describe what the new Soviet writer looked like. In *Commissars*, for example, the sickly Jew Mindlov is ushered off the novelistic stage. No physical weakness is tolerable, and no exchange between bodies, even innocent heterosexual kissing, is approved. *Brider* as a whole, however, is dominated by the image of the grotesque body that is more abject than joyous. Bodies—male bodies as the site of cultural marking—are maimed, hanged, and swollen; the skin is torn from them. Revolution means tearing the skin from flesh and bones (*"m'tut zikh op di hoyt fun layber un fun beyner"*) (1929, 63). In one scene, Markish uses the image of night tearing off its skin to suggest the approach of dawn (*"un s'rayst af zikh di hoyt mit likhtikayt di nakht"*) (153). The revolutionary Lebedev is flayed alive to make him confess (*"opgeshundn Lyebedyevn hobn zey di hoyt—/Im geheysn oyszogn, dertseyln farn toyt"*) (159).

Markish represents the violence and suffering of the Russian Revolution by realizing and literalizing the metaphor of the body politic. In one extraordinary image Markish describes a revolutionary banner that proclaims the end of the old world:

> The fluttering canvas fences with the wind.
> It streams forward, assaulting the heavens.
> Its letters, full of fight, cut themselves, like scars, into the banner
> To spell out: there is no God, no king, and no hero!

> *Un s'fekht zikh mitn vint di flaterdike layvnt,*
> *Zi shpart antkegn himlen, kvalndik un hel;*
> *Un shlakhtndike shriftn, shramike zikh shlayfn:*
> *—Keyner nit! Keyn got, keyn meylekh un keyn held!*
>
> (147)

The poet compares a revolutionary slogan on a banner to an act of self-mutilation. (The slogan is a translation of A. Kots's Russian version of E. Pottier's revolutionary hymn "L'Internationale," which was the Soviet national anthem between 1918 and 1944.[13]) The letters cut themselves into the banner, producing themselves as scars on its flesh. The violence of the assault on the old order extends to the literal sign, the banner announcing the assault, and to the sign as a figure for language itself. Markish makes language change, stretching the meanings of words beyond their limits. Language that is literalized as a kind of writing on the body loses its metaphoricity. The loss of the separation of one body from another, the rending of skin from flesh, and the quantities of waste suggest the destruction of language: the distinctions that make language possible have themselves been destroyed.

Literalization of the metaphor, a common device of modernist poetry, usually serves to defamiliarize worn-out poetic language, but here it also functions as a symptom. Nowhere is the process of literalization clearer than in Markish's depiction of the outbreak of typhus. The infection spreads from the human beings to the entire surrounding world. The day itself grows ill with typhus:

> A cloudy membrane stretches over the day,
> A black-spotted swelling, oozing pus, covers it,
> They threw a sack over the day—
> It will not see the sky, laid out like a dirty bed sheet,
> It will not see the swollen train,
> Which does not go, but stumbles with its wheels across miles and miles . . .

> *S'hot afn tog zikh geleygt un fartsoygn a nepldik haytl,*
> *S'hot afn tog a geshvil zikh tseaytert mit fintstere flekn,*
> *S'hot afn tog zikh farvorfn a zak tsum badekns,—*
> *Vet er dem himl nit zen shoyn, vos hengt, vi a koytiker laylekh,*
> *Vet er nit zen dem geshvolenem tsug af geshvolene vaytn,*
> *Vos geyt nit—vos tapt mit di reder di verstn un mayln . . .*

(216)

The disease escapes all boundaries and spreads everywhere, infecting the vast expanses of the land, which are bloodied and swollen (*"un di vayt iz in blut, un di vayt iz—geshvil"*) (220).

Markish's typhus train resembles Babel's "Syn Rabbi" (The rebbe's son), first published in 1924 and which served as the final story in the *Red Cavalry* cycle in the 1926 edition. Babel writes: "the *polit-otdel* train began to crawl along the dead spine of the fields. The typhus-ridden peasant horde rolled the usual hump of soldier's death before it."[14] Babel represents the massive number of deaths from typhus as a "hump" (*gorb*), suggesting an association between the bulging, excessive body and death.

Again, as in the image of the river of death, the typhus-ridden landscape in *Brothers* is also similar to Markish's own earlier work "Di kupe" (The mound). Markish describes the destroyed Jewish community of Ukraine as a pile of rotting corpses, which overtakes the entire surrounding world. The mound is compared to a pile of dirty laundry, of dead chickens, to a new altar the poet erects in the marketplace, as its high priest. Blood, vomit, pus, and corpses replace the sacrifice pleasing to God. The poet's own body appears as a substitute for the pile of corpses. His body produces vile liquids, and he tells God in the opening line not to "lick my sticky beard" and warns him that "From my mouth run brown streams of tar." He tells God to "caress" and "lick" his hands "as a dog/Licks its scabby, suppurating hide" (Markish 1987, 358).[15] The poem grotesquely transforms the archetypical dyads of mother and child, God and his people, poet and God, poet and people into grotesque images of bodies overflowing their limits. All Levitical prohibitions and separations are turned inside out. The mound is a "breasted cradle of garbage" that the night "tastes"; elsewhere the poet invites God to take a seat on its "bosomy roof" to feed, like a raven. The mound is simultaneously garbage, the mother, and the queen who rejects the Ten Commandments. The continuous rotten flow overwhelms the boundaries between eros, nurture, and death. The pile of corpses knows no limits: "Leap mound, wild fever/Over thresholds, over ditches" (356). The pollution covers the entire earth: "The daylight is stopped up with blood and pus/With a mound of carcasses, a Babel of corpses" (1921, 24). These lines are close to what Markish would write about the typhus train in *Brothers*: "A cloudy membrane stretches over the day, / A black-spotted swelling, oozing pus, covers it" (1929, 216). In both "The Mound" and *Brothers* Markish emphasizes the open, flowing body, not in fecundity but in death, producing an image of what Julia Kristeva describes in her work on abjection as "death infecting life, beckoning to us and engulfing us" (1982, 4).

Riding in the armored train in *Brider*, Shloyme-Ber sits surrounded by maps, the radio, and the telegraph, receiving and giving out orders. Beginning with the first five-year plan, the machine in general and the train in particular symbolized the new, technologically enhanced world made possible by the revolution (Clark 1985, 293–98). Babel explicitly contrasts the moribund world of Hasidism—Gedali's description of the "passionate edifice of Hasidism" with its "oozing eye sockets" not unlike Markish's imagery in "The Mound"—with the brilliant light and clatter of the machines on the agitprop train of the First Cavalry Army (Babel 1990, 2:38).[16] In contrast, in Markish's *Brider*, there is no difference between the armored train and the surrounding world: the train is infected by the typhus of its passengers. The magnitude of the epidemic is emphasized in the description of the train:

> Forty wagons of delirium, lice, and fever,
> Forty wagons groaning, screaming, calling,
> Forty wagons of raw flesh, blood, and pus,
> There was no more space for the fever and heat,
>
> *Fertsik vagones mit hits un mit layz un mit fiber,*
> *Fertsik vagones mit krekhts, mit geshray un mit rufn,*
> *Fertsik vagones mit vund-fleysh, mit blut un mit ayter,—*
> *Mer hot keyn plats far dem fiber un hits nit gestayet,*
>
> (1929, 216)

In his work on Russian revolutionary poetry, Rolf Hellebust describes a symbolic transformation that he calls "flesh into metal" (2003, 28–29). The human body takes on superhuman strength, as in the example of Shloyme-Ber. In contrast, Markish's image of the typhus train reverses the process, transforming metal into flesh.[17]

Brothers is about the revolution, the unmaking of a world before the birth of a new one. It artistically represents the overcoming of all boundaries separating bodies from each other, and the individual from "the people's mass body," to use Bakhtin's language. In Markish, however, Bakhtin's joyful carnival crowd becomes a vast undifferentiated body. As the numerous episodes and images of the separation of skin from flesh reveal, even the most basic of boundaries between inside and outside is destroyed.

The hallmark of Markish's style in *Brothers* is excess. His imagery, writes the Yiddish critic Shmuel Niger, is "swollen," and, Niger continues, he "suffers from a disease which I would call eternal word hunger. He gobbles up word after word and is not satisfied" (1958, 36). Markish's perpetually hungry mouth, as Niger puts it, suggests the process of incorporation, the paradoxical condition of being full of a demanding loss. The superabundance of words and images, the excess of flesh, and the loss of individuation characteristic of *Brider* as a whole give narrative shape to a loss that cannot fully be avowed. The excess of words signals the insufficiency of words. Markish's own ambivalent relation to the Jewish past and the increasing pressure on Soviet writers to overcome "nationalism" meant that the devastation suffered by the Jewish community during the civil war could not be mourned openly. The loss appears instead in the vast, messy corpus of the text, whose words appear as the swollen traces of unacknowledged wounds.

Near the end of the poem, Markish describes the abandoned house of the two dead brothers, where "no one will close the pages of the Bible anymore / Or kiss them" (*Keyner vet dem taytsh-khumesh mer shoyn nit farmakhn, / Mer shoyn nit farmakhn, mer shoyn nit keyn kush tun*) (1929, 265). The people are gone, but the objects momentarily assume living form: "the pages of the bible flutter like the wings of a thin, dead bird." The Bible tells the house everything that happened and then "rises above the shtetl like a beautiful headstone" (*shtelt zikh afn shtetl, vi a sheynere matseyve*) (265). The biblical text loses its meaning as a set of narratives, revelation, law, and history, becoming instead a grave marker, a sign indicating the place of a dead body.

In 1929 Yiddish-language critics were not as generous with their praise of *Brider* as the critics who later commented on the Russian translation. At an event held in Moscow acknowledging Markish's accomplishment, Isaac Nusinov and Moshe Litvakov raised the problem of nationalism. Litvakov asserted that Markish's "leap" into "our Soviet concreteness landed him in an unintentional nationalism." Litvakov went on to say that Markish "has not been able to free himself from the mood of the 'sanctification of the name' [*kidesh hashem*] even in the places where he describes the graves of three fallen Bolsheviks" (Litvakov 1929).[18] He concluded by exhorting Markish to "absorb [*iberkokhn*] dialectically our Soviet revolutionary life and work." Litvakov was right about the atmosphere of mourning that pervades the poem. But he was wrong about Markish's ability to "absorb" or "digest" Soviet life. The world of *Brider* is too full of loss to absorb anything new.

Kvitko's Struggle

Leyb Kvitko's "In roytn shturem" (In a red storm) appeared in a collection of his poems called *Gerangl* (Struggle) in 1929. Kvitko served on the editorial board of the Kharkov journal *Di royte velt* (The red world), and was deeply involved in the Yiddish internecine wars of the late 1920s and early 1930s; among Russian readers he was known as a children's writer.[19] In Kvitko's "In a Red Storm" the conflict between past and present unfolds first as a struggle between generations. The poet's father is dying of hunger:

> He calls for me,
> He asks for me,
> He drenches my name
> In pain.
> I steel myself
> And don't want to hear it!
> I must be,
> And must belong
> To the storm of destruction,
> To the many hammers
> Building what is new.
> I am becoming younger,
> I am becoming younger,
> I am becoming free!
> I breathe in!

Un mikh ruft er,
Un mikh bet er,
Veykt mayn nomen oys
In payn
shtark ikh zikh
Un vil nit hern!
Ikh darf zayn
Un darf gehern
Tsu dem shturem fun tseshtern,
Tsu di hamern di file
Af tsu boyen nay—
Ikh ver yunger,
Ikh ver yunger,
Ikh ver fray
Kh'shep!

(Kvitko 1929, 273–74)

The Hebrew Bible constructs the relation between God and people as a reciprocal process of calling out and answering: Abraham answers God's call to him, and God responds to the suffering of Israel by answering their cry. Kvitko's "In the Red Storm" severs the connection by cutting off the son's response to the father. The process of self-remaking associated with forging—the transformation of "flesh into metal"—takes on the additional psychological dimension of hardening the self against the father's plea for help. The poetic subject wills himself to grow young, emphasizing the distance between generations; he wants to take a breath that is his own, willing his own self-rebirth.

Images of pain in later passages, however, undermine the self-willed autonomy imagined in these earlier lines. Turning away from the father's call amounts to an assault on the poet's own body:

I roast my troubles on my flesh
And I take revenge on myself,
I beat myself with pieces of my own flesh:

Brot mayn tsorn af mayn layb
Un ikh noykem zikh in mir,
Shmits ikh shtiker fun mayn layb:

(276)

The tension between the old world and the freedom, youth, and sense of belonging promised by the new world leads to a split in the poet, who pictures himself as if incarcerated in a gothic torture chamber. The line separating what is part of him from what he rejects as old and dying is impossible to draw, and the punishment he would inflict on others turns out to be revenge on himself.

In the next stanza, the poet feels the heavy burden of his new role:

Bridled to great destruction,
I make my way in the heavy harness
On the mounds of marrow, brains,
The waste flies at me

Ayngeshpant in groysn khorev,
Gey ikhh in dem shpan dem shvern
Af di hrudes markh, gehirn—

(277)

The revolution, and the establishment of Soviet power—the storm of destruction to which the poet yearned to belong—now feels like a constraint, indicated by the term "harness," which the poet uses twice in the stanza.[20] The agent of destruction, the poet, has become its victim. The imagery of the stanza alludes to Markish's 1921 "The Mound." As in that earlier poem, the image of the abject body takes on monumental scale: the landscape itself is strewn with marrow and brains. The modernist and revolutionary myth of the elevation of the single individual to universal dimensions, as found, for example, in the bodily poetics of Vladimir Mayakovsky, here assumes prophetic qualities of universal cataclysm.[21]

Stillbirth

Markish and Kvitko reveal a sense of the competing obligations of past and present, unacknowledged mourning over the destruction of the past, and feelings of ambivalence about both the old Jewish world and the revolution. The metonymy of the body expresses both a joyous and a catastrophic loss of boundaries between the masculine and the feminine, between individuals and the surrounding world, and between the inside and the outside of the body. No single work more powerfully engages this set of themes, and so poignantly, than Markish's untitled poem of 1932:

> Both those,
> from whose death I turn away
> And those,
> whose death is their birth—
> You all are bloodied in my womb,
> You all grow from me
> And fall from me,
> Like fruit.
>
> But I will not free my steps from their shackles,
> I will not allow myself to rest at a well,
> Until I lead the dead into the past,
> Until I bring the newborn to their beginning.
>
> Time that is blotted out!
> Crossroads blotted out in pain
> Which flicker as if drowned in memory
> My one heart has split for you in vain,
> No river can flow on both sides . . .
> There is one way, like my heart and like the pain
> Only my disquieted heart will rock back and forth on the way . . .
>   . . .
> Beat, my heart, and, take breath for both!
> Now you, my heart, must be a stretcher and a cradle
> For all those for whom I have made a vow,
> For all those,
> From whose gaze I turn away!
>
> *Say di*
> *vos kh'ker zikh op fun zeyer brokh*
>
> *Say di,*
> *Vos zeyer brokh—zaynen geburtn—*
>
> *Ir ale zayt farblutikt in mayn yokh,*
> *Ir ale vakst af mir*

Un falt fun mir,
Vi frukhtn.

Nor kh'vel nit oysshpanen di trit mayne fun tsvang,
Kh'vel zikh keyn opshtel bay keyn brunem nit farginen,
Biz kh'vel nit apfirn s'fargangene n'fargang,
Biz kh'vel nit oyfbrengen s'geboyrene n'baginen.

Farmekte tsayt!
Farmekte kreytsvegn—farveyte—
Vos tsanken af, glaykh vi dertrunkene n'gedank—
Mayn eyntsik harts hot zikh umzist af aykh getsveyt dort,—
Es ken nit flisn dokh keyn taykh in beyde zaytn . . .
Der gang iz eyntsik, vi dos harts un vi der vaytik,
Nor vi an umru t'zikh dos harts gevigt in gang . . .
 . . .
Iz klap mayn harts un shlog, mayn otem, zikh far beyde!
Itst muzstu, harts mayns, zayn a mite un a vig
Far ale di,
Vos kh'hob zikh oysgegrint a neyder,
Far ale di,
Vos kh'ker zikh op fun zeyer blik!

(Markish 1987, 464)

The poet does not specify the two groups whom he addresses, those whom he would abandon and those to whom he swears he will lead into the future. Later stanzas associate the figure of the poet with Moses, suggesting a comparison between shtetl Jews on their way to becoming Soviet Jews and the generation of slaves brought out of Egypt.

The problem is that the poet cannot sustain the distinctions between the damned and the saved ("You all are bloodied in my womb"), between rebirth and death, and past and future: "Time that is blotted out!" *Brothers* celebrates the loss of limits and hierarchy as the triumph of the revolution, and mourns the loss of the Jewish world with images of the body overflowing its limits. Here, Markish personifies and psychologizes the loss with an image of abject incorporation, the taking into the self of the lost object, a pregnancy of death. All boundaries are confused. In the second stanza of the poem the poet reveals that the dead are part of his own body: "You all grow from me/And fall from me, / Like fruit." In a later stanza the processes of the poet's body, the drawing of breath, and the beating of his heart are described as taking place for those who are dying and those who are coming to life; his heart is both a "stretcher" and a "cradle." The poet's body serves as both womb and tomb ("*brokh*," destruction, rhymes with "*yokh*," literally, "yoke"). This is not a revolutionary image of the overcoming of nature or the appropriation of reproduction but rather an image of stillbirth.

The ordered succession of generations becomes confused in this work: the dying and dead refuse to disappear into the past, just as those about to be born or reborn never arrive in their future. As in Babel's work, violence supersedes birth, as in the line, "You all are bloodied in my womb." The final stanza underlines the problem of failed natality. The poet, like Moses, ascends a mountain, but on the way up encounters the body of a pilgrim still carrying his pilgrim's sack:

> Because he died with the bag in his teeth,
> And in the bag
> He multiplied
> And increased . . .
>
> *Vayl mit der torbe in di tseyn iz er geshtorbn,*
> *Un in der torbe*
> *Zikh gefrukhpert*
> *Un gemert. . . .*

(465)

This image of stillbirth inverts the biblical injunction to "be fruitful and multiply." The promise of nationhood in the promised land comes to nothing. The pregnant womb, symbolized by the pilgrim's sack, becomes a site of mass death, contained within a single body.

Babel's Ancient Body

Borenstein argues that revolutionary literature placed greater emphasis on the freely chosen bonds of masculine affiliation rather than the inherited bonds of paternal filiation.[22] In choosing "brothers" as the title of his work, Markish it would seem wished to signal allegiance with the new world in which lateral bonds between comrades overwhelm all connection to the past. However, the text's excess reveals the power of the filiative bonds with the past, with the world of fathers. Markish, with his excess of words, and Babel, with an economic use of words, both address events and emotions that words cannot adequately describe. A lack of boundaries—interpsychic, intercorporeal, and intertemporal—dominates both Babel's and Markish's texts. Babel and the Yiddish writers similarly explore the theme of failed birth.

There is a significant body of critical literature on Babel, unlike the other writers discussed in this chapter, and a rehearsal of its major threads will help clarify my readings. One side of the critical debate characterizes Babel as "a seer of the flesh," as Merezhkovskii said of Tolstoy. Aleksandr Voronskii is the prime example of this approach. Babel is the poet of "tactility"; Babel is a "physiological writer," who "worships the flesh"; for Babel, life was a woman with a big belly: these and other images evoke the sunny side of the Odessa writer (Voronskii 1928, 168, 169). Voronskii cautioned, however, that occasionally Babel went too far in his emphasis on "stinking flesh" and gives, among other examples, the episode of Jesus and Deborah from "Pan Apolek." Jesus takes the place of the bridegroom of a young Jewish woman, whose husband rejects her after she vomits on her wedding night: Jesus goes to her "lying in vomit" (Babel 1990, 2:24). This is an example of an abject moment in Babel, comparable to what we have already seen in Markish. Voronskii's approach, which has been adopted by other critics, typically focuses on the way that Babel transforms violence into aesthetic material, and argues for Babel's reliance on Nietzscheanism.[23]

An example of the technique occurs in the story "Berestechko," in the scene describing the killing of an old Jew:

> Right in front of my windows some Cossacks were trying to shoot an old Jew with a silver beard for espionage. The old man squealed and tried to get away. Then Kudria from the artillery squad took him by the head, placing it under his arm. The Jew quieted down and spread his legs. With his right hand, Kudria took out his dagger and carefully cut the old man's throat without spattering himself. (Babel 1990 2:69)

The phrase "without spattering himself" particularly delighted Voronskii, who considered it an exquisite example of Babel's mastery of a Tolstoyan sense of minimalist gesture.[24] The portrait of the old Jew recycles the stereotype of Jewish passivity and impotence. The Jew cooperates in his own death, which is utterly devoid of dignity: "If anyone's interested, they can come get him," Kudria says when he has finished (2:69). The narrator's indifference to the Jew's death has horrified Babel's readers. Efraim Sicher, for example, explains the silence on the grounds that it is the result of Babel's "personal trauma" (1995, 98).

Markish's *Brider* also includes a scene of the killing of an old Jew, a rabbi, also on the grounds of spying. Markish's portrait of the old rabbi is full of dignity and power; his face glows with the white radiance of his eighty years:

Eighty years of snow-white thoughts
Emanate from his beard and brows,

Akhtsik vayse yorn fun zayn ponem brenen,
Akhtsik vayse yorn fun shneyen klore—klerer
Hengen shtil arop fun bord un fun di bremen,

(Markish 1929, 214)

Expressing his surprise over the reverence of this image, Shmuel Niger wrote in 1929, "This is what a Soviet artist says about a rabbi!" (252).

The comparison between "Berestechko" and *Brider* on this single point, however, skews the result. The problem with the exclusive focus on the narrator's lack of affect in this single episode in "Berestechko" (aside from identifying the author with the narrator) is that it ignores the story as a whole. The story as a whole is swamped in death and haunted by the ghosts of the past. On the way to Berestechko, the narrator sees "fantastic corpses lying on thousand year old burial grounds" (Babel 1990 2:69). They pass the watchtower of Bogdan Khmel'nitskii, a name associated with the murder of Jews in the seventeenth century. Invoking Khmel'nitskii sets the events of the present in the framework of the destruction of the past. This is a traditionally Jewish narratological move, which radically shifts the time frame and the model of historical causality, removing an event from its immediate historical context and placing it in a timeless frame. A similar narrative strategy unfolds in the remarkably brief "The Cemetery at Kozin," which opens with the lines: "A cemetery in a Jewish shtetl. Assyria and the secret rot of the East on the overgrown tall weeds of the fields of Volynia" (2:60). As Evgenii Dobrenko rightly points out, the story is outside of time and space: the time referents belong either to three hundred years ago or to the Bible; the spatial referents locate the story both in Ukraine and the ancient near East.

The archetypal Jewish catastrophe is the destruction of the two Temples in 586 B.C.E. and 70 C.E., the first and second "*khurbn*," commemorated in the holiday of Tisha b'Av, about which Babel writes in his diary entry for July 24, 1920:

> The 9th of Av. The old woman sobs, sitting on the floor, her son, who adores his mother, and says that he believes in God in order to please his mother, chants in a pleasant tenor and explains the history of the destruction of the Temple. The terrible words of the prophets: they will eat excrement, the maidens will be forsaken, the men killed, Israel crushed, angry and grievous words. The lamp smokes, the old woman howls, the young man sings melodiously, the girls in white stockings, outside the window Demidowka, night, Cossacks, everything just as it was then when the Temple was destroyed. (1:387)

According to Efraim Sicher, who also discusses the passage above, Babel planned to write a story "about the shtetl of Demidowka which centered on the national tragedy of the Jews symbolized by the destruction of the Temple and the prophecy of Jeremiah" (Sicher 1995, 92). Even though the story did not materialize, the traditional Jewish vocabulary of lament nonetheless enters Babel's text.

In "Berestechko," after the murder of the old Jew, the narrator "began to wander around" the city. His wandering takes him to the Jewish quarter, with its ancient, gloomy architecture and secret entranceways leading to fantastic catacombs: "In times of war people protect themselves in these catacombs from bullets and pillaging. Here human and animal refuse accumulates for many days. Depression and horror fill the catacombs with an acrid stench . . . Berestechko inviolably stinks up to the present day . . . The shtetl stinks in expectation of a new era and instead of people, faded images of border misfortune wander through it" (2:70). In this passage, Torok and Abraham's "secret tomb" is a feature of Berestechko's topography that is hidden but real. The use of the present tense (*spasaiutsia, skopliaiutsia, zapolniaiut*) suggests that there is no difference between the destructions of the past and the present. As Babel put it himself in his diary on July 18, 1920, the Jewish cemetery "saw Khmel'nitskii, now Budennyi, the unfortunate Jewish population, everything repeats itself" (1:377). The dead are not fully dead yet—their presence is not yet erased—but instead they still wander about in ghostly form. Their stink travels across physical and temporal boundaries, filling the town and filling the present tense with the horrors of the past.[25] The suspension of linear time underscores the monumental destruction that has taken place. After catastrophe, the future is uncertain. Babel himself makes this point explicitly in a short piece of 1918, in which he describes "the convulsion of revolution leading no one knows where" (1:162).

Many readers of Babel have remarked on Liutov's attachment to the Jewish world that is dying. "Gedali" provides several passages indicative of this bond. The story opens with an invocation of the narrator's childhood: "On Sabbath evenings the dense sadness of memory torments me. On these evenings my grandfather would stroke the volumes of Ibn-Ezra with his yellow beard. My grandmother in her lace headcovering used to tell fortunes holding her gnarled fingers over the Sabbath candles and sweetly sobbing. My childish heart was cradled on these evenings like a little ship on enchanted waves" (2:29). Entering Gedali's shop resembles a journey into memory itself; the shop is like a precocious little boy's treasure box. "Enveloped in the light odor of rot," Liutov follows Gedali as he "winds his way through the labyrinth of globes, skulls, and dead flowers" (2:29). Some of Babel's contemporaries criticized him for his hero's attachment to the past, as a review published in *Pravda* in 1926 reveals: "the future growth of Babel as an artist is possible only on the condition of his definitive liberation from the dead truth of rotten talmuds" (Ionov 1926). Milton Ehre characterizes Liutov's attachment as nostalgia: "Liutov struggles against the webs of nostalgia that tie him to the mother" (1986, 84). Carol Avins describes Liutov's emerging sense of "bereavement," especially evident in "The Rebbe's Son" (Syn rabbi) (1994). Nostalgia and bereavement tell only part of the story, however, because these terms do not capture the ambivalent and uncanny quality of the text. Babel's narrator in "Berestechko" emphasizes his estrangement from a past that nonetheless "intoxicates" him. Volynia is not Odessa; it is Markish's birthplace, not Babel's. The Jews of Poland were alien to Babel, and this difference emerges clearly both in the 1920 diary and in the *Red Cavalry* stories; for example, in "The Theory of the Tachanka" he characterizes the Jews of Galicia and Volynia as having "unrestrained, jerky movements, offensive to good taste"; in his diary he describes the Jews of Dubno as "misshapen little figures" (Avins 1994, 697).

The emotions of "The Road to Brody" have nothing of the sweetness of childhood: "O Brody! The mummies of your trampled passions breathed their irresistible poison on me. I felt the already lethal chill of your eye sockets full of tears that had grown cold" (*O Brody! Mumii tvoikh razdavlennykh strastei dyshali na menia nepreoborimym iadom*) (Babel 1990, 2:40). Babel used a similar combination of intoxication and poison to describe emotions in "The Church in Novograd": "I see the wounds of your God, dripping with seed, fragrant poison, which intoxicates maidens" (2:9). He stands in the same relation to Brody as the "maidens" do in relation to the crucifix. This is a deadly intimacy with someone else's desires. In "The Theory of the Tachanka" Babel explains what these passions were about: "I understood the burning history of this region, the stories about Talmudists renting out taverns, about rabbis who lent money for interest, about girls, raped by Polish mercenaries and on whose account Polish magnates shot themselves" (2:11). The intoxicating and poisonous passions of Galicia and Volynia were not his own, but they possessed him as powerfully as any native of the region. As Abraham and Torok put it, "the phantom is alien to the subject who harbors it" (1994, 181). In both *Red Cavalry* and *Brider*, the world of the past exerts its lethal force over the living.

What about the revolution and the birth of the new? In Markish's 1932 poem, birth is tantamount to stillbirth. Babel had addressed this theme earlier. In "Berestechko," and in *Red Cavalry* generally, and in Babel's nonfiction writing, the revolution is disassociated from the image of birth. The failure of the new regime to support natality is the central theme of Babel's nonfiction piece of 1918, "Dvorets materinstva" (The palace of motherhood). The eight inmates of this institution have "protruding bellies . . . gray faces" and "swollen legs"; their past consists of "factory sirens calling their husbands to the defense of the revolution;

the heavy anxiety of war and the convulsion of revolution leading no one knows where" (1990, 1:162). The revolution has not yet taken place in "The Palace of Motherhood":

> Children must live. Giving birth to them is necessary for the best arrangement of human life.
> That is the idea. It must be taken to its conclusion. We must at some point make the revolution.
> Taking your rifle on your shoulder and shooting at one another is perhaps, sometimes, not a bad thing to do. But it is not yet the whole revolution. Who knows—perhaps it is not the revolution at all.
> We must give birth to children well. And this—I know for certain—is the real revolution. (1:162)

Passages such as these reveal Babel's ambivalence about the "masculine ethos" that emphasized history, politics, and production over the domestic and over reproduction.[26]

In *Red Cavalry* birth is similarly problematic. The Ratsiborskii castle used to be inhabited by the ninety-year-old countess who beat her son because he did not produce an heir. Birth in Berestechko is an event that belongs only to the past, as in the "yellowed letter" in "faded" ink the narrator finds near the castle, the letter of a noblewoman to her husband, dated 1820, quoted in the story in French, informing him that their son was already seven weeks old, and asking whether it was true that Napoleon was dead. Daily life does not continue in Berestechko, neither the story nor the place: it has been "blown away," as the narrator says. The story ends with the supremely irrelevant speech of the head of the division to the "worried townspeople" and "plundered Jews," announcing that they now hold power in the town. The version of this episode in the diary emphasizes the pointlessness of Vinogradov's words: the Jews "hear about the Russian paradise, the international situation, about uprisings in India" (Babel 1990, 1:405). What Babel characterizes elsewhere in his diary as "what is new—communism" has no reality in this place, no tangible shape or form. Only the horrors of the past have palpable reality.

As in other stories in *Red Cavalry*, by the end of "Berestechko" the narrator's voice is silent, replaced by the words of others. "Crossing the Zbrucz" concludes with the pregnant daughter's lament for her slaughtered, irreplaceable father. The daughter never gives birth; it is her French-speaking Polish sister who gave birth a hundred years earlier, and whose descendents are now infertile. At the end of "Berestechko" the voice of the narrator is lost somewhere in the gothic structures of the Jewish catacombs and the ruined Polish castle. This is not the joyous loss of individuality celebrated by Bakhtin, but a regressive, backward turn to the past. Babel's Liutov, like Markish's heroes in *Brider*, ultimately forms a brotherhood in *Red Cavalry*, but not with the tightly muscled bodies of the new Soviet order. His brotherhood is with the Polish corpse of his "unknown brother" and with Ilya Bratslavskii, the rabbi's son, whose last breath Liutov receives into his own "ancient body" (*"I ia, edva vmeshchaiushchii v drevnem tele buri moego voobrazheniia,—ia prinial poslednii vzdokh moego brata"*) (2:129). Liutov has not grown young with the revolution. By the end of *Red Cavalry* he has grown old, "ancient," full of the past that is and is not his own.

The Grotesque in Gekht

Bodies swollen with disease and bursting with the alien desires of the past litter Markish's and Babel's texts. Their use of the grotesque, repetition, and hyperbole and their backward glance, together with intertexts from traditional Jewish mourning literature, undermines the discipline of the new revolutionary order and disrupts the conventionally autonomous subjects and teleological plot structures of realism. The civil war era works of Semen Grigorevich (Avraam Gershovich) Gekht share a similar perspective on the revolution and civil war and a similar set of narrative devices. In "Prostoi rasskaz o mertvetsakh" (A simple story about corpses), published in 1925, a Red soldier on a punishment detail transports dead bodies, the victims of typhus, from an overcrowded morgue to the cemetery. Hundreds of corpses wait for burial; in exchange for a meal, the solider agrees to take more than his orders require. The ride to the cemetery is full of macabre misadventures: the bodies slip around in his cart; he ends up sitting on someone's head; he loses a corpse on the way; but he himself remains distant and indifferent to what takes place (Gekht 1983, 5–16).

Born in Odessa, Gekht was a close friend of Babel and, later, the poet Semen Lipkin and the prose author Vasilii Grossman. Gekht was a student of the poet Eduard Bagritskii and part of what Viktor Shklovskii identified as the "southwest school" of Soviet literature. He published short prose fiction throughout his lifetime (1903–63), except for his eight-year stint in the Gulag from 1944 to 1952 for the crime of "anti-Soviet activity" (his friendship with Babel played a significant role in his arrest). Gekht also translated the Yiddish authors Sholem Asch and Sholem Aleichem. Yiddish words and expressions, sometimes transliterated and sometimes translated into Russian, appear throughout his writing.[27] Little is known of his early years; one source reports that his parents were killed in the Odessa pogrom in 1905, and that he was raised by his older brother. It seems likely that he grew up in a more traditional home than Babel's, something closer to what Markish or Bergelson experienced. During Gekht's interrogation, when asked about his use of "Semen" instead of "Avraam" (with the implication of duplicity on his part), the author explained that according to Jewish custom, when children became sick, they were given alternate names to try to trick the angel of death. Gekht invoked the traditional Jewish life world in his fiction, including, for example, the rules concerning work on the Sabbath, the laws of family purity, and the custom of seeking intercession from the dead. The effect of the ethnographic detail, however, is more ironic than nostalgic. In the remarkable 1927 story "Chelovek, kotoryi zabyl svoiu zhizn'" (A man who forgot his life), for example, the narrator explains the *eruv*, the space within which it is permissible to carry and to walk on the Sabbath, demarcated by lines hung from poles. During the civil war, Petliura's men called the *eruv* a wireless telegraph and shot ten Jews to stop the practice.

Gekht's story "Gai-Makan" reunites a Jewish victim, the first-person narrator of the story, and a Ukrainian perpetrator on a breadline in Berlin. In the opening scene the gigantic body of the former Ukrainian general Gai-Makan is grotesquely swollen from dropsy; his gigantic head, like a pumpkin, is set deep in his shoulders. The abject landscape of Markish and Babel is here condensed into a single figure. The narrator recounts the events of 1918, when there was no order in Ukraine, when life and death changed places: "Eighteen months of endless misfortune taught Jewish women to meet death calmly, because death was unavoidable, and to fear life, because life seemed to be an accident" (Gekht 1983, 142). Beila Pritsker tries to outwit the inevitable by telling her tormentor, a Cossack, that she is ill with syphilis. At this point, Gai-Makan makes his entrance: "Someone's gigantic legs thundered iron and steel. Someone's gigantic body threw itself at the door. One minute passed and a deafening cough was heard, the rusted door hinges squealed penetratingly and shards of glass spilled" (144). This highly stylized description can be compared to a scene from Babel's "My First Goose":

> Savitskii, head of division 6, stood up when he saw me, and the beauty of his gigantic body amazed me. He stood up, and the purple of his riding pants, his raspberry cap, worn askew, his medals, stuck into his chest, split the hut in two like a standard splits the sky. He smelled of cologne and sickly sweet coolness of soap. His long legs were like girls', encased up to their shoulders in dazzling high boots. (1990, 2:32)

Babel's story was first published in 1924, and Gekht's a year later in a collection of his stories that appeared in Moscow (1925). In both passages the non-Jew's body is gigantic and powerful, but in Babel, unlike Gekht, it fascinates and entrances the Jew. Both stories share the theme of rape. The bespectacled Liutov is told that the Cossacks will accept him if he assaults a woman; in Gekht's story the title character dispatches the syphilis problem by ordering a terrified Jewish doctor to examine Beila. When she is found to be healthy, Gai-Makan begins to get undressed as Beila closes her eyes. In "My First Goose" the old lady says she wants to hang herself; in "Gai-Makan" Beila says, "I won't survive this. I want to die" (Gekht 1983, 143).

In Babel's story the boundaries of emotions and allegiances constantly shift: Liutov is amazed and attracted by Savitskii, repulsed by the Cossacks and eager for their acceptance, and full of desire and guilt. Similarly, in Gekht's story, the opposition between perpetrator and victim breaks down as the Jew and the Ukrainian general find themselves together in exile in Berlin, both suffering from hunger and united by their relation to Beila. The narrator, it turns out, is her husband, and he reassures Gai-Makan that she feels no hatred for him. At the conclusion of the story, the bakery runs out of bread, and the Jew and the general go off together in search of sugar. In both Babel's "My First Goose" and Gekht's "Gai-Makan" the lines separating Jews and non-Jews blur, their bodies intertwined in hunger, enmity, violence, and desire.

Fathers and Children

Revolutionary culture emphasized youth, and revolutionary culture looked forward to the future. The revolution called upon sons to renounce the ways of their fathers. Gekht's story "The Man Who Forgot His Life" sets all these commonplaces on their head. Set in the period of the so-called new economic policy, the story looks back to the civil war years. An anti-Semitic outburst on a tram in Moscow opens the story: a Gypsy with a dark beard declares that the Jewish "kingdom" has arrived, and complains that Russians are being squeezed out. The Gypsy's speech is full of Yiddish, including the words "*shurem-borem*" (muddle, mess) and "*gesheft*" (business). The story retraces the path of Jewish migration from the former pale to Moscow (as one character puts it, mixing Russian and Yiddish, "they flooded Moscow with their *tatele-mamele*"), focusing not on the new type of Jewish worker but on the lives of the old-fashioned Jews who lived in the ghetto called Little Jerusalem in the city of Vinnitsa during the civil war.

Isak Zel'ts, the hero of the story, lives in a topsy-turvy world from beginning to end. Married off in a "black wedding" (a wedding held in a cemetery to ward off misfortune for the community), he is promised money by the rich Jews to buy a shop, but they fail to carry out their promise. Isak's only surviving son, Nakhman (which as the story tells us, means "comfort"), begins reading secular literature in Russian at the age of thirteen and falls in love with a non-Jewish girl. At this time the Austrian and German troops that have been occupying southern Ukraine fall to Ukrainian forces, embodied in the story in the character of Ataman Zaremba. To prove his bravery, Nakhman tries to enlist in Zaremba's militia but is instead arrested. His father's efforts to free him prove fruitless. Forced by Zaremba, Isak eats pork and curses the Jews, only to learn later that Nakhman is already dead, shot by mistake. Isak goes mad from grief and takes up a wandering life; in an inversion of the biblical story of Balaam, he no longer can speak except to curse Jews. Calling himself Ahasveros, the king of Shushan, he leaves history and enters the timelessness of legend.[28]

Time's Rupture: Bergelson and Mandelshtam

The products and symptoms of the body appear as unacknowledged and indirect articulations of mourning in the work of Markish, Kvitko, Babel, and Gekht. Time does not move forward but rather circles back to saturate the present with the past. The problem of time is key to David Bergelson's works of the late 1920s, including "Tsvishn emigrantn" (Among immigrants, first published in 1927), "Hinter a brenendikn shtetl" (Near a burning shtetl, 1926), "Birgerkrig" (Civil war, 1926), and *Mides-hadin* (The harshness of the law, 1929), which were written while Bergelson was still living in Berlin. By this time he had already established himself as a leading Yiddish modernist; *Arum voksal* (At the depot, 1909), "Der toyber" (The deaf one, 1910), *Nokh alemen* (When all is said and done, 1913), and *Opgang* (Descent; also translated as "Departure," 1920) are among his outstanding early works.[29] Bergelson was born in Okhrimove, near Sarne, Ukraine; his father was a wealthy timber and grain merchant and a Talner Hasid. Bergelson received no formal secular education, although he read widely in Hebrew and Russian, and his early attempts at authorship were in those languages. Something of Bergelson's early years can be grasped from his autobiographical fiction *Baym Dnyeper* (At the Dnieper; Vol. 1, "Penek," 1932; Vol. 2, "Yunge yorn" [Early years], 1940).[30] Although Bergelson energetically participated in the development of new Yiddish cultural and literary institutions, including the Kiev Kultur-Lige (an organization founded in 1918 to promote Yiddish culture), the civil war had a profound effect on him, and he left Moscow for Berlin in 1921, where he lived until 1933; he returned to Russia in 1934.[31]

In Markish's poem of 1932, time is "blotted out in pain." In stories such as "Berestechko" from *Red Cavalry*, and in the image of the Bible as a headstone in *Brothers*, the destruction of the past burdens the present. Bergelson develops this backward-facing temporality in the story

"Tsvishn emigrantn" (Among immigrants). A young Jewish man, originally from Ukraine, now living in Berlin, discovers that a Ukrainian leader, notorious for his role in anti-Jewish violence, is staying in the same hotel. As in Gekht's "Gai-Makan," Berlin, a space of exile, unites victim and perpetrator, blurring the boundaries between them. The young man decides that he must assassinate the Ukrainian leader, and having failed to find support from the Jewish community, who try to put him under the care of a psychiatrist, he turns to an unnamed writer, the first-person narrator, for help with his plan.[32] The young man describes his childhood in his grandfather's home, overwhelmed by reminders of death. All of the grandfather's children, including the young man's father, died young, and the grandfather had the strange habit of buying a clock to mark their deaths. The would-be assassin says, "Every clock was a grave, the anniversary of a death" (*Yeder zeyger—a keyver, a yortsayt*) (Bergelson 1930b, 182). The forward motion of time marks only a succession of deaths; the ticking clock more resembles a calendar of remembrances than a timepiece.[33] In *Red Cavalry* and *Brothers* the deaths of the past similarly burden the present.

This strange, backward-facing quality of time permeates the landscape of "Among Immigrants," spreading from the "terrorist" to the writer, and filling the streets of Berlin with "mute ghosts" (*shtume gayster*). The young man, with his strangely crooked face, has an "uncanny" (*unheymlekh*) effect on his environment, stirring up emotions and events from the past (177). Time itself lengthens on the day of the visit: "it was a day like a year, like a long, long road"; "on a day like this, looking back, you think to yourself that you've walked a tremendous distance" (2005, 23) (*af aza min tog, az men kukt zikh um tsurik, dakht zikh: men iz durkhgegangen an umgeveynlekh groyse shtreke*) (1930b, 178). The strange day has no outcome: the self-styled "Jewish terrorist" kills only himself. His attempt to implicate the writer in responsibility for what has happened ("you are as responsible as I am, and even more, because you are a writer") has no obvious result save the writing of the story. The story addresses its readers with the same unanswered questions posed by the young man. To be "among immigrants" is to reside in a world burdened with debts to the past, called upon to answer for and answer to the dead (to be answerable, "*farantvortlekh*") but without the possibility of discharging the balance owed. In the impossibly elongated present, there is no clear future.

The first-person narrator of "Among Immigrants" is unusually prescient about his moment in history. More typically, the characters in the *Storm Days* cycle are unaware of the extraordinary nature of their time. Bergelson's narrator alludes to Jewish history as if to signal the larger meaning of events: the story "Civil War," for example, refers to Betar, the Jewish city that fell to the Romans in 135 C.E., on the Ninth of Av [Talmud Gittin 57a]; and "Near a Burning Shtetl" (*Hinter a brenendikn shtetl*) refers to Lot's escape from Sodom (1930b, 99). The characters in these works, however, pursue their ordinary lives in spite of the enormous, epoch-making events that frame their experience.[34] In "Near a Burning Shtetl" the protagonist daydreams about "first-class" women as he runs from destruction. In "Civil War," Leyzerke, the Bolshevik whom the townspeople of Aleksandrovke blame for the attacks by Petliura's men, finally establishes his authority. He tells Hayml Bashevis, the innkeeper, "I hate you!" (*Hob ikh aykh faynt!*) (1930b, 64). The last word of the story is "hate." The triumph of Bolshevism fails to change the consciousness of the characters. The 1930 Russian translation of these stories features a cover illustration depicting two Jewish Bolsheviks with strong jaws, muscled necks, and in Lenin-style caps. They look off into the future they are earnestly building. The contents of the book belie the image on its cover (Bergelson 1930a).

Written in a deliberately fragmentary style, "Civil War" shifts focus, moving from a pair of non-Jewish Bolsheviks to a non-Jewish wet nurse in a Jewish family, and culminating in the virulent divisions within the Jewish community. Each perspective is estranged, confounding the reader's expectations.[35] Using the technique of cinematic montage, Bergelson shifts emotions from personalities onto disaggregated parts of the body; for example, the Cossacks' outburst of joy in response to the overthrow of the tsar "blazes up" in their hair and shoulders; in contrast, "the Jews look with terror at the soldiers' laughing teeth" (1930b, 21). Bergelson also displaces emotion onto inanimate objects, as in his description of the shtetl besieged by Petliura's men: "fainting, indifferent, the damp rooftop dropped drip after drip of misfortune, demanding mercy from the world" (*in kaltblutikn khaloshes hot dort der naser dakh getript mit umglik a tropn nokh a tropn, gemont rakhmones bay der velt*) (55). It was the Yiddish critic Isaac Nusinov who first characterized Bergelson's style as impressionist, but the odd angles of his prose, the decentered and shifting outlines of people, places, and events, and the sudden personification of inanimate objects more resemble cubism than impressionism in the visual arts.[36] His use of distance and irony, and his polyphonic use of multiple language styles share features of Russian literary modernism of the time, especially Babel.

In Markish's *Brider* the civil war engendered a horrific loss of individuation on the part of his male heroes; the catastrophe of war appears as a monstrous, grotesque body. In "Civil War," in contrast, grotesque motifs appear only intermittently. The economy of their use makes them all the more shocking. The non-Jewish protagonist Botchko goes to see his lover, Frosya, and "his new black boots step into piles of fallen yellow leaves, as if into something rotten and soft" (*vi in epes neveylediks un vaykhs*)(Bergelson 1930b, 22). The term "*neveyle*" can refer to a carcass and can also mean "slut," suggesting the image of the abject body, exceeding its limits. Another strikingly grotesque image is found in Bergelson's description of a Jewish girl who was raped and murdered by Petliura's men:

> So what if on a thin, thin thread of memory hangs the big mouth of a girl—a deep-set mouth, like a pig's? So what if a pair of coarse swollen lips remains twisted in insult forever?
>
> *Iz vos, az af a dinem, dinem fodem fun zikorn iz hengen gebliben a groys meydlsh moyl—a tif-farshnitns vi bay a khazer? Iz vos, az a por grobe gedrolene lipn zenen geblibn baleydikt-farkrumt, af eybik farkrumt?* (55)[37]

The use of synecdoche and the contrast between the girl's fat lips and the delicate "thread of memory" heighten the repulsive absurdity of the image. The Jews and everyone else remain indifferent to the girl's fate and go about their business as usual: "So what?" is their response.

"Civil War" opens in a miserable tavern set "halfway between a great swampy forest and a far-flung muddy village" (*af halbn veg tsvishn a groysn zumpikn vald in a vayt-tsevarfn blotik dorf*) (9). Botchko and Zik, the two non-Jewish protagonists, wander the countryside avoiding

Germans and Whites, halfheartedly looking for Petrun, a Bolshevik leader. Botchko, like Fadeev's Levinson in *The Rout*, is the commander of a Red regiment, but unlike Levinson, who concentrates all of his efforts at preserving his "fighting unit," Botchko gives all his thought to his girlfriend, Frosya, and lets his men loot and desert. Botchko "goes north, while yearning for the south," as the title of the second chapter reads. The chapter focuses on Botchko's memory of the time he spent together with Frosya while his regiment was in Zvil.

The Frosya episode is a miniature drama of the body politics of interethnic relations; as in Babel and Gekht, Bergelson's bodies unite in desire and violence. Frosya, who abandoned her own infant, works as a wet nurse for a Jewish family occupying a big white house on the main street. She smells of mint candy, of "wanton autumn nights," but sometimes her breath is full of onions, which she eats "on purpose to spite her Jewish mistress, who stuffs her with milk and eggs to make the little Jewish bastard fat." In spite of herself, however, Frosya starts to love the Jewish baby more and more, even though she says that all the "Yids" should be shot. The three bodies—the mother, the infant, and the wet nurse Frosya—are intertwined in resentment and love. The act of providing food amounts to a form of assault, as the mother "stuffs" Frosya with milk and eggs, and she attempts to give the infant stomach cramps by eating onions. Violence, love, hatred, and nurture can no more be separated than the bodies of the wet nurse, the infant, and the mother, tied together and dependent on each other in spite of themselves.

In Frosya Bergelson uses language to deepen his ironic distance from the violence he describes. She whispers words of encouragement to Botchko's men as they loot Jewish stores: "She quietly prayed, 'Sin, sin, dear ones'" (*Zindikt, zindikt, tayerinke—hot zi shtil gedavnt*) (25). The use of the term "*davenen*," to pray, usually restricted to Jewish prayer, is strikingly ironic. Jewish terminology is used to refer to what amounts to an incantation against the Jews. Elsewhere in the story cycle *Shturemteg* (Storm days), in which "Civil War" appears, Bergelson uses Russian speech transliterated into the Hebrew characters of Yiddish. Frosya's use of Yiddish and the narrator's choice of markedly Jewish terms to describe her anti-Jewish attitudes emphasize the intimate enmity between

Jews and non-Jews. Using Frosya as the focalizer of emotion in response to the outbreak of anti-Jewish violence maximally estranges the Jewish point of view, challenging readers' expectations of a Yiddish-language narrative of the civil war.

Indirectness and distance characterize Bergelson's treatment of violence in "Civil War" as a whole. Botchko and Zik stay for a time in an abandoned horse stall that had once been owned by a nobleman. The nobleman's house itself is full of torn-up rooms "reeking of abandonment." The walls bear the traces of violence that has already taken place: "Along the papered walls, which were spattered in places with ink and what seemed to be blood from women who had been raped, moved three long shadows searching and rummaging for something" (*Iber di opgerisene topetn-vent, vos zenen ertervayz bagosn mit tint un bashpritst vi mit blut fun fargvaldikte nekayves, hobn zikh gerukt dray lange shotns un epes vi genishtert, gezukht*) (41). Botchko, Zik, and their unreliable comrade, who claims to know the whereabouts of their leader, Petrun, cast the "three shadows" moving along the wall. The abandoned nobleman's castle transforms living people into ghosts, reminiscent of Babel's "Berestechko," in which "instead of people, faded images of border misfortune wander through." The nature of the violence remains unclear, a point emphasized by the narrative repetition of the Yiddish "*vi*," which I have translated "what seemed to be." The violence that seems to have been perpetrated against women in this abandoned horse barn appears as a sign, a mark left on the wall, like the ink from the printing press. There is no direct encounter with violence, unlike Markish, Babel, and Kvitko's images of wounds inflicted on the body. In Bergelson, in contrast, violence is a trace left after the event.

It is difficult for Bergelson's characters and for his readers to decode these traces. The impediments to interpretation are the product of a deliberate strategy of loss and dislocation. Bergelson explicitly announces the loss of all signposts, describing regions in which villages, people, and train stations lost their names. The signs giving the names of villages have been erased "as if to say, 'Villages and people no longer have names'" (45). The loss of the names of people and places signals the loss of orientation, direction, and meaningful action. The unnaming of the world inverts the process of creation and naming in Genesis;

the revolution and civil war unmake the world. As in Babel's "Palace of Maternity" and "Berestechko," in Bergelson's "Civil War" the revolution has not yet created new meaning.

The present moment is both "after," that is, after monumental destruction, and "before"—before some unknown event, also monumental:

> The greatest sin had already taken place throughout the widest possible surrounding area. Now little sins unfold, tiny, slippery ones; with dripping autumn rains they drip and drip, and everything is permitted in this big silent land, although something once again is brewing within its tired wrinkles: a sin is brewing there, something unheard of, if it were a pious act, it would be the greatest ever.
>
> *Dem vaytikdikn arumikn arum iz di greste aveyre shoyn opgeton gevorn. Itst geyen shoyn aveyres pitselekh, glitshik-kleyne; mit klepik-tripndike tishre-regns tripn zey un tripn, un alts is muter in ot dem groysn onloshndikn land, khotsh epes greyt zikh dokh baynays in zayne mide broyznidike kneytshn: an aveyre greyt zikh dortn, an umgeherte, tsi a mitsve, a nisht gevezn groyse*
> (Bergelson 1930b, 45)

All previous limits and authority have been overcome, as in the Dostoevskian line "Everything is permitted." Russia is a vast feminized space, both fecund and aged, like the carnival hag, within whose "folds" something stirs and brews. What exactly is stirring and brewing is unclear, however. Bergelson parodically describes recent history as a movement from tragedy to farce back to tragedy—or salvation.

For Bergelson "now" is poised uneasily between destruction and deferred redemption. The interval in between the collapse of the old world and the birth of the new becomes a moment of time after destruction has taken place but before a new justice is imposed or restitution is made. Bergelson's polemical remarks voice desire for the express train of revolution, but his art says something else. In "Near a Burning Shtetl," the Bolshevik armored train pulls away, leaving behind the homeless refugees who are fleeing the violence of warring bands that roam the countryside. The armored train, sparklingly clean as if washed by rains, stands waiting to depart, but "from the platform eyes, sentenced to death, fixed their gaze at it" (111). From the perspective of the refugees, the rushing train of progress only piles up disaster, to use Benjamin's language again: "the pile of debris before the angel of history grows skyward" (1969, 258). Bergelson looks back to those left behind on the platform and looks out on the world from their perspective.

In "Civil War" the present moment is located between "already" and "not yet." Botchko and Frosya have already had their love affair, and have not yet met again. The chicken in the opening of the story has not yet laid its egg. The "greatest sin" has already taken place, but at the same time, an "unheard-of sin" is still being prepared, which, "if it were a pious act, would be the greatest ever." The revolution causes a fissure to open up in the normal course of events. Instead of coming to fruition, the promise of time breaks under its own weight. Babel, Gekht, Markish, and Bergelson all play the changes of this central theme.

Osip Mandelshtam also saw the 1917 revolution as a catastrophe that severed the connections between events, things, people, and words.[38] Mandelshtam, like Bergelson, calls on the laws of physics to express the new quality of time. In "On the Nature of the Word" Mandelshtam writes that the rapidity and enormity of events has changed time itself: "the concept of a unit of time has begun to falter and it is no accident that contemporary mathematics has advanced the principle of relativity" (1979, 117). In Mandelshtam's prose and poetry of the 1920s, time is shattered into pieces: the "ship" of time is sinking in "Sumerki svobody" (The twilight of freedom, 1918); the poet laments the century's death in "1 ianvaria, 1924" (January 1, 1924) and says that only someone with the helpless smile of a person who lost himself could comprehend the century. Bergelson discovered that "villages and people" had lost their names; Mandelshtam found that people had lost their life stories. The twentieth century destroyed the form of time embedded in human biography that made the novel possible. "Today Europeans are plucked out of their own biographies, like balls out of the pockets of billiard tables," writes Mandelshtam in "The End of the Novel" (1979, 200).

The past, discarded by the revolution, persisted nonetheless, its connections to the present waiting to be discovered. In 1921, in "The Word and Culture," Mandelshtam writes that this revelation is the task of poetry, which "is the plough that turns up time in such a way that the abyssal strata of time, its black earth, appear on the surface" (1979, 113). Poetry's work of excavation could retrieve and reanimate the great poets of the past, including Ovid, Dante, and Pushkin. In contemplating the history of the twentieth century, however, Mandelshtam's backward glance reveals something darker. The backbone of the poet's "beautiful, pathetic century" is broken, and should it look back, like a once agile beast, it will see the "traces left by its own paws" (1991, 103).

Mandelshtam's shifting relation to the Jewish past can be seen against the broad backdrop of his relation to the revolution and its shattering impact on time itself. As Clare Cavanagh points out, he expressed horror at time's backward motion, identifying this turn as Jewish. In an unpublished piece about Pushkin and Skriabin, Mandelshtam says that Judaism "always stood behind [Rome's] back and is only awaiting the hour when it will celebrate its awful, unnatural motion; history will turn back the flow of time."[39] This perspective has a parallel in normative Christian theology, which claims that Judaism was obsolete, superseded by the New Testament. Cavanagh argues that by the 1930s, however, Mandelshtam "himself turned backwards in time to the Jewish past that had horrified him earlier with its own 'awful, unnatural' backward motion" (1991, 324). In "Fourth Prose," Mandelshtam himself experiences time's backward flow (1979, 323). Instead of breaking free from his past, Mandelshtam finds himself in it, thrust back like the billiard ball into the pocket of his own biography, into the "Judaic chaos," the "womb" from which he fled in "The Noise of Time" (1990, 2:13). The turn away from the past and the subsequent backward glance are not unique to Mandelshtam; Perets Markish also bid farewell to his past only to invoke it again. Mandelshtam's trajectory is distinct, however, in that he recuperates himself as a creative artist within Judaism's backward-glancing temporality.

Mandelshtam becomes a part of Jewish time, the "apparition wandering" along the Russian calendar, and the voice of its disjuncture.[40] He becomes one of those people whom he had described in "Egipetskaia marka" (Egyptian stamp) as having only an oblique attachment to contemporaneity (1990, 2:66). In the same essay, Mandelshtam compares memory to a sickly Jewish girl who secretly runs away from home, registering in this albeit less than positive way the fugitive and Jewish quality of memory. He is the poet who never was and never will be anyone's "contemporary" ("*Net, nikogda, nichei ia ne byl sovremennik*") (1:154). He cannot belong to the present moment, because he has already spoken, and the present tense for him is everyone else's past, thereby embodying the principle of relativity in his own poetics. In "Nashedshii podkovku" (Horseshoe finder, 1923), Mandelshtam describes poetry as a physical trace that is left behind after the event producing it has already happened. I quote from the second half, using Cavanagh's translation:

> The sound still rings, although the sound's cause is gone.
> The horse lies in the dust and snorts in a lather,
> But the sharp arch of its neck
> Still holds the memory of racing with legs outstretched—
> . . .
> Thus,
> The one who finds a horseshoe
> Blows the dust from it
> And rubs it with wool until it shines
> Then
> Hangs it above the lintel,
> To let it rest
> It will never need to strike sparks from flint again.
>
> Human lips which have nothing more to say
> Preserve the shape of the last word spoken
> And the hand keeps feeling the weight
> Though the pitcher lost half its water while being carried home.
>
> What I'm saying now isn't said by me,
> It's been dug up from the ground like grains of stony wheat.
>
> (Cavanagh 1995, 160)

Mandelshtam's verse embodies the temporality of belatedness in a series of concrete gestures. What was going to happen has already happened, and what remains is the aftereffect: the arch of the horse's neck, the shape of human lips, and the weight in the hand that was carrying the pitcher. The poem creates an impossible chronology in which the present and the long-faded past unfold simultaneously: what he says "now" (*seichas*) has been excavated from the soil as if it were "stony" or fossilized wheat. "Now" thrusts itself backward into a remote stratum of the past. A few decades later Il'ia Sel'vinskii and Boris Slutskii would use this chronology of immediate obsolescence to describe the catastrophe of the Second World War. Markish, Mandelshtam, Benjamin, Babel, and Bergelson in different ways are working out an aesthetic of temporal disjuncture in which the Jewish world, a fugitive in the present, intrudes as the uncanny past.

The New World

In 1930 Isaac Nusinov argued that Bergelson's 1929 novella *Mides-hadin* "proclaimed the justice of the fact that the revolution had to judge not by mercy, but according to the cruel deeds of the past, for only then could it fulfill its great historic tasks."[41] Nusinov's reading has influenced critics to the present day. Set in an unnamed border town, the novella focuses on the prison, the center of the new "strict justice" of the revolutionary regime. Filipov, the prison head, a former mineworker, suffers great pain from an abscess on his neck; at the end, he heroically sacrifices himself. Dr. Babitski, a socialist revolutionary out of favor with the new government, identifies Filipov as the agent of history. According to Dr. Babitski, when Filipov orders a person to be shot, nothing can help the intended victim, "because it is not he who orders the shooting, but history" (*vayl nisht er heyst shisn—es heyst shisn di geshikhte*) (Bergelson 1929, 75). To read *Mides-hadin* from the perspective of this single character is, however, reductive.[42]

The passage in which the title phrase, "the harshness of the law," appears suggests some of the work's complexities. Dr. Babitski is riding in a cart to see Filipov, and he sees the monastery where the prison is located:

> The monastery walls were broken and had fallen, like the walls of a ruin, and everything seemed to be without an end, as if there were no end there but a beginning.
>
> There very high up the first fires are revealed, and they are not simple ones; they are the cold fires of the strictness of the law, fires, over which "he," Filipov, a worker from the mines, is the boss, they are the fires of a strange new stronger world.
>
> *Di monastir-vent zenen geven opgekrokhn un opgefaln, vi di vent fun khurbes, un gedakht hot zikh alts on oyfher, az dort iz nisht keyn 'ek,' nor an 'onheyb.'*

Ot baveyzn zikh dort zeyer hoykh di ershte ongetsundene fayerlekh, un oykh zey zenen nisht keyn pshute; zey zenen kalte fayern fun mides-hadin, fayerlekh, iber velkhe es iz balebos 'er', Filipov, an arbeter fun shakhtes—zey zenen fayern fun epes a modner nayer shtrenger velt. (78–79)

The point of view floats between Dr. Babitski and the narrator, confusing the question of who is speaking in this passage. The shift in tense between the past and present, and the use of the conjunction "and" instead of a term that would indicate a contrast ("the monastery walls were broken and had fallen, like the walls of a ruin, *and* everything seemed to be without an end") raise questions about the relation between the ruin and the "beginning." Whatever has been destroyed somehow lives on without end, as if to suggest that "the strange new stronger world" takes into itself the old, weak world that has been destroyed.

This structure of events reflects a dialectical model of history, to be sure, but one that is closer to Benjamin's ambivalent messianic vision than a crudely Marxist view of mere historical necessity.[43] In *Mides-hadin* the outline of history is more legible than in other works, but the emphasis on the past makes its ideology ambiguous. The protagonist, Yuzi Spivak, imprisoned and sentenced to death for smuggling socialist revolutionary documents across the border, lies on his bed, in a state between sleep and wakefulness. It seems to him that the sunset is taking a very long time. During the unnaturally long sunset, he thinks that his death originates from his life, and "not only his own life but also the life of previous generations" (*"nisht nor mit zayn eygenem lebn heybt zikh on zayn toyt, nor mit dem lebn fun zayne frierdike dores"*) (97). In these dreamy reflections a tension emerges between the laws of an inevitable historical trajectory and the value of the concrete and specific memory of a specific person's past. The truth and value of these discarded people of the past is not merely their death; there is also the potential for something new. In a passage that is more lyrical than rational, the character's dreamy state connects the distant past with the present. The intermittent fragments of memory, and not merely the rational laws of history, are the gateway to the present.[44]

Filipov makes Yuzi wake up, spurring him to the truth of revolutionary consciousness. Bergelson's portrait of the new man, who presides over "the fires of a strange new, stronger world" does not, however, conform to the decisive men of steel found in Libedinskii, Fadeev, or even Markish. Yuzi enters Filipov's private room and gazes at him with awe and fascination. A single lamp lights the bare room:

> And at the table, wearing trousers and boots, but without a jacket and shirt stands Filipov.
>
> His naked, well-muscled torso is bent over an earthen bowl as if he were going to wash his hair. His bare arms are pressed flat against his chest. A few of the muscles on his shoulders strain and quiver as if from cold, only his face is flushed and bends more and more deeply, then from the swollen wounds on his neck drip drop after drop of pus into the bowl. (140)

Filipov accompanies his ablutions with curses directed at the bourgeoisie. Yuzi, who helps bandage his wounds, starts to feel guilty, and understands Filipov's loathing for the class that he, Yuzi, belongs to—the bourgeoisie, which are "like the pus in his wounds" (*vi ayter bay zikh in di vundn*)(141). The boundaries between the body and its waste products, the Russian and the shtetl Jew, and the champion of history and its waste products blur in Bergelson's text, as in Markish and Babel.

The scene that marks the beginning of Yuzi's rebirth is charged with homoerotic and abject overtones, his transformation more decadent than disciplined. The scene of Yuzi and Filipov in Bergelson resembles Babel's *Red Cavalry* story "The Church at Novograd," in which the narrator also stares at the wounds of a naked God: "I see the wounds of your God, dripping with seed, fragrant poison, which intoxicates maidens." The intoxication, the poison, and the desire have no limits and obey no rational rules. Their importance as motifs in Bergelson's text calls into question the author's alleged turn toward the forward-looking laws of historical necessity.

Russian-Jewish and Soviet Yiddish literature celebrating the revolution represent the present moment as an "intermission" (*pereryv*) from the conditions of ordinary life. Dreamy, frightened Jewish boys become—for a moment—Cossacks and commanders. Fragments of Maimonides mingle with texts by Lenin. In this interval, carnival takes over: order and authority are suspended; social roles and identities undergo rapid metamorphoses; and everything and anything becomes possible. In

Markish, Babel, Kvitko, and Hofshteyn, however, the carnivalesque body exceeding its limits is a symptom of stillbirth and catastrophe. For Gekht the carnival ends in nightmare. In Mandelshtam the catastrophe of the revolution creates a disjuncture in time, thrusting him back into Judaic chaos.

By the end of the 1920s, the intermission was over. To participate in history meant joining the future, and redeeming the dead meant transforming them into proletarians and agricultural workers. Yiddish and Russian authors faced the task of building a new self and a new Jewish space in Soviet society by producing a literature of construction that would inscribe Jews in the bright future.

Two Socialist Construction, the *Luftmentsh*, and the New Jew

> He has a broad face, furrowed by diagonal wrinkles (Rembrandt, Hermitage, upper tier), shaggy brows over his big eyes and veiny hands with long, yellow fingers. His clothing is—it's archeological, ethnographic, right out of an engraving, a mixture of the Five Books of Moses with some sort of joke . . .
>
> Beggars walk along the road to Khmel'nik-Medzhibozh. Kabbala nestles in their old skulls; their inheritance consists of legends of the wonderworking Baal Shem. Human fates are determined by numbers; for example, Lenin is 220, but what this means no one knows. In the evening, in the old *bes-medresh* an old man describes the Shekhine, whose wings are whiter than snow, weeping bitter tears.
>
> Gekht 1923, 14

These passages come from one of Semen Gekht's numerous short pieces (*ocherki*, sketches) published in 1923 in the mainstream weekly Russian journal *Ogonek* (The flame). Rembrandt's 1654 painting "Portrait of an Old Jew" can be found in the Hermitage Museum in St. Petersburg to this day. Gekht's Jewish beggars recall S. R. An-sky's synagogue idlers in *The Dybbuk*; his elegiac and ironic tone anticipates Babel's story "Gedali," published a year after this sketch. Gekht's description also suggests something of *luftmentsh* (person of the air; in Russian, *chelovek vozdukha*) of classic Yiddish fiction, embodied in Sholem Aleichem's stories of Menakhem Mendl. Although he knows he is obsolete, Gekht's mystical *luftmentsh* "refuses to yield his position" even as he makes his way off "to the archive" to become an artifact of an extinct culture. Gekht thus performs a strange double gesture, at once bringing into the Soviet and Russian-language cultural space the figure of the old Jew of the past and at the same time marking him as doomed.

The genre of the "sketch" rose to prominence in the Soviet period as a verbal snapshot of socialist construction, well suited for an ideological campaign emphasizing rapid progress in the vast Soviet empire. Maxim Gorkii wrote that sketches were "for the purpose of informing the mass readership of everything that was being created with the energy of the working class in the entire enormous space of the Union of the Soviets" (Gorkii 1930). However, Gekht's sketch of the old Jew shows not what was being created but rather what was destroyed, the *luftmentsh*. The Jew appears in order to disappear; or he is made to disappear and in so doing to reappear. In his essay on the Yiddish actor Solomon Mikhoels, Mandelshtam describes the "inner plasticity of the ghetto . . . that immense artistic power which is surviving the ghetto's destruction and which shall emerge completely only after the ghetto is destroyed" (1979, 261). The Jews' difference is reinscribed in order for it to be overcome (always again). Their obsolescence keeps them alive in a literary/cultural space even as they and their native environment, the shtetl, undergo radical transformation. This double gesture can be traced in artistic and propagandistic literature and film in Russian and Yiddish produced in the 1930s.

The project of transforming disenfranchised shtetl Jews into productive workers and agricultural laborers was not in and of itself new. The Soviet and Jewish project of the 1920s and 1930s (Soviet and Jewish because it was spearheaded by Jews and depended on abundant help from Jews in the West) continued the efforts of Jewish reformers (*maskilim*) in tsarist Russia and overlapped with the Zionist movement. The project of productivization intertwined with the question of the Jew's body. The Soviet and Jewish project and the Zionist movement shared similar goals and methods to achieve them: the remaking of the Jewish body by means of the resettlement of the Jew on land that was marked as Jewish national territory. The Soviet Union offered Jews the twin opportunities to remake themselves and relocate themselves in a body politic that gave them a home and a national home in Jewish settlements in Southern Ukraine, Crimea, and later the Jewish Autonomous Region of Birobidzhan. Soviet Yiddish and Russian novels, brochures, journals, and films of the 1920s and 1930s written in the newly emerging style of socialist realism explicitly link the reconstruction of the Jew's body with socialist construction and national belonging. This vast project had an impact on hundreds of thousands of Jews; its impact on the Russian cultural space was of similar scale. For example, the Russian-language journal *Tribuna* (The tribune), the official organ of OZET (Society for the Settlement of Jewish Workers on the Land), had published 1.9 million copies by 1932 (Dekel-Chen 2005, 292 n. 76).

This project was not implemented by means of force from above. Socialist construction and socialist realism were not something that happened to Jews and Jewish writers as passive victims. Jews actively participated in antireligious campaigns and other forms of socialist self-reconstruction, yet also maintained Jewish ritual as part of their new lives. In the 1930s socialist realism became the only officially tolerated aesthetic form. Socialist realist literature was characterized by a simple, accessible style, positive proletarian heroes led by wise party officials, and the glorification of Stalin's five-year plans, whose joyous fulfillment was just around the corner. In his novel *Vremia vpered!* (Time forward!)— with its revealing title—Valentin Kataev, a Jewish writer, created a Jewish engineer who outraces time by determining next year's calculations for cement-mixing machines, thereby increasing the tempo of production and bringing the time of socialism closer. In contrast to Kataev, other Jewish artists incorporated traditional Jewish material into their socialist realist plots. Language from the biblical covenant and other Jewish tropes appear prominently in the Soviet Yiddish literary imagination of the new promised land. Perets Markish's and David Bergelson's writings on socialist construction, for example, rework the trope of circumcision for the project of creating a new Soviet Jew in a new Soviet Jewish homeland. Circumcision marks the Jewish male body and signifies belonging in the community. Babel's story "Karl-Yankel" (1931) provides a grotesquely comical fiction of circumcision on trial.

The reconstruction of the Jew's body meant making Jewish men more masculine, overcoming the feminine features that had long been coded as a sign of both physical and political weakness and associated both with traditional Jews and the traditional Jewish community, the shtetl.[1] Yiddish writing by women in the 1930s takes a different tack, however. Shire Gorshman's stories of her experience on a Jewish agricultural commune in Crimea reject the script developed by Markish, Bergelson, and others. Gorshman's work refuses the strictures of belonging, the negative image of the Jewish woman as the obstacle to progress, and traces instead the pleasures and dangers of the freedom of life in the new Jewish space of the commune on the steppe.

The emphasis on new Jews and new Jewish homelands notwithstanding, traditional Jewish life did not come to an end in the 1930s. This chapter concludes by returning to the staged disappearance/reappearance of the shtetl Jew. In Gekht's work and in other Russian-language writing, describing the obsolescence of traditional Jewish life also means inscribing it in a Russian cultural space. A trio of Russian-language films, including *Vozvrashcheniia Neitana Bekkera* (The return of Nathan Bekker, 1932), *Granitsa* (The border, 1935), and *Iskateli schast'ia* (Seekers of happiness, 1936), also performs this double gesture. Each shows the triumph of the new Soviet way of life over traditional life in the shtetl. In *The Return of Neitan Bekker* and in *Seekers of Happiness*, however, the shtetl Jew steals the show. The emblematic figure of the past haunts the project of the future.

The Political Framework

Itsik Fefer, Markish, Bergelson, and other Yiddish writers working in the Soviet Union in the 1930s were acutely aware of anti-Semitism in Germany. Bergelson had only arrived back in Moscow in 1934, and the increasing pressure on Jews in Germany was among the reasons for his return, although Soviet support for Yiddish culture, and active courtship of the author, were also important. Yiddish writers in the Soviet Union could point to the advantages the Soviet Union afforded Jews. As Fefer remarked in his speech at the First Congress of the Soviet Writers' Union in 1934, "at the same time that Hitler's Germany is showing its brutal face, when a dark wave of anti-Semitism has the capitalist countries in its grip, Soviet power has organized the autonomous Jewish region—Birobidzhan" (Luppol, Rozental', and Tretiakov 1934, 167). Fefer emphasized the age-old problem of the Jewish Diaspora, and stressed that Soviet Jewish writers, like Jewish workers everywhere, had one true homeland, the Soviet Union. Palestine, Fefer asserted, was never the home of the Jewish masses but only of Jewish exploiters, and furthermore, Palestine was "now a colony of British imperialism."

With the creation of Birobidzhan as the Jewish Autonomous Region in 1934, the Soviet Union could claim to be the first country in the world to provide Jews with a national homeland, while at the same time addressing political and military concerns in the Far East. As Zvi Gitelman writes, Birobidzhan offered Jews "economic rehabilitation and social respectability through agricultural work; the preservation and promotion of language, culture—and implicitly—of the Jewish people itself—through compact settlement" (1998a, 8). Soviet nationality policy, out of which Birobidzhan developed, promoted the culture of minorities but at the same time undermined national difference and killed members of national groups.

The first stage of this policy, during the 1920s, was an experiment in what Yuri Slezkine and Terry Martin call Soviet "affirmative action," in which the Soviet government actively cultivated national cultures, literatures, and languages, suppressed "Russian chauvinism," and gave nationals preferential treatment in higher education and employment.[2] The use of print culture in the native language of the multiple ethnic groups of the Soviet Union was a key tool in both the support of the national cultures and the inculcation of Soviet socialism in native terms; hence, the policy of *korenizatsiia*—indigenization or nativization. Nonterritorial nationals such as Jews presented a problem since nationality was keyed to territory, but the creation of Birobidzhan resolved this question. Before Birobidzhan, the Jewish section of the Communist Party was charged with responsibility for Jewish affairs. Cultural production in Yiddish, deemed the national language of the Jews, thrived under these conditions.[3]

The Soviet ideological agenda of national cultural production dovetailed with visions shared by Russian-Jewish intellectuals for a secular Yiddish culture (Shneer 2004, 91). The number of newspapers, periodicals, and books published in Yiddish rose significantly in the course of the 1920s (Gitelman 1972, 332). A parallel growth in Yiddish writers' groups, Yiddish theater, and other forms of Yiddish cultural production can also be traced at this time (Shneer 2004, 134–78). Semen Dimanshtein, the leading political figure in the field of Soviet Yiddish during this period (he was, among other things, head of the Nationalities Institute), articulated the link between indigenization and Birobidzhan when he wrote in 1934 that "in the Jewish Autonomous Region, where compact masses of Jewish workers will be concentrated, it will be easier to build a Jewish culture that is socialist in content and nationalist in form" (Dimanshtein 1934, 8).[4] Markish, Bergelson, Fefer, Gorshman, Gekht, Babel, Mikhoels, and Zuskin, however, created art that does not subordinate its "national," that is, Jewish, elements to socialist construction. Their work, a new type of fusion, created a uniquely Jewish space within the Soviet cultural framework of their time.

The emphasis on increased national cultural production, however, had a dark side: "diaspora nationalities were definitively categorized as enemy nations and subjected to mass deportation, arrest, and execution" (Martin 2001, 423). Soviet nationality policy of the 1930s sought to fix identity, language, nationality, and national territory in a totalized grid of relations. Slezkine describes the shift toward a fixed structure of national and personal identity: "The triumph of real *korenizatsiia*, as in taking root . . . pinned buildings to the ground, peasants to the land, workers to factories, women to men and Soviets to the USSR. At the same time and in the same basic way, each individual got stuck with a nationality and most nationalities got stuck with their borders" (1994, 444). This was not an environment that supported fluidity, fusion, or hybridity in daily life or art. Nonetheless, the artists who created new forms of Jewish culture and the people who actually lived it unsettled this grid, producing work that joined socialist realism, socialist construction, and Jewishness in new ways.

The contradictory nationality policy of the late 1920s and early 1930s led to both the creation of Birobidzhan and the subsequent arrest of its leaders and the closure of Yiddish schools. Bergelson's "Barg-aruf" (Uphill), published in the journal *Forpost* (Outpost) in 1936, accurately reflects the problem by both celebrating the foundation of the Jewish Autonomous Region and also attacking Jewish nationalism. In the opening vignette, the secretary of the district committee receives a negative report from his boss. He regrets his poor record of accomplishment but nonetheless counts as a positive step the beginning of a "struggle against Jewish nationalism and against great-Russian chauvinism" (*a kampf . . . kegn yidishn natsionalizm un kegn groysrusishn shovinizm*) (Bergelson 1936a, 38). The contradiction lies in the simultaneous development of "Jewish nationalism" in the Birobidzhan project as a whole (and in this story in particular) and the struggle against it.

Reconstructing the Jew

The problem of Jewish belonging in the new Soviet body politic necessarily involves the problem of remaking the Jew—morally, physically, and sexually. In order for the Jew to join the Soviet socialist collective, the Jew had to be overcome. The ideology behind the makeover goes back at least as far as the fin de siècle, and can be traced to the writings of Otto Weininger and Max Nordau. The Jewish male was sickly, physically weak, pale, anemic, both effeminate and oversexed, and Jews as a group were dirty, vulnerable to disease and a source of contamination, unproductive and parasitical in their economic practices, clannish, unconnected to the land, and lacking in allegiance to the countries in which they lived and the communities that surrounded them.[5] The representation of Jews of the former Pale of Settlement in literature written by Jews and non-Jews fits these stereotypes. Their bodies and characters were distorted by Jewish religious observance, traditional Jewish occupations, and the anti-Semitism found in tsarist officials and shared by the surrounding population. Nordau's "muscle Jews," their bodies strengthened by gymnastics and their spirits renewed by agricultural labor in their own homeland, were in large part a response to this negative image.[6]

Representations of Jews' bodies in Soviet works of the 1930s linked their deficiencies to the problem of class. In Markish's *Eyns af eyns* (One by one) the professional beggars are resettled in collective farms and given work in factories. These subhuman beings, whom the narrator calls "rubbish" (*brokhvarg*), want to be like human beings, to achieve "*mentshn-endlekhkayt*" (Markish 1934, 223). The problem of becoming a human being was a common theme in the literature of the national minorities of the 1930s. The collection *Tvorchestvo narodov SSSR* (The works of the people of the USSR), published in 1937 on the occasion of the twentieth anniversary of the revolution, contains numerous poems paying tribute to Stalin for granting the new status of "person" to members of the national minorities. The concluding lines of a poem, translated from Kirgyz, addresses Stalin as follows: "Under your watchful gaze, / A person has become a person" (Gorkii and Mekhlis 1937, 21). The members of the oppressed national minorities achieve personhood thanks to the cultural gifts of literacy, new hygienic practices, and new agricultural methods that Stalin bestows on them. The Jews of the marketplace in Markish's *One by One* achieve personhood by means of the proletarianization that the five-year plans make available to them.

One of the goals of socialist construction was the construction of a new Jew. Khaizekil' Dunets, for example, a Jewish critic from Belorussia, killed in 1938, spoke at the First Congress of the Soviet Writers' Union about the "remaking of the Jewish worker on the basis of the construction of socialism" (Luppol, Rozental', and Tretiakov 1934, 446). The stoop-shouldered, anemic, sickly Jewish male, the *shtetl luftmentsh*, was to be transformed into an able-bodied, muscled, heroic worker. Fefer's speech at the first congress emphasized that the *luftmentsh* was disappearing from Jewish life and from Jewish literature. As Bergelson wrote in a brochure on Birobidzhan: "In the struggle to master and develop the natural resources of this region a new type of Jew has emerged" (1936b, 48). Birobidzhan propaganda literature featured images of clean-shaven, smiling Jewish agricultural workers with bulging muscles and sun-browned skin, their gaze directed toward their bright future. In Emmanuel Kazakevich's *Sholem un Khava: Roman in ferzn* (Sholem and Khave: A novel in verse), a Birobidzhan love story published in 1941, the narrator says, "And one lives life with the future / Because 'now' has no worth" (*un lebn lebt men mit der tsukunft / Vayl s'hot keyn vert nit der 'itst'*) (Kazakevich 1941, 28). Mikhail Kalinin, the president of the Soviet Union, said that Birobidzhan was "giving birth" to a new kind of Jewish nationality, "to people with big fists and strong teeth."[7] In Kazakevich's novel, the Jews settling the taiga "sate their bellies with coarse food / And glow with a quiet fire" (*Mit shverer shpayz dem boikh gezetikt, / Un vi geglit mit shtiln bren*) (74). Bergelson's hero Molover in "Barg-aruf" is similar: "His healthy white teeth chew quickly, his cheek muscles bulge" (*Zayne gezunte vayse tseyn kayen gikh-gikh, zayne bak-muskuln zaynen ongetsoygn*) (Bergelson 1936a, 39).

The physically powerful positive hero of literature, film, and visual culture of the 1930s is a hallmark of the socialist realist aesthetic.[8] The single most important message of socialist realism was the transformation of the individual through the transformation of the surrounding world, the overcoming of nature, and the defeat of the class enemy. The process was to be a joyous struggle. In his speech at the First Congress of the Soviet

Writers' Union, Maxim Gorkii said: "Socialist realism affirms existence as action, as creativity, the purpose of which is the unceasing development of the most valued individual capacities of the person, for the sake of his triumph over the forces of nature, for the sake of his health and longevity, for the sake of the great joy of living on the earth" (Luppol, Rozental', and Tretiakov 1934, 17). In his brochure, Bergelson describes Birobidzhan as "the scene of a joyous struggle," and in "Barg-aruf" the character Velvl has the nickname "happy-go-lucky" (*freylekh khapenish*) (Bergelson 1936a, 42). As Velvl works on the new building in which the community will celebrate November 7, revolution day, he experiences intense happiness: "the higher he lifted himself together with the scaffolding under the hot sun, the more he felt that what he was doing was more joyous play than work" (*vos hekher er ineynem mit di reshtovanyes hot zikh unter der heyser zun afgehoybn, alts mer hot er gefilt, az yede zakh, vos er tut do iz mer a shpilevdike freyd eyder an arbet*) (42).

Works by Kazakevich, Markish, and Bergelson thus conformed, in some ways, to the emerging template of socialist realism; however, to view them as nothing more than "national in form, and socialist in content" neglects their richness and complexity. Characterizing Soviet Yiddish works of the Stalin period, as Irving Howe did, as what Jewish writers "*had* to compose" is historically misleading.[9] To speak of Jews as only recipients of Soviet policies, and not as active participants, is inaccurate. As Gitelman points out, even before Birobidzhan, the Jewish sections of the Communist Party promoted campaigns, which "cleared the way for a new type of Jewishness and Jewry" (Gitelman 1998a, 6). Instead of describing the Jews as merely passive victims of Soviet nationality and culture policies, it is preferable to borrow a grammatical term and use the middle voice, in which subjects perform actions on themselves. The action that Markish's and Bergelson's heroes perform on themselves directly relates to circumcision.

The Wound and the Covenant

Soviet propaganda of the 1920s and 130s targeted Russian Orthodox, Jewish, and Moslem religious institutions and practices. Print media as well as agitprop theatrical performances were the chief weapons of the antireligious campaigns. An article published in *Der apikoyres* (The atheist) in 1934 used a newspaper item about a collective farm worker who made money on the side as a kosher butcher, a cantor, and a *moyel* (ritual circumciser). The article, titled "A gesheft-firer—a shoykhet-moyel" (The moonlighter—a butcher-*moyel*) was accompanied by a cartoon showing all these services (Figure 1).

The caption reads, "The Art of Transformation: (1) The Moonlighter Sorkin; (2) The Same as a Butcher; (3) The Same as a *Moyel*; (4) The Same as a Cantor" (Leytes 1934). The enormous hooked nose and bulbous lips create an unflattering portrait of the moonlighter. Another article, titled "Kempfn kegn altn shteyger" (The struggle against old ways), appearing in *Der apikoyres* in 1935, used the occasion of a court case in Minsk in 1931 against a *moyel* who had maimed an infant. The article argued that circumcision was fundamentally a pagan ritual, a form of sacrifice used to generate a good harvest (Kheytov 1935).

The articles in *Der apikoyres*, as well as agitprop trials of circumcision (which took place in Kharkov and Odessa in 1928), reveal that the practice continued to take place. Ordinary Jews, including Communist Party members, continued to perform circumcisions. Elissa Bemporad writes that "during the 1920s circumcising one's son was the norm among Soviet Jews, not the exception" (2006, 157). The continued practice of circumcision and other religious rituals points to the gap between policies established from the center and the daily life of the time, especially in the former Pale of Settlement.[10] Soviet Jews did not necessarily see a sharp divide between Jewish life and Soviet life.

Jewish artists working in both Yiddish and Russian appropriated and transformed the trope of circumcision in their work about Soviet Jewish life. In the Hebrew Bible, the covenant creates a relation among the members of the Jewish collective body, between the collective body and God, and between the collective body and land. In Genesis, circumcision is the sign of the everlasting covenant between God and the Jewish people: "You shall be circumcised in the flesh of your foreskins, and it shall be a sign of the covenant between me and you" (Gen. 17:11).[11] God promises Abraham that from him will come "nations" and kings, and that the land of Canaan will be their possession. Circumcision is the

Figure 1 Cartoon by A. Leytes, in *Der apikoyres* (The atheist) 1934 (3):17.

sign of the mutual obligation *between* God and the Jews, and it is a sign *among* Jews of their belonging to the nation of Israel, synchronically and diachronically. The Genesis circumcision commandment obliges fathers to circumcise their sons, the next generation. Circumcision is the wound that signals a promise of plenitude. Elsewhere in the Hebrew Bible circumcision is used metaphorically. Moses tells the recalcitrant Israel of God's love and urges a recommitment from them: "circumcise therefore the foreskin of your heart, and be no longer stubborn" (Deut. 10:16). Other traditional Jewish texts reemphasize the corporeal and corporate nature of the covenant. For example, after eating bread, Jews, both men and women, thank God for "the covenant, which You sealed in our flesh."

A poem by Itsik Fefer of 1925 denies that circumcision makes a difference:

> So what if I've been circumcised,
> The field winds have darkened
> My white, sleepy legs.
> The Jews dream of Sabbath stew—
> But the men yearn for smoke and flame.
> I spent eight years in the field and valley
> Near the sky-blue sea.
> People know me for a good, quiet type,
> For many, my honesty is hard.
> I didn't wind the straps around my arm
> Or ply my trade in the market.[12]

> *Nu, iz vos, az m'hot mikh gemalet,*
> *Un gepravet, vi bay yidn, a bris.*
> *S'hobn feldishe vintn farsmalyet*
> *Mayne vayse fardrimlte fis.*
> *Do troymen nokh yidn fun tsholnt—*
> *Yatn benken nokh roykh un nokh flam.*
> *Akht yor in felder un toln*
> *Unter himlish bloyen yam.*
> *Me ken mikh far a gutn un shtiln,*
> *Far a sakh iz mayn erlekhkayt karg.*
> *Kh'ob keyn mol nit geleygt keyn tfiln*
> *Un keyn mol nit gehandlt in mark.*[13]

The "white, dreamy legs" suggest the effeminacy and softness long associated with the circumcised body. Active participation in the revolution, according to the poet, changes the Jewish male body and the Jewish characteristics of dreaminess, passivity, and otherworldliness. The poet claims that he never used phylacteries or plied his trade in the market. The physical otherness of the Jew can be overcome, if traditional Jewish religious and economic practices are abandoned. The outcome of the transformation remains unclear, however, as the poet finds himself neither among those who yearn for the Sabbath nor among those who yearn for smoke and flame. His own desires remain unstated, except the desire to deny his circumcision. The poem ends by repeating the opening line, "So what if I've been circumcised." The marked Jewish body can coexist with the new Soviet order.

Instead of denying the force of circumcision, Markish and Bergelson rework it as a trope that fits the needs of the new Soviet covenant. Markish's *One by One* tells the story of Neytn Bekker, who returns to his native Russia after twenty-eight years of "hard labor" as a bricklayer in New York City. His Yiddish name "Nosn" becomes "Neytn" in New York, and the narrator and all the characters in the novel refer to him using his Americanized name, except his father. He returns because he wants to "lay bricks for socialism" (Markish 1934, 20). The Soviet Union functions as the new Zion, the place where exiles are restored to their home. The novel uses many of the motifs of Soviet socialist realism of the 1930s, including the competition between the United States and the USSR, scenes of nighttime labor, gigantic construction sites, the remaking of nature, and the remaking of the human being. At the same time, however, the work incorporates traditional Jewish themes and tropes, including the legend of the Golem and the biblical trope of circumcision, into its conventional socialist realism. The Jewish critic Moshe Litvakov had harshly criticized Markish for the so-called nationalist apologetics found in his previous novel *Dor oys, dor ayn* (The generations).[14] Markish's decision to use Jewish traditional material in his new work is significant especially in light of the challenges of the Soviet literary environment of the time.

The novel reveals a striking duality about the price of transforming shtetl Jews into model Soviets. Listening to a powerful communist agitator at a meeting in Madison Square Garden, Neytn sees his life as a construction worker on New York skyscrapers in a new, harsh light. He sees himself

> chained to a stone wheelbarrow up in the heights of tens of stories, crawling with his bricks over the conical and diamond-shaped concrete athletes, magically covering their flat heads with brick, and from there, from the skyscraper's sixty story height, he hears the orator declaiming that the Soviet Union, harnessed to the Kremlin, is rushing toward him and millions of other convicts like him like a mighty locomotive to free them from their lofty prison. He hears the thunderous call of the flaming Kremlin, 'Rise up, all you who are as slaves.' (Markish 1934, 14–15)

Neytn, the magician who lays bricks with extraordinary speed, is also the victim of capitalist oppression and is shackled to his lofty prison, the skyscraper. The mighty locomotive of the Soviet Union will liberate him, but at the risk of destroying him. The train, the symbol of a new social order and technological progress, is rushing straight at the hero. The danger of bodily harm appears even in the metaphor of socialist emancipation.

Neytn's main problem in the Soviet Union is to accommodate himself to the methods of Soviet labor. He laughs at what he calls the "theater" in the workers' training institute, where he and others learn not only dialectics but also the ergonomically correct technique of lifting and placing bricks. The trainees pretend to lay bricks as the teacher calls out the count, "one, two, one, two." The scene evokes the biomechanics of Vsevolod Meyerhold and the science of work developed by Alexei Gastev, which influenced Meyerhold. According to Rolf Hellebust, the fundamental idea uniting the two was the transformation of the human body into a machine, with precisely regulated and maximally efficient movements (Hellebust 2003, 65). The emphasis on physical culture is both a means of producing the "new person" and transforming work into a "joyous enterprise" (Hoffman 2003, 35). In contrast to the dangerous mechanical labor of capitalism, socialist labor carefully nurtures the well-being of each worker, while at the same time forging each separate individual into a part of the whole.

Significantly, the image of the socialist corporate body in Markish borrows elements both from Russian literature of the 1920s and from

Jewish legends. Markish depicts the new construction as a vast, fantastical figure:

> A huge area of twelve miles, paved with stone, cement, steel, sand, lime and wood, shaped by tens of thousands of workers, mixed together into one amazing force, will be kneaded and formed by one will, by one intent. They cry out, as if one, through the roar and rush of the future rising before them. All together, like blood vessels, they circulate in the new, raw life, which is just about to be born, which is awakening, which stutters the first, new, marvelous *'alef.'* (Markish 1934, 246)

The image of a giant made of steel and cement is found most prominently in such works of proletarian poetry as Gastev's "We Grow Out of Iron" and Vladimir Kirillov's "Iron Messiah."[15] These poems celebrate the triumph of socialist construction and industrialization, the victories of Soviet technology, and the forging of a new collective society. What makes Markish's giant unique, however, is his relation to the legendary Golem, most famously associated with the sixteenth-century rabbi Judah Loew of Prague. On its forehead is inscribed the Hebrew and Yiddish word for truth: *alef, mem, sof*. Every night, the *alef* must be removed, turning the Golem into a corpse, *"mes"* (*mem, sof*)—lest the Golem overpower his human creators. Every morning, the *alef* must be reinscribed in order for the Golem to come to life.[16] In contrast to the silent Golem of legend, Markish's Soviet Golem says his *alef* out loud, proclaiming his freedom from his rabbinic creators.

According to Katerina Clark, the socialist realist "master plot" involves the hero's arrival at a factory, kolkhoz, or other socialist microcosm, and the delineation of a problem and its solution, leading to the completion of the task and the hero's rising in the ranks or achieving some form of more successful integration into the community after overcoming the obstacles in his path (Clark 1985, 93–113). Markish's Neytn Bekker, however, never achieves integration, even though he is both circumcised and scarred by years of capitalist labor. The covenant of the socialist collective requires yet another form of circumcision, both on the body and on the heart. Access to the promised land and to the corporate Soviet body comes at the price of pain. Bodily injury dominates the novel, as if there were a deficit of pain that could never be made up.

Socialist Construction, the *Luftmentsh*, and the New Jew   81

In the bizarre opening scene, Neytn remembers the funeral held in his shtetl for his grandfather's leg, severed in a workplace accident: the gravedigger "carried Eli-Leyb's leg under his arm, as if it were a small child who had died" (*trogt Eli-Leyb's aropgenumenem fus unter der pazekhe, vi a kleyn kind a geshtarbns*) (Markish 1934, 3). The gravedigger complains bitterly that no one will put any money in his charity box for this funeral, because "such a little piece of a corpse under the arm" (*mit aza a shtikl mes unter der pazekhe*) gives no credence to the belief that "charity redeems us from death." Various problems arise as to where the leg should be buried and what prayers should be said over it. Like Gogol's "Nose," the severed leg in Markish's novel takes on a life of its own, with the clear ideological purpose of showing the brutality of labor conditions under tsarism. The value system of traditional Judaism, the novel suggests, was no less brutal: the size of the remains determines the amount of charity, reducing and demeaning the worth of the person.

The conditions of labor in the capitalist West resemble those under tsarism. Neytn, like his grandfather, is also injured. His years of labor as a bricklayer in America left him a broken man. He suffers from a terrible hernia, which is described as his "cash savings from his American years" (*der mezumener opshpor fun zayne amerikane yorn*) (16). The savings in the bank that capitalism promises turn out instead to be a painful deposit on the body of the worker.

Injury, debility, and pain are not, however, limited to the capitalist side. The Bolshevik leader Kholodenko is disfigured by wounds he received at the front during the civil war. "A scar of sewn-up flesh ran from the top of Comrade Kholodenko's jawbone to his throat" (*Funem ek kinbeyn biz tsum haldz iz dem khaver Kholodenko gegangen a heft fun farneyt layb*) (83). The scar has a powerful effect on Neytn: "it seemed that Kholodenko answered him with a cut-off part of his face" (*az Kholodenko entfert im mit an afgerisenem teyl fun zayn ponem*). Neytn imagines that the mouthlike wound on Kholodenko's face will remain open his whole life and that it will "speak to the entire world" (83). The metamorphoses made possible by socialist construction include the transformation of injury into enhanced capacity, here realized in the bizarre image of the speaking wound. The opposition between the conditions of capitalist and Soviet labor, and the contrast between Neytn, whom Markish calls a "slave" (*a knekht*), and Kholodenko, the "master" (*a hersher*), do not hold water, however, because both men are wounded (205). Neytn feels a kinship between himself and Kholodenko based on their common pain. As the two argue the merits of Soviet and American methods of construction, Neytn observes Kholodenko taking aspirin and concludes that he must also suffer from a "rupture" (*gebrekh*) somewhere in his body, only "not in his groin, but a little higher, somewhere in his heart, or in his lungs." Using Neytn, with his outsider's point of view, his constant questioning, and his anguish about belonging, Markish points to the central problem of the novel, emphasizing and marking the problem of entrance into the new Soviet covenant. The grotesquely wounded bodies of his civil war epic *Brothers* speak to the poet's mourning over the destroyed shtetl; the pain in *One by One*, in contrast, is supposed to accomplish a positive transformation in the hero and in the world he wants to join. The excess of pain, however, suggests that the price to be paid for the new socialist collective is exorbitant. No matter how great the suffering of the Jews in the past, more is required.

Markish creates a relation between the stamp on the heart and the new productivity of the land promised by Soviet industrialization. In Leviticus, the fulfillment of God's promise that the land will be abundant depends on the humbling of the "uncircumcised heart" (Lev. 26:40). While still in New York, Neytn looks eagerly at his visa, stamped with the Soviet hammer and sickle; when he arrives in the Soviet Union, he looks "in the same way at the land, which was stamped with new construction, factories with their high chimneys, and manufacturing plants," and he "cannot tear his eyes away from the newly-stamped earth" (*fun der nay-oysgeshtemplt erd*) (Markish 1934, 53). The Soviet visa, stamped with the hammer and sickle, leaves a symbolic imprint on the land, as well as on the heart.

Neytn's progress toward gaining a place in the new Soviet society is difficult. He puzzles over what the Soviet definitions of work and "qualifications" are. He wants to shout on the street that he too is a worker, that he labored together with Chinese, Italians, and blacks and "built entire cities" (133–34). But this de facto membership in an international workers' union, so to speak, is inadequate. Neytn begins to understand that he is not a worker in the true Soviet sense, and that he does not know what the term "qualifications" means here. The question alone is a shock, "the first Soviet bullet, which wounded the tormented American brick-layer" (*dos iz geven di ershte sovetishe koyl, vos farvundet ot dem gut-oysgemutshirn amerikanerishn tsigl-leyger*) (134). The language of injury here is significant in light of the novel's overarching metaphor of covenantal wounding.

Markish compares joining the Soviet collective to crossing a boundary. Attending classes (on dialectical materialism and physical culture) with other trainees, Neytn wonders whether there is "another boundary, inside the land" and what sort of document has to be shown there (*"iz, heyst es, take faranen nokh a grenets? Inveynik in land? Iz vos-zhe veyzt men do, af der grenets, ha?"*) (140). Neytn shows the teacher his hands, which he calls his "working passports" (*horepashne pasportn*), and demands to know what papers he has to show "at the border," that is, the symbolic boundary separating him from the Soviet workers. The teacher answers that what is wanted in the Soviet Union is not passports but hearts: Neytn must show his heart. The reality was quite different. In 1934, when the new Soviet passport system was in full swing, hundreds of thousands of people deemed unacceptable—former kulaks, for example—were denied passports and subject to expulsion from urban areas (Holquist 2001). Jews were not singled out at this time, but those whose professions were deemed incapable of proletarian transformation entered the ranks of the *lishentsy*, those denied rights. Markish transforms the mass violence into the violence meted out "one by one" as a tool in remaking the individual, involving both psychological and physical suffering. In the course of his exchange with the teacher, Neytn asks whether a Soviet visa can be stamped on his heart. The language about the heart, and the visa and stamp on the heart, echoes language found in the Bible: in Deuteronomy Moses speaks of circumcising the heart (Deut. 10:16), and Jeremiah exhorts the people to "remove the foreskin of their hearts" (Jer. 4:4).

Markish may well have had this biblical language in mind when his hero Neytn examines his heart and sees "with his own eyes how the armor of twenty-eight years of work in America was becoming thinner and thinner and transparent as glass. And the glass began to crack" (*mit di eygene oygn, vi der pantsir fun zayne akht un tsvantsik yor arbet in amerike vert ale diner un diner un durkhzikhtik, vi gloz, un vi dos dozike gloz heybt an trasken*) (Markish 1934, 254). Entrance into the Soviet community requires softening of the heart, a breakdown of psychological defenses. Markish transforms the biblical language about the removal of the foreskin of the heart into the modern, technological idiom of "armor." Making the hero by breaking him down departs from what Hellebust calls the "narrative of flesh into metal" characteristic of the hero of socialist realist literature of the time—"the acquisition of the physical or psychological qualities of iron that must precede any development of revolutionary consciousness" (Hellebust 2003, 22). The removal of the "armor" surrounding the heart suggests the reverse process, one that is consistent with the trope of wounding as a qualification for membership in the new society.

Markish emphasizes the visible sign of the wound. In the exchange with his teacher about visas stamped on the heart, Neytn remembers Kholodenko, the Cossack with a "scar stamped on his face" (*mit an opgeshtempltn shram ofn ponem*) (Markish 1934, 140). Neytn understands that unlike Kholodenko, he did not serve at the front during the civil war and lacks the token of that service: "And he did not have any scars on his face, like Kholodenko, no" (*Un keyn shramen afn ponem, vi er, Kholodenko, hot her nit, neyn*) (255). He discovers a substitute, however, in the scars on his hands: "But the scars on his overworked hands, from twenty-eight years of hard labor are scars? Right? Scars or not scars?" (*Ober di shramen fun zayne farhorevete hent, fun akht un tsvantsik yor horevanye zaynen shramen? Ha? Shramen, tsi nit keyn shramen?*) (255). In Neytn, Markish embodies the socialist realist hero's desire to possess a visible scar as the token of belonging in the new covenant. Neytn wants his scarred hands to serve as his "qualification" for the status of a true Soviet worker, just as the scar on Kholodenko's face signifies his status as a member of the party.

Kholodenko provides a gloss on what the scar on his face means when he says that "the revolution has inscribed on our flesh where we ought to go, just as it has written our party cards with our blood" (*Afn layb bay undz hot undz di revolutsye ongeshribn, vuhin mir zoln geyn, punkt vi zi hot undz mit undzer blut ongeshribn undzere partey-biletn*)(254). The scar is the writing of history on the flesh, indicating the future direction of the revolution. Kholodenko's scar functions as the equivalent of a new, terrible form of circumcision.

The trope of the wound as circumcision and the problem of reinoculation come together in the central image of the novel, the speeding locomotive of the Soviet Union. When Neytn attends the communist meeting in Madison Square Garden and listens to the orator's stirring words, he has a vision of the Soviet Union rushing at him like a locomotive to free him from his skyscraper prison. He feels a great strain and experiences an attack of his hernia. The Soviet Union and the episode of pain are directly linked:

> From the great strain he unexpectedly had an attack of his hernia and his stomach cramped. Without looking he quickly pressed his right hand to his groin and with a piercing wheeze thrust his intestines, which had come loose, back in place.
>
> *Fun groys ongeshtrengkayt, hot im demolt geton oykh umgerikht a khap geton dos gebrekh un im a kortshe geton dem boykh. Nor er hot nit kukndik shnel tsugeleygt di rekhte hant tsu der dikh un mit a svishtshendikn khorkhl zey arayngeshtoysn, di apgerisnene kishkes, tsurik.* (15)

The end of the novel uses the same image of the locomotive, "harnessed with the Kremlin" rushing straight at the hero, Neytn, as if to reopen his wound. Despite his terrible injury, the Soviet collective rejects him, leaving him suspended between America and the USSR. Neytn thus returns to the pre-Soviet, traditional role of the *luftmentsh*, a "person of the air." The symmetry of the opening and closing undermine the novel's explicit agenda of socialist mobility, because the hero ends up where he began, shackled to his lofty prison. Markish himself had returned to the Soviet Union in 1926, and although he rose rapidly through the ranks of Yiddish writers, his work was not always well received. It is difficult not to see Markish the artist in Neytn the magician/acrobat: the author himself had mixed feelings about being "harnessed to the Kremlin" in his own new home.

Bergelson and Birobidzhan

David Bergelson's "Barg-aruf" also raises questions about the new Soviet covenant by focusing on the twin problems of the wounded body and the Jewish homeland. The so-called taking root of a national history and culture in the confines of a national territory (*korenizatsiia*) is key to the story. In 1934 Bergelson was present at the First Congress of the Soviet Writers' Union, at which he received high acclaim from Fefer and the Yiddish critic Iakov Bronshtein. Bronshtein, using the overblown language of the time, said that Bergelson's autobiographical novel *At the Dnieper* (Baym Dnyeper) "guillotined" the formerly idealized bourgeois nationalist Jewish environment (Luppol, Rozental', and Tretiakov 1934, 271) (Bronshtein himself was arrested and shot in 1937). Bergelson's own remarks at the congress, however, were far more enigmatic. On the one hand, he praised Stalin as the "great leader of the world proletariat," but he also said that "as a Jewish writer" one of the strongest speeches he had heard at the congress, given by the national poet of Dagestan, Suleiman Stal'skii, was one he did not understand a single word of (Luppol, Rozental', and Tretiakov 1934, 271). To praise a text that is completely opaque falls outside of the socialist realist demand for utter transparency, clarity, and cohesiveness. Bergelson's statement belongs to the same theater of the absurd as Babel's characterization of himself at the same event as a master of the genre of silence. Bergelson used the technique of the absurd, the opaque, and the unsaid with particular skill in "Barg-aruf."

In the doctrine of socialist realism, the transformation of the individual through socialist construction also has the effect of binding the individual to the collective. To use Bergelson's language from the first congress, the socialist realist writer must "illuminate all the bonds that tie the laboring unit to the collective" (*osvetit' vse perepleteniia, kotorymi sviazyvaetsia trudovaia edinitsa s kollektivom*) (Luppol, Rozental', and Tretiakov 1934, 271). In the Jewish tradition with which Bergelson was familiar, circumcision binds and obligates members of the community to God and to each other. In the Soviet context of the 1930s the wound that obligates becomes the "obligation to be wounded," and this is precisely what "Barg-aruf" (Uphill) reveals.[17] The biblical trope of the covenantal sign and the socialist realist aesthetic intertwine in powerful and disturbing ways in Bergelson's text, undermining the socialist realist aesthetic of clarity and optimism.

Birobidzhan was supposed to solve the Jewish problem by providing Jews with a national territory. Bergelson's narrative explicitly links the problem of territory with Jewish experience. The construction worker Velvl and the editor of the Birobidzhan newspaper engage in a dialogue about the current new moment in Jewish history. The choice of these two interlocutors, the worker and the editor, is stock-in-trade in socialist realism, because the two represent the proletariat and party consciousness. The language they use, however, departs from the norm. Velvl recites the prior history of the Jews in marked language:

> their fate tossed them from land to land, and not anywhere in any land was their history written on the ramparts, the walls, the towers, not with the roads that went through them, or the bridges that were thrown across them, or with the building of cities.
>
> *un in ergets in yene lender iz ir geshikhte nit farshribn gevorn nit af keyn moyern, nit af keyn vent un nit af keyn turems, nit mit durkhleygn vegn, tsi mit ibervarfn brikn, tsi mit oysboyen shtet.* (Bergelson 1936a, 42)

The Jews could not leave a record of their presence on the great public works of civilization and progress. The editor continues the metaphor of history as inscription, adding that the Jews "carry their history around like a type of little prayer book under their arm" (*un zeyer geshikhte trogn yidn arum vi epes a min siderl unter der pakhve*) (42). Up to now, up to the dawn of socialism, the history of the Jews had no material, positive existence; it was a deterritorialized, depoliticized tale of exclusion and homelessness, and it was a history, moreover, known only to them, like the prayer book they would carry to the synagogue. But with the rise of socialism, everything changed. The tale of woe is no more, and instead the text of Jewish history is to be realized materially and territorially. The editor continues:

> And now the party tells you: "Jews, take part in our great socialist construction, write your history on the walls, write it on the ramparts, write it on the factories, on the cities, and on the land!"
>
> *Un itst zogt tsu aykh di partey: "Yidn bateylikt in undzer groyser sotsyalistisher boyung, shraybt ayer geshikhte af vent, shraybt zi af moyern, shraybt zi af fabrikn, af shtet un af land!"* (43)

This language echoes the ideology of the "taking root" of a national culture in a specific territory, but also the text of the traditional Jewish prayer "Hear, O Israel." Israel is enjoined to "write" God's words: "And thou shalt write them upon the doorposts of thy house and upon thy gates" (Silverman 1984). Bergelson's text repeats and transforms the biblical commandment in the party's commandment to the Jews to "write your history on the walls, write it on the ramparts."

The metaphor of history as inscription can be found in other Soviet Yiddish works of the 1930s. Markish's Birobidzhan play *Mishpokhe Ovadis* (The Ovadis family) uses a similar image to signal Jewish participation in Soviet history.[18] The play tells the story of a Jewish family's resettlement in Birobidzhan, focusing on the struggle between the older generation, who want to preserve Jewish traditions, and the younger generation, who reject them, embracing the new Soviet way of life, including intermarriage (Veidlinger 2000, 174–77). One of the grandsons, Shlyomke, dies heroically while patrolling the border: with his dying breath he points in the direction of the enemy. The patriarch of the family, Avrom, writes the date of his beloved grandson's death in a book, the same book in which his birth date was noted. One of the other grandsons protests, "it's not the same," because the hero died for the sake of the whole country, and his "death will be inscribed in the hills" (*vet forshribn vern af di sopkes*) (Markish 1938, 153). The Jews are no longer the people of the book, rootless and outside of history; the creation of Birobidzhan has given them the opportunity to "take root" in a territory, and their stories leave palpable traces on the land.

Fefer's Birobidzhan poem "Di tayge vart" (The taiga waits), written in 1937, similarly links history, territory, and inscription:

Who goes there? Who steps there?
The song leaves a trace,
It's our step and our word
At the shores of the Amur.

Ver gayt es dort? Ver tupet dort?
Di lid nor lozt a shpur
S'iz undzer trot un unzer vort
Af bregn fun Amur.

(Fefer 1967, 113)

This poem attempts to fulfill the charge of *korenizatsiia*, the taking root of a culture that is national in a specific place; the poet affirms the presence of a Jewish community and culture in Birobidzhan.

However, in "Barg-aruf," Bergelson, in contrast to Fefer, shows that the inscription of the Jewish people into socialist history comes at a price. As in Markish's *One by One*, in Bergelson's text the new covenant of the socialist collective requires a new form of circumcision, a wound that is not a sign but an injury. The punishment is only suggested. Receiving his negative report from the regional committee, the district "secretary had the face of a man who allows himself to get a whipping, only he himself must think whether the whipping comes for him alone, and if not, for whom else?" (*hot er gehat a ponem fun a mentshn, vos lozt zikh gebn shmits, nor aleyn darf er nokh a trakht ton, tsi di shmits kumen nor im eynem, un oyb nit—iz vemen nokh?*) (Bergelson 1936a, 38). Bergelson repeats the motif of metaphorical and self-inflicted pain in the worker Velvl. Velvl misses the girl he left behind, and foolishly asks for leave just as the work reaches its most frantic pace. Sensing his error, he "grimaces harshly as if he had hit his own finger himself while hammering a nail" (*zikh shtark farkrimt, vi er volt bam farshlogn a tshvok getrofn mitn hamer in an eygenem finger*) (48). Here again is the middle voice, in which the subject performing the action and its recipient are the same. In another emblematic scene, the semaphore at the train station is torn from the ground by the ferocious Birobidzhan wind. As the worker Sholem Bubes labors to replace it, his face takes on the appearance of a "fiery wound." Leaving a trace in history—the semaphore in the taiga—requires bodily injury.

Bergelson's vignettes describing socialist construction in the taiga of Birobidzhan shift the emphasis from the transparent message of victory to the unsaid and the unfulfilled. The new covenant is not between God and Israel, but between Stalin and Israel. The sign of the father works through absence and distance. Stalin enters Bergelson's text through terror and fear, his great power signaled by an enormous portrait, an icon, that Velvl carries as he rushes off to complete his tasks in the new building. Stalin, the new father of the people, is a punishing and wrathful God. I quote the enigmatic opening of the story:

> Nonetheless, this time, as always after the late rains, the work began anew in the young city and in all the young human nests, in the

mountainous and in the flat places of the entire area. Like flaming fiery horses the days before the October holidays rushed in, and with them, the summer warmth returned . . . Like flaming, fiery horses, the days before the October holidays chased over villages and settlements along hidden trails, along mountain peaks, and around fields, everywhere throwing off sunny embers, everywhere kindling the desire to mount them, hold them by the manes and ride and ride . . . They brought joy to some. Others they frightened. (37)

The opening line suggests without articulating clearly a prior condition that would obviate the yearly cycle of renewed work and the return of warmth. In spite of this circumstance that would interrupt the cycle, what usually took place happened this time as well. The unspoken negative is the founding moment of the story, and constitutes one of its dominant motifs. The story's ending contains a string of unspoken negatives. An American family arrives in Birobidzhan, and as they make their way in a snowstorm from the station to their quarters, their escort shouts, "'It's like Winnipeg,' as if someone had frightened them with 'it's worse than Alaska.'" He points out the post office, "as if someone had frightened them with, 'it's the end of the world, a wasteland'" (*ek velt, a midber*) (66).

The "October holidays" twice repeated in the opening passage refer to a time of special significance in the Jewish calendar: the New Year, and Yom Kippur, the Day of Atonement, and especially the days between the New Year and Yom Kippur, the period known as "the days of awe," when Jews wait to see whether they have been inscribed in the "book of life." The link to the Jewish tradition of the fall holidays, with their communal confession of sins of commission and omission, emerges in the opening vignette. The secretary of the Birobidzhan regional committee learns that he has not fulfilled a single plan: the necessary plots of land have not been cleared; the required number of apartments and barracks have not been constructed; not enough hay and silage were prepared; and so forth. The enumeration of the secretary's list of sins, together with the mention of the October holidays, unmistakably echoes the Yom Kippur confession. Ironically, for Bergelson's district secretary the only indication of positive accomplishment is the lack of negative consequences. The secretary considers that given all his failures, the regional committee ought to remove him and the entire leadership in the area, and that if they have not done so, it is a sign that something was accomplished (*iz a simen, az epes iz in rayon dokh opgeton gevorn*) (38). Evidence of accomplishment, which would consist in the abundance of food, provisions, land, and the positive presence of socialist construction, can be seen only in the absence of punishment. "Barg-Aruf" never arrives at its own happy conclusion. The characters he portrays in the story, and its readers, remain in the position of unfulfilled anticipation, waiting for something that could be wonderful or terrible. This condition of dreadful expectation hearkens back to the temporality Bergelson used in his own earlier civil war stories, suggesting that little in the way of socialist construction has actually taken place.

In his introduction to a collection of Birobidzhan stories published in 1980 in Russian and English by Progress Publishers in Moscow, Chaim Beider quotes the last lines of "Barg-aruf." The story as a whole, notably, is absent from the collection. I cite from the English translation: "The sifting snow has stopped, the wind had died down and everywhere you look the snow lies smooth as a counterpane. And the sun . . . The sun above you, below you, in the hillocks and in the sky, so bright—could it possibly be any brighter?" (Beider 1980, 16). According to Beider, this passage shows that "the story ends on a joyous note." Another interpretation is more likely. The Stalinesque brightness of the sun on the white snow calls to mind Bergelson's words from the tribune of the First Congress of the Soviet Writers' Union about the blinding whiteness of the sheet of paper on which the Dagestani poet wrote his completely incomprehensible poem about Lenin and Stalin. Bergelson said, "I did not understand a single word of this speech, but nonetheless this extraordinary poem about Lenin's and Stalin's national policy was written on a piece of paper of blinding whiteness" (Luppol, Rozental', and Tretiakov 1934, 271). The Stalinesque sun shining on the snow of Birobidzhan is also blinding, and the blinding sun on the snow "everywhere you look" makes it impossible to read the traces of human habitation there. The all-important material inscription of the Jews on the land is illegible, and the meaning of Birobidzhan as a solution to the Jewish problem remains opaque.

Babel's Bris and the Specter of Beilis

Unlike Markish, Bergelson, Kataev, and many others, Babel never published works about massive construction projects. His writings published after *Red Cavalry* reveal an increasing ambivalence about the transformation of traditional Jewish life in the new socialist order.[19] And in "Karl-Iankel'" (Karl-Yankel, 1931) the question of the new Jew is tied to circumcision.[20] Whereas Markish uses wounding to suggest the covenantal meaning of circumcision, Babel makes the theme explicit.

As the twin names of the title indicate, the story concerns the double legacy of Marxism and Judaism. The infant Karl-Yankel "is to receive the Soviet kingdom," but his pious Hasidic grandmother needs an heir who could listen to her tell legends of the Baal Shem Tov, and while her son-in-law is away, she has Naftula Gerchik the *moyel* circumcise her grandson, adding "Yankel" to his name.[21] It is likely that this dimension of the story is based on real-life cases in which fathers blamed their religious in-laws for carrying out circumcisions.[22] In the story, the child's father, outraged, takes the grandmother and the *moyel* to court.

In 1933, a Yiddish translation of Babel's story appeared in *Der apikoyres*. The illustration accompanying the work emphasizes the benefits of the "Karl" side of the controversy (Figure 2). The caption reads, "The struggle for the young generation." The "Karl" proponents are schoolchildren, some wearing the ties of young pioneers. A Torah scroll lies on the floor, abandoned and blasphemed. On the "Yankel" side are old Jews with side curls and beards; they carry the Torah in their arms. The figure in the foreground, wearing a bowler hat and carrying an umbrella—the costume used by the Moscow State Yiddish theater to signify the *luftmentsh*—also carries the *moyel*'s knife.

What is strikingly present in the story, and conspicuous by its absence in the accompanying illustration, is Babel's horrifying portrait of Naftula the *moyel*:

> Cutting off what he was supposed to, he did not filter the blood through a glass tube, but sucked it with his own raw lips. The blood spread over his clotted beard. Drunk, he approached the guests. His bear's eyes glowed with joy. Red-haired, like the first redhead on earth,

he intoned the blessing over the wine through his nose. With one hand, Naftula flung vodka into his overgrown, crooked, fire-breathing maw, and with the other he held a plate. On it lay a little knife, stained crimson with the little boy's blood, and a piece of gauze . . . "Fat mamas," the old man would yell, flashing his coral eyes, "conceive boys for Naftula." (Babel 1990, 164–66)[23]

In his grotesque description of the satanic *moyel*, Babel conjures the image of the predatory Jew from the late tsarist era, an image that circulated during the ritual murder trial of Mendel Beilis in 1913. Babel was in Kiev when the trial took place.[24] While Babel's story "Karl-Yankel" refers most immediately to actual agitprop trials of circumcision that took place in the 1920s, the specter of the Beilis trial haunts his text. Each of these layers can be examined in turn. At the Beilis trial the prosecution charged that the victim was killed in such a way as to yield the maximum amount of blood from his body. It was alleged that Jews needed Christian blood to compensate for the loss of blood at circumcisions. The emphasis on the profuse flow of blood and the startling picture of Naftula's voracious mouth may allude to one of the most

Figure 2 "The Struggle for the Young Generation," in *Der apikoyres* (The atheist) 1933 (3):11. Illustration accompanying Isaac Babel, "Karl-Yankel," pp. 11–13.

notorious Judeophobic writings of the time of the Beilis trial, Vasilii Rozanov's article "The Jews' Olfactory and Tactile Relation to Blood." Babel read Rozanov, and if he did not refer to this article directly, he was familiar with the image of Jews as bloodsuckers found in other works by Rozanov.[25] Rozanov stressed the image of the blood on the *moyel*'s mouth: "around the tongue and lips of the *moyel* is the infant's blood; he feels it, hot, sticky, red" (Rozanov 1932, 52).[26] Rozanov explicitly linked circumcision with the fecundity of the Jews, understanding circumcision as a form of sacrifice and fecundity as its compensation. In Babel's story, Naftula urges Jewish mothers to conceive boys to slake his thirst for their blood, and he is rewarded for his efforts. The courtyards "swarmed with children like the mouths of rivers with roe. Naftula dragged himself around with his bag, like a tax collector." Lust for money and lust for blood, both of which circulate, are the twin hallmarks of the vampiric Jew.

Hasidism is another key link between Babel's story of 1931 and the Beilis trial of 1913. Karl-Yankel's grandmother attends a Hasidic synagogue, pays tribute to emissaries from Galician *tsadikim* (leaders), and needs a Jewish grandson to whom she could tell legends of the Baal Shem Tov, the founder of Hasidism. She belongs to the "ethnographic" Jews that Gekht describes in his sketches of the 1920s, but she is not quite obsolete. Among the spectators who gather in the court in Babel's story are the Galician *tsadikim*, convinced that "the Jewish religion" was on trial. Russian newspapers made Hasidism the particular target of the Beilis case: according to their reports, "*tsadikim* instructed Jews how to employ kabbalistic symbols to extract the blood of Christian boys" (Petrovsky-Shtern 2006, 97). Efraim Sicher says that Naftula is "accused of being a fanatic follower of a villainous cult," but does not link "Karl-Yankel" to the Beilis trial (Sicher 1985, 100).

In contrast to the Beilis case and the accompanying newspaper campaign, the agitprop trials of circumcision that took place in the 1920s did not promote the image of the bloodthirsty, predatory Jew. In her study *Soviet and Kosher: Jewish Popular Culture in the Soviet Union: 1923–1929*, Anna Shternshis includes an account of the Odessa agitprop trial of circumcision of 1928 (Babel's story is set in Odessa, and the *moyel* Naftula is described as an Odessa institution). According to the author of the memoir, the *moyel* at the Odessa trial defended himself by pointing out that he had performed circumcisions on many members of the audience: "I look at you, my audience, and I see that 90 percent of you are 'my productions'"(Shternshis 2006, 95). In Babel's story, Naftula does something similar when he reveals that the chair of the court, "Orlov," was born with the name Zusman, and that he, Naftula, performed the circumcision at Orlov-Zusman's *bris* thirty years before. Both at the Odessa trial and in the Babel story the *moyel* performs a figurative act of uncovering identities—uncovering is another meaning of circumcision—but the Odessa case does not exploit the alleged bloodlust of the Jews, as the Beilis case did.

Why go back to Beilis? In reverting to the image of the Jew as Naftula the *moyel* with his fire-breathing mouth, Babel is not giving credence to this stereotype. He is asking rather whether at the dawn of the new Soviet era the ghost of Beilis has to be exorcised again. Babel's version of circumcision on trial reveals Jewish and non-Jewish anxieties about transforming Jews into Soviets. His portraits of the most Jewish Jews, including the Hasidim in all their stereotypical "fanaticism," the wig-wearing grandmothers who pay tribute to *tsadikim* and believe in the Baal Shem Tov, and especially the *moyel* whose ardor for his profession borders on demonic lust, provide an uncomfortable mirror for assimilated Jews and raise questions about the image of Jews and Jewish tradition in the new Soviet world. Babel seems to be asking, is this who we are to ourselves; is this who we remain to non-Jews? Babel's story ends without any clear resolution but instead poses a question about the future happiness of the newly circumcised Karl-Yankel, the heir to both Marxism and Medzhibozh. "Is it possible," the narrator asks, "that you will be happier than I?"

Semen Gekht's *Pouchitel'naia istoriia* (An edifying story, 1939) answers this question about the next generation in the affirmative. Like Markish's *One by One* it describes the transformation of a shtetl Jew into a proletarian. Unlike Markish, Bergelson, and Babel, Gekht's writing does not focus on the male Jewish body and its difference. The tropological structure of covenantal wounding, central to Markish and Bergelson, does not dominate Gekht's story, even though his youthful hero suffers an injury and a false accusation. And yet the remnants of the past, the stories and legends, religious practices and sacred texts of Jewish tradition, and Babel himself find their way into Gekht's text.

A young boy, Moisei Gubler, leaves his native shtetl for the Dneprstroi construction site. He faces many difficulties, including his family history (his father was a "*chelovek vozdukha*," a *luftmentsh*); he is accused of "wrecking." Show trials against alleged industrial saboteurs took place in Moscow in 1928 and 1931, leading to the mass arrests and executions of the later part of the 1930s. Gekht's plot takes a fanciful turn when Moisei's mother travels to Moscow, where Kalinin agrees to help her son. By the end of the story, Moisei is well on his way to becoming a successful engineer. The happy ending also includes intermarriage, one of the stock elements of Soviet Jewish propaganda of the time, found also in, for example, Markish's *Family Ovadis* and the film *Seekers of Happiness*.

The socialist realist fairy tale of successful integration into the proletarian collective requires that heroes reject the past. As in his sketches for *Ogonek*, in *An Edifying Story* Gekht inserts Jewish religious motifs, customs, and institutions into his text in the guise of the past that is to be overcome. The description of these devalued remnants of the past is explicit and detailed and includes: the institution of heder, the Jewish elementary school; Onkelos and Rashi, biblical commentators that were studied at the elementary level; Kabbala and the Zohar, the Jewish mystical tradition and its chief text; the founder of Hasidism, the Baal Shem Tov, known as the Besht, and the custom of leaving intercessionary notes at his grave; and references to Passover and the Yom Kippur liturgy. Gekht describes the emotional high point of the Yom Kippur service, the "*unsane-tokef*" prayer. The prayer, from which Gekht quotes, lays out God's plan for "who shall live and who shall die" and lists the various kinds of deaths, by drowning and by disease, for example. This reference to the Day of Judgment alludes to real events, the ongoing terror that was taking place in the Soviet Union at the time.

The Jewish material that Gekht inserts into his socialist realist fairy tale also includes ancient and more recent Jewish history, including references to nineteenth-century culture—for example, Gutskow's tolerance play *Uriel Acosta*, which was performed well into the Soviet period. The novel refers to twentieth-century Jewish history with its mention of OZET, the society promoting Jewish agricultural resettlement; and

Palestine, the discarded alternative to the Soviet Union. Gekht wrote an entire novel on the theme of disenchantment with Palestine: *Parakhod idet v Iaffu i obratno* (The steamship travels to Jaffa and returns). In the 1939 *Edifying Story*, Moisei's elder brother returns from Palestine to resettle in Birobidzhan.

Published under the imprint of "children's literature," Gekht's didactic novel about proletarianization also includes a condensed and simplified curriculum in Jewish culture, history, and Judaism. The didactic agenda of atheism, industrialization, and intermarriage includes a short course on traditional Jewish life in the shtetl, complete with explanatory footnotes. Indeed, in his review of the novel for the mainstream *Literaturnaia gazeta* (Literary gazette) in 1939, the noted critic and author Konstantin Paustovskii praised the first half of the book for the force of depiction of the "dying Jewish shtetl," and criticized the "dryness" of the description of the new Soviet life in the second half of the book (Paustovskii 1939). The dying Jewish shtetl has more warmth and life than the living socialist construction site. Gekht's *Edifying Story* performs the same double gesture as his "sketches" of the previous decade: staging the death of traditional Jewish life simultaneously brings about its reanimation in a Russian literary and cultural space.

Gekht's novel also reanimates the literary voice of his friend and patron Babel. In the novel, the young hero's mentor reproaches him for his initial passivity. Moisei draws a diagram in his notebook of the "good" and "bad" people in his life. His teacher attacks him: "No, Moisei, I am beginning to worry about your political education. What kind of classification is this? Where did you get these old-fashioned ideas? What are you aiming at? An international of good people, or what?" (Gekht 1939, 293). The "international of good people" is a direct quotation from Babel's *Red Cavalry* story "Gedali," first published in 1924. Gedali, the quixotic owner of a Dickensian curiosity shop, a figure conjured out of the narrator's own "dense sorrow of memory," wants the impossible, not a revolution of blood, bullets, and requisitions but "an international of good people," in which "each soul is registered and given the best quality rations" (Babel 1990, 2:73).

The dismissive allusion to "Gedali" ostensibly teaches Gekht's young readers that naive idealism can only be harmful. Moisei had to learn to defend himself and not rely on the "international of good people." The allusion, however slight, also serves another purpose. By the mid-1930s, Babel had largely fallen silent. Gekht's novel entered the production queue in September 1938 and was released for printing in April 1939. Paustovkii's review came out in June. Babel was arrested in May 1939 and shot in January of the next year. Whether Gekht knew or suspected that Babel was about to be arrested cannot be ascertained. His quotation nonetheless brings before his reading audience a powerful literary voice that was about to be permanently silenced.

Jews in the Cinema

Cinema, that most important of art forms, played a particularly important role in the project of transforming the shtetl Jew into a productive Soviet worker. As a visual art, cinema staged the remaking of the Jew right before the very eyes of the spectator, substituting the particularistic visual semiotics of beard, cap, wrinkles, old age, and stooped shoulders (as in Gekht's description of the "archeological Jew") for a new visual code that emphasized the universal features of youth, strength, and belief in the future. The Soviet Union made this new universal body, unmarked by the burden of ethnic difference, available to all the minorities who lived within its borders and to those who immigrated to the Soviet Union in search of the brotherhood and tolerance that was denied them elsewhere. In the 1930s a number of films were made that emphasized the theme of the brotherhood of peoples, including the 1932 film *Vozvrashchenie Neitana Bekkera* (The return of Nathan Bekker), in which Kador Ben-Salim played Nathan's African American friend, who immigrates to the Soviet Union with him from the United States. In the 1936 musical *Tsirk* (The circus) the Soviet Union provides a home for a mother with a black child. In its climactic apotheosis of multiculturalism, representatives of each national minority sing the child a lullaby—including Mikhoels, who sings to the child in Yiddish that all paths are open for him.[27]

In *The Return of Nathan Bekker*, the otherness of the Jew's language and body is linked to race. The appearance of Kador Ben-Salim as Nathan's African American friend points to a racial otherness that both the Jew and the black share. In the Russian-language version of the film, Nathan's father, upon seeing Ben-Salim, asks whether he is "also a Jew." The inhabitants of the shtetl rush to the Bekker's house when Nathan arrives, because they think he is a member of an American charitable commission. Nathan steps into a back room as they crowd in, and Ben-Salim appears in his place. Mikhoels, not noticing the substitution, tells the crowd, "this is my Nosn." During the bricklaying competition, Nathan's face grows darker and darker with dirt and sweat, until he seems to appear in blackface. The conditions of capitalist labor under which Nathan works make him "black." In the Soviet Union, however, everyone, including blacks, Jews, and other minorities, have a chance to become "white" or, at least, to more closely resemble the teacher at the training institute, whose chiseled face and blond hair reflect an Aryan ideal.

The story of the making of *Nathan Bekker* is complicated. The archive of the Moscow State Yiddish Theater (GOSET) contains a Russian-language screenplay *Puteshestvie Neitana Bekkera* (The journey of Nathan Bekker, 1931) with Perets Markish and Rashel' Mil'man listed as the joint authors. The same archive contains a 1932 contract in which Solomon Mikhoels agrees to play the role of Nathan's father, Tsale, in both a Russian and a Yiddish version of the film. The film premiered in 1933; however, I have been unable to find a copy of the Yiddish apart from a few frames attached to the Russian version, available at the National Centre for Jewish Film.[28] After working on the Russian screenplay, Markish wrote a Yiddish novel, *One by One* (Eyns af eyns), using the same plot (I discussed the novel earlier); the film, however, is quite distinct from the novel. I base my discussion on the Russian-language film, directed by Mil'man and Boris Shpis, and starring David Gutman in the role of Neitan, with Mikhoels as his father, Tsale.[29]

The film, like the novel that followed it and like other films of its time, advertises the superiority of the Soviet way of life over the capitalist West. The bricklaying competition that is the culmination of the film shows that Soviet work methods are more efficient and more humane. The competition takes place in a circus tent, performed before an audience; the scene stages the theme of work as a source of aesthetic pleasure, as a joyous spectacle. The screenplay emphasizes the project of national and individual transformation of the 1930s: the particularistic ethnic self was to be made anew by means of participation in vast construction projects. Markish recycles the image of the rotting, abject body that he had used in his work of the 1920s, including the pogrom poem "The Mound" and the civil war epic *Brothers*. In these earlier works, the rotting, oozing body signified the collapse of divine and human order. Here, however, similar imagery accentuates the transformation of the shtetl that will take place with industrialization: "we will take people from the streets, from the train stations, from the small shtetls, rotting in the marketplaces, and we will make them into workers and useful people." These "denizens of waste heaps . . . hold in their minds, their will, and their hands the birth of a new socialist city." In the screenplay, "the building of socialism in one country" leads to the wholesale transformation of people and places. The Jews and their shtetls are remade from top to bottom, leaving no trace of the past.

The film, however, departs from its own script. The past refuses to rot away, and the shtetl is beautiful, touching, funny—even transcendent. Contemporary reviews picked up on what Miron Chernenko calls the film's duality with regard to remaking Jews. One review noted that in spite of the author's "good intentions," the film's depiction of socialist competition does not show "the signs of the times," that is, the true spirit of the first five-year plan. As Chernenko points out, the *Return of Nathan Bekker* was the first sound film with a Jewish theme. The use of sound, and in particular Mikhoels's voice, allowed the film to escape the strictures of its script. Whereas the screenplay gives Tsale Bekker a minimum role, Mikhoels as Tsale takes over the film. He performs the role almost entirely without words, replacing them with a combination of gestures, facial moments, and *nigunim*, wordless melodies. The film opens and closes with Mikhoels's *nigun*. In the first shot, of the dilapidated shtetl with its broken-down roofs and broken, idle men, and in the last, we hear Mikhoels singing his *nigun*. Even the visual elements of the opening shot belie the ostensible purpose of depicting the "rot" of the shtetl, since the images capture and preserve the appearance of the shtetl, the very thing that the new Soviet way of life was to destroy. The shop signs, for example, use words in both Russian and Yiddish to inform customers about the shops' wares; a prominent sign reads "kosher" in Yiddish.

Mikhoels opens, closes, and steals the show.[30] In a dramatic departure from the screenplay, the first sounds we hear in the film are of Mikhoels singing and of his stuttered Yiddish version of the name Nathan—"N-n-n-Nosn." Mikhoels's repertoire of gestures includes, for example, putting on and taking off his glasses, pushing his cap forward and back, removing his folding measure from his breast pocket, stroking the electric teakettle that his son has brought from America, and picking up a bust of Marx and cradling it, while comically noting the similarity between his beard and Marx's. When Nathan returns home to tell his wife the joyous news of his acceptance as a Soviet worker, he and his father perform a duet using Mikhoels's melody of monosyllables and gestures. The words "we are building" (*stroim*), "we are working" (*rabotaem*), and "socialism" serve merely as points of departure for an extended wordless acoustic ballet. Gutman as Nathan and Mikhoels as his father conduct an entire conversation by changing the intonation of the words "well," "yes," and "no," with the longest exchange between father and son accomplished by the single word *nu*, a word that in both Russian and Yiddish expresses a full range of meanings, from approval to doubt to impatience, and everything in between.

Tsale Bekker Mikhoels lacks articulate speech; he cannot even sign his own name, and when he speaks, he stammers. A musical polyphony is created in the interchange between his stammering speech and his wordless *nigun*. The words lose their meaning and function only in relation to the melody. This was a technique that Mikhoels had developed in his work at the Moscow State Yiddish Theater, particularly in his role in Mendele's "The Travels of Benjamin the Third." In an article published in a Russian theater journal in 1935, Markish wrote that in Mikhoels's performances, the actor engraved on his "face the previous epoch and romance of Jewish poverty, it could seem, that on one side sat Mendele, who dropped by for a visit, on the other, Sholom Aleichem, and one story above, I. L. Peretz" (Rudnitskii 1981, 348). Mikhoels had previously played in the 1925 silent *Evreiskoe schast'e* (Jewish luck), an adaptation of Sholem Aleichem's Menakhem Mendl tales, directed by Alexander

Granovsky.³¹ Mikhoels rendered Menakhem Mendl, the insurance salesman turned hapless matchmaker, as an ethereal Jewish Charlie Chaplin, dressed in a bowler hat and carrying an umbrella, with a mincing gait, a bobble head, and ever-gesticulating hands conveying a full range of emotions. As Tsale Bekker, he translates the bewildered, comically detached *luftmentsh* of the traditional Yiddish theater into the idiom of film. The constant gesticulation and wordless song separate Tsale Bekker from the Soviet reality unfolding around him, creating an alternative space that is not of this world. The last shot of the film shows Mikhoels and Kador Ben-Salim sitting on top of the vast scaffolding of a construction site (Magnitogorsk) as Mikhoels teaches Ben-Salim how to sing his *nigun*. The wordless melody is a form of traditional prayer in the Hasidic community: it is an act that links the singer to the soul, to God, and to the community.³² The vertical axis of the last shot, showing Mikhoels perched at the very tip of the scaffolding, visually underscores the role of the Jew as *luftmentsh*, "a person of the air," and further suggests a link between the *luftmentsh* and the divine.

Mikhail Dubson's 1935 Russian-language film *Granitsa: staroe Dudino* (The border: Old Dudino), with Veniamin Zuskin in a lead role, also uses music and improvised *nigunim*, but in contrast to *Nathan Bekker*, the triumph of the new world edges out the old. The film tells the story of Jews in the shtetl of Dudino, located four kilometers to the west of the Polish-Soviet border. In Dudino, all the Jews live in thrall to the capitalist Novik, who colludes with the local authorities. As the characters in the film repeat, "Four kilometers to the East, Jews are people, but here?" Zuskin plays the role of Arye, bookkeeper to Novik. As the film unfolds, Arye gains the courage to join the small group of revolutionaries in Dudino, led by Boris Bershtein (played by N. K. Val'iano). The film consistently and monotonously reiterates the distinction between "here," that is, the old, bad, traditional way of life, and "there"—across the border, the new, good, Soviet way of life. As in other films and other artifacts of the time, *The Border* shows traditional Jewish life in the shtetl under the sign of what is to be overcome. The film reveals a certain duality, because on the one hand, it depicts the life of Jews in the shtetl as obsolete and corrupt, but on the other hand, it preserves in a Russian cultural space the very thing that is obsolete and corrupt.

Compared with *Nathan Bekker*, however, Dubson's film is far less sympathetic to the old life.

Music plays a central role in the staging of the Jew's remaking. Just as the sound of Mikhoels's singing opens and closes *Nathan Bekker*, music opens and closes *The Border*. The film begins with a scene in the synagogue: the cantor chants the *kedusha*, the prayer that proclaims God's holiness. In the middle, however, he protests when other members of the congregation attempt to steal his thunder, and he has a wordless conversation with an apparently Gentile woman across the balcony, suggesting an illicit relationship with her. Wordless conversation during prayer, preserving only the appearance of holiness, reveals the hypocrisy of religion. In *Nathan Bekker*, in contrast, Mikhoels's inchoate *nigun* provides an ironic commentary on the changes taking place before our eyes. When we first meet Mikhoels, he is chanting, and similarly when we first meet Zuskin as Arye, he is beautifully singing his way through his bookkeeping calculations. By the film's end, Zuskin sings a "new song," a term that clearly alludes to the motif of the "new song" in the Hebrew Bible (Ps. 40, 96, and 98). The "new song" is the new Soviet Jewish way of life. As Zuskin says, describing the Jewish collective farm that he saw on the other side of the border, the Jewish farmers were singing "a new song," a song that was undoubtedly Jewish and even, as he says, "in a minor key," but with "a major content." At the end of *Nathan Bekker*, in contrast, Mikhoels is singing the same *nigun* with which he opens the film.

In 1936 Zuskin and Val'iano played together again, this time on opposite sides of the ideological divide: Zuskin as the intractable *luftmentsh* Pinye Kopel'man, and Val'iano as the new Jew who embraces life as an agricultural worker in Birobidzhan. *Iskateli schast'ia* (Seekers of happiness), like *Nathan Bekker*, is a story of return. Directed by V. Korsh-Sablin with Mikhoels serving as "artistic consultant," the film tells the story of Old Dvoira, her son Leva (Val'iano), daughters Rosa and Basia, and Basia's husband Pinia (Zuskin), who return from "abroad" (presumably Palestine)—where Jews could pray but there was no work—in order to resettle in Birobidzhan. The film opens with the family on a steamship. Rosa, dressed in a leather coat, stares into her bright future through binoculars. Pinia, bearded and in a bowler hat and scruffy suit, sings an improvised *nigun* with the words "we are going, we are going [*edem, edem*]" and asking what the steamship costs:

> Tell me, please, how much, approximately of course, could a steamship like this cost?
> What, you want to buy it?
> No, I'm just curious.[33]

Zuskin himself came up with these lines. They perfectly capture the essence of Pinia's role as a hopeless schemer and daydreamer, the *luftmentsh* of Yiddish literature and theater here thrust into the new Soviet utopia of collective labor.[34] Zuskin's performance of the role of Pinia, down to the detail of the bowler hat in the first scene, recapitulates his own and Mikhoels's performances in the Moscow State Yiddish Theater's stage and film adaptations of Sholem Aleichem's Menakhem Mendl stories, including particularly the 1928 play *Luftmentshn* (People of the air), with Zuskin in the role of Menakhem's "shadow," Kapote.[35] By the end of *Seekers of Happiness*, Zuskin has become dirtier and more bedraggled, more and more like the perpetually sagging Kapote (the word means "coat"). The stuffing goes out of Pinia when the extra bulge in his pocket, the bottle of fool's gold, is forcibly removed during his arrest.

While the other characters in the film "found their places" (as the film titles inform us) as agricultural workers on the collective farm "Royte feld" (Red Field), Pinia alone keeps his critical distance. When the barn the family lives in starts leaking, only Pinia sarcastically points out how "cozy" it is; when the other workers—remade, new Jews—assemble to go off to the fields, Pinia notes that "they don't even look like Jews." Pinia's commentary resembles the disembodied ironic critical voice in Bergelson's Birobidzhan story "Uphill"—the voice that names Birobidzhan as a "wasteland." Instead of working in the fields, Pinia pans for gold, singing his *nigun* as he digs. Pinia dreams out loud of what his newly discovered fortune will bring: "I can buy . . . a house . . . No! . . . A factory . . . A factory that makes . . . suspenders! And the suspenders will have my trademark, a crown and the inscription: Pinia Kopman—the king of suspenders!" (Zuskina-Perel'man 2002, 151). As Zuskina-Perel'man points out, Pinia delivers this speech as his pants fall down. His plans, of course, come to nothing: he assaults Leva, who tries to steal his bottle of gold dust, and he is arrested trying to cross the border into China. His fortune turns out to be fool's gold. In *Seekers of Happiness*, Zuskin does what Mikhoels had done in the *Return of Nathan Bekker*. Zuskin uses the *nigun*, the wordless melody that accompanies him in practically every scene, as Mikhoels had. The "king of suspenders" (*korol' podtiazhek*) recalls Mikhoels as Menakhem Mendl, in *Jewish Luck*, proclaiming himself to be the "king of matchmakers." Zuskin in *Seekers*, like Mikhoels in the earlier film, takes the role of the hopeless, obsolete shtetl Jew, the intractable but incompetent capitalist—the *luftmentsh* that is to be replaced by the productive Soviet worker—and transforms the role into the transcendently wise fool.

Shire Gorshman's "New Way"

In Shire Gorshman's works from the late 1920s, the productivization of the shtetl inhabitant, as well as the trope of covenantal wounding in Stalin's new order, does not appear. Markish, Bergelson, Fefer, and Babel rework biblical tropes to link inscription on the Jewish male body and inscription in the new Jewish spaces of the Soviet Union. Rather than describe the marking of the body, Gorshman's stories focus instead on its pleasures. Her stories of Jewish communal life in Crimea imagine a space unmarked by the strictures of Soviet construction and free from the confines of traditional Jewish life.

Born in the shtetl of Krok (Krakes) in Lithuania in 1906, Shire Gorshman emigrated to Palestine with her first husband, returning to the USSR in 1929 to work on a socialist commune in Crimea named Vojo Nova, Esperanto for "New Way."[36] Menakhem El'kind led the immigrants. The commune, which had approximately one hundred members, was located in an abandoned gentry house near Evpatoria in Crimea. It was organized more like a kibbutz than a Soviet-style kolkhoz: children lived in separate quarters, and no money was used. Gorshman had separated from her husband in Palestine. Her autobiographical stories describing life on the commune emphasize the heroine's sense of freedom there, including the freedom from worry about her children, who lived in the children's home. She visited them every few days. The artist Mendl Gorshman, who became Shire's second husband, was sent to Vojo Nova as a member of a team whose mission was to produce publicity materials about Jewish agricultural settlement in Crimea. In 1931 the family moved to Moscow, where Gorshman began her writing career, with encouragement from the Yiddish poet Leyb Kvitko and the critic Meir Viner. By 1937, Vojo Nova had been dismantled and its leaders arrested and shot (Dekel-Chen 2005, 101).

Gorshman's early stories appeared in the 1930s in such publications as *Der shtern* (The star) and *Zay greyt* (Be ready), a Yiddish magazine for youth. The illustrated journal included poetry, prose, chess problems, puzzles, games, and articles about sports and Stalin. The work that Gorshman wrote about Vojo Nova was collected and republished in various editions and Russian translations in the 1960s and subsequent decades. The collection *33 noveln* (33 stories), which includes more than a dozen of these short pieces, was published in Yiddish in Warsaw in 1961, and in Russian translation as *The Third Generation* in 1963.[37] Gorshman's longer autobiographical novel, *Khanes shof un rinder* (Khane's sheep and cattle), also touches on the commune years.[38]

Gorshman's life is a Soviet Jewish success story; the poverty-stricken Jewish woman from a shtetl transformed herself into an agricultural laborer and then into a successful Soviet writer from one of the "national minorities." Her work, however, does not conform to the emerging aesthetic demands of socialist realism, in which reality is enhanced and heightened by the socialist reconstruction of the self and the world. Stalin makes no appearance in her writing. This is not to say that her stories are entirely free from Soviet sensibilities. In one, for example, commune members show their awareness of the epoch-making significance of their experiment in collective living. The food in the dining room is a thin, tasteless, barley gruel. Relief comes in the occasional tomato or cucumber taken from the garden (the produce is supposed to be sold, not consumed). The gardener worries whether future generations will be insulted by the way commune members broke with their principles out of mere hunger.

Gorshman's stories about life at Vojo Nova emphasize the heroine's pleasure in the physical environment and her close connection to the natural world. In *Khanes shef un rindner*, for example, the heroine sings

Socialist Construction, the *Luftmentsh*, and the New Jew 107

a wordless melody, a *nigun*, accompanied by her horse, named Borukh, who whinnies in tune with her. When she encounters a group of horses locked in a barn and apparently abandoned, her empathy for their suffering makes her milk flow. She comes to a place on the steppe where it seems that the very edge of the earth is visible. Exhausted from riding, she flings herself belly down on the grass and "breathes in the peace that comes to her from the earth" (*aynzapndik in zikh di ru, vos hot geotemt tsu ir fun der erd*) (Gorshman 1984, 15). The narrator emphasizes the heroine's sense of freedom and of her power to direct her own life; as she says, "I do what I want" (*vos ikh vil*) (24). In contrast, in Markish's *One by One* and in Bergelson's story "Uphill," women play an incidental and passive role, even though Bergelson's earlier work, notably *Nokh alemen* (The end of everything), centers on a woman who rebels against the conventions of Jewish daily life. Free love is also part of communal life, and the lack of privacy leads members to conduct their love affairs at the grain silos, nicknamed "towers of love" ("Der turem fun libe" is also the title of one of Gorshman's stories).

Free from biblical and Soviet grand narratives, Gorshman's stories provide a portrait of a presocial world of individuals—regardless of their setting in a socialist and Jewish collective. The space she describes, unlike Markish's, Bergelson's, and Fefer's image of a land inscribed with the traces of the Soviet Jewish homeland, is unmarked and without boundaries; there is no need to show passports or scars in order to gain entrance. The heroine's attitude towards animals, with whom she feels a physical bond; the "towers of love"; and the emphasis on maternity, not paternity, show that Gorshman's representation of Vojo Nova corresponds to something like Rousseau's state of nature. Gorshman avoids the question of the Jew's entrance into the Soviet body politic and the masculine covenant that binds its members in the flesh. She represents the commune in Crimea as an alternative, a precovenantal or pre-Abrahamic, space that exists prior to the institution of God's or Stalin's law. Commune members make up their own law on the spur of the moment. In "Hoykhe shveln" (High barriers), for example, a single mother wards off the unwanted advances of a young man who accosts her while she is sleeping. Wrongly assuming that she is available to everyone, he is expelled from the commune. Gorshman herself left the historic Jewish homeland of Palestine to live in the socialist utopia of the Soviet Union. "Utopia" means "no place," and in Gorshman's location in the "no place" called Vojo Nova she is free from the traditional Jewish polarity of exile and home.[39]

Gorshman was not a writer of ideas, and her stories do not explicitly refer to the concepts of foundation, history, and national narrative or to the question of women's participation in them. In contrast, Dine Libkes, a woman poet writing in Yiddish in the same time period, directly engaged these issues.[40] Libkes's "In a loytern baginen" (In a sheer beginning, 1923) questions the notion of the foundation of society:

> In a sheer beginning
> I found a brother,
> In a sheer beginning.
>
> In a sheer beginning
> My husband came to me,
> In a sheer beginning.
>
> In a sheer beginning
> I begat a small child,
> In a sheer beginning.
>
> In a sheer beginning
> I was nothing, I disappeared,
> In a sheer beginning.
>
> *In a loytern baginen*
> *Hob a bruder mir gefunen,*
> *In a loytern baginen.*
>
> *In a loytern baginen*
> *Iz mayn man tsu mir gekumen,*
> *In a loytern baginen.*
>
> *In a loytern baginen*
> *Hob ikh a kind a kleyns gevunen,*
> *In a loytern baginen.*
>
> *In a loytern baginen*
> *Bin ikh nishto, ikh bin antrunen,*
> *In a loytern baginen.*
>
> (Korman 1928, 309)

In the "sheer" or "absolute" beginning, the foundation of society, the woman, the first-person voice of the poem, receives the roles of sister, wife, and mother, but at the same time, at this very instant, she is already absent. The repetition of the moment of foundation, furthermore, undermines the possibility of an absolute beginning: if it happens over and over again, it is not unique and not absolute. The female narrator's absence has a negative sense: she is invisible and passive in this moment (*bin ikh nishto*, "I was nothing"). The foundation or "absolute beginning" excludes her. However, her absence also carries a positive meaning, because she "escapes" the sheer beginning, making off with herself (*"ikh bin antrunen"*) to find her existence elsewhere and in another time. Gorshman's novella about a woman living in a Jewish utopian commune in Crimea fills out the picture of what this other time and place might have felt like.

By the end of the 1920s, the shtetl and its inhabitants were declared obsolete. The Russian-language Jewish journal *Tribuna* (The tribune), for example, portrayed the shtetl as a starving, dying place that "was quietly going to its eternal rest without protest" (Zil'pert 1928, 9). Markish himself had made similar statements in his poetry and in the filmscript to the *Return of Nathan Bekker*. Nonetheless, in other works and in literature and film of the time, the past, the shtetl, and the *luftmentsh* coexist with the new and far from joyous life of socialist construction. The obsolete forms and practices of the Jewish past took hold in the cultural and artistic space of the socialist future. Inscribing themselves in the new Soviet collective life, Markish, Bergelson, and Babel turned to the most traditional and Jewish trope of the biblical covenant. In contrast, in their imagination of the time before the "absolute" beginning, Libkes and Gorshman rejected both the new covenant and the old.

One of Gorshman's postwar stories describes how the members of Vojo Nova retained something of their collective identity even after the commune became incorporated into the "Friendship of Nations" kolkhoz. They were betrayed to the Nazis by one of the inhabitants of the collective farm, giving the lie to its name. Gorshman laments not only the physical extermination of the commune members but also the loss of the memory of their world. No one knows that the grain silos used to be called "towers of love." This and other little-known sites of memory represent one dimension of the problem of commemorating the destruction of Soviet Jewish life during the Second World War. No less important is the representation of Jews as heroes of what the Soviets called the Great Patriotic War. This monumental event far outweighed the October Revolution in the formation of the Soviet imperial narrative. The next chapter turns to the role of Jews in fighting the war and telling its story.

Three Fighting the Great Patriotic War

Shortly after Hitler invaded the Soviet Union on June 22, 1941, his forces quickly occupied the Baltic region, Belorussia, the area of Poland that had been ceded to the Soviet Union in the secret Molotov-Ribbentrop pact, Ukraine, and parts of Russia. With the invasion, Hitler put into action his plan for the systematic and total annihilation of the Jews.[1] German forces used a new type of killing team to achieve their goal, the *Einsatzgruppen*, who worked with local collaborators. Jews in the German-occupied parts of the Soviet Union were usually taken just outside the cities where they lived, and shot: the most famous of these killing sites is Babi Yar, but numerous other ravines and ditches outside other cities served the same purpose, including Bagerovskii, an antitank ditch outside Kerch' (in Crimea), and Ponary (near Vilnius). Mobile gas vans were also used. Jews living in the Soviet Union did not, for the most part, die at Auschwitz, and Auschwitz never became a prominent symbol of the Nazi genocide.[2] German forces and their collaborators killed 2.6–2.7 million out of the approximately 4 million Jews that lived in German-occupied territories of the Soviet Union.

This chapter and the next are devoted to what the Soviets called the Great Patriotic War, during which twenty-seven million Soviets, including Jews, lost their lives. The impact of the war on Soviet and post-Soviet Russia cannot be overestimated: an exhibit in the State Museum of Political History from May 2010 describes the war against the Nazis as "unprecedented in the history of mankind." To discuss the war and the Holocaust on Soviet soil means contemplating two parallel singularities. Both events took place in the same time and space, and yet paradoxically, subsequent accounts rendered them invisible to one another. Soviet Jewish participation in the war effort is the focus of this chapter; Chapter Four concentrates on responses to the Nazi destruction of the Jews. Since the term "Holocaust" was not used in the West in the 1940s and did not appear in Russian until the collapse of the Soviet Union, I will avoid it. The two phenomena, the war and the killing of Jews as Jews, overlap: Soviet Jews were Red Army soldiers who fought and died on the front; they were victims of the Nazis, and witnesses; they were also photojournalists, propagandists, literary authors, and newspaper correspondents, whose accounts significantly shaped the narrative of the war as it unfolded. Whether they wrote in Yiddish or Russian, the war compelled such authors as Boris Slutskii, Vasilii Grossman, Boris Iampol'skii, Der Nister, David Bergelson, Emmanuel Kazakevich, Il'ia Erenburg, and Perets Markish to confront their own implication, both as Soviets and as Jews, in the problem of describing, imagining, remembering, mourning, and testifying to what took place in the ravines, ghettos and camps, killing fields, and battlegrounds. In its May 1965 issue, on the occasion of the twentieth anniversary of the end of the war, the Soviet Yiddish journal *Sovetish heymland* (Soviet homeland) included a pictorial and verbal memorial of twenty Soviet Yiddish artists who died fighting for their country. Each author was shown in uniform, and a brief excerpt from the author's work accompanied each photograph. The introduction sounded an uncanny note by calling upon the writers to address the readers directly, as if printing their work could resurrect them from the dead. The photographs and accompanying text emphasized that the Yiddish artists died as Soviet soldiers and Soviet citizens ("Zey hobn opgegebn dos lebn farn heymland" [They gave their life for their homeland] 1965). Approximately three hundred thousand Jews served in the Red Army during the Second World War (Arad 2009, 87).

The relation between the two identifications—Jew and Soviet—is complex, and it undergoes particular stress in the aftermath of the war. Rather than insisting on a firm boundary separating the two, it is more accurate historically and more productive analytically to trace how the lines between them blur and cross. The historical actors who are the subject of my discussion were not playing a zero-sum identity game, especially not during the war years. During the war Jews were particularly good Soviets, because they were Jews, because they were doubly the target for annihilation in Hitler's war against "Judeo-Bolshevism." The Soviet government encouraged ethnic identification at this time.[3] For example, in 1925, Fefer wrote a poem downplaying his particularity as a Jew ("So what if I've been circumcised"); in 1942, in contrast, he published his proclamation in verse—"Ikh bin a yid" (I am a Jew). The poem repeats the proud refrain "I am a Jew" as the poet travels through centuries of Jewish suffering, and concludes with a triumphant dance on Hitler's grave.[4] Ten years later, during his interrogation, Fefer characterized the poem as "nationalistic" (Rubenstein and Naumov 2001, 92).

Some authors explicitly named themselves as fighting both for the Jewish people and for their Soviet homeland. Indeed, the title of one of Markish's wartime anthologies was *Far folk un heymland* (For my people and homeland). This perspective was not limited to the elite. A 1944 letter from a Jewish soldier to Il'ia Erenburg asks for the formation of Jewish detachments, arguing that Jews as both "patriots of the homeland" and avengers of their fellow Jews' deaths would fight the Fascists with "tenfold hatred" (Altshuler, Arad, and Krakowski 1993, 132). During the war, the Soviet Jewish community, furthermore, actively cultivated its relationship with the international Jewish community. A document produced by the Jewish Anti-Fascist Committee on the occasion of a rally held on August 24, 1941, appealed to "fellow Jews the world over" to join the Soviet people's and the Red Army's "holy war" against Hitler: "it is not by memorial candles but by fire that the murderers of humanity must be destroyed, [n]ot tears, but hate and resistance to the monsters" (Redlich 1995, 175). In addition to emphasizing hatred of the enemy, the appeal names Soviet Jews as both members of the world Jewish community and members of the Soviet people. An article in *Eynikayt* (Unity), the newspaper of the Jewish Anti-Fascist Committee, from December 27, 1942, announced that Hitler's army was carrying out its plan to exterminate the Jewish population of Europe, thereby linking the Soviet and Soviet Jewish war effort with the defense of world Jewry ("*Vi azoy di Hitlerishe makht firt durkh dem plan fun oysratn di yidishe bafelkerung fun Eyrope*").

The double designation of Soviet and Jew also appears in Markish's poem of 1943, "Dem yidishn shlakhtman" (To the Jewish soldier). The poet's address to his readers is a call to military duty: "You! Jew! Citizen! Soldier!/You! Jew! Red Army Man!" (*Du! Der yid! Der birger! Der soldat!/Du! Der yid! Der roytarmeyer!*) (Markish 1943a, 3). In response to the poet's call, the addressee is to inhabit all the roles listed by Markish, including the role of citizen, Red Army soldier, and Jew. Noticeably absent on the list is the role of victim. Naming Jews as Soviet soldiers was of prime importance to Jewish writers during and after the Great Patriotic War.

This chapter and the next explore the overlap and conflict between the two terms of Markish's address, "Jew" and "Red Soldier." One of the best examples of Jewish identification with Soviet Russia is Boris Slutskii's wartime prose writing, not published until the collapse of the Soviet Union. Works published by Il'ia Erenburg, Iurii German, and Emmanuel Kazakevich during the war years reveal other dimensions of this identification: the Soviet Union meant freedom from past limitations imposed internally and externally on the Jewish community. These authors represent the Soviet homeland as a place of progress, tolerance, and enlightened internationalism. Proud membership in the Soviet homeland and a fervent belief in the values of the nineteenth-century Russian intelligentsia transcended a specific identification with Jewry and Judaism; their Soviet identity, however, coexisted with Jewish secular culture. From this perspective, fascist anti-Semitism was a throwback to the oppression of a previous era. The first part of the chapter examines wartime writing that emerges out of this equally Soviet and Jewish perspective.

Internationalism, however, could not provide the right ideological platform for mobilizing the Soviet people; it would be difficult to fight an enemy who was a brother-worker. The early 1940s saw the emergence of a new perspective, the campaign of hatred for the enemy. Slutskii puts it somewhat sarcastically in his wartime writings: "Our ancient internationalism was shattered by a fresh hatred for the Germans" (2006b, 25). Il'ia Erenburg was chiefly responsible for this campaign; he was, as Slutskii says, "like Adam and like Columbus, the first to enter the land of hatred" (26). A letter to Erenburg in 1944, written by a Jewish major in the medical service, emphasizes the transition from brotherhood to revenge: "I was raised in the tradition of Russian humanism, but my heart demands the enemy's blood" (Altshuler, Arad, and Krakowski 1993, 127).

Erenburg was not the only Soviet Jew who helped to shape Soviet wartime print culture. Drawing on the roles of David Ortenberg, Erenburg, Grossman, and the photojournalism of numerous Jewish reporters, David Shneer argues that "Soviet Jews were the ones charged with telling the war to all their countrymen" (2007, 248).[5] In the second part of the chapter, I focus on the specifically Jewish voice of this narration, tracing the Jewish dimensions of what Evgenii Dobrenko calls the literature of mobilization (1993).

Expressing hatred of the enemy and remembering victims do not necessarily conflict. The Jewish source-texts to which Soviet Jewish writers allude demand acts of violence and acts of commemoration. A remarkable story by Bergelson explicitly raises the question as to whether hatred and revenge are proper Jewish emotions. The final part of the chapter examines works by Der Nister and Shmuel Halkin that transcend the wartime ideology of revenge by invoking compassion, hope, and comfort.

A Soviet Jewish Soldier

The poet Boris Slutskii served as a military procurator, soldier, commissar, and propagandist with the Soviet Army advancing through formerly occupied Russian territory and on to Europe during the last period of the war. Slutskii's essays, *Zapiski o voine* (Notes on the war), written in 1945 but not published until 2000, track the author's journeys and encounters at this time. Slutskii characterizes the war as the defining event of his life. In an extraordinary poem that begins with the line, "*A v obshchem, nichego, krome voini!*" (And on the whole, there is nothing besides the war!), Slutskii describes the fissure in time created by the war:

My yesterday passed a long time ago.
My war still fires its guns right next to me.

Moe vchera proshlo uzhe davno.
Moia voina eshche streliaet riadom

(Slutskii 2006b, 311)

Both the war and the poet's unspecified "yesterday" occurred in the past, a coincidence emphasized by the parallelism of the first part of each of these lines. The ending of the second line, however, shatters the parallelism. The shift from two-syllable to three-syllable words and from masculine to feminine rhyme (stress on the penultimate syllable), and the sound pattern created by *"streliaet riadom"* (fires its guns right next to me), with its repetition of *"ia,"* all serve to create a punctuated, staccato effect akin to the sounds of shooting. In these lines, the war is not merely a memory but an ongoing experience, continuing into the present, which contrasts to the "yesterday" that paradoxically took place in the remote past (*"davno"*). The difference in the sound patterns between the two lines enhances the fractured temporality that is the poem's theme. Bergelson fractured time to describe the double perspective of Jews who had experienced the revolution and were still waiting for its benefits; Mandelshtam portrayed his own instant obsolescence in the 1920s; here, Slutskii similarly creates the effect of temporal disorientation to suggest the shattering experience of the war. In another poem, "Odnofamilets" (Namesake), Slutskii describes the uncanny discovery of the gravestone of another soldier having the same seven letters of his own last name—his double. The war destroyed this other unknown self, now buried in the ground. The war has split open the integrity of time and of self, leaving them fractured and doubled. There is a past that is over and a past that the poet keeps reliving.

It is important to note that it is not as a Jew or at least not from the perspective of the Nazi destruction of the Jews that the war gains its all-pervasive importance in these works. The relative silence about the Nazi genocide is not the result of external pressure, since Slutskii did not attempt to publish his war memoir during the Soviet era. Slutskii's wartime writings make a full claim on the roles named in Markish's poem, the roles of the Soviet citizen and Red Army soldier. The role of Jew emerges in a subtle fashion that is at times surprising. As a procurator, commissar, and propagandist, Slutskii articulates the values of Soviet society and carries out judgments in its name. Indeed, in one poem that describes his work as a political commissar, Slutskii writes, "I spoke in the name of Russia" (*Ia govoril ot imeni Rossii*) (2006b, 214). The men whom he addresses "in the name of Russia" are cold, hungry, tired, and short of bullets. He cannot offer them bread or bullets but only his words. As a military procurator responsible for cases of self-mutilation and desertion, he holds the "terrible rights" of judgment over his fellow soldiers, whom he can sentence to death, again in the name of the Soviet Union (243). Speaking "in the name of Russia" does not mean that Slutskii glorifies the Soviet war effort; on the contrary, he acknowledges the shortages, brutality, and abuses suffered by and perpetrated by the Soviet Army and by Soviet citizens. Slutskii shows the consequences of living in the "land of hatred" that Erenburg had helped to create. In one revealing episode, he describes a convoy of German prisoners who have been starved by their Soviet guards. The local population of Soviets offers the prisoners snow (dirty February snow, as Slutskii points out) in exchange for their watches and rings. Among the prisoners are Yugoslav Jews, taken from German work battalions, and one of them pleads with his new Russian captors that he wants to work and not to die of hunger. In another episode, a Viennese Jewish woman who survived the war sheltered by Austrian peasants now finds herself the victim of rape by Soviet soldiers. In Slutskii's account the Soviet Army is not always the savior of the Jews. The portrait he provides is a far cry from the hagiographical terms used in the newspaper of the Jewish Anti-Fascist Committee, *Eynikayt*, in which the term "Red Army" does not occur without the adjective "heroic." It is significant that what Slutskii registers is not Hitler's annihilation of the Jews of Europe but their ill treatment at the hand of their Soviet liberators. This is not to say that Slutskii fails to write about the Nazi genocide; on the contrary, descriptions of the killing of Jews can be found in his poems "Kak ubivali moiu babku" (How they killed my grandmother) and "Teper' Osvenstim chasto snitsia mne" (Now I often dream of Auschwitz).[6] In the wartime writings, however, Slutskii's identification as a Jew and with his fellow-Jews is more closely linked to his position as a captain in the Soviet army, in whose name he acts.

Sustaining all these roles at once involves a delicate balance. Slutskii speaks in the name of Russia and yet maintains a critical distance from Russia; he is completely identified with the war effort, yet his right to do so is constantly challenged. Slutskii's description of his war service is reminiscent of Babel's account of his work with Budennyi's army during the civil war. Babel read Lenin's speeches to Cossacks who could not understand them; in *Red Cavalry* and his civil war diary, and in Slutskii's wartime writings, Jews serve as mouthpieces for Soviet culture and values, in spite of their own doubts about them and, what is more important, in spite of persistent attacks on their legitimacy as representatives of Soviet values. In the poem "Pro evreev" (About the Jews), Slutskii restates the problem by quoting anti-Jewish stereotypes:

> Jews do not plant grain,
> Jews trade in the shops
> Jews grow bald sooner,
> Jews steal more.
>
> Jews are evil people,
> They make bad soldiers:
> Ivan fights in the trenches,
> Abram trades in the market.
>
> I have heard all this since childhood . . .
>
> I never traded,
> I never stole,
> I carry in myself, like an infection,
> This accursed race.
>
> The bullet missed me,
> So that it could be said:
> "Jews were not killed!
> They all came back alive!"
>
> (Slutskii 2006b, 298)[7]

The phrase "this accursed race" should not be taken as Slutskii's own evaluation of Jews but as his citation of others' negative view of them. Written in all likelihood in the early 1950s, the poem pokes a hole in the myth that there was no anti-Semitism in the Soviet Union before the Second World War.[8] In the last stanza, Slutskii's own survival ironically confirms the assertion of the Jews' failure to serve the Soviet Union and their failure to fight the Soviet war.

The essay titled "Evrei" (Jews) is the longest section of Slutskii's wartime notes. Structured as a series of vignettes, the essay describes the author's encounters with Jewish soldiers and survivors in Europe and in Russia. His voice in these miniatures moves over a range of positions. In, for example, a discussion of the reasons that Jews and other national minorities are perceived as bad soldiers (their traditional low participation in careers in the military), he takes on the voice of a detached ethnographer who fully accepts Soviet terms and categorizations. Elsewhere he becomes an impassioned advocate for starving Soviet Jewish refugees, whom he names as Soviet citizens. He serves as a confessor of sorts to a Ukrainian Jew named Gershel'man. The man, writes Slutskii, approached him with "an unheard of request, 'Comrade Captain, give me permission to tell you my life'" (*razreshite rasskazat' vam svoiu zhizn'*) (2006b, 135). The "Jew Gershel'man" describes his prewar existence as a member of the party and the head of a printing press. Married to a non-Jewish woman, he says, "I completely forgot that I was a Jew," reasserting a glorified image of Soviet tolerance and inclusivity. The German occupation changed everything. The acts of survival that the Jew Gershel'man confesses to include betraying his wife by living with another woman, who finally threatens to betray him to the Germans; living off the property of murdered Jews; and begging for his life on his knees. Slutskii's account of this confession does not reveal whether he as confessor revealed his own identity as a Jew. In the last vignette, however, the roles are reversed. The scene takes place in Bulgaria. Slutskii recognizes a Jew in the man who guards the now abandoned German consular building. He asks the man whether he is Jewish and when he receives an affirmative answer adds, "Me, too" (*ia tozhe*), and the two men embrace.

The multiplicity of voices, the dialogic quality of "Jews," give the account a novelistic complexity. His position as a captain in the Red Army enabled him to defend Jews victimized by the Germans and again victimized by the Soviets. Slutskii's wartime writings show how the categories of Jew and Soviet overlap—not seamlessly but closely enough, regardless of the bitterness expressed in the poem "About Jews." The emotions and attitudes his writing reveals are typical of Jews of his generation who served in the war.

A Jewish Passion for the Universal

An inclusive vision of the Soviet Union as embodying an ideal of universal humanism, together with enhanced Jewish self-awareness, resonated broadly among Soviet Jews during the war. One of the most important figures of this time, Il'ia Erenburg, the chief Soviet war propagandist, articulated this attitude.⁹ Erenburg was the author of numerous articles for *Pravda* and several significant Soviet novels, including his depiction of the war, *Buria* (The storm, 1948), and was the coeditor of the *Black Book*, a compilation of testimony about the destruction of the Jews that was published only after the collapse of the Soviet Union. Erenburg's relation to his own Jewishness was undoubtedly complex, but to say that he became conscious of it only in relation to Hitler is misleading. In one of his early novels, *Julio Jurenito*, published in 1922, Erenburg imagines the future annihilation of all the Jews of Europe. In his memoirs, Erenburg attempts to reconcile hatred with internationalism. He writes that he hated the German invaders "because they were fascists. I confronted racial and national arrogance in childhood, I suffered from it considerably in my life, I believed in the brotherhood of nations and suddenly saw the birth of fascism" (Erenburg 1990, 251). Later in the same work, Erenburg asserts, "any form of nationalism is alien to me, whether it is French, English, Russian, or Jewish" (352). Nazi anti-Semitism is, from this perspective, a throwback to a system that the Soviet Union overcame.

This demurral notwithstanding, Erenburg's deep attachment to Jews as a community is clear, as is his image among them as a Jewish leader. He received numerous letters from Jews throughout the war years and beyond, including pleas for material help, demands that he speak up about specific issues, as well as letters that provided evidence for the *Black Book*. One letter writer called him "our Moses," and another characterized the *Black Book* as the "Kinot" of its time (Kinot, or Lamentations, are recited on the Ninth of Av, the day commemorating the destruction of the Temple).¹⁰ Erenburg brought the great Yiddish poet and Vilna ghetto fighter Avrom Sutskever to Moscow in 1944 and to the Nuremberg trials as a witness in 1946. In an article published in 1944, "Tvorchestvo cheloveka" (The deeds of a man), Erenburg described Sutskever as a man with "an automatic in his hands, the lines of a poem in his head, and a letter from Gorkii on his heart" (1944).¹¹ The characterization evokes both Jewish prayer and typical Soviet rhetoric. In the morning prayer recited after the "Hear o Israel," Jewish men and boys thirteen and older place phylacteries on their foreheads and arms and recite, "let these matters that I command you today be upon your heart . . . bind them as a sign upon your arm and let them be *t'fillin* between your eyes." Erenburg is symbolically binding Sutskever in a Soviet and Jewish covenant.

The belief that Erenburg articulated—in the Soviet Union as the most progressive nation, the nation that transcended the barriers of nationalism and racism—provides the framework for a significant body of Soviet wartime and postwar fiction. Erenburg's novel *The Storm* (Buria) also provides ample information about the German killing of Jews, in Europe and in Russia. Erenburg's novel was published in 1948 and received a Stalin Prize. The novel describes the killing of Jews at Babi Yar and at Auschwitz. Its scenes of the selection lines at the death camp and the striped uniforms of the inmates rely on what became iconographic images of the Holocaust in the West. The scene in the gas chamber leaves no doubt as to the identity of the victims or to their number. Erenburg emphasizes Jewish defiance: an old man refuses to strip and curses the Germans in language that echoes Deuteronomy.[12] This is only one episode out of many. The novel as a whole weaves together the story of the war and of the German occupation of Europe and Russia with the stories of Jews; yet at the same time, it reduces all these incidents to the single framework of the contest between socialism and fascism, understood as a variant of capitalism.

Like so many other Soviet war novels that imitated Tolstoy's *War and Peace*, *The Storm* is organized around the fate of three families, one in France and two in Russia—the Vlakhovs and the Al'pers. Before the war, Raia Al'per was a spoiled woman who neglected her husband and daughter. After the Germans kill her daughter at Babi Yar, she becomes a sniper in the Red Army and kills several dozen German soldiers in revenge. She learns to love her husband, Osip, a stern communist who became a commander in the Red Army. When the Soviets return to Kiev, Osip retraces the steps his mother and daughter took to the killing site, attempting to remember each landscape along the way. But when he arrives, an uplifting and banal message of the triumph of love subsumes his grief. As he lay "on the sands of Babi Yar, he thought of Raia and life was victorious. You could kill a defenseless person, and in terror of retribution, burn the body, scatter the ashes, remove the witnesses, but it was impossible to destroy the highest thing in a human being—love. Raia turned out to be stronger than the murderers" (Erenburg 1960, 597). The story moves from war to victory, from hatred of the enemy to the affirmation of life afterwards, with only the briefest pause for mourning the dead. Erenburg, it seems, reserved the problem of testimony and mourning for the *Black Book*. In the transcript for a meeting of the editorial committee of the *Black Book* held in October 1944, Erenburg emphatically stated that the only criterion for the inclusion of a document in the work should be its "impact" and "emotion" (Grossman n.d.). In the novel, however, the haste to affirm human nobility and the victory of life at Babi Yar has the effect of muffling the importance of what took place there. Erenburg does not remove Jews from his picture of the war; on the contrary, he emphasizes their participation as frontline soldiers and as defiant victims. What is missing from his picture, in spite of all the deaths, is the impact of destruction on the lives of individual characters on the forward motion of history. Erenburg's lack of artistic depth flattens the significance of the deaths at Babi Yar. They do not interfere with the tale of progress that *The Storm* describes.

The *Izvestiia* review of the novel underscored the importance of the theme of victory. The reviewer, N. Zhdanov, saw the fate of the Al'per family in terms of the conflict between capitalism and socialism. Before the war, Osip's father went to France, taking with him Osip's brother, Leo. Leo became a partner in a major industrial firm, but when the Germans took over, he died in a concentration camp; in contrast, his brother, Osip, "became a victor, like his country" (Zhdanov 1948). The fate of Jews under German occupation, the deaths of the character's mother and daughter, have no weight; what matters is the superiority of the Soviet way of life.

Grossman's "The Old Teacher" (Staryi uchitel') uses a similar framework and yet reserves particular emphasis on the German destruction of the Jews. The story was published in the mainstream Russian literary journal *Znamia* (The banner) in 1943, and in the Yiddish anthology *Heymland* (Homeland) in the same year under the title "Der alter lerer" (Grossman 1943); Robert and Elizabeth Chandler's English translation appeared in 2010 (Grossman 2010, 84–115). "The Old Teacher" is absolutely clear about the target of the German mass killing: "in the morning it was announced that the Jews living in the city had to appear the next day at six o'clock in the morning" (Grossman 1985b, 135). The story provides a detailed description of the technology of death used in the actions, including the required use of handguns as opposed to artillery (to make resistance more difficult), the number of bullets assigned to each man, the psychological profile required for the volunteers chosen to carry out the killing, and the special requirements for the killing of children. As John and Carol Garrard and Shimon Markish point out, Grossman transformed eyewitness testimony that he had been gathering for the aborted *Black Book* into the scene of the mass killing in "The Old Teacher." It is impossible to read the story without coming to the conclusion that the mass killing of Jews was a key dimension of the German occupation.

The foregoing, we can say, is the information the story gives about the German destruction of the Jews. The "old teacher," Boris Isaakovich Rozental', provides the interpretative frame. Grossman emphasizes the teacher's Jewishness, defined not in terms of religious observance but in certain habits of mind, his personal history, and most importantly, his sense of belonging among Jewish people. Rozental' used to be religious but became an atheist. Before the revolution, he taught children in a Jewish vocational school; afterwards, he became a math teacher in an elementary school in a small town. He shared in the ideals of the nineteenth-century Russian intelligentsia and loved the Russian people, in whom he saw "compassion" for the Jews. He also, however, felt a deep attachment for the Jews: "He spent his whole life with these people, and it was with them that he would spend his last bitter hour" (Grossman 1985b, 136).

The portrait of the old schoolteacher, Boris Rozental', is important to the larger concerns of this study. Grossman's schoolteacher challenges the presupposition that the Jew and the Soviet are necessarily opposed, that whatever is Soviet compromises what is Jewish. Russocentric chauvinism, which Erenburg argues began to arise as early as 1943, conversely saw the Jew as a corruption of the Soviet ideal. For Grossman in this story, the Soviet and the Jew are not only not opposed; they are, on the contrary, interdependent: Soviet life brings out what is best in the Jew, and the best, ideal Soviet is a Jew, the old schoolteacher Boris Rozental'. He was the only one in the town whose behavior—attentive, courteous, and considerate—did not change during the time of the German occupation.

The German war against the Jews, according to the teacher, is part of the fascist attack on the nations of Europe as a whole, part of the vast "hierarchy of oppression" in which the Jews occupy the lowest possible rung in order to frighten the other nations into submission. There is, to be sure, universalizing rhetoric in this explanation, but it does little to undermine the impact of what the story as a whole describes in almost documentary detail: the systematic mass murder of Jews. Grossman's story disproves the oft-repeated claim that Soviet-era artists failed to represent the Nazi genocide of the Jews on Soviet territory.

Boris Iampol'skii's novella *Doroga ispytanii* (The road of trials), in contrast, focuses more on the glorification of the Soviet way of life. The novella tells the story of a young history student attending university in Kiev, caught up in the early months of the war. He returns to the apartment building where his girlfriend lived, and when he rings the doorbell, the only response is from a woman who regards him with suspicion. When she notices his soldier's cap, however, her attitude changes, and she lovingly calls him "comrade": "Perhaps she [the woman] cried out 'comrade' in Babi Yar, calling us from hundreds of miles away, or from some miserable hole in Berlin, from a bloody wooden bench, or from a wooden scaffold in a village, when the hangman put her in the noose" (Iampol'skii 1964, 46).

In the passage, "Babi Yar" registers as a place where something terrible happened, and yet its mention fails to have a particular impact separate and distinct from other terrible places. The inclusion of Babi Yar in the list of places where German atrocities took place may very well have been understood by readers to signify Jewish deaths. The meaning of those deaths is, however, subsumed under a narrative of the brotherhood and solidarity of the Soviet way of life, which the Russian word for comrade, "*tovarishch*," embodies.

At the end of the novel, the young hero hears a popular science radio lecture about the universe: "The universe as a whole has no limits, no boundaries in either space or time" (236). The hero thinks that the words apply to him and to his country, not only because of its power and permanence but, more importantly, because it and only it embodies the features of universal inclusivity and progress. The Soviet Union gives its citizens the opportunity for limitless accomplishment, for the overcoming of every kind of barrier. As we saw in Chapter One, a similar sentiment informs the ending of Markish's civil war epic, *Brothers*: "now our fatherland is the whole round earth."

Another example of Soviet wartime universalism can be found in Iurii German's novella *Podpolkovnik meditsinskoi sluzhby* (A lieutenant-colonel in the medical service), published in truncated form in 1949. The complete work first appeared in 1956. German (1910–67) was a prolific and popular Soviet writer, the author of a well-known trilogy set during the war and of a historical novel set during the time of Peter the Great; several of his works were made into films. During the war, he served as a correspondent for TASS attached to the Soviet Navy fighting in the north.

The hero of German's novella, Aleksandr Markovich Levin, is a sixty-year-old navy doctor, selflessly devoted to the cause, who refuses treatment in Moscow for his cancer and dies at his post. Levin learns how to ignore his fear over his illness from the men he serves, men who had "the feeling of duty. These were communists, Soviet people, the strongest people in the world, people dedicated to a great idea [*liudi velikoi idei*], and he was obligated to be like them" (German 1976, 114). In *A Lieutenant-Colonel in the Medical Service*, the only "Jewish" moment takes place when Dr. Levin confronts a Nazi pilot rescued from the sea. The pilot refuses any medical treatment, as he says, "from a Jew" (*ot "iude"*) (96). The word "Jew" appears in Russian transliteration of the German "*Jude*." The novella as a whole makes no reference to mass killings or death camps, or to any other wartime reality, including the brutality that German and Russian prisoners of war received from one another. This is the single episode that mentions the Nazi attitude toward Jews. Dr. Levin's response to the Nazi's statement is worth citing in full: "He knew what the man said, he heard everything word for word, but he couldn't believe it. During the years of Soviet power he had forgotten this curse, only in nightmares did he see Jews being beaten—he was a lieutenant-colonel in the Red Army, and here this despicable creature reminded him again of the repulsive time of the pogroms" (96). The "curse" referred to in this passage is the term "Jew." The point of view attributed to Dr. Levin empties the term "Jew" of all positive association and content. From this perspective, the only way to fight German racial superiority is not with more nationalism—whether Russian or Jewish—but with the form of universalism that was uniquely possible in the Soviet Union.

What "The Old Teacher," *The Storm*, and *The Road of Trials* reveal is the role of Jewish writers and public figures in creating and sustaining the Soviet narrative of the universal suffering caused by the war. For German, Erenburg, Kazakevich, and similar writers, the term "Soviet" referred not to Russians alone but to a broad, inclusive, and multiethnic universality. Soviet Jewish writers maximize the exemplary role of Soviet Jews as the personification of Soviet ideals. Scholars have not acknowledged the importance of the Jewish contribution to this narrative. Furthermore, the analysis of specific passages in Erenburg and Iampol'skii shows that the linear and teleological structure of their works obscures the particularity of *any* suffering—Jewish or otherwise. The problem is that these works fail to register suffering as such. Babi Yar, Auschwitz, and German prisoner-of-war camps have little impact as sites of overwhelming loss, because love, the friendship of nations, and the superiority of the Soviet way of life have already triumphed, before pain can be felt. Victory supplants the loss of the mere human being and the loss of what is merely human.

Universalist ideologies of various kinds held a particular attraction for Jewish intellectuals seeking acceptance in the larger, predominantly non-Jewish world. In *Anti-Semite and Jew*, published after the war, Sartre wrote that Jews were distinguished by a "passion for the universal" (1948, 111). What others saw as a negative Jewish hyperrationality, Sartre interpreted as a desire to transcend the exclusions created by national cultures. Sartre's characterization accurately describes the mentality of many prominent Soviet Jewish figures who fought both for their people and for their Soviet homeland.

In the late 1940s, however, the Stalinist government came to identify the "passion for the universal" as a negative, "rootless cosmopolitanism." The reason that German succeeded in publishing only the first half of his novella in 1949 has to do with Stalin's anticosmopolitan campaign. A hero with a Jewish surname who occupied a prominent place in a work of fiction was unacceptable. The exchange between the Jewish doctor and the Nazi appears in the second half of the story, which meant that readers in 1949 did not see it. Instead of the continuation of *A Lieutenant-Colonel in the Medical Service*, the third issue of *Zvezda* (The star) contained a letter from the author recanting the work.[13] German wrote that his hero, "locked into his own intimate little world . . . does not have the right to be called a positive hero" (1949).

German is a good example of the "too Jewish"/"not Jewish enough" conundrum that plagues the Western reception of Jewish literature in twentieth-century Russia. There is nothing Jewish about Dr. Levin, and the question may be raised as to whether German himself was a Jew.[14] Regardless of the answer, readers in Russia have come to associate German's work with the tradition of Russian-Jewish literature in the twentieth century, even though it is completely lacking in obvious Jewish themes, let alone references to the traditional Jewish life world. For the Soviet censor, however, German's hero was too Jewish.

Emmanuel Kazakevich (1913–62) was the antithesis of German. He began his writing career as a Yiddish poet who lived in and wrote about the Jewish Autonomous Region of Birobidzhan, publishing in *Birobidzhaner shtern* (The Birobidzhan star); his romantic novel in verse about Birobidzhan, *Sholem un Khava* (Sholom and Khava), was published in 1941. Unlike German and Erenburg, Kazakevich was not a correspondent during the Second World War. He volunteered for the army, starting out as a rank and file soldier in reconnaissance and moving up to the position of assistant head of reconnaissance for the Forty-seventh Soviet Army.[15] Kazakevich's first work in Russian, *Zvezda* (The star), was published in 1947 in the literary journal *Znamia* (The banner) and received the Stalin Prize in 1948. Kazakevich went on to write other major works in Russian and served as the editor of a major Moscow literary journal, where he performed the unsavory task of rejecting some of Vasilii Grossman's stories for publication. Kazakevich, like Slutskii, registers the hard labor involved in the Jew's love of Russia. In a notebook entry for 1961, Kazakevich described his intention, never realized, to write a novella titled *Rabinovich* (the name of the typical protagonist of Jewish jokes in Soviet Russia) about a man "who tragically and profoundly felt and loved Russia and the Russian individual, but did not always experience reciprocity" (Kazakevich 1990, 219).

Praised at the time as a realistic, "bitter," yet "optimistic" work, *The Star* tells the story of a reconnaissance mission in German-occupied Western Ukraine.[16] The scouts move through the center of German activity, taking the occasional informant—in military jargon, a "tongue"—every one of whom they kill. Their silent and deadly presence intimidates the German rank and file, who give them the nickname Grüne Gespenster (green shadows), because of their green camouflage gear. The Yiddish translation of the novel, published in Warsaw in 1954, used *Green Shadows* (Grine shotns) for its title (Kazakevich 1954).[17] The reconnaissance team succeeds in informing the Russian military command about a new major German offensive, led by Himmler's elite tank division, but they are hopelessly outnumbered and none return from the mission.

The novella has no obvious Jewish themes and, unlike German's story, does not have an identifiable Jewish hero. Even though the story is set in Western Ukraine, there is no mention of the effect of the German occupation on the Jewish population of the region. In contrast, Kazakevich's wartime letters, written in Russian and published in 1990, register the particular fate of the Jews of Europe. For example, in a letter of 1945, he describes himself as feeling pity for the Germans on occasion, "but then suddenly you remember the ravine at Kerch', Majdanek, the murdered women and children, and the destruction of Jews throughout Europe, who were guilty only of belonging to this nation, and then you begin to think, that it is just this way and could not and should not be otherwise" (Kazakevich 1990, 284). Kazakevich implies that the suffering of Germans is a just recompense for the suffering they inflicted on the Jews. His letters to his family and to his commanding officers show his sincere desire to fight at the front, and his unfailing good spirits in spite of the destruction he sees (252, 274).

As is clear from his novella and his wartime letters, Kazakevich shares with German and Erenburg an ideological commitment to universalism. In *The Star*, the leader of the reconnaissance mission is Lieutenant Volodia Travkin, a former physics student. Young, handsome, and serious, Travkin resists the advances of Katia, the radio operator who falls in love with him. Like German's Dr. Levin, Travkin has one distinguishing characteristic: his "fanatical dedication to the fulfillment of his duty" (Kazakevich 1984, 319). Travkin feels a particular sense of kinship for another reconnaissance officer: "They called one another 'kinsmen' because they were both from the same country, the country of those who believed in their cause and were ready to give their lives for it" (319). This single-minded dedication to an abstract idea of duty in Kazakevich's and German's heroes is reminiscent of the Jewish hero Levinson from Fadeev's civil war epic *The Rout*—a work that was praised in 1945 as a model for Soviet literature of the Second World War (Reznik 1945, 289). The country imagined by Kazakevich's hero grants the right of citizenship, not on the basis of blood or nationality but on the basis of an idea. This was the sort of country in which a Jew—or anyone else—could find belonging. Two years later, in 1949, German would write that his Dr. Levin did not have the right to be called a positive hero, and although German said the problem had to do with Levin's personality, the real problem was his hero's last name— his nationality as a Jew. In avoiding a particularly Jewish perspective and emphasizing the transcendent and abstract dedication to the cause—in his "passion for the universal"—Kazakevich, like Erenburg and German, is attempting to create a space for Jews.

The Literature of Mobilization

The passion for the universal evident in Kazakevich, Erenburg, and others conflicts with another crucial trajectory of Soviet wartime writing, the literature of hate. What binds the reconnaissance team together in *The Star* is the task of destroying the enemy. Alone in German-occupied land, the men see "traces of an alien, hated way of life . . . everywhere was the smell of the German, the Frits, the Hans, the Fascist" (Kazakevich 1984, 335). The dehumanization of the enemy goes hand in hand with the dehumanization of the soldier fighting the enemy. The task at hand, to which Travkin is so fiercely devoted, transforms the men into unearthly creatures. Participation in the neutral public space of a universalist political community requires that the particularities of nationality, religion, race, ethnicity, and other markers of identity be left behind. Participation in a reconnaissance mission carries this requirement to an extreme. The team members have to give up everything that makes them individuals:

> When he puts on his camouflage . . . the scout no longer belongs to himself, his bosses, or his memories . . . He attaches grenades and a knife to his belt and hides his pistol under his shirt. In so doing he refuses all human institutions, placing himself above the law, and relying from this point on only on himself. He gives his chief all his papers, letters, photographs, orders, and medals; his political commissar gets his Party or Komsomol card. In so doing he rejects his past and his future . . . his brain carries only one thought: his assignment. (327)

In Vasilii Grossman's account of Treblinka, the surrender and destruction of personal documents is one of the crucial stages of the dehumanization of the death camp: "the documents flew to the ground, no longer needed by anyone on earth, the documents of living corpses" (*a dokumenty leteli na zemliu, uzhe nikomu ne nuzhnye na svete, dokumenty zhivykh mertvetsov*) (1985c, 162). The parallel between the processes the two writers describe is significant. The removal of personal artifacts and the forced suspension of memory are powerful tools in the reshaping and ultimate destruction of the human being. The extermination of the Jewish victim and the creation of the Soviet soldier mirror one another: Grossman and Kazakevich are describing the same technology of war and death.

In Kazakevich's story, the team's radio code is "star"; home base is "earth." Going into enemy territory is like going into outer space, and Travkin feels that "here, on this lonely Star, they were all part of a single whole"; the other men seem to him "parts of his own body" (Kazakevich 1984, 336). In camouflage the men lose all sense of their individual humanity; their weapons become part of their bodies, and their bodies merge together into a single weapon. No longer located on the earth but instead in outer space, the men become an artificial collective human being; what is more, this artificial being, part of the technology of war, functions as a weapon. Kazakevich, however, unlike other writers who similarly imagine the transformation of human beings into weapons, refuses to glorify this metamorphosis.

Itsik Fefer's poem "The Oath" (Di shvue), in contrast, pumps up the rhetoric to cosmic proportions. Published in 1942 in the first issue of the Soviet Yiddish newspaper *Eynikayt*, the organ of the Jewish Anti-Fascist Committee, the poem also appeared in Russian under the title "Kliatva" (The oath) in the mainstream literary journal *Znamia* (The banner) in the same year, in a section that also included translations of works from Ukrainian and other languages. In naming his poem "Di shvue," Fefer acknowledges the importance of S. An-sky's prerevolutionary work of the same title, which became the anthem of the Bund.[18] Two distinct goals, however, animate the two poems: An-sky's "Oath" reveals his passion for the Jewish community, but Fefer's displays an obsession with violence that is ultimately self-annihilating.

In "The Oath" Fefer swears by the sun, the stars, "by everything that a simple person can swear" that his hatred and wrath will not be spent until he feels his enemy's blood on his own flesh (*ikh shver . . . mayn has vet nit oysgeyn . . . biz kh'vel af mayn orem dos blut funem faynt nit derfiln*):

> And if the dark whirlwind tears off my hand
> I will choke off the enemy's hateful breath with my other hand
> And if a bullet destroys my other hand,
> My sacred hatred will dull the pain . . .
> If the night darkens my eyes with blindness
> My hatred—my sister in battle will not let me
> Bow my head . . .
> The flame of my hatred will obliterate his memory forever.
>
> *Un oyv s'vet der fintsterer vikher a hant mir tseflikn,*
> *Vel ikh mit der tsveyter dem fayntlekhn otem dershtikn;*
> *Un oyb s'vet a koyl mir di hant oykh di tsveyte tsedroybn,*
> *Vel ikh mit mayn heyliker sine dem veytik fartoybn . . .*
> *Un oyb s'vet di nakht mir mit blindkayt farleshn di oygn,*
> *Mayn sine—mayn shvester in shlakht vet nit lozn farnoygn*
> *Mayn kop . . .*
> *Der flam fun mayn has vet af eybik zayn zeykher farmekn.*
>
> (Fefer 1943, 3)

Fefer's image of the soldier as a supreme engine of destruction has precedents in Russian and Yiddish literature. The transformation of the human individual into a super being was a central trope of proletarian poetry of the 1920s. Perets Markish's hero Shloyme-Ber, for example, forges himself in the fire and speaks "words like bullets." Fefer's soldier also recalls Ostrovskii's Pavel Korchagin from *How the Steel Was Tempered*. The civil war hero lost his vision, the use of his legs, and the use of one arm but continued to serve the cause by writing novels. An article published in *Znamia* in 1944 proclaimed that Pavel Korchagin had entered real life (Tregub and Bachelis 1944).

The difference between Markish's civil war hero and Fefer's Second World War hero has to do with the acknowledgment of loss. Markish's expression of ambivalence about the revolution, with his images of swollen, putrefying bodies, is pregnant with loss, what I called in Chapter One the "stillbirth of the revolution." Fefer's hero, in contrast, fails to experience the injuries inflicted on his own body as anything but the next stage of his metamorphosis into a more efficient weapon. Eric Santner's concept of "narrative fetishism," based on his analysis of German war stories of the 1980s, also sheds light on this dimension of Soviet wartime mobilization literature. Narrative fetishism is a "strategy of undoing, in fantasy, the need for mourning by simulating a condition of intactness" (Santner 1992). As the uplifting message of Erenburg's novel *The Storm* reveals, socialist realism generally offers an improved version of reality. The literature of mobilization takes this principle to an extreme, transforming it into something new. Fefer's "Oath" changes injury into gain: in his mini–science fiction fantasy, the mutilated body of the fighter is not only fully intact but even better than it was before. The poem fetishizes the loss of body parts as a gain in fighting capacity.

The transition from one stage to another happens quickly. The poem jumps from injury to consequence, from the infliction of violence to the production of hatred and more violence. There is no pause for the expression of pain. This accelerated temporality is a key dimension of the literature of mobilization. To be mobile is to be capable of a rapid shift from one position to another; to be mobilized is to be ready for war, and Fefer's "Oath" unites the two meanings. The rapid-fire temporality of works such as "The Oath" contrasts with Slutskii's "And on the whole, there is nothing besides the war!" (*A v obshchem, nichego, krome voini!*). Slutskii elongates time by juxtaposing the remotely distant past of "yesterday" and the ongoing past that is the war. The repetition of the past in the present is a crucial feature of the literature of mourning and remembrance. The rapid and relentlessly linear time structure of the literature of mobilization, however, allows no opportunity for mourning.

During the war years Soviet Jews played a central role in creating and circulating the literature of mobilization; Fefer's poem provides a key template. It should suffice to mention the titles of Erenburg's numerous articles that appeared (in Russian) in *Krasnaia zvezda* (Red star) and *Pravda* in 1942 and 1943, among which were included "Opravdanie nenavisti" (The justification of hatred), "Im ne zhit'" (They must not live), and "Ubei!" (Kill!).[19] In "The Justification of Hatred," for example, Erenburg describes German soldiers as "monsters" and "savages armed with the latest technology." He provides both a genealogy of and an incitement to hatred of the German enemy, affirming that "hatred did not come to us easily. We paid for it with whole cities and provinces, with hundreds of thousands of human lives" (Erenburg 1943, 7). In Erenburg's article, hatred supplants every other emotion: "Death to the German occupiers—these words sound like an oath of love . . . The death of every German—this is a pledge that children will no longer know grief" (8). As in Fefer's poem, swearing an "oath" is also important in this work, where it is offered as a security against all future evil. The structure of the narrative works in a series of steps, each replacing what came before: (1) hatred for the enemy replaces the awareness of loss; (2) hatred becomes attached to love; and (3) hatred is a guarantee of future happiness. Other texts by Erenburg show a similar pattern. For example, Sergei, the hero of Erenburg's war novel *Buria* (The storm) finds himself physically overcome by his hatred of the enemy, his body transfigured by the war: "Now the war became his life; everything in him fought—his blood, his bile, his breath" (Erenburg 1960, 290). Erenburg's article "Evrei" (Jews), published in *Krasnaia zvezda* in 1942, is another example: the meek Jewish male—in his Soviet incarnation, that is, not the yeshiva student but the student of philology and literature—becomes a daring soldier at the front. Erenburg uses rhetorical questions to challenge the stereotype of the Jew, as in the line "Perhaps the Germans thought that Jews don't ski?" (Erenburg 1942). In his article, Jews use technology to overcome the limits of nature and overpowering enemy force; they single-handedly destroy enemy tanks. Other writers working both in Yiddish and in Russian widely used this pattern of the transformation of the hero into a weapon. Boris Polevoi's *Povest' o nastoiashchem cheloveke* (The story of a real man), published after the war, in 1946, is an important Russian-language example of this genre. It tells the story of a double amputee who resumes his mission as a bomber pilot and experiences the sensation of fusing with his plane. Polevoi wrote *The Story of a Real Man* during a nineteen-day period in the coverage of the Nuremberg trials in the spring of 1946.[20]

Soviet Jewish works written in the 1940s and in subsequent periods emphasize rage, hatred, and the desire for retribution—in contrast to what became canonized as Holocaust literature in the West. Il'ia Sel'vinskii's "I Saw It" (first published in the newspaper *Bolshevik* on January 23, 1942) describes the sight of seven thousand corpses in a tank ditch outside Kerch'; the last stanza hammers away at the theme of retribution:

> The ravine . . . ? Can you describe this in a poem?
> Seven thousand corpses.
> Semites . . . Slavs . . .
> Yes! But not with words,
> Only with firepower!
>
> *Rov . . . Poemoi li skazhesh' o nem?*
> *Sem' tysiach trupov.*
> *Semity . . . Slaviane . . .*
> *Da! Ob etom nel'zia slovami:*
> *Ognem! Tol'ko ognem!*
>
> (Sel'vinskii 1971, 1:355)

The only language adequate to the mass killing is the language of revenge, the central motif of Soviet Yiddish wartime literature. Markish's 1943 "Dem yidishn shlaktman" (To a Jewish soldier), like Sel'vinskii's poem, changes the pain of the victims into a call for revenge: *"Un blut af ale vegn shrayt: nekome!"* (The blood on every road cries out: revenge!) (Markish 1943a, 3).[21]

In the West, in contrast, Jewish rage was suppressed. Naomi Seidman's comparison of the Yiddish, French, and English versions of Elie

Wiesel's *Night* reveals that the original Yiddish emphasizes the theme of revenge. The Yiddish version reproaches the survivors for failing to carry out revenge; the subsequent translations into French and English praise them for transcending revenge (Seidman 2006).[22] The motif of revenge has subsequently reappeared in popular culture. Quentin Tarantino's 2009 film *Inglourious Basterds* raises the specter of Jewish revenge in fantasy celluloid form.[23]

Recognizing the significance of the Jewish contribution to Soviet war narrative—which includes the literature of hate and revenge—does not deny that Soviet Jews were also victims of Nazi destruction, or that they failed to write as powerful and moving literary witnesses to the Nazi genocide (which is the subject of Chapter Four of this study). An either-or approach would impose yet another form of totalizing narrative that obscured the self-awareness of the authors and the nuances of their works. It was particularly important for writers like Erenburg, Grossman, and Fefer to show that Jews were not merely victims, that they were heroic fighters—and precisely because they were Jews. In an article published in 1942, Erenburg wrote: "Once upon a time, the Jews dreamed of a promised land. Now a Jew has a promised land: the main line of defense."[24] In his article "Jews," Erenburg took pains to deny assertions that Jews did not shoulder their fair share of the burden of fighting the war; Erenburg rebuts this claim by saying, "Jews are fighting side by side with Ukrainians, with Belorussians" (Erenburg 1942).

Evgenii Dobrenko argues that Fefer's poem "Di shvue" (The Oath), in its Russian form, was more than a literary representation; it provided a ritual of allegiance between the mass reader and Soviet power. According to Dobrenko, the poem contains the "grammar" of the entire genre of the oath found in countless other poems and works of wartime literature and film. Both the Russian and the Yiddish versions of the poem lay out the terrible consequences of the poet's failure to keep his word. The Yiddish text reads: "let my people pierce me with the shaft of contempt . . . / Let my name remain on the roll call of shame / Let the earth reject the ash of my flesh" (Fefer 1943, 3). The Russian text has a similar list of dire punishments but concludes with a repetition of the poet's oath to the fatherland.

What Dobrenko does not discuss, however, is the Jewish framework for Fefer's poem. Answering Markish's appeal to both the Soviet citizen and the Jew, Fefer's "Oath" is both to the Soviet Union (in the original Yiddish, "*der land fun di rotn*") and "to my ancient people" (*mayn uraltn folk*), namely, the Jews. The poet makes the twofold addressee absolutely explicit:

This is my oath, which I swear now to the land of the Soviets,
To my ancient people, and to my old mother and father,
And this is my vow: if I break my bond,
Let my people spit on me with contempt!

Ot dos iz mayn shvue, vos kh'shver itst dem land fun di ratn,
Mayn uraltn folk, un mayn altinker mamen un tatn,
Un dos is mayn neyder; un oyb ikh vel bayde zey brekhn,
Zol demolt mayn folk mit der shpiz fun farakhtung mikh shtekhn!

(3)

The Russian translation preserves the twofold addressee, referring both to the "fatherland" (*otchizna*) and to the poet's "ancient people" (*narod drevneishim*).[25]

The source of the poet's vow is Psalm 137, which begins, "By the rivers of Babylon, there we sat down, yea, we wept when we remembered Zion." The historical event around which the psalm is built is the destruction of Jerusalem in 586 B.C.E. and the subsequent Babylonian captivity—the first in a series of catastrophic destructions in Jewish history, which according to traditional Jews culminates in "*der driter khurbn*," "the third destruction," what the Soviets did *not* call the Holocaust. In the psalm, the captors demand that their prisoners sing to them. The Jews' response turns compliance into resistance. It begins in uncertainty, "How shall we sing the Lord's song in a foreign land?" and moves to action, first with an oath of remembrance: "If I forget thee, O Jerusalem, let my right hand forget her cunning. / Let my tongue cleave to the roof of my mouth, if I remember thee not." It culminates in a prophecy of Babylon's destruction, depicting in grisly terms the joy of revenge: "O daughter of Babylon, that art to be destroyed; happy shall he be that repayeth thee as thou has served us. / Happy shall he be that taketh and dasheth thy little ones against the rock." Psalm 137 is structured around a promise made by the poet and the enumeration of the consequences of its violation.

Fefer's "Oath" works in a similar fashion, building from the consequences of his own oath and vow: the speaker swears that if he loses one arm, he will kill the enemy with the other; if he loses his other arm, his hate will give him strength to continue fighting. If he fails to erase every trace of the enemy and obliterate the memory of his enemy, if he fails in his oath and vow to the Soviet land and the Jewish people, his own name will remain forever on the roll call of shame. The psalmist's promise to remember what has been destroyed, lest he suffer injury, is also a demand that God remember Israel's torment and carry out revenge on its behalf. In both Psalm 137 and Fefer's "Di shvue" the intertwined motifs of memory and revenge work together to produce a single horrific effect. Like other Soviet Yiddish writers, who in the 1930s adapted Jewish tropes in their works about socialist construction, Fefer reworks Psalm 137 to create a uniquely Soviet and Jewish "pledge of allegiance" during the war.

Perets Markish's 1943 "Dem yidishn shlakhtman" (To a Jewish soldier) also refers to the Jewish textual tradition. The poet envisions a union of man and weapon:

> It is all the same whether you fuse yourself into the helm of a tank . . .
> Whether you become one with the machine gun,
> Whether your power blazes up in the shells bursting over the fields,
> No matter what, with every salvo your heart flows over with
> Bless God, oh my soul!
>
> *Altsayns—tsi shmeltsst zikh ayn in ruder fun a tank . . .*
> *Tsi inem koylnvarfer ayngeglidert bist,*
> *Tsi durkh granatn blitst ibern feld dayn kraft-shayn,*
> *Nor fun dayn yedn zalp ibern hartsn zikh tseflist*
> *Aza farfleytsndike borkhi nafshi!*
>
> (Markish 1943a, 4)

The line "Bless God, oh my soul," which appears in Hebrew in the Yiddish text, is the opening of Psalm 104. The psalm recounts the creation of the world and describes God's majesty and power over his creation; for example, the winds are God's messengers. The poem incorporates the psalm's images of God's glory and nature's obedience to him in its praise of the glory of the Jewish soldier, as in, for example, lines that describe how the "language of the winds, the stillness of the mountains" and the "colors of the rainbow" polish the soldier's weapon to a blinding brightness. At the same time, the poem also calls for revenge and praises hatred ("I do not know the color of hate / I know its power"), and it deifies the Jewish war hero, whose body is dispersed into his weapons. The poet promises the Jewish soldier that his country will award him a "gold star" and that his people, meaning the Jewish people, will include him as a link "in the golden chain" of Jewish memory (*"dikh in der keyt der goldener vet aynshlisn dos folk, / A shtern onton vet a goldenem dos land dir!"*) (7). The use of language from Psalm 101 and the references to the Jewish people provide a Jewish framework for what is essentially a paean to the soldier as cyborg.

The literature of mobilization spends no time reflecting on the damage caused to the hero in his metamorphosis into a super warrior. As soon as pain is inflicted, hatred sutures it, transforming the wound into a weapon. The enhancement of human fighting capacity comes at the cost of the loss of humanity, which war literature ignores. In contrast, in his extraordinarily powerful work "Heshl Ansheles," Der Nister takes a critical approach to this literature without flinching from the brutality of the circumstances that gave rise to it. Der Nister ("The Hidden One") was the pseudonym of the Yiddish writer Pinkhes Kahanovitsh (also Kaganovich) (1884–1950). Influenced by the writings of the mystic Rabbi Nakhman of Bratslav, Der Nister began publishing in the early years of the twentieth century; his story "Under a Fence" and his novel *The Family Mashber* have been translated into English, but his wartime works, including his series of stories about occupied Poland, are relatively unfamiliar to the English-language audience.[26] During the first few years of the war, Der Nister lived in Tashkent; his daughter died during the blockade of Leningrad.

Published in the anthology *Heymland* in 1943, "Heshl Ansheles" also appeared with similar works by Der Nister in a collection called *Karbones* (Victims, 1943). The story, set in Poland, begins with a gentle, timid Jew named Heshl Ansheles. A scholarly, learned man, well-known among the city's intelligentsia for his expertise and his extensive library, Heshl lives with his father and his father's old steward. Their peaceful life is marred, however, by the family history. Heshl's mother suffered from postpartum depression and killed herself shortly after Heshl was born. His own health is frail, and the family doctor warned that stress must be avoided. The mother's *"yerushe"* (inheritance) comes back to haunt Heshl when the Germans invade Poland. A German officer demands quarters in the Ansheles house. He also demands that his bags be carried up to the study, and singles out Heshl for the task. This straightforward and seemingly harmless request comes with a twist: Heshl must carry the heavier bag in his hand but the lighter one in his teeth. The entreaties of Heshl's father and the servants are to no avail. The German has discerned Heshl's weak point—his frail mental health.

It is at this point that the narrative departs from a realist account of events. All the members of the household understand that no entreaties would help Heshl "and that whoever had eyes and could look at what must happen here next, let him look. And whoever could not withstand it should turn his head and look away" (*un az ver s'hot oygn un kon tsukukn, vos do vayter darf farkumen, zol er kukn. Un ver s'iz dos nit imshtand, der zol dem kop opkereven un avekukn*) (Der Nister 1943, 33). The reported speech of what "everyone" understands also contains an extradiegetic address to the reader, as if the narrator were speaking to the reader directly, warning of the danger of looking at what would come next. The address breaks the illusion of mimesis characteristic of conventional narrative, because it disrupts the ongoing flow of events. The biblical cadences of the line, with its echoes of Ezekiel ("who have eyes to see, but see not," Ezek. 12:2) and Habakkuk ("Thou who art of purer eyes than to behold evil and canst not look on wrong," Hab. 1:13), shatter the unity in time of the event being described. The "now" of the moment is also linked to the eternal biblical warning. The warning is reiterated to any and every reader who encounters the text.

The narrative elides the moment when Heshl takes the suitcase in his mouth:

> he bent toward the bag with the heavy suitcase in his hand and without any choice bent his face closer . . . A little bit later one could see how he hesitated, his back twitching, bending up and down, but soon he stopped hesitating . . . A calamity took place . . . A man named

Heshl had bent over toward the bag, and the one who stood up with the bag in his teeth was someone else, another man, one could say, not a man at all, in any case, it was not he.

hot er zikh tsum gepek ongeboygn, dem shvern chemodan mit der hant genumen un tsum tveytn, beeyn breyre, mitn ponem zikh derneent . . . a vayle nokh hot men gezen, vi der rukn kvenklt zikh im, zikh arop un afheybndik, nor bald hot zikh oykh zayn rukn afgehert kvenklen . . . ober vey di yorn . . . ongeboygn tsum gepek hot zikh eyner a mentsh mitn nomen Heshl, un afgeshtelt, dem chemodan shoyn in di tseyn trogndik, hot zikh afgeshtelt an anderer, a tsveyter shoyn, kon men zogn, nit keyn mentsh, alnfals, nit er. (33)

The gaps in the text, indicated by the author's ellipses, indicate the moment of violence. Heshl is reduced to something other than what he was, which the text cannot determine exactly: he is no longer a person, or in any case, he is no longer Heshl. The mother's "inheritance" plays its part in this transformation. Heshl's eyes become opaque "as if his mother's milk had entered them" (*glaykh der mames milkh volt im in zey gekumen*) (33). Afterwards, when the bag is already in his teeth, the servants and Heshl's father follow him.

Heshl, whose life was devoted to texts and to speech, no longer speaks. His mouth remains open, but there are no words in it. Der Nister plays on this trope in his description of the "funeral procession" when Heshl's father and the servants accompany him with the bag in his teeth. They follow him "as if they were following a corpse, speechless" (33). What I have translated as "speechless" is in the original Yiddish, "when there are no words in your mouth" (*ven keyn verter in moyl zaynen nito*). The open mouth lacking words reiterates the elision in the text. With no direct act of physical violence, the officer's command reduces Heshl to a subhuman state, because the command deprives Heshl of speech. The violence of the officer's command leaves its mark on Heshl's body, horrifyingly on the part of the body that produces speech. From the moment he takes the bag until the end of the story, Heshl's mouth remains open as wide as necessary to accommodate the officer's bag. He is no longer aware of his surroundings and, reduced to an infantile state, must be led by the hand.

In the story's final dramatic scene, Heshl sees a German soldier wearing a uniform similar to the officer's. The German carries a small bag.

Heshl feels the compulsion to repeat the earlier act, and bends forward to take the bag in his teeth; but instead he bites off a piece of the German's finger. For the first time since the officer's command, Heshl closes his mouth and, as the text emphasizes, with "great pleasure" (*mit fuler hanoe*). The Germans shoot him, but neither they nor anyone else recover the finger from his mouth. The narrative emphasizes the symbolic and material importance of this act of closing the mouth: "for the first time since his misfortune he now closed his mouth with great pleasure, no, he did not close it, he locked it, no, he did not lock it, he sealed it" (*far der gantser tsayt, zint zayn umglik iz im geshen, hot er itst mit fuler hanoe dos moyl tsugemakht,—neyn, nit tsugemakht, nor tsugeshlosn,—neyn, nit tsugeshlosn, nor azoy farkhasmet*) (37). Closing his mouth, Heshl signed and "sealed" his statement. Closing his mouth around the German soldier's finger substitutes for the words he can no longer utter. The term *farkhasmen* has a legal dimension: the signatory attests that he or she is indeed the author of the statement. Heshl has no identity; he cannot "seal" or "attest" to anything except his own destruction. To author, sign, and seal a statement in the face of the author's own destruction (he is not a person, not Heshl; he is like a "*mes*," a corpse) is to offer testimony in the face of overwhelming death. The mark left on Heshl's body—his open mouth—becomes a weapon used to inflict injury on the German soldier. The open mouth without words, the sign of injury, was at the same time a rehearsal for an act of compensatory violence. Heshl is already dead by this point in the story and is only temporarily reanimated by his act of revenge. His open mouth cannot speak, cannot provide testimony, but it can inflict violence.

Der Nister's hero resembles the warrior heroes created by Fefer and Markish. As in "Di shvue," in which hatred compensates for a missing arm, in "Heshl Ansheles" injury becomes an instrument of revenge. Unlike these other works, however, in Der Nister's story compensatory violence does not erase the traces of the damage already done. Der Nister's human weapon died in the beginning of the story when he picked up the German's bag with his teeth. Heshl's mouth, forced open by an act of violence (the German's command), closes, but the closing of the mouth does not provide restoration or narrative closure. There is something disturbing about the "pleasure" that Heshl takes in biting off the

German's finger. He is buried with the remains of the finger, the "little bone," still in his mouth. The pleasure, the focus on the mouth, the text's reminder that Heshl's madness is the legacy of his mother—specifically in the phrase "his mother's milk"—combine infantile innocence and sadism in a grotesque fantasy of incorporation. The speech act of biting off the German soldier's finger represents the illusion of taking back what has been lost, in this case both the mother and the gift of speech. Der Nister's Heshl Ansheles uses his mouth not for speech but for an act of violence that mimics and repeats his own injury. The story does not absorb the violence it describes into a comfortable narrative of loss and restoration but instead reinflicts it.

Jewish Hate and Jewish Compassion

The numerous examples of the literature of mobilization in both Russian and Yiddish, by Jews and non-Jews, reveal its importance during wartime. As we have seen, leading Jewish writers of the time, including Erenburg, Fefer, and Markish, portrayed Jews as super soldiers motivated by hatred of the enemy and a desire for revenge. This message may be particularly difficult for readers in the early twenty-first century nurtured on the convention of the timid, gentle Jew and accustomed to the image of the Jew as victim of the Holocaust.[27] It is remarkable that Bergelson's story "Geven iz nakht un gevorn iz tog" (It was night and became day), published in 1943, should respond to the question about the Jew's image in similar terms. Bergelson, like Slutskii and Erenburg, was trying to counter stereotypes about Jewish passivity, cowardice, and greed—the accusation that Jews avoided frontline duty and instead kept up their commerce while Russians fought in the trenches. Bergelson's story, however, addresses the question more broadly, because it challenges the fundamental idea of a predefined image of the Jew.

Set in the mountains of the Caucasus, the story is about three Germans and their prisoner, a young Jewish student named Godashvili. Lost in the "labyrinth" of the mountains, the Germans kill Godashvili's parents and attempt to force him to lead them out, but hunger, exhaustion, and lack of discipline lead to the Germans' undoing. Godashvili alone survives, even though the Germans deprive him of food and water. The descriptions of Godashvili's intense feelings of love for his country and hatred of the enemy, and the schematic and fanciful plot, do not make for particularly compelling reading.

The story is of interest, however, in its reflections about the character of the Jews and their values. These reflections, furthermore, are not neutral; they do not come from the narrator or the Jewish student himself but from one of the German soldiers, Hans Messer, a Nazi propagandist. Messer tries to read the student's personality from the expression in his eyes. He compares Godashvili to a famous Jewish humorist whom he used to see in a café in Berlin during the Weimar years. The humorist used to lend Hans Messer money; one day he offered him his entire wallet, as if he had no further need of money, and explained that his only child, a daughter, had died. Hans remembers the look in the Jew's eyes as he recounted the death: "and in his eyes there was more than pain and more than suffering, it was something that you never see in Germans' eyes" (*un in zayne oygn hot zikh bavizn epes mer, vi veytek un mer, vi leydn, un geven iz es epes azoyns, vos ba daytshn in di oygn bavayzt zikh es keynmol nit*) (Bergelson 1943, 17). Hans Messer sees something similar in the student's eyes, something that is lacking in his two comrades, in himself, and "in the millions of Germans who love the Third Reich," namely, "compassion" (*mitleyd*)—and it is this Jewish compassion, according to Hans, that will save him. The student will take pity on him and help him get out of the mountains alive. The Nazi brings a fixed template of the Jewish personality to the situation on the ground, and it is his misreading of the Jew that leads to his undoing. At the end of the story, Hans is horrified to see Godashvili's "German eyes" (*daytshishe oygn*) (29).

Bergelson does not permit his Nazi character to have the last word on the Jewish personality. Hans Messer turns out to be both right and wrong about the Jewish student. He does have compassion, but not for Hans. Instead, his compassion is for the Nazis' victims, as he tells Hans, leaving him to die alone. In providing this reading of Jewish character, but from the point of view of a German soldier, Bergelson estranges readers' expectations about the Jewish personality and Jewish suffering, challenging stereotypical images of Jews.

Bergelson, like Erenburg, Grossman, Fefer, and other Jews writing in the Soviet Union during the Second World War, helped to create the template for the literature of mobilization; they enlisted the aid of the West; and they fought the claim that Jews were rearguard soldiers and passive victims. Their engagement on multiple fronts included what may appear to be an objectionable effort to stoke the emotions of hatred, inciting their audience to acts of revenge. To read their works as nothing more than Soviet propaganda, distanced from Jews, Jewish emotions, and Jewish tradition does an injustice to the impossible burden these authors shouldered during the war.

Looking Beyond the Machinery of War: Halkin and Der Nister

Bergelson's "It was night and became day" also challenges the image of the human fighting machine. Bergelson's Godashvili is a far cry from Fefer's terminator in "The Oath" or Markish's Jewish cyborg. The story as a whole suspends the transformation of the human being into a weapon, and the ending, far from providing an uplifting message of loss overcome, reminds readers of the overwhelming devastation suffered by Jews under the Germans. Making his way down the mountain, the student thinks only of the "destruction" (*khurbn*)—the traditional Jewish term for "catastrophe"—that awaits him at home.

Unlike more propagandistic works, the story also looks forward to the problem of postwar justice. It confronts the problem of gathering evidence for the mass killings carried out by the Germans in occupied territory. One of Godashvili's captors, a big man with a red face, was an avid participant in the killings. Hans, the Nazi propagandist, teases him about the consequences:

> In the eyes of each [victim], you should know, is a negative, as in a camera—everything is reflected there. Experienced murderers take the trouble to close the eyes of their victims so that afterwards their photographs cannot be retrieved. This is no small matter for you . . . when the Russians win, they will extract your red image from the eyes of all the people whom you murdered. (Bergelson 1943, 21)

The perpetrator's crime, the injury inflicted on the body of the victim, is at the same time evidence that can be used against the criminal.

Unlike typical wartime writing, in this story there is no recovery for the victims, only the recovery of what they saw and experienced. In his story, Bergelson imagines that the materialization of what the victims saw—the image engraved on their retinas—could be preserved and harvested after their deaths. In what is almost a piece of science fiction, the dead provide material evidence of their own experience. Bergelson registers the problem of witnessing as formulated by Lyotard: when the best witnesses are dead, who will provide evidence as to how they died?[28] Hatred and revenge are impotent in the face of this problem. In the literature of mobilization, hatred of the enemy extends the human body beyond its limits in space and time; in Bergelson's story, in contrast, what is extended beyond death is the record of violence from the victim's perspective. This is an extraordinary fantasy of an impossibly perfect testimony.

There are other significant works that interrupt or in other ways question the dominant trope of the literature of mobilization. Shmuel Halkin's wartime poem "Zol zayn mayn shtub a hafn dir" (Let my house be a harbor) was published in the anthology *Homeland* (Heymland) in 1943. Halkin (1897–1960), a poet, playwright, and translator, began publishing in Yiddish in the 1920s, during which time he also wrote poetry in Hebrew. During the war he was a member of the Jewish Anti-Fascist Committee and served on the editorial board of its newspaper, *Eynikayt*. He wrote a dramatic poem about the Warsaw ghetto uprising, which appeared in a volume of selected works in Moscow in 1948 (Shmeruk 1964, 759–61).

Halkin's poem imagines a moment of peace in the midst of the war. I quote from the middle section:

Old, embittered
Torn to bits, shot
Full of suffering
I will welcome him, embrace him.

Guiltless brother
Purified a hundred times over
Time makes us patient
But never distant

> Tell me what clothing to make ready for you,
> And what joy to prepare?
> For you, entangled in misfortune still,
> My house shall be a harbor.
>
> Not to comfort you, not to be a guarantee
> With what balm shall I sooth your catastrophe?
> In your destroyed nest
> You will not see your children anymore.
>
> Your house was not flooded
> No eagles carried off your children
> It was a German plane that killed them from on high.
>
> Let your blood be ignited,
> A fire set aflame
> Your courage kindled,
> An unheard of force arise,
>
> That conquers cities and countries
> That destroys fortresses,
> And when it encounters the tiniest gift
> It yields in agreement, from the depths of its heart.
>
> (Halkin 1943)[29]

The theme of solace and the mood of almost holiday-like renewal (the speaker asks what clothing and what special "joy" to prepare for the visitor) contrast sharply with the violence of the war and the sorrow it engenders. In this poem, unlike other works by Halkin, the war is not a monumental catastrophe that destroys the continuity of time. The traditional Jewish cycle alternating weekday and holiday time persists in spite of the war.

This theme goes back to Halkin's first published poem, "Di lipn baym tatn" (The lips of my father), which describes the dead body of the poet's father as if he were still alive, his lips as if they were "blessing someone." The poem ends with the lines "O keep the weekday cloth off the table a while longer / Let that much of the Sabbath remain" (Halkin 1987, 512). The domestic detail adds immediacy to the scene and underscores the importance of the cycle of profane work and sanctified rest time. Indeed, Halkin later said that this first work contained the most substantive motif of all his poetry: "the painful transition from holiday to workday time and the attempt to elevate the weekday to the time of holiday" (Shmeruk 1964, 759).

Similarly, the 1943 poem "Let My House Be a Harbor" stages a holiday-like intermission from the war and in so doing interrupts the force of hate and revenge. Within the framework of the poem, the poet's "house" (*shtub*) offers temporary shelter; reading the poem offers temporary respite from the surrounding violence of war—even as it urges the soldier on to battle in the stanza "Let your blood be ignited." As in other wartime poems, pain turns to revenge, but unlike the implacable warriors in Fefer, Markish, and other writers, Halkin's soldier restrains his force and yields in the face of even the smallest overture of peace. The poem suspends the transformation of the human into a hate-driven machine. The story that the poem tells so beautifully offers no uplift or decisive, final transformation; the offering of a safe harbor is neither "comfort" nor a "guarantee" but only a moment of peace in the ongoing war.

Der Nister's article of 1944, "Has" (Hate), published in *Eynikayt* (Unity), also looks beyond the immediacy of hatred—in spite of its title—to the act of giving comfort.[30] Even though Der Nister's piece can easily be located within the genre of war literature, at the same time it also functions within another type of literature entirely. Der Nister's "Hate," in contrast to works by Fefer and Markish, has nothing to do with mobilizing the population to kill the enemy; it is instead oriented toward the prophetic literature of comfort. A series of quotations from and allusions to prophetic literature transforms the work from propaganda to something approaching messianic literature. The article embeds the first-person narrative of a young boy, Shloyme, who saw his "entire shtetl of Jews" killed by the Germans. He witnessed his own father's death and endured the loss of his little brother. Der Nister punctuates the narration of these events with words from Isaiah traditionally recited on the Sabbath after Tisha b'Av (the Ninth of Av), the holiday marking the destruction of the first and second Temples. On the Sabbath of Comfort, as it is called, the opening of Isaiah 40 is read: "Comfort, comfort my people, says your God" (Isa. 40:1). Der Nister takes this language directly, quoting it twice in Yiddish: "*Ober lomir zikh treystn, Shloymke*" and "*Iz lomir zikh treystn, Shloymke*" (Let us be comforted, Shloymke). He continues in the same vein, referring to an unspecified text that Shloymke "has learned": "You have learned this. He who has seen the jackals in the desolate places of our mountain will also see building take place there" (*Ver s'hot gezen di shakaln af di khurves fun unzer barg, der vet oykh zen, vi me vet dort boyen*) (Der Nister 1944). The jackals, the desolate places, and the mountain are also prophetic references. Der Nister repeats this language and this imagery, building to a crescendo at the end of the work. I quote at length from the final passage, which opens by shifting Isaiah's words of comfort to Der Nister's own words of "fantasy":

> Let us, I say, fantasize. *V'haya bayom ha'hu*—one wants to use the prophets' fiery language; and it will come to pass on that day, the kingship of evil will expire . . . and then when you Shloymke little by little forget your father, about whom you do speak, and even your unlucky brother, about whom you cannot speak, will not speak, because it is your unhealed wound, this also will be healed, then (we hope, and with this hope we live) we will see you among the builders and saviors of the desolation on our mountain. (Der Nister 1944)

In contrast to conventional Soviet war narrative, Der Nister leaves the wound unhealed and does not transform injury into a weapon. The Hebrew words "and it will come to pass on that day" appear in the original in the Yiddish text. The use of prophetic language lifts Der Nister's article out of its own space and time, framing the events it describes in a messianic perspective. Der Nister, however, inserts an ironic distance between messianic time and his own. The messianic time, God's day—"and on that day it will come to pass"—is a time of restoration and redress in Isaiah, Amos, and other prophets; in Der Nister, in contrast, it is not a certainty or even a likelihood but a hope, and even a "fantasy" ("let us, I say, fantasize"). It cannot be decided *in what voice* Der Nister is speaking; that he is speaking by quoting these multiple voices—the use of a multivocal register—is what is important. Der Nister is not saying that the Nazi destruction of the Jews is part of a divine plan of destruction and restoration. In appropriating prophetic language, Der Nister both couples and uncouples his text from its framework of reference. In the gap between "Let us take comfort" and "Let us fantasize" there is an affirmation of and a longing for redemption, as well as a denial of its possibility. Comfort itself remains something of a fantasy. There is no single, definitive interpretation of the events of Shloymke's story. Its terrible emotional force cannot be subsumed under any unitary framework of meaning. The irreducibility of the work suspends the closure of typical (socialist) realist narrative.

Narrating and propagandizing the war to their fellow Soviets and fellow Soviet Jews in both Russian and Yiddish, Soviet Jewish writers produced a body of literature that fueled the war effort. They adapted traditional Jewish texts, including most importantly Psalm 137, to suit the work of mobilization. At the same time, they also questioned the fundamental principles of the literature of hate, as the writings of Slutskii, Der Nister, and Halkin attest. In these works, the wounds inflicted by the fighting and by the Nazi assault on the Jews do not heal, but linger. Bergelson's story of a student turned warrior raises the question of how the dead victims' experience would or could be remembered, of what form their testimony could take. It is this question having to do with testimony, memory, and commemoration that would reveal the fissures separating the Soviet and the Jew.

Four In Mourning: Responding to the Destruction of the Jews

Only now in mourning the answer comes to me,
In the pain of being melted down—I understand as if on fire
The pain of wanting to see myself whole in the mirror.

Ersht itster kumt tsu mir in troyer der basheyd,
In vey fun ibershmelts—bagrayf ikh flamik
Dem payn fun veln zen zikh in shpigl—gantserhayt
    Perets Markish, "Ho Lakhmo" (The bread of affliction)
                   (1943a, 8–9)[1]

Weren't you ashamed of your Red Army rifle?
Did your five-pointed star dedicate itself to revenge?

Tsi hostu nit farshemt dayn roytarmeyerishe biks?
Tsi zikh geheylikt in nekome hot dayn finf-ekediker shtern?
      Perets Markish, *Milkhome* (War) (1956, 2:535)

Why was there no Holocaust in Soviet Russia?[2] Western scholars as well as some circles of the general readership are acquainted with such works as Evgenii Yevtushenko's poem of 1961, "Babi Yar," which opens with the line "There are no monuments at Babi Yar"; Anatolii Kuznetsov's novel of the same title (published in Russia in expurgated form in 1966, and also available in English); and Anatolii Rybakov's 1978 *Heavy Sand*. The 2001 edition of Kuznetsov's *Babii iar* shows a black-and-white picture of a Jewish family on the cover (the family is identified in the front matter of the book) with yellow stars superimposed on the picture (Kuznetsov 2001).[3] The illustration's emphasis on the specificity of the Jews' fate reflects the publisher's marketing savvy more than it does the content of the book, which does not tell its story from a Jewish perspective.[4] Millions of Jews died on Soviet soil, but the killings were not officially memorialized—"There are no monuments at Babi Yar." The killings did not take on the same meaning as in the West, where the Holocaust emerged as a unique and paradigmatic set of events, and where

Responding to the Destruction of the Jews   151

it forms, especially in America, a crucial part of Jewish identity.[5] With the Eichmann trial, as Michael Rothberg and others have argued, the term "Holocaust" began to carry a set of assumptions about the unique fate of the Jews and their meaning for world history, even though Jews remembered their murdered brethren before this event.[6] In what has come to be a discipline in its own right, scholars explore the history and meaning of the Holocaust, the limits of its representation in literature and art, and the varieties of its commemoration.[7] In American academic discourse, a certain exhaustion has set in regarding the Holocaust, and the distance between the events and the present has led some scholars to speak of "postmemory" and "prosthetic memory" (the use of technology to simulate memory), but as far as the study of the Holocaust in Russian and Soviet Yiddish literature is concerned, the problems of representation, memory, and testimony have hardly been broached.[8] In the Soviet Union, in contrast to the West, the Holocaust had a different trajectory. Its contours are still unfolding in the twenty-first century as new and older works, both literary and scholarly, are published and republished.

The term "Holocaust" (*kholokost*) did not enter Russian scholarly discourse until the last decade of the twentieth century; the word *katastrofa* (catastrophe) was used in its place.[9] In Yiddish-language works published in the Soviet Union and elsewhere in Eastern Europe in the 1940s, other terms were used for both the event and those it killed, including, for example, *khurbn*, a word that referred originally to the destruction of the first and second Temples; and *karbones* (victims), the biblical meaning of which is "sacrificial offerings."[10] In a speech given in Moscow in May 1942 and published in the first (June) issue of *Eynikayt* (Unity), the newspaper of the Jewish Anti-Fascist Committee, David Bergelson used the term *karbones* when he asked the Jews of the entire world to respond to the call of the dead: "our victims [*karbones*] have not yet been counted and not even brought to their graves" (Tsu di yidn fun gor der velt 1942, 2). Neither *khurbn* nor *karbones* is identical to the term "Holocaust," which began to circulate in the late 1950s; however, both Yiddish terms link the events of the war to traditional Jewish forms of responding to catastrophe.[11] The absence of a Russian term for "Holocaust" for much of the twentieth century does not mean that

Jews in Soviet Russia did not share wider Jewish views of the events of the war. To see this requires a broadened definition of what constitutes a Jewish response to the Holocaust and, furthermore, a critical awareness of the limitations of the term "Holocaust" itself as representing a quite specific phenomenon not necessarily found outside twentieth-century American and Israeli culture. This chapter focuses on the war and immediate postwar period, when the meaning of the events of the war had not yet become fixed.

As David Shneer points out, Western scholarly neglect of Soviet Holocaust literature is due in part to the silence in Soviet historiography about the role of Jews in the war.[12] Amir Weiner argues that the Soviet version of the "Great Patriotic War" made Jews disappear—both as soldiers and as Holocaust victims.[13] Weiner writes, "the mass murder of Jews was never denied in Soviet representations of the war, but in the official accounts and artistic representations, memory of the Jewish catastrophe was submerged within the universal Soviet tragedy, erasing the very distinction at the core of the Nazi pursuit of racial purity" (2001, 231–32). In *Bitter Legacy*, Zvi Gitelman characterizes the dominant response to the Holocaust in Soviet historiography, not as complete repression but rather as a matter of less emphasis and a more universalist interpretation. The Soviet response saw the destruction of the Jews as "part of a larger phenomenon . . . a consequence of racist fascism" (1997, 18). It cannot be denied that Operation Barbarossa did make Slavs the objects of racist fascism.

The Soviet Union's failure to memorialize Jewish victims of the Holocaust may also be seen as part of a larger neglect of the war's victims generally. The Soviets also failed to memorialize and indeed even to acknowledge "the estimated two to three million unburied soldiers who lost their lives in the Great Patriotic War" (Tumarkin 1994, 12). The Soviet war narrative, as the May 2010 celebration of the sixty-fifth anniversary of the "Great Victory" reveals, rationalizes the "unprecedented" suffering of the Soviet people as the price paid for their unprecedented defeat of the Nazis.[14] One enormity, the enormity of the victory, justifies the other, the enormity of unacknowledged pain.

The few critical studies of the representation of the Holocaust in Soviet literature focus on the absence of the Jew.[15] The emphasis on Soviet neglect of the Holocaust has influenced the reading and interpretation of Soviet literary works on this subject. The apt condemnation of the Soviet policy of purging Jews from the record of the war, together with a general neglect of literature of the period, has led to an unintended consequence. Soviet literary responses to the destruction of the Jews remain largely unexplored territory. The few available studies are dominated by the Soviet refusal to acknowledge the unique tragedy suffered by the Jews. In his groundbreaking *The Making of the State Writer*, Evgeny Dobrenko writes, "It is fully worth recognizing an essentially surprising fact: every attempt to historicize Soviet literature has ended with a *loss of the* object" (2001, xiii). Dobrenko's argument about the lack of work on Soviet literature applies to Soviet literature about the Nazi genocide with particular force.

I do not dispute the universal consensus about Soviet historiography and official commemoration; when the discussion turns to "artistic representations," however, the argument requires modification, beginning with the term "representation" itself. Scholars of Holocaust literature (the study of which nearly always excludes anything created in the former Soviet Union) argue that the Nazi genocide challenges the possibility of realistic, referential, or mimetic representation. The chief symptom of trauma, according to Cathy Caruth, is the victim's failure to recognize that an overwhelming injury has taken place. What "constitutes trauma and points to its enigmatic core [is] the delay or incompletion in knowing, or even in seeing, an overwhelming experience" (Levy and Rothberg 2003, 194). Trauma is an unknowable experience, partly accessible only through the symptomatic repetition of the event. Caruth characterizes trauma as "a pathology of history of itself," because of the split between the event and knowledge about it. "The traumatized . . . carry an impossible history within them" (Levy and Rothberg 2003, 194). At the heart of what came to be known in the West as the Holocaust is the problem of knowledge and this "impossible history." Works of Soviet literature, almost completely neglected by scholars and critics on both sides of the Atlantic, also grapple with the impossible history of the destruction of the Jews, but not in the same terms as Holocaust literature in the West. To return to my opening question, there indeed was a Holocaust in Soviet Russia, but it looks different from what came to be understood as the Holocaust in the West. In the former Soviet Union and in post-Soviet Russia, the scholarly and artistic response to the destruction of the Jews takes on its own distinct outline in which the perspectives of Jewish victims, Jewish avengers, and Jewish victors overlap. My readings in this chapter attempt to restore the literary value of Soviet works about the Nazi destruction of the Jews, and to restore them to the Jewish narrative tradition from which they have been artificially severed.[16] Instead of focusing on the ideologically orchestrated absence of Jews, this chapter explores memory, memorialization, mourning, and testimony as literary problems, as problems of language and representation. Il'ia Sel'vinskii's poetry; Bergelson's "An eydes" (A witness, 1945); Vasilii Grossman's *Za pravoe delo* (For a just cause; published in 1952) and *Zhizn' i sud'ba* (Life and fate; not published in Russia until 1988); Der Nister's "Vidervuks" (Offshoots, 1946); and Perets Markish's poem "Ho Lakhmo" (The bread of affliction) and his epic *Milkhome* (War) all respond to the killings of Jews. These works address the problem of insurmountable loss, using poetry and literary narrative, not to improve reality, as the ideology of socialist realism demands, but to face irrevocable destruction. An emphasis on language choice alone as the ground of analysis, with the assumption that only the Yiddish works address the uniqueness of Jewish suffering, would do an injustice to the works. It would, furthermore, obscure their engagement with the problem of language itself: its specificity and its universality, its inadequacy, and its fragmentation and destruction in the wake of mass death. The problems of memory, mourning, and testimony that these works engage are central to the larger problem of responding to the war and the Holocaust and, indeed, central to the problem of (Jewish) mourning in the twentieth century.

The Ravine: What Sel'vinskii Saw

Il'ia Sel'vinskii (1899–1968) was born in Simferopol, attended gymnasium in Evpatoriia, and fought there during the civil war. He rose to prominence in the 1920s, when he was associated with the literary movement known as "constructivism." One of his best-known early works, "Uliaevshchina," describes an anti-Bolshevik uprising and includes an anarchist named Shtein. A narrative poem about a gangster, titled "Mot'ka malkhamoves" (Mot'ka angel of death, 1926), uses Yiddish and Hebrew expressions transliterated into the Russian text. In this regard his early writing resembles the work of Russian-language Jewish writers of the time, including Babel, Bagritskii, Veniamin Kaverin, and Semen Gekht, who employed similar heterolinguistic devices in their work. During the Second World War, Sel'vinskii served in the army in Crimea, the Caucasus, and the Baltic Front, and published with several army newspapers. He achieved the rank of colonel.[17] His war poetry was published extensively throughout the 1940s and in the subsequent decades of Soviet rule; readers could have access to it.

"Ia eto videl" (I saw it), first published in the newspaper *Bol'shevik* on January 23, 1942, reprinted on February 27, 1942, in the army newspaper *Krasnaia zvezda* (Red star), and included in many collections of the poet's works, describes Sel'vinskii's reaction to the sight of seven thousand corpses in a ditch outside the Crimean city of Kerch'.[18] Two subsequent poems—"Sud v Krasnodare" (The trial in Krasnodar) and "Kandava" (Kandava, a city in Latvia)—return to this scene. These poems are among the earliest artistic responses in any language to the Nazi mass killings of Jews. They form a cohesive narrative, building from murder to trial to commemoration. Sel'vinskii's writing confronts the impossible knowledge of what was not yet called the Holocaust, even within the Soviet framework of the universality of the suffering that took place under German occupation. His poetry attempts to speak the pain of the victims but at the same time sounds the call for revenge. Finally, a distinctly Jewish voice, which resonates with Soviet Yiddish writing, emerges in his work. Sel'vinskii wrote to his wife on January 12, 1942, that he "visited the ditch outside Kerch', where 7000 women, children, and old people lie shot to death . . . And I saw them. I don't have the strength now to write about it in prose, my nerves have stopped reacting, what I could do, I expressed in verse" (Sel'vinskii 1971, 1:678). The key phrase is "And I saw them," which the poet uses both here in the letter and as the title of his poem. The Germans completed their bloody work in December 1941; the Soviets retook Kerch' in January 1942, leaving the Germans no time to cover the evidence, as they did at Babi Yar; indeed, the frozen bodies of the dead could be clearly seen.[19] The sight of the dead produced a physiological change in the witness that is characteristic of trauma: the cessation of response. Sel'vinskii nonetheless responds to the dead, choosing what he defines as the less demanding genre of poetry.[20]

The very opening stanza claims the role of the eyewitness as offering the most credible evidence of the mass murder:

> You may ignore folk tales,
> Doubt the newspaper,
> But I saw it. With my own eyes.
> Understand? I saw it myself.
>
> Here's the road. And over there—hills.
> Between them
> Like this—
> A ravine.
> From this ravine grief rises.
> Without limit.
>
> No! you can't use words for this . . .
> You have to howl! Scream!
> Seven thousand shot dead in a frozen pit,
> That turned red, like rust.
>
> Who are these people? Soldiers? No.
> Partisans, right? No.
>
> (1:352)

The first stanza raises the question of what kind of account is credible, discarding both "folk tales" (*narodnye skazaniia*) and newspaper reports (*gazetnye stolbtsy*) as susceptible to doubt, and offering as irrefutable the evidence of an eyewitness. The distinction between evidence that is not compelling and evidence that is carries with it an obligation on the part of the witness and those who hear his testimony. The opening words "*mozhno ne slushat'*," which I translate "you may ignore," can also be rendered more literally as "It is possible not to listen to," in the sense of hearken, attend to, obey. The opening line "*mozhno ne slushat'*" (you may ignore) contains an implied commandment, "*nado slushat'*" (you must listen to): you must listen to this poem, because it speaks for the dead.

The "Seven thousand shot dead in a frozen pit" have to be heard, and Sel'vinskii struggles to create an impossible language that could adequately translate the victims' pain:

Every cry that flies from their lips
Corresponds to an implacable grammar.

Here you would have to . . . call an assembly
From every tribe
And extract from each all that is human,
Everything that burst through the centuries,
Shrieks, cries, sighs and groans,
The echo of attacks, pogroms, butchery . . .
Wouldn't this
Utterance
Of bottomless torment
Be equal to the word that is sought?

K neumolimoi grammatike sveden
Kazhdyi krik, sletaiushchii s gub.

Zdes' nuzhno by . . . Nuzhno sozdat' by veche
Iz vsekh plemen ot drevka do drevka
I vziat' ot kazhdogo vse chelovech'e,
Vse, prorvavsheesia skvoz' veka,-
Vopli, khripy, vzdokhi i stony,
Ekho nashestvii, pogromov, rezni . . .
Ne eto l'
narech'e
muki bezdonnoi
Slovam iskomym srodni?

(1:355)

Sel'vinskii imagines a language that has no words but only inchoate cries. Each cry nonetheless corresponds to an "implacable grammar," the grammar of pain, which has no grammar and which destroys articulate speech.[21] To speak this language properly is to submit to torment, to be reduced to what is less than human. Each "correct" utterance brings the speaker closer to death. To conform to this implacable grammar means to cease speaking. Kerch' thus creates an impossible poetics.

The theme of impossibility is important. Adorno, Lyotard, Derrida, Cathy Caruth, and others address the problem of impossibility in relation to the Holocaust, the impossibility of poetry itself, the impossibility of traumatic knowledge. Lyotard in *The Differend*, and Derrida in his writing on Paul Celan, focus on the impossibility of testimony and witnessing.[22] The "differend" is "the unstable state and instance of language wherein something must be able to be put into phrases yet cannot be." Sel'vinskii's "I saw it," which has never been discussed in the context of the Holocaust, engages one of the central issues of Western writing about the Holocaust: the failure and impossibility of the language of pain.

The victims, whose pain the poet translates into an impossible language, must then be listened to and obeyed, as in the eighth stanza, in which the dead command the poet:

> Go on then! Brand them! You stand before the massacre,
> You caught them red-handed—condemn them!
> You see how the butcher's bullet
> Smashed us to pieces,
> Thunder forth like Dante, like Ovid,
> Let nature herself cry
> If
> You yourself
> Saw
> All this
> And haven't gone out of your mind
>
> (1:354)

The first stanza, with its delineation of what does and what does not have to be "listened to," anticipates this order from the dead.

In three succeeding stanzas, Sel'vinskii picks out details from three different victims of the mass murder: a young man with an amputated leg; a peasant woman, a Christian, who reproaches the Virgin Mary for what the Germans have done; and a Jewish woman with her child (*isterzannaia evreika/pri nei rebenok*). The mention of the Christian conforms to the Soviet cliché of the universality of suffering. The description of the Jewish mother and child, however, is the longest and most emotional:

> Next to her a tormented Jewish woman.
> With a child. Completely as if in a dream.
> With what care the child's neck

Is wrapped in mother's gray scarf . . .
A mother's heart doesn't change:
Going to be shot, under the gun,
An hour, a half-hour before death
The mother protected the child from catching cold.
But even death is no parting for them:
The enemy has no power over them now—
And a red stream
From the child's ear
Drips into the mother's
Cupped palm.

(1:353)

This description of the stereotypical Jewish mother dramatically changes in a subsequent stanza when the poet declares that the mother's hands, now a fist, will "burn through" the Germans' "blue waltzes." The image of the Jewish mother's fist transforms Jewish suffering into Jewish revenge, an important dimension of the Soviet Jewish response to the Nazi genocide. Sel'vinskii develops the theme of revenge in "I saw it" and in subsequent poems.

No Mercy

Sel'vinskii returns to the mass killing at Kerch' in a later poem, "Sud v Krasnodare" (A trial in Krasnodar), first published in the mainstream literary journal *Znamia* (The banner) in 1945, and republished in an anthology of the author's work (Sel'vinskii 1947, 147–55). The poem describes the first war crimes trial, conducted by a Soviet military tribunal in Krasnodar from July 14 to July 17, 1943.[23] The Germans occupied the North Caucasus city of Krasnodar beginning in the fall of 1941, and they and their collaborators killed over fifteen hundred Jews there, and several more thousands in the larger Krasnodar region; in addition, they murdered several hundred inmates of a psychiatric hospital, and tens of wounded Soviet officers.[24] The Germans introduced mobile gas vans, known in Russian as *dushegubki*, in these locations. In the poem, one of the defendants accused of collaborating with the Gestapo attempts to exonerate himself by saying that he worked for the Germans only as a driver, without killing anyone. Turning on the ignition of a dushegubka, however, was what released the gas into the chamber of the vehicle, making the driver the executioner. I. I. Kotov, who survived a gas van killing, gave key testimony at the trial by identifying one of the defendants as the driver (Sel'vinskii writes, "I was in the fourth group, driver,/Don't you recognize my ghost?"). Eight collaborators were sentenced to death.

The poem contrasts different responses to the verdict. A newspaper correspondent asks the poet whether he feels pity for the condemned; the first-person narrator, the poet, answers that he does not. The correspondent, skeptical about the poet's denial, calls it "propaganda" ("*Etot vash, otvet/sovsem ne bolee, kak propaganda*"). The poet cites what he saw at Kerch'—"seven thousand corpses" (*sem' tysiach trupov*)—as the basis for his lack of pity for the collaborators.

In the earlier poem, "I saw it," Sel'vinskii wrote, "Whoever saw you, from now on/Will carry your wounds in his soul." The wound makes itself felt in "Sud v Krasnodare." Sight provides the grounds for the poet's credibility, as if the line "I saw it" was marked, "I *saw* it" (*Ia eto videl*); now another accentuation emerges—"*I* saw it" (Ia *eto videl*). It was *I* who saw it, and therefore I am marked, wounded by it; the victims' pain inscribes itself in me, I am implicated in it, I must answer it, I belong again and already to this community. There is something like the Deuteronomic circumcision of the heart playing just under the surface of the poem ("Circumcise the foreskin of your heart," Deut. 10:16). *I* saw it and have been circumcised in my heart; I now carry your wound and therefore cannot and must not feel pity for the perpetrators.

As an eyewitness to the aftermath of the mass killing of Jews, he cannot feel sorrow for anyone who aided in similar killings. The poem explicitly links religious affiliation and the emotional response to the verdict. The poet's interlocutor, the correspondent, tells him that as a Christian he is obliged to pity the condemned: "*Kak khristianin, ia dolzhen pozhalet' seichas vot etikh.*" The poet's extraordinary response, with which the poem ends, is worth quoting in full:

An unthinkable pain stopped my breath
nausea filled my throat . . .
Get out!

The "Christian" was taken aback.
Get out!
Thank God no one
heard that phrase.
Get moving!
I am very sorry for your Christ

Nemyslimaia bol', kak ot udara,
na mig oborvala moe dykhan'e—
i toshnotoi pod gorlo . . .
—Ukhodite!
Khristianin opeshil.
—U-kho-di-te!
Blagodarite boga, chto nikto
ne slyshal etoi frazy.
Nu!
Stupaite!
Mne ochen' zhalko vashego Khrista.

(Sel'vinskii 1947, 155)

The poet names his interlocutor as a Christian in the line "The 'Christian' was taken aback," and by implied contrast names himself as a non-Christian. He expresses pity, not for the condemned defendants but for Christ instead: "I am very sorry for your Christ." Note the possessive adjective "your." This line about pity for "your Christ" can be parsed as a Jewish response, a way that the poet names himself as a Jew. It can also be parsed as a Soviet, atheist response to the demand for Christian compassion; however, Sel'vinskii does not mention Russia, the Soviet Union, Stalin, or communism in the passage above, just the contrast between the Christian and the non-Christian. The rejection of Christ and the rejection of mercy for the perpetrators are equally Soviet and Jewish responses to the mass killings of victims, whom the Soviets did not identify as Jews.

A Double Dream

"Kandava" (the title is the name of a city in Latvia) is the final and most important of the triad of poems written by Sel'vinskii in the 1940s in response to the destruction of the Jews. In this work, published in 1947, the poet describes himself both as a Jewish victim of the Nazi genocide and also as a triumphant Soviet and Jewish army officer accepting the German surrender at Kandava. Sel'vinskii in fact participated in the ceremony in May 1945 as a Soviet officer.[25] The poem, remarkably, frames its account of military triumph with the Jewish nightmare of the death camp:

> Last night I had a dream: I was walking
> with my wife somewhere either in Auschwitz or Majdanek.
> I was walking past rows
> of blue-gray fascist soldiers
>
> *Mne snilsia nakanune son: idu*
> *s zhenoiu riadom gde-to v Osventsime*
> *ili v Maidaneke. Idu pred stroem*
> *fashistskikh sero-golubykh soldat*
>
> (Sel'vinskii 1947, 209)

"Myriads of eyes—filled with hate, contempt, mockery, malice, and even curiosity" watch the poet and his wife as they go to their death. The opening stanza poses the question of the relation between the death camps and Kandava. The stanza that follows, however, does not answer the question but introduces yet another location, the scene of the poet's childhood. The poet remembers himself as a little boy, trying to see how long he could hold his breath; this section ends with a philosophical reflection on the real suffering that dreams can inflict. The first part of the poem concludes:

> If there is a "landscape of the soul" and a map,
> on which you could draw it—
> mark on mine: "Majdanek."
>
> *Tak esli est' 'peizazh dushi' i karta,*
> *gde mozhno by ego izobrazit'—*
> *otmet'e na moei: "Majdanek."*
>
> (211)

The repetition of the sounds "m" plus "e" in "*otmet'e*," "*moei*," and the first syllable of "Majdanek" (which I have tried to capture with "mark," "mine," and "Majdanek") embody what Roman Jakobson calls paronomasia, sound mirroring (Jakobson 1987, 86). The reflection of the sound of the previous word in the succeeding syllables impedes the forward motion of the line; the sound-image that is thereby formed serves to fix the place of the poet's nightmare as the death camp, pinning him down to this spot on the map, and no other. The poet does not name himself as a Jew, and he never claims firsthand knowledge of Auschwitz, Majdanek, or Treblinka, all of which he mentions in the poem. However, he explicitly contrasts his own map of nightmares with that of some dreamer for whom the nightmare would take place in some other location; some other dreamer would dream of being chased by a panther in the jungle. In labeling his own space on the map of nightmares with the name of a death camp, Sel'vinskii signals his belonging among murdered Jews.

The second part of the poem dramatically changes register from dream and memory to documentary detail, giving the precise date and place and specifying the division of the German army that surrendered. As I mentioned earlier, this section of the poem reflects Sel'vinskii's real-life experience as a Soviet officer. The poet identifies himself as one of "seven Soviet officers" who enter the base to accept the surrender. The nightmare of "Majdanek" and other scenes of the mass killing of Jews disrupt the victory at Kandava. As he walks in front of the ranks of Germans, the poet remembers his nightmare of the previous evening and recognizes the same look of contempt in the eyes of the defeated soldiers. A German captain in particular draws his attention, because he wears a little bronze badge on his sleeve depicting the most beloved places of the poet's youth in a now destroyed Crimea. One place stands out:

> And finally, gray with age,
> covered in ash, like Pompeii,
> spattered with blood and brains
> the height of all my torments—"Kerch'"!

> *I nakonets, ot drevnosti sedaia,*
> *zavalennaia peplom, kak Pompeia,*
> *zabryzgannaia krov'iu i mozgami*
> *vershina vsekh moikh muchenii—Kerch'*

>> (Sel'vinskii 1947, 215–16)

The mass killing at Kerch'—the subject of his poem "I Saw It"—which took place only three years earlier, is thrust back from the recent to the remote past; covered with ash like Pompeii, it impossibly belongs simultaneously to antiquity and to the immediate present. It is covered with ash but still gory with blood and brains. Kerch' happened in the ancient past, and it is still happening now; time doubles and repeats itself.

The poet tears the badge from the German officer's sleeve and thinks the captain must be dreaming his, the poet's, dream from the night before, the poet's dream of Auschwitz or Majdanek in which he and his wife were Jewish victims and the Germans were triumphant. The captain must be dreaming that one of his prisoners dared to assault him, "an S. S. officer, an Aryan."

But on the day of his own surrender the German does not respond to the Jew's act. He keeps quiet. The poem ends by describing what can be heard in that silence:

> And in that vivid silence
> I heard Red Army banners
> The blare of the trumpets and the din of drums,
> and the exultation of dead voices
> made of ash, poems, and dreams!
>
> *A v etom iarostnom molchan'i*
> *ia slyshal shum krasnoarmeiskikh stiagov,*
> *bravadu trub i grokhot barabanov,*
> *i likovan'e mertvykh golosov*
> *iz pepla, iz poem, iz snovidenii!*
>
> (217)

The last lines of the poem bring together the incommensurable elements of the interior space of the poet's nightmare, the voices of death camp inmates turned to ash, the triumphant sounds of victory, and poetry itself, without subordinating any one voice to another. It is important that the victory of the Soviet Army does not drown out the voices of the Jewish dead.

Far from making Jews disappear as soldiers or as Holocaust victims, as Amir Weiner contends, "Kandava" makes Jews vividly legible in both roles. The "memory of the Jewish catastrophe," to use Weiner's language, is *not* submerged in the grand narrative of the universality of Soviet suffering. The Jewish catastrophe escapes temporal boundaries in the poem "Kandava": it is ahistorically and impossibly part of the poet's childhood terror and is as ancient as the disaster at Pompeii; it disrupts the poet's triumph in the place called Kandava. The poem's embedded narratives of childhood terror, adult nightmare, mass Jewish death, and military victory suspend the linear, teleological motion toward a single message of Soviet triumph. The poetic use of mise en abyme—the placement of the image of the death camp both as the frame for and at the center of the narrative of victory at Kandava—makes it impossible to decide which narrative dominates. It is this undecidability that is so crucially a part of the distinctly Soviet but nonetheless universally impossible history of what Sel'vinskii does not call the Holocaust.

Cinema

Sel'vinskii translates the spectacle of what he *saw* at Kerch' in the sounds that he *hears* at Kandava. Seeing the bodies in the ditch makes him a witness who feels compelled to testify to the massacre. One of the earliest cinematic representations of the mass killings accomplishes something similar. Boris Gorbatov's *Nepokorennye* (The unvanquished), published in 1943 and the recipient of the Stalin Prize in 1946, includes a scene of the German roundup of Jews in a Ukrainian town. The hero, Taras, a Ukrainian metalworker, bows down before the Jewish Dr. Fishman, honoring him and his great suffering (Gorbatov 1987, 18). Semen Gekht's short story "Zhena podvodnika" (The submariner's wife), published in 1963, describes the deportation of the Jews from Kharkov, offering a far less idealized picture of Ukrainian-Jewish relations than Gorbatov.[26]

In 1945 a film version of Gorbatov's *Unvanquished* was released, directed by Mark Donskoi, with the renowned Yiddish actor Veniamin Zuskin playing the role of Dr. Fishman.[27] In contrast to the story, the film treatment gives the Jewish theme central importance by focusing on Zuskin's character. Dr. Fishman (Zuskin) opens the film; we see the impact of the arrival of the Germans in the town through his hesitation, fear, and utter isolation. In a later scene in the marketplace, he wears an armband with a Star of David. The action pauses as the viewer watches Taras bend over to inspect the armband. As the camera moves in, the Jewish star grows bigger and bigger. When the Germans come to the market with their dogs to hunt for Jews, Dr. Fishman again is the focus. The film, unlike the story, gives prominence to the mass killing of the town's Jews. The story merely mentions that "the Jews were shot somewhere outside of town." Dr. Fishman's last thoughts as he walks in the procession with the other Jews have only to do with Russia: "the damp Russian evening . . . the smell of the Russian earth . . . the Russian rooftops, the Russian rain were unbearably dear to him" (Gorbatov 1987, 34). The film replaces the Russian landscape with Jewish music that accompanies the scene of deportation. Where the story Russifies, the film Judaicizes. A line of soldiers moves through the crowd, systematically shooting as they walk, and then, as survivors struggle to get up, the soldiers use pistols to complete their terrible work. Images of the crowd alternate with close-ups of Zuskin's face. The cinematic metonymy transforms the anonymous victims into a crowd made up of Zuskins, made up of Jews. What is more, the film provides its viewers with the perspective of eyewitnesses to mass killings. The members of the audience, like Sel'vinskii, can say, "I saw it." According to Miron Chernenko, the film was the first in world cinema to directly depict the annihilation of Jews (2003, 168).

Aftermaths

In Sel'vinskii's trio of poems, the Jewish story of mass death and the Soviet victory story uneasily inhabit the same narrative space. In works by Der Nister and Perets Markish, in contrast, the integrity of narrative and self break down; as Markish put it in "The Bread of Affliction," "I understand as if on fire/The pain of wanting to see myself whole in the mirror" (1943a, 8–9). Der Nister's Yiddish story "Vidervuks" (Offshoots), published in New York in 1946 and in Moscow in 1969, focuses on the aftermath of the war.[28] One of the "offshoots" the story traces is the gap that grows between the Soviet and the Jewish experience. The work disrupts the stability of the Soviet Jew as the subject constituted by the narrative of Soviet victory. The story combines allegory, realism, dream, and fantasy in its account of the postwar experience of two assimilated Jews, Dr. Zemelman, a widower, whose only son died heroically in battle in the beginning of the war; and Mrs. Zayets, a teacher and widow, whose only daughter was also killed. Der Nister emphasizes that dying in battle and dying as a Jew were radically different.

The significance of this difference becomes particularly important to Dr. Zemelman. He learns what happened to his older brother, a professor, who lived in a border city. When the Germans ordered the Jews to leave, the brother was forced to carry his sick wife on a stretcher; both died en route. Dr. Zemelman starts to dream of the dead. He dreams that he has to carry the stretcher, and when he begins to pant from the unaccustomed exertion, his dead brother, "enraged," asks: "What made him out of breath? Was the Jewish yoke hard for him? Did he want to escape it?" (*Vos sopet er? Der yiddisher shpan iz im shver? Er vil zikh fun im oysshpanen?*) (Der Nister 1946, 46). This passage, which emphasizes the particularity of Jewish suffering and expresses Jewish rage, and Jewish reproach, was tellingly cut from the Soviet edition.

The bitter reproach of the dream hits home. A formerly silent and self-contained man, devoted to his work as a surgeon, the hero becomes emotionally involved with the fate of the Jews, the "community" (*klal*) and "collectivity" (*kibuts*) from which he had been previously so distanced "that he did not know who he was or where he came from." He develops a "sense" (*khush*) of the community and is troubled not only by "the unheard of number of victims" but also by "the taint of their deaths, as if the source of their life had been besmirched" (45).

By the end of the story, Dr. Zemelman adopts a son in memory of his dead child, and has convinced his neighbor to do the same. He decides to fulfill the biblical commandment to be fruitful and multiply by marrying Mrs. Zayets. The meaning of the story's title is to be found both in the rebirth of the hero's family and in the renewal of his Jewish consciousness. There is more to the story, however, than the mere summary of its plot can convey. The story of rebuilding and new growth has a dark and fantastical lining. Dr. Zemelman's dreams, memories, and fantasies, and fragments of biblical stories and Jewish legends, crowd out the realistic moments of the narrative. He dreams of Hitler,

Moses, Abraham, and Sarah and finds it difficult to free himself "from his dreams and night-visits, which even began to border almost on illness" (*khaloymes un nakht-bazukhn, velkhe hobn zikh shoyn afile bay im ongehoybn grenetsn kimat mit krenklekhkayt*) (46). In the beginning of the story, Dr. Zemelman, the devoted Soviet doctor, a man of science, resembles German's Dr. Levinson; but unlike Dr. Levinson, who remains unchanged by his confrontation with Nazism, Dr. Zemelman becomes unhinged. He begins to live in a Jewish dreamworld.

Der Nister's use of a fantastical style is particularly striking when it comes to the narration of well-known Nazi atrocities. The description of a mass killing site is a case in point. The place is far away from human habitation; it is well known and often described; one can still find there "remnants of clothing . . . woman's hair, a hat, a lone sleeve from a man's or woman's shirt" (46). Dr. Zemelman does not visit this place like Osip in Erenburg's *Storm*; he only imagines it, and never by day but only at dusk or dawn. And another fantasy accompanies his image of this site: a couple, dressed in clothing from the East, approach the place, remove their shoes, and stare at the "now silent and poorly buried bones." It seems to Dr. Zemelman that this couple must be Abraham and Sarah. It is possible, the narrator says, that Dr. Zemelman's image of the couple came from a childhood memory of the religious observance of a day of mourning for the "*khurbn*." The term refers to the destruction of the first and second Temples, and the day of mourning presumably is the Ninth of Av, although it is not specified in the text. According to legend, the narrator continues, God himself would summon Abraham and Sarah to help him "weep over the destruction of his and their children" (*veynen afn brokh fun zayne un zeyere kinder*) (46–47). The use of the term *khurbn* clearly links the events of the war to a specifically Jewish religious narrative.

Unlike Erenburg's treatment of Babi Yar, which hastens to affirm the victory of life in general and the victory of Soviet life in particular, Der Nister's account suspends realist narration and opens up the time frame to the cyclical and ever-recurring chronotope of legend. There is no victory. God himself weeps. The story never reconciles the gap between the realist plot of postwar rebuilding and the haunted fantasies of the surviving Jews; the conflicting motifs jar against one another without resolution. The waking nightmares interrupt the forward motion of the narrative toward its seemingly happy ending of *"vidervuks,"* in the sense of "renewal."

For Perets Markish as for Der Nister the end of the war brought no closure but only intensified the split between the Jewish tragedy and the mainstream Soviet narrative of victory. In Moscow in 1948 Perets Markish published a monumental two-volume narrative poem titled *Milkhome* (War); the title, significantly, dispenses with the usual Soviet formulation, the "Great Patriotic War."[29] Nakhman Mayzel called this the "greatest Yiddish literary work" about the war and said that it provides a "superb rebuff" to those who claim that Soviet Yiddish literature is empty of Jewish content and cut off from Jewish tradition (Mayzel 1956). The gallery of heroes in *War* includes Jews and non-Jews; its panoramic scope covers Stalingrad, Moscow, Ukraine, and Berlin. But for all its range, the poem emphasizes one theme above all else: the agony of the Jewish tragedy. As in Der Nister's *Aftermaths*, in *Milkhome*, Markish the Soviet confronts Markish the Jew. Markish concludes the work by asking whether the Soviet victory over Germany will also mean a revival of Jewish life and culture: "Will the thousand-year old Jewish melody / Awaken from the dead stillness of Berlin?" (Markish 1956, 2:604). In "The Trial at Krasnodar" Sel'vinskii accuses Christians of misplaced compassion; in *War* Markish accuses Christ. If Jesus went to the ghettoes, he would encounter "countless Jewish children / who are holier and purer than you, Nazarene" (1:113).

The roles of Soviet and Jew that overlapped in Markish's poem of 1943, "To a Jewish Soldier" (Dem yidishn shlakhtman), split apart in this work. In "To a Jewish Soldier," the poet promises the soldier that his people will include him as a link in the "golden chain" of Jewish memory and that his country, which gave him his rifle, will award him a gold star. The opening lines read: "I know: you kissed your rifle on the day / That your people's life hung in the balance" (Markish 1943a, 3). In contrast, in *Milkhome*, the Soviet rifle failed to save the Jewish people. One chapter in particular—"Geshprekh mitn shotn" (Conversation with a ghost)—stands out. Mayzel compares its artistry and vision to that of Bialik's writings. The protagonist is a Jewish Red Army soldier with the Hebrew name "Gur Arye" (which means "young lion"); he is symbolically associated with the image of Israel in the Bible. Having miraculously survived Babi Yar, he ends up in a deserted synagogue.

The inscriptions on the synagogue walls scream at the hero, and the shades of the dead press in on him, demanding that he speak and recognize his place among them:

> The screaming silence crushed him,
> Day and night became confused;
> The shadows from the walls besieged him—speak!
> Don't you recognize your hand in the engravings?
> Don't you know your own blood, abandoned, that flows together with
>   your mother's tears?
> You carry a rifle in your hand now
> And on your cap a star.

> *Es hot di shrayendike shtilkayt im geplet,*
> *Der tog hot mit der nakht genumen zikh farplonten;*
> *Balagert hobn im fun vent di shotns:—Red!*
> *Host in di oyfshriftn dayn hant do nit derkont den?*
> *Tsi host den nit derkont dayn hefker-blut, vos flist*
> *In zey ineynem mit dayn mames trern?*
> *Du trogst atsind in hant a biks*
> *Un af dayn hut a roytn shtern.*
>
> (Markish 1956, 2:535)

The Jewish Red Army soldier impossibly occupies two places at once; he is at once alive and dead, joined to his murdered people, his blood mingled with theirs. The blood no longer flows in people but instead in the inscriptions on the walls and in the writing of the Jews, in which the poet Perets Markish has also had a hand.

Unlike Sel'vinskii's poem "Kandava," the tension between the hero's two selves, the Red Army soldier and the murdered Jew, cannot be reconciled:

> Weren't you ashamed of your Red Army rifle?
> Did your five-pointed star dedicate itself to revenge?
>   . . .
> Did your luck in battle, soldier, comfort you
> For our shame, for our misfortune?
>   . . .

Did you accomplish anything with your rifle?
Did you gain anything with your star?
Do you know how big a sea of blood
Would suffice for the wild animal world?

Tsi hostu nit farshemt dayn roytarmeyerishe biks?
Tsi zikh geheylikt in nekome hot dayn finf-ekediker shtern?
   . . .
Tsi hot in shlakht dos mazl dikh getreyst, soldat,
Far undzer shand, far undzer umglik?
   . . .
Tsi hostu epes vos gepoyelt mit der biks?
Tsi hostu epes vos dervorbn mitn shtern?
Tsi veystu nit af vifl ot der yam mit blut
Vet far der velt der khaye-reyediker klekn?

(2:535–36)

The poem expresses the insurmountable gap between the Soviet socialist triumph over fascism and the overwhelming destruction suffered by the Jewish community. In this poem, the tokens of Soviet power—the rifle and the red star—are objects of contempt.

The powerful expression of the extraordinary nature of Jewish pain, brought by the war and the world's indifference, coexists, however, with the recognition of other suffering. It is not only the voices of Jews that call out to Gur Arye in the synagogue; the poem also quotes the voices of prisoners of war and partisans in the woods, "tormented to death, with their last cries of 'Stalin.'" The poem asks a question about the measure of suffering:

Is there a line painted somewhere
In the highest, purifying suffering,
Between an old man killed in the synagogue
And the prisoner burned on a piece of wood?

Iz ergets den gemolt a gevul,
In hekhster leyd un vey gelaytert,
Tsvishn dem zakeyn farpayniktn in shul
Un dem gefangenem farbrentn af a shayter?

(2:537)

Milkhome makes a clear statement about the unique suffering of the Jews, and yet it also raises a question about the experience of suffering itself, and whether it is possible to distinguish one kind of suffering from another. Markish is searching for a way to talk about the universality of suffering without diminishing any particular suffering. To frame the discussion about Soviet responses to the Holocaust solely in terms of universality versus uniqueness is to neglect the more subtle approach that writers such as Markish explored. Where, indeed, is the boundary between pain and pain?

In Markish's *Milkhome* it is not merely the Soviet and the Jew that split apart, but the unity and stability of self, voice, and language. In *War* the hero no longer recognizes himself, and language itself is fractured: "the letters have ruptured from screaming" (*gebrokhn hobn zikh di oysyes fun shrayen*) (2:533). The poet no longer speaks in his own voice but instead bears the traces of the dead voices in his own body: the inscriptions on the walls engrave themselves on him "with fire and pain." The experience of the survivor, writes Derrida, "consists in carrying the other in the self, as one bears mourning—and melancholy" (Derrida 2005, 159). In *War*, reading the inscriptions on the synagogue walls means suffering a terrible branding, as if experiencing the fate of Kafka's hero of "In the Penal Colony" many times over. Sel'vinkskii's "I Saw It" also conveys this sense of bearing another's pain. Markish's language, in contrast to Sel'vinskii's, has the effect of a direct assault on the reader, as if his own poetic "inscription" carries the same fire and pain as those left on the walls of the destroyed synagogue. The poem implicates the reader in the burden of survival.

Grossman: A Space for Mourning

Carrying the other in the self is the burden of the survivor, as Markish and Sel'vinskii attest. In Russian prose no writer bears this burden as fully or as powerfully as Vasilii Grossman. Grossman did not have the Jewish background of a writer like Perets Markish or Der Nister; whether he understood Yiddish is a matter of debate. The Jewish textual tradition, including the Bible, the prophets, and other works, does not appear in his writings as a poetic source—with two notable exceptions. Shimon Markish, Perets Markish's son, discusses one such instance in his essay on Grossman (1985, 391). Markish points out that the cadences of Grossman's "Ukraine Without Jews," particularly in the repetition of the phrase "cruelly killed" (*zlodeiski ubit*), call to mind Jeremiah, the Book of Job, and the Jewish prayer book. There is another exception, which Markish does not discuss, found in Grossman's essay "The Murder of Jews in Berdichev," which was written for *The Black Book*: "Dread hung over the city. Dread entered every house, it stood over the heads of the sleeping, it rose with the sun, it walked the streets by night . . . Dreadful were the dark cloudy nights, and the nights lit by a full moon, dreadful was the early morning, and the bright noon, and the quiet evening in the town" (Grossman 1993, 27). The passage resembles the curses in Deuteronomy: "your life shall hang in doubt before you; night and day you shall be in dread, and have no assurance of your life" (Deut. 28:66). The Deuteronomy passage is read in the synagogue during the time leading up to the new year, which occurs in the fall. In his essay, Grossman notes that the German "action," which began with the roundup of the Jews, started on August 28. The timing of the action and the time when the passage would have been heard in the weekly service in the synagogue are similar.

These examples of textual parallels from the Bible do not typify Grossman's writing generally. The differences between his work and that of a Markish or a Der Nister still obtain when it comes to Jewish intertextuality. Nonetheless, the sense of insurmountable loss in his work corresponds to what the Yiddish writers evoked in their poetry and prose. The emotion is similar, but Grossman has to be read in his own terms, and that requires looking beyond his socialist realist style in *For a Just Cause* and, some would say, even in *Life and Fate*.[30] Eric Santner is helpful in making some distinctions among shades of realism. Santner defines "narrative fetishism" as the "construction of a narrative designed to expunge the traces of the trauma or loss that called the narrative into being in the first place" (Santner 1992). Erenburg's depiction of Babi Yar in *The Storm* is an example. Santner, LaCapra, and Hayden White, among others, have criticized conventional storytelling, in particular realism, for its tendency to provide restoration and premature closure to the narration of traumatic events (LaCapra 1999, 12–17). The literature of mobilization, as in the example of Fefer's "The Oath" (Di shvue), improves reality by immediately and automatically transforming injury into a new and better capacity for warfare. The poetics Grossman employs, in contrast, allow the traces of loss and destruction to remain legible in the text. In *For a Just Cause* the representation of the hero's loss breaks open the closed structure of socialist realist narrative. In *Life and Fate* the use of the address to the reader has a similar effect.

During the war, Grossman served on the frontline as a correspondent; his articles for *Red Star* achieved extraordinary popularity (S. Markish 1985, 376). He was the author of "The Hell of Treblinka," one of the earliest accounts of a death camp to be published in any language, and "Ukraine Without Jews," which first appeared in the Yiddish newspaper *Eynikayt* in 1943 and was back-translated into Russian in 1985 (Grossman 1985d). As is so often the case, Grossman's stature in the Soviet Union during the war and his stature in the West after the war come from different works. His reputation in the West is associated with *Zhizn' i sud'ba* (Life and fate), a profoundly oppositionalist novel that argued for the similarity between Hitler's destruction of Jews and Stalin's murderous collectivization campaigns. In comparison to *Life and Fate*, which has garnered great critical acclaim, critics have dismissed *For a Just Cause* for its conformism. Shimon Markish and E. Etkind contend that "the author of *Life and Fate* has almost nothing in common with the Vasilii Grossman who wrote *For a Just Cause*" (Grossman 1980, 11). A closer look, however, suggests otherwise.[31]

Written during the years 1943–46 and published in 1952 and 1959, *For a Just Cause* was one of the most widely read novels of the war. It went through significant revisions, however, before it was published. One of the obstacles to its publication was that it had too many Jewish characters, including the Jewish physicist Viktor Shtrum.[32] In *Life and Fate* Viktor "thought about what he never thought about before and what the Fascists made him think about—his Jewishness, the fact that his mother was a Jew" (Grossman 1980, 40). This revelation should not be taken at face value as the expression of the author, Grossman, who had thought about Jewishness before the war. In 1934, for example, Grossman published a story "V gorode Berdicheva" (In the city of

Berdichev) about a pregnant commissar billeted with a Jewish family during the civil war. The story includes a scene at the end in which the hero explicitly thinks about Jews: he reflects on the difference between the Bundists' attitude toward political struggle and his own passivity. The story was reprinted as a separate edition in 1947 and later became the basis for Aleksandr Askol'dov's film of the late 1960s, *Commissar*. Viktor Shtrum's attitude, again not necessarily shared by his creator, was nonetheless typical of the early years of the war.

The argument has been made that Jewish self-consciousness that is only a product of Hitler is not an authentic or sufficient form of Jewishness. To put it in a word, Shtrum, his creator, and others like him, on this account, are not Jewish enough.[33] The Soviet objections that there was too much Jewishness in Grossman's wartime fiction and the later objection that there is too little Jewishness are strangely symmetrical. Instead of retracing the steps of this discussion about the overabundance or insufficiency of Jewish identity markers, I am interested in what follows artistically and philosophically from the sudden and terrible forced reminder that "I am a Jew." In Grossman's case, the results were extraordinary; in Erenburg's and Fefer's artistic work, less so. *For a Just Cause* has a direct connection not only with Grossman's widely acclaimed *Life and Fate* but also with key works of Soviet Yiddish literature published in the 1940s and beyond. Grossman, like the Yiddish writers, creates a symbolic space for confronting loss.

In *For a Just Cause* the description of the hero's relationship with his mother opens up an alternative space for mourning the destruction of the Jews within the confines of a conventional socialist realist narrative of the war. The juxtaposition of the conventional and alternative narrative emerges clearly in the episode of Stalin's first radio speech of July 1941. In Grossman's novel, Viktor in Moscow gets up in the morning and hears Stalin naming the war "the all-national Patriotic War" (*On nazval etu voinu vsenarodnoi Otechestvennoi voinoi*) (1956, 152).[34] This was Stalin's first public address of the war, but his words have little effect on Shtrum, who is more concerned with the fate of his mother, left behind in German-occupied territory. The night before, Viktor had an uncanny dream:

> he dreamed that he entered a room, full of pillows and sheets that had been thrown on the floor, and he went over to the armchair, which, it

seemed, preserved the warmth from the person who had just sat in it. The room was empty; apparently, the inhabitants left it suddenly in the middle of the night. For a long time he stared at a shawl hanging from the chair, and suddenly understood that his mother slept in that chair. It now stood empty in an empty room. (152)

This is an empty room crowded with the traces of a person who has just departed it, and crowded also with the emotions of the one who arrived too late for the longed-for meeting. Violence is muffled and indirect, conveyed through the bedclothes left on the floor. Violence is something not to be seen or heard but whose effects and consequences are decoded afterwards. The passage does not attempt an eyewitness account of the Jews' deportation; the word "Jew" does not appear at all. Grossman's emphasis is instead on belatedness: arriving too late, the hero senses the palpable presence of the absent person. This narrative technique recalls Bergelson's use of a similar effect in works of the 1920s, such as "Civil War." The theme of belatedness is a key feature of traumatic narrative; it also appears in Bergelson's works addressing the German murder of the Jews.

The scene of the radio speech in Grossman contrasts powerfully with similar scenes from Konstantin Simonov's classic war novel *The Living and the Dead*. The outbreak of the war and the opening pages of the novel find the hero, Sintsov, a correspondent, and his wife separated from their one-year-old daughter, left behind with her grandmother in what has suddenly become German-occupied territory. Except for one brief scene in the opening, and one reference later in the novel, the daughter subsequently disappears from the text, as if she never existed. The plot focuses not on the recovery of the child but instead on the recover of Sintsov's party card and other personal documents, which he loses in the first days of fighting with the Germans. *The Living and the Dead* explicitly encourages readers to "erase" the traces of negative experiences. One of the characters (Serpilin) spent time in the camps, and the ordeal made his wife's hair turn gray prematurely. He was released to join the army, and his wife dyed her hair back to its original color. He says that he "erased that time," and she describes her own gesture in the same terms (Simonov 1960, 410).

The engine driving the mechanism of forgetting and erasure is none other than Stalin himself. Every major war novel describes Stalin's first radio address following the entrance of the Germans onto Russian soil, but in *The Living and the Dead* the scene links Stalin's voice with the destruction of personal memory. Lying in a hospital bed, Sintsov remembers a soldier who was killed, and dwells on other painful memories, including a disagreement he had with his editor, but

> In a few hours an event took place that for a long time replaced all other thoughts and feelings in Sintsov's mind.
>   He heard Stalin's speech on the radio.
>   . . .
>   Usually people ask themselves such questions when they are young, but Sintsov asked himself the question for the first time at the age of thirty in his hospital bed: "Would I give my life for Stalin, if someone just came up to me and said, 'Die, so that he would live!' Yes, I would, and today more than ever!" (70)

It is not merely that Stalin's speech thrusts the hero's own thoughts into the background, crowding out other emotions. Stalin's speech destroys the hero's awareness of himself. He is suddenly overwhelmed by the desire to die for Stalin's sake. Grossman's hero hears the same words but is overwhelmed by his haunting dream of his mother's disappearance.

For a Just Cause is not a dissident, anti-Soviet novel; on the contrary, "large parts" of it, as Alice Nakhimovsky has shown, are "standard socialist realism" (Nakhimovsky 1992, 126). Praise for the new socialist order can be found in such passages as: "The new Soviet Russia leapt forward a century, leapt with all its enormous weight, with its trillions of tons of earth, with its forests, it changed what seemed for centuries unchangeable, its agriculture, its roads, and the flow of its rivers . . . Destroyed and dispersed by the revolution, enormous numbers of people, whole social strata, the backbone of the exploitative class, disappeared" (Grossman 1956, 47). Unlike its banned sequel, *For a Just Cause* does not draw a parallel between Stalin's collectivization and terror and Hitler's annihilation of the Jews. *For a Just Cause* does not focus on the Nazi war against the Jews in particular, although the opening pages make it clear that this was Hitler's goal. Hitler says, "Jewish laughter will be silenced forever" (Grossman 1956, 7–8). The language used to characterize the German war relies on the universalist truisms of Soviet-speak: the "occupiers intended to establish on Soviet soil the unimaginable, senseless pre-revolutionary order" (201); "the fascists decided to destroy Soviet unity with racial division" (210). A more concrete description of specifically anti-Jewish violence can be found not only in Grossman's own earlier story "The Old Teacher" (1943) but also in other Russian-language works, including Erenburg's *Storm* and Alexei Nedogonov's 1945 poem "Kogda uchenik v 'messershmitte'" (When the student pilot in the Messerschmitt), which describes at least the initial phases of the German persecution of Jews in the couplet "We put stars on Christmas trees/They put them on Jewish backs" (*my stavili zvezdy na elke—/oni na evresikoi spine*) (Nedogonov 1977, 184). Where readers might expect to find mention of Jews in Grossman's *For a Just Cause*— for example, in descriptions of refugees fleeing west—there are none. Simonov, in contrast, in *Zhivye i mertvye* (The living and the dead), includes a Jewish photojournalist, killed in the early days of the fighting, and also describes the countless Jewish refugees from the shtetls of western Belorussia, including old men with beards and side locks, and fashionably dressed young women (Simonov 1960, 27). The lack of explicit reference to Jews in *For a Just Cause is* due in large part to the conditions of censorship in 1952, the year that most of the members of the Jewish Anti-Fascist Committee were murdered (S. Markish 1985).

If, however, we read the novel only from the perspective of its reliance on the approved Soviet ideology of fascist racism, we miss Grossman's construction of an alternate space of unresolved mourning, and we fail to experience the vivid, wrenching emotions of loss. Viktor Shtrum is the center of these emotions. Grossman fought long and hard to keep Shtrum in the novel. In a diary he kept of the battle to publish *For a Just Cause*—from August 1949 to the end of 1951—he records a conversation with Aleksandr Tvardovskii, the editor of *Novyi mir* (New world), in which Tvardovskii tells him to remove all the Shtrum chapters or else the novel would not be printed. Grossman refused to comply with the ultimatum. At a meeting held in 1950, one of the editors of the journal expressed his unease with Shtrum and said that he had "no right to be different from other Soviet characters in Soviet society." This criticism of Shtrum offers an invitation and a justification to read him as attentively as possible. The alternate reading that I am suggesting focuses on the problem of mourning. In a diary entry for August 1949, the same time that the publication battle for his novel began, Grossman has a significant note about mourning. He had been reading the classics, and quotes a line attributed to Pericles, which I translate from the Russian, "Because of me, none of the Athenians has experienced the relief of mourning" (Grossman n.d.). In his funeral oration, quoted in Thucydides' *Peloponnesian War*, Pericles admonishes the Athenians not to mourn. It is fair to assume that Grossman was reflecting on the parallel between injunctions against mourning in his own time and in ancient Athens.

Grossman, however, wants his readers to mourn the killings of Jews, and he structures the problem of mourning in *For a Just Cause* around Shtrum's mother. As Alice Nakhimovsky writes, Viktor's mother, and her letters to him, constitute "the core fact of his spiritual life" (1992, 128). Shtrum's reading of his mother's last letter, a chronicle of her forced move to the ghetto and the last days of the Jews there, offers a model for reading the novel as a whole.

Grossman organized both *For a Just Cause* and *Life and Fate* with *War and Peace* as his model, just as Erenburg did with *The Storm*. At the center of both of Grossman's works is the family of Alexandra Shaposhnikova, her daughters, Zhenia, Marusa, Liudmila, and their husbands, lovers, and children, and friends of the family, including, for example, the "old Bolshevik" Mostovskoi, the Jewish doctor Sof'ia Osipovna Levinton, and a young woman, Tamara Berezkina, who loses contact with her husband during the first days of the war. The letters from Shtrum's mother, however, disrupt the stability and continuity characteristic of the great family chronicles of nineteenth-century realism and twentieth-century socialist realism. Linear time and forward motion break down as Viktor reads and rereads his mother's last letter. The readings themselves erupt as a kind of episodic symptom that coexists with the normal flow of life.

Before the war, Anna Semenovna, Shtrum's mother, "lived in a green, quiet little town in Ukraine." She was supposed to join Shtrum's family at their dacha outside Moscow, but the outbreak of war makes the trip impossible. The last letters Shtrum has from her are dated March and June 1941. The June letter, colorless and bland, expresses her fears and her resolve to bear what will happen to everyone. The March letter, however, seems prophetic. It was unseasonably warm, and the storks arrived early. When the weather suddenly turned cold, they gathered together for the night in a park on the outskirts of the town. A snowstorm began at night, and tens of storks perished, "many, half-dead, driven mad, hardly able to stand, went out to the road apparently seeking help from people" (Grossman 1956, 148). The dead bodies of the birds line the road. It is hard to imagine that this little episode is anything other than an allegory for the killing actions carried out by the Germans in the occupied territory. Grossman is clearly linking the German invasion with the disappearance and deaths of multitudes of Jews, although he does not say so directly.

A hundred pages go by without any significant mention of Shtrum's mother until Viktor receives a letter, which looks "as if it had lain in a basement for two years" (245). Already undressed for bed, he begins reading:

> He recognized his mother's handwriting, threw off the blanket, and began to get dressed, as if a calm, collected voice had summoned him from the darkness.
>
> Shtrum sat at the table and leafed through the letter—this was a set of notes that Anna Semenovna had kept from the first days of the war until the day of the inevitable destruction that had been hanging over her from beyond the barbed wire of the Jewish ghetto, built by the Hitlerites. This was her farewell to her son . . .
>
> He lost all sense of time. He did not even ask himself how the notebook ended up in Stalingrad, from across the front. (259)

In the morning Viktor looks in the mirror expecting to find his face altered by the reading of the letter, but his face appears the same. The text of the letter does not appear in *For a Just Cause* but only in its suppressed sequel, *Life and Fate*. Shimon Markish suggests that the censors deleted it from the first novel because of its emphasis on Jews.

I will quote just one passage from this extraordinary letter:

> They say that children are our future, but what can you say about these children? They will never be musicians, shoemakers, cutters. And this evening I clearly saw that this whole noisy world of bearded, worried fathers, grandmothers who mutter as they prepare honey cakes and

goose necks, this world of wedding customs, sayings, Sabbath holidays will disappear forever into the earth, and after the war, life will once again make itself heard, but we won't be there, we will have vanished, like the Aztecs. (Grossman 1980, 53)

The absence of the letter and of Viktor's immediate reaction to it, however, does not diminish its importance to the text of *For a Just Cause*. Grossman is not simply "erasing" suffering, as Simonov's husband and wife "erase" the years spent in the Gulag. The missing letter as it appears in *Life and Fate* is not a fictionalized account of a German killing action, but more a diary of Anna Semenovna's growing attachment to her fellow Jews. Whether the gap in *For a Just Cause* is the censor's doing or Grossman's, the author made no effort to mitigate its effects on the narrative, to smooth over the rough edges of the missing text. The blank is left a blank.[35] The blank space only underscores the problem of addressing catastrophic loss.

Several hundred pages later, the narrative returns to the scene of Viktor's reading the letter, using language that draws attention to the emotion of his response:

When he reread his mother's last letter, when between the calm, restrained lines of this letter he guessed the horror of the helpless people doomed to destruction, driven beyond the barbed wire of the ghetto, when his imagination filled in the picture of the last minutes of Anna Semenovna's life on the day of the mass killing, about which she had guessed from the stories told by people from the surrounding shtetls, who miraculously survived, when with pitiless stubbornness he forced himself to measure the suffering of his mother, standing in the crowd of women and children in front of the barrels of the SS automatics, an overwhelmingly powerful feeling gripped him. But it was impossible to change what happened and what death had forever sealed off from him. (Grossman 1956, 479)

In *The Bones of Berdichev*, John and Carol Garrard remark that Grossman "found it impossible to portray [his mother's] terrible death directly even in fictionalized form" and that as a consequence, "Anna Shtrum's own letter in *Life and Fate* breaks off before the death march" (Garrard and Garrard 1996, 251). In contrast to *Life and Fate*, the passage above from *For a Just Cause* contains what the hero forces himself to imagine as his mother's last moments. The stress, however, is what the reader of the letter imagines and, moreover, what he forces himself to imagine: there is no direct account as if from an eyewitness. Grossman had access to testimony about the mass killings yet here decides to avoid even the fiction of an eyewitness account. The question is, what is the effect of the artistic choices Grossman made? Grossman structures what could have been a fictitious first-person account into an act of imaginative reading that makes a maximum demand on the reader. Shtrum "fills in" the gaps that his mother's letter necessarily leaves; he is merciless toward himself as he imagines what her last moments were like. Grossman departs from a realist and socialist realist aesthetic in his depiction of Jewish deaths. Instead of filling in the gaps in his text, he marks the missing places. The consequences of Grossman's artistic choices are clear. Literature that attempts to represent mass killings must make the greatest possible demand on readers, implicated as bystanders and survivors. *For a Just Cause* makes such a demand. The letter, which must be reread and decoded, its gaps filled in, serves as a model of a particular type of text, different from other texts and messages in the same work. The letter strikingly contrasts the simplicity, transparency, and optimistic teleology of standard wartime socialist realism, as in the passage from *For a Just Cause* that I quoted earlier: "the anger, pain, suffering of the people was transformed into steel, explosives, and armor, into the barrels of firearms." The intensity of Viktor's belated emotion cannot undo what has happened.

Grossman focuses on Viktor's emotional relation to the letter as a material object:

> Several times a day he patted his chest in the place where the letter lay in the side pocket of his jacket. Once, when he was seized by an attack of unbearable spiritual pain, he thought: "if I hid it farther away, I would gradually calm down, it is like an open, uncovered grave in my life."
>
> But he knew that he would rather destroy himself than part with the letter that had reached him by a miracle. (Grossman 1956, 479)

The comparison between the letter and an "open grave," the earlier description of the letter's "torturous path" to him (to use Nakhimovsky's language), and the truncated contents of the letter open up an alternate space of mourning in what is otherwise a socialist realist war novel. Der Nister's Heshl Ansheles, as we saw in Chapter Three, uses his mouth not for speech but for an act of violence that mimics his own traumatic injury, the act of being forced to carry the German soldier's suitcase with his teeth. Viktor Shtrum, unlike Heshl, carries on his daily life as before; Heshl has a permanently open mouth, and Viktor, a permanently open grave. Unlike Erenburg's novel *The Storm*, in *For a Just Cause* the victory of love does not obscure loss. Instead, the traces of loss persist both in the representation of the hero and in the broken surface of the text.

Anxiety about his mother's "fate" (the word the author himself used) runs like a red thread through the letters Grossman wrote to his father in 1941 and 1942 while serving as a frontline correspondent. On September 9, 1941, for example, he writes that he is healthy, feels good, and is in a good mood but "worries day and night" about his mother and her niece (Grossman n.d.). A letter of September 14, 1941, expresses his urgent wish to know whether there is any information about them. On March 20, 1942, he reports that he dreamed of his mother "all night and saw her, as if she were alive." What he saw in the territories liberated from the Germans led him to believe, however, that she could not be. "The desire to exchange my pen for a rifle grows all the stronger in me" (Grossman). Dreaming of the dead, as Der Nister observes, comes as no surprise in the aftermath of the German occupation. An undated letter, possibly from 1944, describes the uncanny experience of visiting his former apartment and learning from a neighbor that Vasilii Semenovich "died last winter from tuberculosis." The neighbor may have been referring to a relative of Grossman's father, but the name and patronymic are the author's own. Grossman writes in this same letter, "People say that the entire Jewish population of Berdichev was killed, that the city is destroyed and empty" (Grossman). In this bizarre moment, his own death and the deaths of the Jews of Berdichev, including his mother, merge together. Grossman remarks on his own emotional state at the end of the letter: "It's very hard for me" (*na dushe u menia ochen' tiazhelo*).[36]

The epistolary relationship with his mother continued in the postwar years but with a major shift. On the anniversary of the killings in

Berdichev, on September 15, 1950, and September 15, 1961, Grossman wrote to her "as if she were alive" (Garrard and Garrard 1996, 352). In the first letter Grossman writes:

> I learned about your death in the winter of 1944 . . . But as early as September 1941 I felt in my heart that you were gone. I had a dream one night at the front. I entered a room, knowing that it was your room, and saw an empty armchair: I knew at once that you had slept in the chair.[37]

He uses this dream in *For a Just Cause* in the scene of Stalin's radio speech, as I have already discussed. In the second letter, Grossman reflects on his own state ten years earlier: "Ten years ago, when I wrote you my first letter after your death, you remained just the same as then you were alive, my mother in my body and in my soul."[38] This extraordinary language expresses the anguish of melancholic mourning: the son refuses to let the mother depart, taking her into his own body. The real-life letter of a son to his dead mother and the fictitious letter of a dead mother to her son mirror each other. In *For a Just Cause* the letter is both a text to be read and a thing that is hidden, lost, and found, as in the narrator's exaggerated emphasis on the letter's journey, the episode of its concealment, its place near Viktor's body, and his compulsion to touch the place on his own body near where the letter is hidden in his pocket. Irrevocably "sealed off" from her by her death, Viktor nonetheless bears his mother's death in himself, even though he appears both to himself, to other characters in the novel, and to some of its readers as unchanged by the event. In writing the episode of the letter, Grossman, like Markish and Sel'vinskii, expresses the experience of the survivor, "carrying the other in the self, as one bears mourning—and melancholy" (Derrida 2005, 159). Grossman's heavily censored socialist realist novel carries another poetics of loss inside itself, just as Viktor Shtrum carries the letter from his dead mother in his jacket pocket.

The novel's sequel, *Life and Fate*, continues the saga of the Shaposhnikova family and the circles of characters around them. Again, *War and Peace* continued to serve as the model. There are, however, differences between the two Grossman works and their model. In *For a Just Cause* Viktor is haunted by the letter from his mother. In the next novel the integrity of the realist subject undergoes further pressure, spreading to other characters. Grossman talks about the "shadow" (*ten'*) that haunts not only Viktor but his wife, Liudmila, whose son Tolia was killed; and the shadows that haunt her nephew, whose parents were in the Gulag (Grossman 1980, 471). The camp, a new form of human association not imagined in Grossman's model *War and Peace*, dominates *Life and Fate*.[39] "Camps," writes Grossman in the opening pages of the novel, "were becoming the cities of a new Europe" (3). The novel begins with a scene in a German camp and closes with a scene in a Russian one. Viktor Shtrum, comparing the German murder of the Jews with Stalin's collectivization policies, identifies a new, terrible stage of what he calls "egoism" in humanity—"zoological, class, racial, governmental, and personal egoism"—and predicts that humanity will transform "the entire world into a galactic concentration camp" (478).

The emphasis on the camp and the new type of human being that makes the camp and is made there shatters the conventions of realist narrative in *Life and Fate*. Grossman imagines a new literary subject whose action is stamped by the new reality of mass death. What this new reality meant, how it could be addressed and described, preoccupied Grossman throughout the war years but took on particular urgency with regard to the *Black Book*. Grossman and Erenburg and other members of the editorial committee of the *Black Book* discussed what kinds of materials to include in the work and, what is more, how to make it readable. Erenburg insisted on the criterion of emotional impact. Grossman felt that too much emphasis was being placed on accounts by the few who miraculously survived. He argued that the task of the book was "to speak in the name of those who lie in the earth and cannot say anything." The uplifting message of survival was not as important as the fact of irrevocable loss and the challenge of speaking in its shadow. On another occasion, Grossman formulated the problem differently. He said that the book should be a memorial (*pamiatnik*) to the dead. Mikhoels disagreed, arguing that the book not only was for the dead but had to serve the living by prompting them to action (*eta kniga dolzhna sluzhit' dlia aktivnykh deistvii*). All of these concerns enter Grossman's description of a Nazi death camp in *Life and Fate*. Grossman struggles with the problems inherent in the task of creating a verbal memorial that speaks *to* the living reader while avoiding speaking *for* the dead.

The problems of testimony, memorial, and fiction in the face of mass death preoccupied Grossman not only in the *Black Book* but also in *Life and Fate*. One of the most important discussions of these questions is found in Hannah Arendt's *The Origins of Totalitarianism*. It is helpful to back up a step and begin with her description of the failure of witnessing in the camps. She describes the forms of legal, political, and social death that paved the way for the actual killings. It is not merely that the ideal community of witnesses is already dead; it is also that they suffered a form of political death before they died. Arendt's language is important: "The insane mass manufacture of corpses is preceded by the historically and politically intelligible manufacture of living corpses" (1973, 447). This process includes first the destruction of the juridical person, second, the destruction of the moral person ("grief and remembrance are forbidden"), and third, the killing of the individual as an individual. All of this takes place before the person is physically destroyed. Grossman himself (before Arendt) in "The Hell of Treblinka" paints a similar picture, emphasizing the deprivation of the personal archive (letters, photographs, and official documents) as a preliminary stage to death. Grossman's novelistic style provides a vivid image of this moment: "the documents flew to the ground, no longer needed by anyone on earth, the documents of living corpses" (*a dokumenty leteli na zemliu, uzhe nikomu ne nuzhnye na svete, dokumenty zhivykh mertvetsov*) (Grossman 1985c, 162).

Arendt dwells at length on the murder of the moral person, which she defines as a problem of isolation and inability of the inmate to form any sort of bond, even the most ephemeral bond of communication with another inmate. In a passage that she quotes from David Rousset, Arendt uses the key notion of witnessing as action beyond death:

> How many people here still believe that a protest has even historic importance? This skepticism is the real masterpiece of the SS. Their great accomplishment. They have corrupted all human solidarity. Here the night has fallen on the future. When no witnesses are left, there can be no testimony. To demonstrate when death can no longer be postponed is an attempt to give death a meaning, to act beyond one's own death. In order to be successful, a gesture must have social meaning. There

are hundreds of thousands of us here, all living in absolute solitude. That is why we are subdued no matter what happens.[40]

The passage emphasizes the difficulty of witnessing in the absence of a human community, in the absence of those who could hear the message. *Life and Fate* uses the resources of narrative to mitigate the problem of isolation without resorting to the narrative fetish of the uplifting message or to the false community of the "friendship of nations."

Grossman imagines this possibility of a meaningful utterance by staging a kind of action beyond death that takes the form of a direct address to the reader. In "The Hell of Treblinka," as Shimon Markish points out, Grossman says that what people experienced in the gas chamber is unimaginable, but in *Life and Fate*, again as Markish points out, Grossman does the impossible and imagines the unimaginable. The scene of Sof'ia Levinton and David in the gas chamber situates the present moment as "now," in which as the narrative repeatedly emphasizes, there is no future, but nonetheless the moment extends impossibly into the future by drawing the reader into its orbit. Readers travel inside the overcrowded train car with Sof'ia Osipovna and the boy, David, follow them as they arrive at the camp, hear the music that the orchestra plays, hear the call for skilled artisans and physicians to step forward, enter the room where the victims undress and watch as the women's hair is cut, enter the gas chamber with its cold, slippery walls and floor, and trace what Grossman calls the Brownian motion of the mass of people who no longer move of their own individual accord but find themselves compelled to follow the movements of others. Readers learn David's last feelings, and hear Sof'ia Osipovna's last thought as she grasps the little boy's body, "I have become a mother" (*Ia stala mater'iu*).[41]

The scene emphasizes the irrevocable fact of death as eliminating the future. There is no future but only the past, and "now" is situated at the very edge of the abyss separating life from death (*nastoiashchee—krai zhiznennogo obryva*). In this narrow strip of time, Grossman imagines his character thinking, feeling, remembering, and acting: she experiences the utterly unique sense of her own life, she decides not to save herself by withholding the information that she was a doctor, she feels a bond with the naked men, women, and children in the changing room, and she adopts David as her son. When David, pressed by the crowd in the gas chamber, is forced to let go of Sof'ia's hand, she "immediately receded into the past. Only now existed" (*No tut zhe Sof'ia Osipovna sdvinulas' v proshloe. Sushchestvovalo tol'ko seichas, teper'*). "Sof'ia Osipovna had no future, she had only the life she had lived" (*U Sof'ii Osipovny ne bylo budushchego, byla lish' prozhitaia zhizn'*) (Grossman 1980, 375). One final, important reiteration of the same idea raises and immediately dismisses the possibility of speech and action in the gas chamber: "Speech no longer could serve people, action was senseless—it is directed toward the future, but in the gas chamber there was no future" (*Rech' uzhe ne sluzhila liudiam, deistvie bylo besmyslenno—ono napravlennoe k budushchemu, a v gazovoi kamere budushchego ne bylo*) (382).

Sof'ia Osipovna's thought about becoming a mother was her "last thought," but an almost physiological form of thought and emotion succeeds her death: "But her heart still lived: it contracted, pitied, and ached for you, living and dead people; overcome by nausea, Sof'ia Osipovna pressed David, who had become a doll, to herself, she died and became a doll" (*A v ee serdtse eshche byla zhizn': ono szhimalos', bolelo, zhalelo vas, zhivykh i mertvykh liudei; khlynula toshnota, Sof'ia Osipovna prinimala k sebe Davida, kuklu, stala mertvoi, kukloi*) (383). The strange syntax of the Russian emphasizes the activity of Sof'ia's heart beyond her death, with particular focus on the object of her heart's pity, the "you" (*vas*).[42] Grossman extends this speck of time after her last thought and before she "becomes a doll" into the unlimited future. As long as there are readers to read this text, they will stand in the place of the addressee, the "you." The striking and even peculiar second-person address to the reader found in the "you" breaks the closed frame of conventional realist narrative. It situates readers in a relationship with the character as if the action of the novel were taking place now, involving them in a past that is never over.

Bergelson: Testimony as Translation

Grossman's construction of an impossible time frame—a "now" that has no future and yet carries forward into the future—registers the irrevocable nature of loss. Bergelson's "An eydes" (A witness), first published in Soviet Russia in 1946, accomplishes a similar end.[43] Bergelson uses his temporality of belatedness that he had developed decades earlier to confront the obliteration of the Jewish people. As in his civil war work, the story constructs the present moment as the aftereffect of catastrophe; only here the catastrophe is so overpowering that it dehumanizes the survivors and radically undermines the entire enterprise of speaking and writing. Bergelson questions the assumption that writing is the expression of the emotion or experience of a unique individual and estranges testimony as the transparently factual account of an eyewitness.[44] Bergelson renders testimony as a problem of transcription and translation, showing it to be fundamentally impossible. Writing about the destruction of the Jews, his language becomes inhuman, exposing writing as the "materialization of memory" that cannot recover the person who once had the memory.[45]

"An eydes" opens with a description of "a Jew" (*a yid*) standing in the entranceway of a dilapidated building in a newly liberated city. He looks more dead than alive. Just above the figure of the Jew in the entranceway is "a sign that had been blotted out, on which only the word 'mash' could be read" (*an opgemekte shild, af velkher me kon iberleyenen nit mer, vi dos vort 'mash'*) (Bergelson 1961, 683). In another story written at the same time as "An eydes," entitled "Yortsayt-Likht" (Memorial-Light), Bergelson says that his protagonist, Dr. Soyfer (whose name means "scribe"), "lost his entire people" (*er iz eyner fun yene, vos farlirn a folk*) (1961, 709). To write and to bear witness is to write and bear witness to the loss of an entire people and to do so in the face of the obliteration of their memory. Bergelson confronts the danger that the remembrance of the Jewish people would be "blotted out." The Jew and all Jews are under the sign of erasure.

In "An eydes" the traces of memory are not legible. The lettering on the sign is virtually destroyed. The lack of transparency, both for the fictitious reader of the fictitious sign and for the reader of Bergelson's story, is key to the text's meaning. The loss of the entire people and the near obliteration of their memory cannot be grasped. The process of reading this story (Bergelson's and the Jewish people's) is of necessity a process in which reading is impeded. Viktor Shtrum's reading of his mother's letter is similarly interrupted and repeated.

Bergelson compares the immobility of the Jew's figure to the immobility of the word on the sign (*"der yid rirt nit mit keyn eyn eyver, vi es rirt zikh nit dos vort 'mash'"*) (1961, 683). The description continues:

> And from the side it seems for a minute that he was not alive, that he was only an image painted in the dark emptiness of the missing door, and something seemed to be missing from his face, exactly like something was missing from the word 'mash' on the sign over his head.

> *un fun der zayt dakht zikh minutnvayz, az er iz nit keyn lebediker—az er iz bloyz oysgemolt in der tunkeler pustkayt fun der felndiker tir un tsu zayn gezikht felt zikh epes, punkt vi s'felt epes tsum vort 'mash' af der shild, vos iber zayn kop.* (683)

The Jew, who is never named, is like the sign from which something is missing. Bergelson emphasized his likeness to something printed or painted. Bergelson's portrait of the witness shifts the problem of testimony from speech of the witness to the problem of textualization, which always includes a lack, the "something" that is missing from the Jew's face. The survivor is a piece of a materialized text.

A passerby, Dora Aronski, asks the Jew in the doorway whether he needs help. He seems to her to be a blind man, and she thinks he needs her help to cross the street. The Jew answers that he is the sole survivor of over a million who perished in a death camp outside Lvov and that "everything that he saw must be written down" (*me darf, meynt er, farshraybn alts, vos er hot gezen*) (687). The use of the third-person form of reported speech heightens the distance between the words that were spoken and their reporting in this statement. The structure maximally removes the listener/reader from the utterance. Near the Jew is a wall on which "a useless and senseless inscription can be read: 'Khane was taken from the ghetto very early in the morning of the 27th'" (*Khane hot men avekgefirt fun geto dem 27-tn gantsfri*) (684). Did Khane write the inscription, or did someone else? Who is, or was, Khane? Is the inscription useless because there is no one left to read it? The story continues without answering these questions. When the Jew makes his request to Dora, it seems to her that "from all the remaining walls here in the city countless other useless and senseless inscriptions scream at her" (*fun ale gantse gebliebene vent do in shtot shrayen itst tsu ir arop on a shir azelkhe umnutslekhe un umzinike oyfshriftn*). The function of the inscription shifts from a statement that conveys information to a form of address. Markish also uses the trope of the screaming inscription in *Milkhome* to create the effect of an assault on the reader. In this story the screaming inscriptions produce more inscription: Dora agrees to serve as the witness's scribe.

It is important to stress what Bergelson is *not* doing. The cries of countless other useless and senseless inscriptions do not restore the voices of the dead, with their unique cadences, lexicon, and forms of expression. Instead, the screaming inscriptions make a demand on those who both survived and came after the event—not to make sense of them, or grasp their import, but to answer them and in some way answer for them. The gap between those who are gone and those who remain cannot be filled.

The theme of translation serves as a trope for this problem of loss and death. The way in which Bergelson represents the problem of testimony as a problem of transcription and translation maximally emphasizes loss. In "An eydes," the witness, the sole survivor of a death camp, speaks in Yiddish, but Dora first translates his words into Russian before writing them down. "Dora writes carefully and without hurrying, careful, moreover, that in her translation into Russian of what the Jew said in Yiddish there would be no mistakes and no distortions from the Russian language" (*Dore farshraybt getray un nit gekhapt, bamiendik zikh, deriker, az inem ibergebn af rusish dos, vos der yid dertseylt af yidish zol nit arayn keyn grayzn un keyn farvildungen fun der rusisher shprakh*) (691). Dora reads her translation aloud before the Jew and asks whether she has properly understood his words. He answers: "You are asking for my expertise? . . . What can I tell you? The suffering was in Jewish" (*Mikh fregt ir do meyvines? . . . Vos ken ikh aykh deruf zogn? . . . Di tsores zaynen geven af yidish*) (692). The last line can also be translated as, "The suffering was in Yiddish," but the old-fashioned way of referring to the Yiddish language as "Jewish" captures more of Bergelson's meaning.

At first glance, the statement "The suffering was in Jewish" seems only to emphasize the uniqueness of the Jewish tragedy, the difference between Jewish and Russian suffering under German occupation. The phrase was omitted from the 1957 Russian translation of the work (Bergelson 1957, 374). There is, however, another set of problems that it raises. Suffering is not in any language, or alternatively, as Sel'vinskii implies, it is in all languages at once, and thus similarly incomprehensible. Suffering is the deprivation of language, the reduction of the human being to mere body without speech. Suffering radically isolates the sufferer from the interlocutor.[46] The suffering of a victim makes no sense to another. Testimony about suffering, even if the original language of the speaker is preserved, is always a translation across a boundary. Representing the problem of the witness as a problem of translation is one among a series of moves, or transfers, that underscores the exteriority and belatedness of testimony. The very thing that extends the memory into the world as a material object and thus preserves it necessarily remains always outside it, something that comes later. The witness's oral testimony comes after the events that took place in the death camp. Transcribing his testimony takes the place of speaking it; translating takes the place of the original language in which it was spoken; and describing in Yiddish the process of translating and transcribing Yiddish testimony into Russian situates the reader at yet another remove from the original events and words. The description of the procedures and processes of the inscription of the witness's testimony thus distances readers from it. The excessive framing thus contributes to the effect of loss.

Structuring the problem of testimony as a problem of translation emphasizes that the testimony is about loss and death. In "The Task of the Translator" Benjamin writes, "a translation proceeds from the original. Not indeed so much from its life as from its 'afterlife' or 'survival' [*Überleben*]" (Rendall 1997, 153). Death is the "original," the originating experience, from which the testimony as translation "survives." The witness is a living corpse and a living document. He has no name but is referred to only as "*a yid*" or "*der yid*" (a Jew; the Jew). We know only that he was a tinsmith from Western Ukraine and that he is about sixty years old. He has no desires, preferences, habits, or dislikes, no memories of his own, and no emotions—except grief. He has no personality but is only a witness. Another way to say this is that he has no life. Bergelson emphasizes the witness's moribund condition. His face is darkened as if it was burnt, and he gives off the smell of burned bones. His "face resembles the waxen face of a corpse" (1961, 694). He is so weak that he cannot sit up straight, and Dora attaches a plank of wood to the table where they work, so that the witness can half recline as he speaks. At the end of the story, Dora fears that the Jew is dead, but he cries out: "How can I die? I am a witness!" (703). Giving testimony does not return his life to him; it is, in contrast, an alternative to dying or, better, as Hannah Arendt says, a form of action that is "beyond one's own death" (1973, 451). The act of testimony resembles the task of Benjamin's translator. Both testifying and translating take place beyond the death of the original.

Bergelson's "An eydes" rethinks the problem of testimony. It is not the first-person oral account of injury, violence, or atrocity but instead a particular form of writing, a materialization of memory. To speak even of the authorship of testimony in the context Bergelson creates is misleading, because authorship suggests individual creativity and expression, but the story, in contrast, emphasizes the collective, mediated, and material production of text. An overriding sense of compulsion pervades the witness's testimony, evidenced, for example, in the line "everything he saw must be written down" and in the senseless graffiti that "screams" at Dora, who transcribes and translates the testimony. The significance of this defamiliarization of testimony is that the story avoids the mimesis of death. The artwork does not imitate the act of killing; there is no pleasure obtained out of death. In structuring the time frame of the story as "after" and beyond the death of the victims, or to use Benjamin's idea of translation as the afterlife of an original, the story asks that readers acknowledge their own position in relation to the events. The representation of testimony as action beyond death, the image of the witness as the embodiment of the camp's collective memory, and the trope of translation work together to make a maximal demand on the reader.

Disparate Stories, Multiple Plots

In "I Saw It" Sel'vinskii searches through the entirety of world history for a language adequate to convey the suffering endured by the victims of the mass killing at Kerch'. In Grossman's *Life and Fate* the new reality of the camps destroys the unity of the national languages, producing in their place a polyglot, in which the Russian contribution is "*dokhodiaga*," referring to a prisoner on his or her last legs. The author himself provides the gloss for the term in the body of his text. Bergelson's "Witness" is remarkably free of biblical and liturgical references, and his emphasis on translation suggests the author's own position as addressing a transnational audience with a text that should hold a place in world literature. In the story proper, each reader of the witness's testimony adds more testimony to the pages of the transcript, collectively creating a palimpsest of multiple and disparate accounts of their own losses.

In his important essay "Historical Emplotment and the Problem of Truth" Hayden White asks whether Nazism and the Final Solution, unlike other events, "must be viewed as manifesting only one story, as being emplottable in one way only, and as signifying one kind of meaning" (1992, 38). Yiddish and Russian literature from the Soviet Union does not emplot the destruction of the Jews in the same manner as Western readers might expect—with a story that describes the unique suffering of the Jews and the unique possibility of their restoration in the state of Israel. The different and disparate texts that this chapter examines, however, do not merely conform to the standard Soviet narrative that both Jews and non-Jews constructed. An alternative poetics of mourning erupts in Grossman's otherwise conventional war novel *For a Just Cause*, the prequel to *Life and Fate*. In Der Nister and Perets Markish, the narrative subject created by Soviet socialism splits apart under the pressure of the mass killings. Der Nister in particular uses biblical images to connect the destruction of the Jews in the 1940s with a timeless, transcendent history. In Grossman, Markish, and Bergelson, writing itself—whether in the form of a packet of papers, an inscription on a wall, or a piece of handwritten testimony—takes on a terrible, haunted reality.

"Speech no longer served people," says the narrator in *Life and Fate*; Bergelson's witness is like a painted sign whose text is illegible. Bergelson, Grossman, and Der Nister (and there are others) struggle to save Jewish history from oblivion; they ask how an artist can speak to overwhelming violence without making violence an object of aesthetic pleasure; and out of long years of silence and neglect they address us as readers. Bergelson, who insists on testimony as translation; Grossman, who imagines pity extended to us from the gas chamber; and Der Nister, who knows the wound remains unhealed: all use literature as a form of action beyond death and oblivion—their own as well as that of the victims of the Germans.

Part II *Postwar Reconstructions*

Introduction

The year, 1946; the place, Berlin. Erika Hamburg, a Jew and a camp survivor, informs the Soviet military administration of the whereabouts of a famous war criminal, one of the inventors of Zyklon B. The Soviets arrest him, preventing the illegal sale of a ton of saccharine, a crime also involving British and American officers. One of the Americans, a former shtetl Jew, now a businessman in New York, has no qualms about dealing with a Nazi. The war criminal turns out to be none other than Erika's father, the non-Jewish Hugo Von Hamburg. When the Nazis took power, he allowed his Jewish wife to be killed and his daughter to be sent to a camp. Having survived the war, Erika, a former champion swimmer and member of the upper crust of Berlin society, rejects her old acquaintances and her former privileges, rediscovers her Jewish roots (she starts to sign her name "Esther"), and comes to admire the Soviet way of life. Only in the Soviet zone with her new Soviet friends, who speak Yiddish and for whom Jewishness carries no stigma of the camps, does she feel that a new life is possible: for Erika "a world is born." This is the far-fetched plot of Natan Zabare's Yiddish novel *Haynt vert geboyrn a velt* (Today a world is born), published in the Soviet Yiddish journal *Sovetish heymland* (1965) and translated into Russian three years later (Zabare 1968).

Zabare's Berlin novel is based in part on his own experience working for the Soviet military administration in Berlin after the war. Zabare (1908–75) grew up in impoverished circumstances, served in the Soviet military in the 1930s, and attended the Institute of Jewish Culture (at the Ukrainian Academy of Sciences), a product of the Soviet development of Yiddish. Zabare was arrested in 1950 for "betraying the motherland": he had distributed Zionist materials in Yiddish and Hebrew. He served four years of his ten-year term in Magadan and was permitted to return to Kiev in 1956.

Today a World Is Born uses the standard clichés of Soviet literature. The plot of the child who "heroically" betrays a parent recalls the famous real-life case of Pavlik Morozov, who turned in his father to the KGB. Zabare depicts Lenin in hagiographical terms: Erika survives the camp because of the inspiration she derives from his portrait, tantamount to a wonder-working icon. The novel touts Soviet nationality policy, showing that only in Soviet Russia, in this case in the Soviet zone in Berlin, can Jewish culture experience rebirth. Zabare repeats the Soviet version of the Holocaust: in the West, Jews went to camps, but in the Soviet Union, they served in the army. As in so much Soviet literature and art generally, the meaning of "today," as the title indicates, is its capacity to give rise to the bright future. This stock-in-trade Soviet kitsch coexists with the novel's Jewish agenda, which stresses the importance of Yiddish and Hebrew.

Zabare also wrote, among other works, *Galgal hakhoyzer* (The wheel of eternity), which portrays Jewish life in thirteenth-century Provence and Spain. It was published serially from 1972 to 1975, with a separate edition in 1979 and a Russian translation in 2004. *The Wheel of Eternity* highlights the knowledge, sophistication, and social preeminence of early modern Sephardic Jewry: the characters are physicians, poets, philosophers, scholars, translators, and merchants. They govern their own affairs and speak many European languages in addition to writing scholarly and literary works in Hebrew. The novel's broad panoramic scope includes many actual historical figures, and describes the birth of Yiddish. In one pointed scene, addressed to the Soviet Jewish audience, a stranger from Russia appears, a young Jewish man who speaks only Russian—characterized as the language of "slaves"—and whose only Hebrew is a few words from the prayer "Hear O Israel." Zabare's Cold War and historical novels instruct readers didactically about the perils of assimilation and emphasize a separate Jewish national consciousness.

Zabare's work and the work of numerous other Yiddish- and Russian-language Jewish authors in the postwar period have gone virtually unnoticed in Western critical literature. The neglect stems in large part from Cold War cultural politics on both sides of the Atlantic. The United States and the Soviet Union competed over which country protected the interests of minority groups; as Zabare's novel shows, the Soviets claimed that Jewish culture flourished only in their sphere of influence. Each side used the conventional narrative of destruction and redemption; the difference was where redemption would take place: in the West or in the Soviet Union. The Western Holocaust narrative, as Saul Friedlander shows, revolved around passivity and heroism, catastrophe and redemption. Most Jews were led like sheep to the slaughter; the heroic few ghetto fighters and partisans mostly belonged to Zionist youth movements. "Implicitly, the catastrophe of European Jews," Friedlander notes, "is linked to the redemption of Israel" (1998, 347). The Soviet war narrative also casts the Jews of capitalist Western Europe as victims, casting Soviet Russia, in contrast, in the starring role. The victorious Red Army, which united the peoples of the USSR, including Jews, Ukrainians, and others, and most importantly, Russians, saved Europe from Hitler.

The typical Western account of postwar Jewish literature in the Soviet Union boils down to this: Hitler killed the readers, and Stalin killed the writers. The only way to "save" the remaining silenced and oppressed Soviet Jews was to reawaken their national consciousness and send them to Israel.[1] One source, for example, characterizing the postwar years of Russian-Jewish literature (without mentioning Yiddish), states: "the period of 'silence' in Russian-Jewish literature lasted until the second half of the 60s, in essence, until the rebirth of Zionism in the Soviet Union and the beginning of repatriation in the State of Israel" (diaspora, . . . 2005). The Soviets, for their part, condemned Zionism as Nazism, making it difficult for Westerners to see anything produced in the Soviet Union as participating in or supporting Jews and Jewish culture, especially anything published in its official Yiddish journal, *Sovetish heymland* (Soviet homeland).[2]

Hitler's genocide, and Stalin's murderous anti-Jewish campaign, which culminated in the deaths of the Yiddish writers Bergelson, Der Nister, Kvitko, Hofshteyn, Markish, Persov, and Fefer, and the Yiddish actors Mikhoels and Zuskin, did not destroy Jewish culture and literature in the Soviet Union. The mid-1950s saw the release of Jewish writers who had been in the Gulag, including Semen Gekht and the Yiddish writers Moshe Altman and Zabare, among others. The posthumous rehabilitation of previously repressed writers, including the Yiddish authors killed by Stalin, also began at this time with the prominent example of Isaac Babel in 1955; a volume of his work was republished in 1957 with an introduction by Il'ia Erenburg. Yiddish publication resumed in 1959, and translations from Yiddish into Russian began appearing in the same year, including a multivolume edition of Sholem Aleichem's works (Estraikh 1995). The monthly *Sovetish heymland* (Soviet homeland), the only Yiddish journal aside from *Birobidzhaner shtern* (The Birobidzhan star), started publication in 1961.[3] As Bernard Choseed points out, "the successive issues of *Sovetish heymland* gave material proof that the overwhelming majority of established Soviet Yiddish writers who had flourished through 1948 had survived the holocaust," including Shmuel Halkin, Note Lurie, and Itsik Kipnis (1968, 104). The 1970s saw major new Yiddish literary publication, including the work of Rivke Rubin, Zabare, Altman, Shmuel Gordon, and others.

Russian-language works with Jewish content were published at the end of the 1950s. Aleksandra Brushtein's enormously popular *Doroga ukhodit v dal'* (The road disappears into the distance), published in 1959, is a fictionalized autobiography that traces the life of a prosperous liberal Jewish family in the early twentieth century. The central figure is the kindly Jewish doctor. The work, aimed at adolescents, became a widely read sourcebook for Jewish history of the period, neglected in official Soviet history books. Boris Iampol'skii's *Mal'chik s golubinoi ulitsy* (The boy from Golubinaia Street), published in 1959, takes up the story of his prewar *Iarmarka* (The fair). It focuses on the same little boy and includes some of the same characters as *The Fair*, and it is set in a similarly fantastical and unreal shtetl, although with accurate and detailed descriptions of Jewish holidays and institutions. Iampol'skii's work inserts a markedly Jewish thread into Soviet literature of the time, which typically emphasized the factory, the collective farm, and building socialism after the war. Postwar Soviet Yiddish and Russian literature maintained intense connections with the shtetl and with other sites of Jewish memory; Shmuel Gordon and Shire Gorshman's travelogues are examples.

Now that the Cold War and its cultural politics are over, it should be possible to focus less on suppression and more on the continuity and reinvention of Soviet Yiddish and Russian-Jewish literature after the war, without mitigating the catastrophe of either the war or Stalin. It is not merely a question of correcting the historical record. Postwar work written in the Soviet Union powerfully engages the central question of twentieth-century literature: living in the aftermath of disaster.

Boris Slutskii's "Liberating Ukraine" (Ia osvobozhdal Ukrainu) is an extraordinarily moving example of the delicate and difficult balance required of postwar literature. The poem confronts the overwhelming destruction of the war, focusing on the destruction of Yiddish culture, the "murder," as Slutskii puts it, of the Yiddish language itself. At the same time, the Russian-language poem enfolds Yiddish into itself, thereby creating a space for Yiddish in Russian:

> Liberating Ukraine,
> I walked through its Jewish villages.
> Yiddish, their mother-tongue, has long been a ruin.
> Three years ago it went extinct, like something ancient.
>
> No, it did not die—it was excised and extinguished.
> They were too sharp-tongued, apparently.
> Everyone perished, and no one survived.
> Only their sunrises and sunsets are left.
>
> In their poems, now sweet, now sad,
> Now burning hot, aflame with bitterness,
> In the past, perhaps too barbed,
> And in the present—too real.
>
> Described by Markish and Hofshteyn
> In stories by Bergelson
> This world, which not even Einstein
> Could bring back to life.
>
> Not sown as a kernel of grain, or chaff
> But as black ash,
> So that words would arise one-hundred fold
> Where the open mouths of ruins gape wide.

It has been three years since this tongue, like a person, was killed.
In three years, how ancient it has grown.
For three years we poke our fingers in its books,
In its alphabet, forgotten, like cuneiform.

Ia osvobozhdal Ukrainu,
Shel cherez evreiskie derevni.
Idish, ikh iazyk,—davno ruina.
Vymer on i goda tri kak drevnii.

Net, ne vymer—vyrezan i vyzhzhen.
Slishkom byli, vidno, iazykovaty.
Vse pogibli, i nikto ne vyzhil.
Tol'ko ikh voskhody i zakaty

V ikh stikhakh, to sladkikh, to goriuchikh,
To goriachikh, gorech'iu goriashchikh,
V proshlom slishkom, mozhet byt', koliuchikh,
V nastoiashchem—nastoiashchikh.

Markishem opisan i Gofshteinom,
Bergel'sonom tshchatel'no rasskazan
Etot mir, kotoryi i Einshteinom
Nesposoben k zhizni byt' priviazan.

No ne kak zerno, ne kak polovu,
A kak pepel chernyi rassevaiut,
Chtob sam-sto vzoshlo liuboe slovo
Tam, gde rty ruiny razevaiut.

Goda tri kak dreven, kak antichen
Tot iazyk, kak chelovek, ubityi.
Goda tri perstami v knigi tychem,
V alfavit, kak klinopis', zabytyi.

(Slutskii 2006a)[4]

The Nazi genocide destroyed the "sharp-tongued" inhabitants of Ukraine's Jewish villages, and with their deaths, their language, Yiddish, also died. Yiddish was not only the language of their everyday life but also the language of their poetry, which burned with passion, grief, and wit. The last two stanzas raise the question of resurrection using a set of motifs from the Gospel of John, including the "word" ("In the beginning was the Word," Jn. 1:1); the kernel of grain ("unless a grain of wheat falls into the earth and dies, it remains alone, but if it dies, it bears much fruit," Jn. 12:24); and doubting Thomas, who thrusts his fingers into Jesus' wounds to make certain that he really died and came back to life ("Except I shall see in his hands the print of the nails, and put my finger into the print of the nails, and thrust my hand into his side, I will not believe," Jn. 20:27). In Slutskii's poem, it is not grain that is sown to bring forth new fruit, but dead Jews, in whose place words will arise "one-hundred fold." Slutskii replaces the single word "Jesus" with the multiple and heterogeneous words of the barbed, pointed, Yiddish language. He creates an aural association between the sound "*i*" and the Yiddish language, as in the line "*Idish, ikh iazyk,—davno ruina*" (Yiddish, their mother-tongue, has long been a ruin) and then uses this sound sign in his Russian text; the stanza beginning "v ikh stikhakh, to sladkikh, to goriuchikh" (in their poems, now sweet, now sad) uses the sound eight times. The sounds of Yiddish multiply inside Russian.

The last lines of the poem, "For three years we poke our fingers in its books / In its alphabet, forgotten, like cuneiform," substitute the corpus of Yiddish for Jesus' body. The survivors "poke" their fingers into the cuneiform-like script, just as Thomas thrust his finger (*perst*) into Jesus' wounds. The use of the Old Church Slavonic *perst* instead of *palets* for "finger" underscores the comparison between the survivors and the disciples of John's Gospel (the locus classicus for "*perst*" is the line from John). Unlike the story of doubting Thomas in John, however, for postwar Soviet readers of Yiddish there is no reward of redemption. Jesus died and was resurrected in three days, and Thomas thrusts his hand into a living body. In Slutskii's poem, three years replace the three days, but there is no resurrection yet. The Messiah has not yet come for the Jews.

Slutskii's poem registers the catastrophic nature of the destruction of Ukraine's Jews by describing the complete death of Yiddish. In the span of three years, Yiddish, a vital part of the ongoing present, became a part of ancient history, its alphabet comparable to the alphabet used by the Babylonians. The leap forward was the repeated refrain of Soviet culture; this work, in contrast, chronicles the precipitous leap back of an entire culture into antiquity. As in his poem "And on the Whole There Is Nothing Besides the War," Slutskii fractures and elongates time. "Liberating Ukraine" also echoes Sel'vinskii, who describes Kerch' as the site of an ancient catastrophe, "covered in ash, like Pompeii."

The "grain" of the Jewish word sown like "black ash" and the allusion to cuneiform call to mind Mandelshtam's "Horseshoe Finder" (Nashedshii podkovu). Mandelshtam creates an impossible chronology in which the present and the long-faded past unfold simultaneously: what he says "now" (*seichas*) has been excavated from the soil as if it were "fossilized" wheat. Similarly, in Slutskii's poem, Yiddish, which was alive just three short years ago, has become a fossil, like Mandelshtam's utterances turned to stone. The catastrophe of the revolution for Mandelshtam and the catastrophe of the German occupation for Slutskii thrust individuals and an entire civilization outside the normal course of time's unfolding. The reference to Einstein is significant: "This world, which not even Einstein/Could bring back to life." Even if space and time could be warped, as in Einstein's theory of relativity, it would be impossible to resurrect Jewish life in Ukraine. The rupture between the present and the recent past is insurmountably wide, and yet the Yiddish word will be renewed. Slutskii insists on the impossible possibility of restoration, at once outside the laws of space and time, and yet embodied in his own poem.

To pursue the simultaneity of overwhelming destruction and continuity in postwar Jewish literature—bitter, sweet, sad, and "sharp-tongued"—requires a modification in the chronological structure that I have pursued thus far. Part I focused on events: the revolution, the civil war, the five-year plans, the "Great Patriotic War," and the Nazi genocide. Instead of tracing the course of Soviet Yiddish and Russian-Jewish literature decade by decade through the well-worn stages of oppression, stagnation, immigration, and collapse, Part II is organized thematically, focusing mostly on postwar work but also showing its relation to prewar literature. Babel, Bergelson, and Mandelshtam were killed by Stalin, but they reappear in Part II because authors writing in the 1960s and beyond read and quote their work. Their writing thus remains alive. Chapter Five, "*Yeder zeyger a yorstayt*: The Past as Memory in Postwar Literature," shows how Jewish postwar writers avoid the teleology of Soviet historical narrative, in which the past serves as a stepping-stone to the bright future. In Gekht, Rivke Rubin, Dina Kalinovskaia, and other writers, the past as memory disturbs the continuity of everyday life. In Gekht's collection of stories *Obligations of the Heart* (Dolgi serdtsa, 1963) the intergenerational conflicts created by the war erupt in the present. Rivke Rubin's "Aza min tog" (A strange day), whose title quotes a line from Bergelson's Berlin story "Tsvishn emigrantn" (Among refugees); Kalinovskaia's marvelous "O, subbota" (Oh Saturday), written in Russian; and the short fiction of the Yiddish writers Moshe Altman, Shire Gorshman, and Shmuel Gordon were written in the late 1970s and 1980s but evoke the time of the prerevolutionary past, the civil war, and the Second World War.

The past exists as something more concrete than memory, however. The Pale of Settlement was formally abolished in 1917, and the shtetl declared obsolete even before then, but the forms of life characteristic of the shtetl persisted in this region and elsewhere, as did the literary imagination of a sealed-off Jewish universe in which there was only one way to do things: the Jewish way. Chapter Six, "Jewish Spaces and Retro-Shtetls," explores the connection between the classic Yiddish literary imagination of the shtetl and the work of pre- and postwar Yiddish authors, including Bergelson, Itsik Kipnis, and Gordon, and the Russian-language authors Fridrikh Gorenshtein, Grigorii Kanovich, and Inna Lesovaia.

Chapter Six emphasizes the Jewish Jew living in a Jewish world; Chapter Seven turns to the non-Jewish Jew in the non-Jewish world. "Translating Empire" considers the position of Jews as "enlighteners" in Soviet imperial spaces; in Central Asia, for example, as emissaries, not only of the new Soviet way of life but also of the best of Russian high culture. What happens to the Jewish past in these spaces; what transformations in self-consciousness does this cultural mission require? I discuss the origins of the "friendship of nations" policy in the 1930s, explore the critical work of several Jewish translators, including Kornei Chukovsky, David Vygodskii, and Mandelshtam, and then turn to the figure of the Jewish translator/cultural emissary in fiction by Felix Roziner, Semen Lipkin, and Dina Rubina. I conclude with Liudmila Ulitskaia's post-Soviet novel *Daniel' Shtain, perevodchik* (Daniel Shtain, the translator), published in 2006. The chapter as a whole reevaluates the role of the Jew as cosmopolitan in Soviet culture.

Chapter Eight, "Afterwards," turns to fiction and art produced after 1991 in Russia and abroad. The chapter traces the response to the collapse of the Soviet Union as enabling a new relation to the past. Seeing the present in light of the past and not the future is the traditional Jewish response to catastrophe. Something approaching this Jewish lens can be found in dozens of works written in the first decade of the twenty-first century. The backward glance has become the obsessive focus of the Russian intelligentsia at the beginning of the post-Soviet century.

Five *Yeder zeyger a yortsayt*:
The Past as Memory in Postwar Literature

In his 1930 speech in Warsaw, Bergelson used the image of the speeding train to exalt Soviet Yiddish literature and to castigate Yiddish literature written elsewhere. Nonetheless, his own preoccupation as an artist was with the Jews who arrived too late for the train that was to bring them to their future. In his 1946 play "Prince Ruveni," Bergelson raises the question of renewal again but with a greater sense of urgency:

> In the spirit of the time of rebirth—
> Columbus's time . . . what happened?
> I stand and ask of this great time:
> Whether you give your gift to everyone
> Except my Jewish people? . . .
> Will *we* alone remain guilty?
>
> *In gayst fun ot der tsayt fun oyflebung—*
> *Kolumbus tsayt . . . is vos iz den geshen?*
> *Ikh shtoyn un freg bay ot der tsayt der groyser:*
> *Tsi den oykh du vest alemen bashenken*
> *Un nor mayn yidish folk aleyn farteyln? . . .*
> *Tsi efsher veln* mir *bloyz shuldik blaybn?*
>
> (Bergelson 1946, 103)

The fifteenth-century era of exploration and discovery meant expulsion for Spanish and Portuguese Jews: will twentieth-century postwar rebirth similarly elude the Jewish people? The history of progress repeatedly omits the Jews, who remain "guilty," left behind in a past unredeemed by the future promised by Christianity, modernity, and postwar Communism.[1]

The burden of the war and its legacy constitutes the central theme of Soviet postwar Jewish literature in Russian and Yiddish. The Jewish focus on the past contrasts with the entire thrust of revolutionary culture, in which Jews, of course, played a significant role. Revolutionary culture did not "acknowledge memory," focusing instead on youth and newness, and the remaking of the self and the world (Belaia 1999). Beginning in the 1930s, another competing tendency emerged, emphasizing the greatness of the Russian past—a past that led inevitably to the present state of alleged perfection. I call this attitude "looking back to the bright future."[2] The sociologist of architecture Vladimir Papernyi labels these conflicting approaches toward history and memory *"kul'tura 1"* (culture 1, the effort to destroy the past) and *"kul'tura 2"* (culture 2, the effort to enshrine the past in a particular form of Soviet teleological history). The ascendance of "culture 2" during the war years did not, however, supplant the revolutionary striving toward new beginnings. Papernyi cites Khrushchev's promise of the late 1950s: "the present generation of Soviet people will live with communism" (2006, 53). Evidence of the new, postwar break with the past—with direct consequences for Yiddish—emerged even earlier. When Soviet bureaucrats met in February 1949 to disband Yiddish publication, the failure of Yiddish literature to display adequate contemporaneity was one of the rationalizations for their decision. Criticizing one work, they said the following: "the representation of the remnants of the past in the consciousness and behavior" of the characters takes up more space than showing the growth of what is new (Grossman n.d.). The term for "remnant" (*perezhitok*) was usually used to designate despised vestiges of the past, such as feudalism and capitalism.

The promotion of happiness was not new in 1954 or unique to the Soviet Union; Disneyland is an example of the postwar American version. In Soviet proletarian literature of the 1920s, the prescribed emotion was joy, "the great joy of living on the earth," as Gorkii affirmed. The five-year plans of the 1930s gave the motif of joy new impetus: Stalin himself said that life had become more joyful. The postwar narrative of the "Great Patriotic War" picked up the theme of joy, linking it to Soviet unity and Soviet victory. In 1949, on the occasion of Stalin's seventieth birthday, the film *Padenie Berlina* (The fall of Berlin) was released.

While giving a speech at the workers' club, the heroine turns to the large portrait of Stalin on the wall and joyously thanks him for giving her and all Soviet children such happy childhoods. When Stalin arrives in Berlin to greet his victorious army, representatives of the various Soviet national minorities spontaneously break into their native folkdances to express their joy. The friendship of nations, under the leadership of the Russian people, sustained the Soviet peoples during the war years—this was another crucial component of the official myth of the war.

In 1963, Khrushchev described plans for a monument that was to be called "Pobeda nad fashismom" (Victory over fascism), designed by Evgenii Vuchetich. Vuchetich's sculpture "The Motherland Calls," a colossal Soviet-style goddess of victory, had already been unveiled as part of a complex of monuments honoring the fallen soldiers of the battle of Stalingrad (Palmer 2009). The emphasis of the new monument, similarly, was to be on the superhuman strength of the Soviet Union, without any acknowledgment of loss. "Victory" became a key word in Soviet official discourse in the postwar and post-Soviet period; the term also found a place in literary criticism of this time. In 1961, in an article for the new Yiddish periodical *Sovetish heymland*, the Yiddish author Moshe Notovitsh, relying on an earlier speech by Khrushchev, said that the task of the Soviet writer was to "demonstrate the struggle between the old and the new and the inevitable victory of the new" (1961, 109). Joyous socialist construction was the therapy for those who had suffered under "fascist oppression." More than a decade later, the critic Arn Raskin takes pains to find an affirmation of the joy of Soviet life even in the sad writings of Yiddish authors: "The mournful reminiscences about yesterday make the joyous rhythms of the peaceful present more emphatic" (1976, 95). The official Soviet emphasis on the "victory of the new" produced an atmosphere in which historical amnesia about the war and the Terror flourished.

Semen Lipkin's "Voennaia pesnia" (War song) from 1981 confronts the emotional prescriptions and prohibitions of this atmosphere:

> In the uncovered belly of a cart
> You can see a child's body. The arc of a gramophone.
> It seems the wind spins the record.
> Listening takes too much strength. Weeping is prohibited.

> In the death camp the ovens have gone cold.
> They play the song everywhere. We won.
> Mother, wrap your daughter in her shroud.
> Play, balalaika, weeping is prohibited.
>
> (Lipkin 2008, 283)

In a tone of savage irony, the poet calls for music to celebrate victory, reiterating the prohibition against mourning the dead. The reference to the "ovens" and the "death camp" directly confronts the Nazi genocide of the Jews; the child's body in the cart could refer to the non-Jewish victims of German occupation, or to the famine engineered by Stalin's government during the years of collectivization. For all the victims and their suffering, there is only one answer: the song of victory, "Play, balalaika." The line "Play balalaika" (*poi balalaika*) is a Russian translation of the Jewish riddle song "Tum balalaika"; "*plakat' nel'zia*" (weeping is forbidden) ironically twists "*freylekh zol zayn*" (let's rejoice).[3] Lipkin acknowledges violence that otherwise goes unobserved. Referring to the Jewish folksong heightens the bitterness of unmourned destruction. Reading the poem and experiencing the defiant emotions and memories that it produces violates the prohibitions and prescriptions that it ironically cites.

Lipkin, Gekht, the Yiddish author Moshe Altman, and the other authors who are the subject of this chapter do not fit easily into "culture 1" or "culture 2" but instead trace out their own unique poetics of memory, haunted by the "remnants" of the past. In some texts, the past takes the form of an unforeseen and unwanted intrusion into the present, a hidden, unacknowledged wound carried over from one generation to the next; in other works, the past appears as an intertextual reference to a work of an author previously repressed; for yet another set of writers, the past is embedded in the material objects of daily life. The sudden infusion of memory that these writers describe has more to do with their broken relation to the present than with a sentimental journey to the past.[4] Gekht's collection of stories *Dolgi serdtsa* (Duties of the heart, 1963) retraces the wounds left by the war. The unfinished violence of the past haunts Rivke Rubin's "Aza min tog" (A strange day), Dina Kalinovskaia's "O, subbota" (Oh Saturday), and the short fiction of the Yiddish writers Moshe Altman and Shire Gorshman. The characters in these fictions do not perform actions so much as remember the past. The colors and contours of what they recall are not all somber, however. What has been buried under the surface imbues everyday life with a palpable lyricism.

The Postwar Pursuit of Happiness

Before addressing these works, a discussion of Il'ia Erenburg's novel *Ottepel'* (The thaw, 1954) will provide a more detailed context for the postwar period. Usually dismissed as hopelessly conformist and lacking in obvious Jewish themes and characters, the work nonetheless beautifully illustrates the dilemmas of the new postwar campaign in favor of the future. It provides distinct points of contrast with Gekht, Altman, Rubin, and Kalinovskaia. Set in a factory town in 1953, *The Thaw* describes a group of characters who struggle with the consequences of the war, campaigns of suspicion, and the oppressive demands of the workplace, but who still pursue happiness in their personal lives. They find themselves poised between the demands of culture 1 and culture 2, between overcoming the past and living with perfection achieved.

In *The Thaw*, moods are upbeat, "everyone's mood is elevated, people's spirits have cheered" (*u vsekh nastroienie prepodnialos', na dushe poveselelo*) (Erenburg 1954, 108). Konstantin Simonov's article about the novel emphasizes this point: "Using the example of the personal fates [of the characters] the author wants to depict everything good and joyful [*to khoroshee i radostnoe*], which is growing greater and greater every day in our life, which on the state scale is expressed in the many decisions and practical measures taken by the party and government" (Simonov 1954). The bizarre review ends up attributing to the government not only the divine attribute of producing happiness in life but also the aesthetic quality of expressing happiness in its decisions.

The characters in Erenburg's novel live in the bright future of happiness achieved; however, their illnesses, hysterical outbursts, and difficulty in speaking to one another indicate the weight of an intolerable burden. In *The Thaw*, the war is a closed topic. When, for example, the young engineer Koroteev and Zhuravlev, the factory director, talk about their experiences during the war, Koroteev "felt that closeness which arises between former front-line soldiers: they knew something that others did not see and did not experience" (Erenburg 1954, 89). The war transcends ordinary conversation and approaches something like the sublime in its indescribability and overwhelming power. Those who experienced that sublimity, however, are left incapacitated by it. The men and women of steel, who had been reforged in the early years of the Soviet Union and who were mobilized into human weapons during the war, appear a decade later as "half-finished products" (*nedodelannyi polufabrikat*) (93).

Not only have the characters lost the armor of their hatred for the enemy; they appear to have lost form and definition, as if overwhelmed by something like Freud's death drive, the desire to revert back to a less organized state. Civil war texts by Perets Markish and other authors focused on grotesquely distorted bodies and landscapes. In *The Thaw*, in contrast, bodies do not ooze but freeze. Simonov castigated Erenburg for portraying Soviet art as "a frozen puppet" (1954, 2). The epithet fits. Erenburg's characters act like frozen puppets, who desire their own mechanization. Sonia Pukhov is an apt example. She loves literature but pursues a technical education; attempting to kill her own memories, she destroys the souvenirs of her childhood; she rejects the man she admits to loving and frenetically repeats official-sounding dictates about the necessity for control over the emotions, and the importance of literature's didactic function, even as she tells herself that she is "dying" (*vot prosto pogibaiu*) (Erenburg 1954, 73). Most of the other characters are semimoribund; the older project director Sokolovskii, the hero of the main romantic plot, spends most of the novel ill and delirious. The psychological "thaw" has not yet taken place.

The Thaw is both a phenomenon of the great hulking leviathan of Soviet culture, its near-death, and an active intervention, an attempt at reanimation. What is at stake for Erenburg is nothing less than Soviet culture as a whole, and whether it returns to life. The only solution that the novel proposes, however, is more of the same, more remaking: "we must reeducate our feelings . . . we need our Soviet humanism" (93). Erenburg depicts the moribund state of Soviet culture and perpetuates the conditions of its continual reproduction.

The prescribed Soviet humanism appears in the novel's portrait of its Jewish character, Dr. Sherer. Dr. Sherer has impeccable war credentials: her husband was killed fighting on the front, and her mother and sister were killed by the Germans when they occupied Orsha. Dr. Sherer lives under the shadow of the "Doctors' Plot," the anti-Jewish campaign of 1952, including the arrests and torture of physicians both in and outside the Kremlin, and the newspaper tirade against "murderers in white coats."[5] When she diagnoses a sick child with ordinary flu, and not pneumonia, the girl's mother expresses doubt but then apologizes. Dr. Sherer responds: "Forgive me, it's my fault. My nerves gave way. Sometimes these days you have to listen to certain things . . . after the bulletin . . . It's bad when a doctor behaves like I do" (21).

In his essay "Jews in Officially Published Russian Literature," Shimon Markish observes that even though in the early 1990s the above scene seems toothless and colorless, "at that time it gladdened our hearts and straightened our usually stooped backs," helping Jews to affirm that they were Jews "like Sherer, like Il'ia Ehrenburg" (1991, 221–22). The apparent paucity of Jewish heroes and Jewish themes in the novel does not indicate how the novel was read in the 1950s by a Soviet Jewish audience. Other references in the novel—including a brief discussion of a Grossman novel, presumably *For a Just Cause*, which was pilloried in the press; Shostakovich's tenth symphony, the first work he wrote since the attack against him in 1948; and the occasional utterances of the characters along the lines of "Now they trust people" (108)—indicate potential moments in the novel that might have had a similar effect on readers whose backs were stooped by the particularly oppressive conditions of Stalin's last years.

Erenburg, a Jew, publishes a novel that names the decade—the "thaw"—and gives Soviet Jews characters to identify with, but to the post-Soviet and Western audience the novel contains little that is Jewish in theme. The German destruction of the Jews and Stalin's anti-Jewish campaign remain shameful secrets. *The Thaw* depicts the dawn of new happiness even as it questions official language about the emotions. It exposes the pitfalls of human reengineering at the same time that it calls for more human remaking.[6] The characters in the novel are unable to free themselves from the past and unable to confront it. They are stuck in the ever more joyous present. For all its flaws, *The Thaw* is not mere propaganda. The traumatized, frozen state of nearly all its characters reveals the unhealed devastation of the war and the immediate postwar period.

Fictions of Return: Nekrasov, Gorshman, and Gekht

While *The Thaw* remains uneasily poised between symptom and diagnosis, other works published at the same time provide an alternative approach to the problem of the past. Among the postwar narratives of return and reintegration, Victor Nekrasov's novella *V rodnom gorode* (Native town, 1954), Shire Gorshman's Yiddish story "Vilde hopn" (Wild hops), and Semen Gekht's cycle of short stories *Dolgi serdtsa* (Duties of the heart, 1963) present a striking contrast to the widely prevalent theme of joy. These works address the lasting emotional consequences of the war.

Nekrasov's "Native Town," published in the literary journal *The New World* in 1954, was praised for its honest depiction of the problems of reintegration after the war (Nekrasov 1954). The story's description of the difficulties of living under German occupation, the sympathetic portrait of the relationship between a married woman and a Soviet soldier whom she nurses, and the honest statement of the near impossibility of talking about the experience directly confront the shame associated with survival on the home front. Nekrasov, who was not Jewish, became well known earlier for his war novel *V okopakh Stalingrada* (In the trenches of Stalingrad, 1947) and was an important voice in liberal circles in the 1960s. Subject to increasing governmental pressure for his outspoken opinions, including his protest against plans for a development at Babi Yar, Nekrasov left the Soviet Union for Paris in 1974. "Native Town" includes a positive depiction of a Jewish couple, a pair of professional illustrators who industriously contribute to what was called the "lacquering over of reality." They paint posters of returning soldiers who stare victoriously into the bright future. The narrative does not explain how this Jewish couple survived the German occupation.

"Native Town" opens with images of a destroyed Kiev. The hero, Nikolai Mitosov, returns to Kiev near the end of the war to receive treatment for his injured arm. He finds piles of burned bricks and half-demolished apartment buildings, and walls covered in nearly illegible messages written with chalk. One message gives the new address for the "Vayntraubs," presumably a Jewish family. This description is reminiscent of the opening of Bergelson's "A Witness" (An eydes, 1946) discussed in Chapter Four, in which a Jew stands in the doorway of a dilapidated building. Above him is a sign on which only a fragment of a word remains. An inscription on a nearby wall states the date when an unknown person, "Khane," was taken from the ghetto. The argument for Bergelson's direct influence on Nekrasov is difficult to make, because "An eydes" was not translated into Russian until 1961. The parallel is significant for the contrast it reveals. Bergelson's depiction of the devastation of war quickly abandons realism for an intensely emotional, expressionistic style; the inscriptions begin to "scream" at the witness's scribe, Dora. Bergelson's narrative resonates with the Jewish biblical tradition of memory and forgetting, and the story confronts the problem of testimony about the destruction of an entire people. In Nekrasov, in contrast, the scribbled message on the wall provokes a warm memory of the Vayntraub family. The episode remains confined within a realistically depicted universe, in which interrupted lives resume their normal course.

The hero of "Native Town" is preoccupied with memory. In the opening pages of the work, he remembers the Vayntraubs, his life with his wife before the war, his fellow soldiers during the war; he remembers Stalingrad; indeed, remembering the past marks every new turn in his life. His wife remembers her life under German occupation, and the particularly difficult time of the death of her mother. The two time frames of past and present unfold almost simultaneously with each other, especially in the first part of the story. The example of "Native Town" shows that memory is not the unique province of Jewish authors. Nekrasov's hero, however, sheds his habit of remembering as he achieves reintegration in Soviet society. Recovery means amnesia.

For Shire Gorshman, in contrast to Nekrasov, the wounds left by the overwhelming destruction of the immediate past make normalization impossible. Gorshman's "Vilde hopn" (Wild hops) appeared in a collection of her stories, *Der koyekh fun lebn* (The power of life), published in 1948, the last year of Yiddish publication until 1959. Nokhem, a blacksmith, returns to his native town in Belorussia, even though his parents, siblings, wife, and children are dead. The town is so empty that even when he takes off his boots, "the tread of his bare feet were heard in the congealed stillness" (*di trit fun zayne borvese fis hobn apgehert in der farglivertkayt*) (Gorshman 1948, 6). Nekrasov's hero cannot stop remembering the past; Gorshman's hero is unable to remember, and instead becomes part of the "congealed stillness" of the present, a stillness broken by the screams of the deserted houses. As in Bergelson's "Witness" inanimate objects take on a life of their own: Nokhem "felt with all his might that the empty Jewish houses were screaming at him" (*er hot mit ale koykhes gefilt, vi tsu im shrayen di leydike yidishe hayzer*) (11–12). The houses serve as memorials to the lives they no longer contain.

The hero keeps track of time by quoting the opening of Genesis: "it was morning, it was evening of the second day"; "it was morning, it was evening of the third day" (*es iz geven fri, es iz geven ovnt fun tsveytn tog, es iz geven fri, es iz geven ovnt fun dritn tog*) (9–10). Time stops and starts all over again, as in the first week of creation; the vast scale of the irrevocable loss requires a new creation. The sole remnant of the past is a little Jewish girl who wanders into the smithy where the hero works. The only words she speaks are the tragic answers to the questions "Whose child are you?" (*vemens bistu*) and "What is your name?" (*vi ruft men dikh*). The girl's answers are "No one's" (*keynems*) and "No one" (*keynem*) (14). By the end of the story, Nokhem adopts the girl and stops counting the days: "the remaining survivor of a family of blacksmiths no longer counted the days" (*un der eynstik geblibener fun der mishpokhe shmidn hot mer di meslesn nit getseylt*) (22). Time resumes its normal course.

In work published more than thirty years later, Gorshman returned to deserted places and empty Jewish houses. In "I Love to Travel" (1981) Gorshman includes a vignette about a visit to an old friend, who remembers a trip she took to the shtetl of Kaydan (in northern Lithuania) at the end of the 1950s:

> When I got to Kaydan at the end of the fifties, I was overcome by memories. You can imagine, there wasn't a single Jew! . . . I wandered around the city, like a madwoman, I didn't know where I was! Listen,

you and I are stronger than iron, because we are alive. I start thinking, and it comes to me that my Lipe [the speaker's husband] and your Mendl [the addressee's husband], may they rest in peace, were lucky people. They died their own deaths . . . When I looked at the Jewish houses in Kaydan, I couldn't believe that my friend Rokhte, my sister, my mother and father weren't going to come out. I was there for one day, and that day turned my soul over a hundred thousand times.

Az ikh bin gekumen, sof fuftsiker yorn, in Keydan, hob ikh zikh shir nit gerirt fun di gedanken. Kentst zikh farshteln, keyn eyn yid! . . . Ikh bin arumgegangen iber der shtot, vi a mishugene, kh'hob nit gevust, af voser velt ikh bin! Her zikh ayn, mir zenen shtarker fun ayzn, az mir lebn. Ikh gib a kler, kumt bay mir oys, as mayn Lipe un dayn Mendl, olev hasholem, zaynen gliklekhe mentshn. Zey zaynen zikh geshtorbn mit zeyer toyt . . . Az ikh hob gekukt in Keydan af di yidishe shtiber, hob ikh nit gegleybt, az s'vet nit aroysgeyn mayn khaverte Rakhte, mayn shvester, der tate mit der mamen. Ikh bin dartn geven eyn tog, un der tog hot mir ibergekert di nishome hunderter toyznter mol. (Gorshman 1981, 28)

This miniature narrative contains multiple displacements. The frame narrator, Shire Gorshman, travels to see her friend, who recalls the trip she (the friend) took thirty years earlier and recounts the experience she had at that prior time. Unlike the earlier "Wild Hops," time does not resume its normal course. The Jewish houses are at once empty and at the same time full of the people who used to live in them. In Kaydan, in the late 1950s, time stopped, and memories of the prewar past erased the present. To live on after the war is to remain vulnerable to a particular kind of haunting.

For Gekht this haunting is sharpened by remorse. Moral failure in the past sharpens the bitterness of loss in the present. Gekht completed eight years of his ten-year sentence for anti-Soviet agitation in 1952, and worked in the Kaluga city park before his rehabilitation in 1955. In all the stories included in the cycle *Duties of the Heart*, the past revisits the present by making demands on survivors who failed to fulfill their obligations to others. The title had particular resonance for Gekht, who had also used it earlier. One of the first works he published after his rehabilitation was an autobiographical essay that linked his early years in Odessa with a trip he made there in 1944, right after the Soviets liberated the city from the Germans. The essay, published in 1959, concludes with the line "I bear the burden of many unpaid debts of the heart [*dolgi serdtsa*]" (Gekht 1959, 234). The phrase likely reflects a well-known Jewish moral tractate, "Chovot Halevavot" (usually translated as "Duties of the Heart"), by Bahya Ben Joseph Ibn Pakuda. The work, written in the eleventh century, became a popular text in the moral and spiritual movement known as "Musar," which attained prominence in the nineteenth century and the first part of the twentieth century in Jewish communities in the Pale of Settlement, especially Lithuania. The extent of Gekht's Jewish education cannot be established definitively; however, it is highly likely that the work would have been referred to in the environment in which he was raised. The medieval "Chovot Halevavot" discusses both ethical and religious obligations. In Gekht's story cycle *Duties of the Heart*, ethical obligations and relationships of the past, disrupted by the war and by incarceration in the Gulag, return to haunt the present.[7]

"Begunok" (Release papers), the first story, captures the theme of the work as a whole. The title refers to a document issued at the end of employment, attesting to the return of government property. Unlike the *begunok*, which certifies that nothing is owed, the story attests to the impossibility of fulfilling the debts of the past. There is no release. A Jewish couple, a carpenter who works in a park (like Gekht himself) and his wife, lost track of their son during the war. She remained in occupied territory and gave her son to the care of "a good person" in order to go to the market on the same day that the Germans invaded the town. The mother survives the war but fails to find her son afterwards, and develops a nervous illness. Years later, on the day that the father is to receive his *begunok*—his release document—his son, now a married man, turns up; he has a letter from his adoptive parents, inviting the couple to move to their city in Kazakhstan. The letter from the adoptive father, which says that he could tell right away that the child was not Russian, and which offers the old couple the prospect of a reunited, single family, but in two houses, produces an outraged response from the biological mother. To her, the offer sounds "just like the slogan: the family of nations, the friendship of nations" (Gekht 1963, 42). In her opinion, "nations are different." In the story, Jewish ethnographic difference emerges only in the names of the Jewish couple, Lazar Abramovich and Tsila, and in the cookies, spiced with cinnamon and saffron, that Tsila bakes for her son. The spices provoke one of Lazar Abramovich's coworkers to say, "You want to return him [the son] to his faith?" Gekht's story is not aimed at the restoration of Jewish observances (or foodways); its reflections on the obligations of the past disrupt any comfortable postwar affirmation of victory and progress. Moreover, the rejection of the "family of nations" and the insistence on difference, no matter how slight Jewish ethnographic markers may appear, are remarkable given the time the work was published. The end of the story brings no reconciliation: the son survived, but not as a Jew; the family is not reunited; the wounds of the war remain open.

"Syn Iulian" (Julian, my son), another story in Gekht's *Duties of the Heart*, develops the theme of the obligations between parents and children, and at the same time pays homage to Odessa and the writers associated with the city, in particular, Isaac Babel. Gekht's "duties of the heart" include a sense of obligation toward the great Odessa writer, but not merely in the spirit of a memorial to the dead. Without mentioning the author by name, Gekht's story directly quotes Babel's language. The protagonist, Platov, journeys to Kovel, a small city in Western Ukraine:

> There was a street, there were people, there was life on the street, and this life ended. Whoever survived began a new life in the same place as the old, destroyed life. There are apiaries in the area. Again in Volynia there are many apiaries . . . Platov once read, "I mourn for the bees. They were destroyed by warring armies. In Volynia there are no more bees." And there was another war after the civil war, the most terrible war, and Volynia is once again rich in bees. (Gekht 1963, 210)

The quoted lines that the hero reads are from the opening of Babel's *Red Cavalry* story "The Road to Brody," a miniature series of vignettes that focus on the mindless destruction of the civil war while hinting at the possibility of redemption. It includes a folktale about the bees who protect Jesus on the cross because he, like them, is a carpenter. "The Road to Brody" ends with the intertwined emotions of passion, poison, death, and desire. By putting Babel's language about the devastation of the civil war into the new context of the Second World War, Gekht constructs a link between his text and Babel's, between Babel and himself, and between the two events of the civil war and the Second World War. The linking of separate episodes of monumental destruction into a series recalls the Jewish tradition of linking recent and prior history, as in the reference to the Holocaust as *"der driter khurbn"* (the third destruction), the first two being the destruction of the Temples.[8] In Gekht's story, Babel's lament over the destruction of the bees marks the destruction of the life of Volynia in both time frames—the more distant and the immediate past. The reverberation of the past in the present, a particularly Jewish form of historical imagination, constitutes the central theme of the story.

The story opens in May 1940 in Lvov. Elisei Platov arrives from Odessa in Lvov to provide assistance to the director of orphanages and to visit his son, serving in the army. The father insists that Germany has no designs on Russia. Touring the city, Platov makes a metaphorical journey back in time. He sees the city's medieval buildings and its Galician Jews, dressed in traditional Hasidic garb, which are long gone from Odessa (Gekht's birthplace and the subject of his writings from the 1930s); he visits well-known civil war sites, and he becomes intrigued by a document from 1939, which he finds in his hotel room, addressed "To my son, Julian," the title words of the story. The traveler, Platov, learns the melodramatic tale of a teacher at the gymnasium, Fandrikh, his girlfriend, and their son, whose father does not learn of his existence until many years later. The father's efforts to get in touch with his son fail.

Gekht pushes the action forward to the year 1948. Platov travels once again to Lvov. He learns more about the father, Fandrikh, and his search for his son. It turns out that Fandrikh had two girlfriends at once, and both were pregnant at the same time. His daughter died as a young woman, and his son, Julian, the object of his search, was killed by the Germans in 1943. The meeting that could have taken place in the first part of the story will never come to fruition. The motif of the missed meeting, the wrong turn, arriving too late or too early, is central to Bergelson's vision of Jewish history. Similar failures dominate Gekht's story cycle. The gap between two parallel series of events is never overcome; the longed-for meeting never takes place; the glimmer of redemption fails to touch the course of everyday life. Gekht's reconstruction of discontinuity and failed outcomes contrasts with the monolithic pronouncements about happiness quoted in such works as Erenburg's *The Thaw*.

In "Julian, My Son," Gekht's concern with tracing the gaps in the historical narrative appears in small but telling detail. In the interval between the two parts of the story, history itself changes. All the Polish monuments in Lvov are gone, galloped off, to use Gekht's language, back to Poland. The monuments Gekht names are specifically Polish, but the larger story that Gekht is telling by implication is about the removal and lack of other kinds of memorials, including those having to do with Jewish history. The work Gekht produced after his incarceration in the Gulag reflects the painstaking effort to reconstruct what happened in the face of this other form of destruction, the forced and willful amnesia of this time.

The story of loss and return also reflects Gekht's own biography. The entire literary milieu from which he had appeared was long gone in the early 1960s. This milieu included people (Shklovskii, Babel, Ilf, Bagritskii, and the visual artist Genrietta Adler), the places in Odessa where the young writers met and read their works, and something else, which is far more difficult to pin down: the atmosphere of excitement and anticipation that emerged from his letters of the 1920s about the possibilities for a vibrant Jewish literary culture in Russian.[9] His relation to Babel was central to his conviction on the charge of anti-Soviet agitation in 1944; far from denying his closeness to Babel, Gekht underscored it during his interrogation, insisting that he was "in solidarity with Babel." His sensitivity to Jewish issues was another central theme of his 1944 interrogation. Gekht reported to his interrogator that he had said in public that the venom of fascism was spreading on Soviet soil, repeating more than once his stated conviction that anti-Semitism was on the rise in the Soviet Union in the 1940s. In his published work of the 1960s Gekht returns to the very issues that landed him in the Gulag in the first place, not only by attacking Stalin's "friendship of nations" and avowing his link to Babel but also by acknowledging the overwhelming importance of the past. The committee reviewing his post-Gulag manuscripts for publication rightly concluded that Gekht's heroes "live outside time, outside the epoch and its revolutionary tasks."[10]

While imprisoned, one of Gekht's fellow Gulag inmates, inventing an apt form of literary *gematria*, decoded Gekht's name as if each letter stood for a word. GEKHT spelled out and translated from Russian reads as "Sad Jewish Artistic Text" (*grustnyi evreiskii khudozhestvennyi tekst*).[11] In his post-Gulag fiction, Gekht brings this text to life. Coming across the passage from "The Road to Brody" in "Julian, My Son" is like discovering a message in a bottle. The ocean of silence surrounding Babel was beginning to recede at this time. What hope and despair Gekht must have felt performing his own act of literary resurrection for his friend and mentor.

Moshe Altman and the Tomb of Memory

The troubled relation between fathers and children, a prominent theme in Gekht, has broad resonance in the Yiddish prose of Moshe Altman. There are very few published accounts of Altman's life and work in either Russian or Yiddish, and no discussion of him in English.[12] Altman was born in 1890 in the shtetl Lipkany (in Yiddish, Lipkon) in Bessarabia, into an impoverished and uneducated family: his father could not read Yiddish and his mother was completely illiterate. Altman attended heder, matriculated at but did not graduate from a gymnasium in Kamenets-Podolsk, and was mobilized in the Romanian army during the First World War. He worked as a lecturer with the Jewish Cultural Federation in Bessarabia and lived in Bucharest until 1930, when he emigrated to Buenos Aires to work as the director of an orphanage. He returned to Bucharest after a year and became a member of the Writers' Union during the Soviet takeover of Bessarabia and Bukovina in 1940. He spent the war years in evacuation in Central Asia, and resettled in Chernovtsy, Ukraine, after the war. One of his autobiographical writings marks the exact date (July 6, 1941) when he lost his archive of manuscripts and correspondence—"the work of decades"—during the wartime evacuation (Altman 1957). Altman was arrested in 1949 (the charges included nationalism and Trotskyite conspiracy) and imprisoned in the Gulag in Eastern Siberia until 1955, when he returned to Chernovtsy and remained there until his death in 1981. Altman began his writing career with a novel called *Blendenish* (Delusion) in 1926. A novella, *Di viner karete* (The Viennese carriage), first published in 1935, was included in a collection published in Moscow (Altman 1980). Two chapters included in that collection first appeared in a novel published in Bucharest in 1936 (Altman 1936). Altman wrote for *Eynikayt*, the newspaper of the Jewish Anti-Fascist Committee, during the war; his articles appeared in the Yiddish newspaper *Yidishe shriftn* (Yiddish writings) in Warsaw in the late 1950s, and he also served as a staff writer for the Soviet Yiddish journal *Sovetish heymland*, which published his "Skeynishe notitsin" (Notes of an old man) in the 1970s. *Der vortsl* (Roots), a selection of war stories, was published in Yiddish in 1948 in the Soviet Yiddish journal *Heymland* and translated into Russian a decade later (Altman 1948; 1959).

Altman's work, including his fiction and nonfiction prose, is at once worldly, cosmopolitan, and intensely Jewish. References to the classic Yiddish writers I. L. Peretz and Sholem Aleichem appear together with allusions to the writings of Freud, Henri Bergson, Einstein, Paul Verlaine, the Bible, and Rashi (the twelfth-century scholar whose work was studied by Jewish children together with the Bible). For Altman, Yiddish is a mobile, literate world language. His practice of Yiddish contradicts Soviet linguistic policies, according to which the literature of the national minorities was to be national in form, socialist in content. Altman's writing, and indeed that of the other writers in this chapter, challenges the critics who continue to claim that postwar Soviet Yiddish is nothing more than the product of oppression. Altman's work explores the simultaneity of multiple time frames in acts of remembrance that open the present to the past. The present is not the end point of the great events of the past, as in Papernyi's model of Soviet history, "culture 2," but neither is every clock in Altman "the anniversary of a death," as in Bergelson. Altman's preoccupation with the past is not driven by the *khurbn* alone; his all-consuming interest in the past characterizes both his prewar and his postwar writings; for example, in the opening of his prewar *Medresh Pinkhes*, we read, "*Der roman iz a restovrirungs-pruv fun a vinkl fun a svive in a geviser tsayt*" (The novel is an attempt to restore a corner of a world from a particular time) (Altman 1980, 17). Altman, like other writers in this study, was ready to respond to overwhelming catastrophe, even before the Nazi destruction of the Jews. He had already worked out his poetics of memory and restoration.

"A mayse mit a nomen" (A story about a name), written after the war, reworks the Jewish legend of the thirty-six hidden righteous men. The most well-known precedent from classic Yiddish literature is Peretz's "If Not Higher," in which a rabbi disguises himself as a peasant to perform menial tasks for a bedridden woman on the holiest Jewish holiday. In his nonfiction writing, Altman singles out Peretz as the Yiddish writer who had the most important meaning for him and his generation. Altman's version of this story begins in the interwar period with the sudden appearance of a madman in an unnamed city in Bessarabia. Motye performs menial tasks and fixes clocks, asking only for bread as payment. He maintains absolute silence until another madman in the town gets annoyed and demands to know why. Motye's answer is, "And what do you accomplish with your talk?" (*un vos makhstu mit dayn redn?*) (Altman 1974, 326). It later emerges that Motye is not only literate but highly educated, and that he left behind a wife and children in another city. His renunciation of home, family, and normal social life take on another significance, as a form of penance. When the war begins, Romanian and German soldiers begin killing Jews. On a scorching summer day, the Germans drive the Jews out of town and force them to march to their deaths, depriving them of water. At a stop along the way the German soldiers mock the Jews' suffering by pouring water on the ground. Disguised as a peasant, Motye brings the Jews water.

The source of this narrative is none other than Motye himself, now a very old man, who provides this account to the narrator. The narrator's prefatory remarks deftly frame the story in the broad context of Jewish history. Mulling over what to call the story, he considers including it among the "tales of the destruction" (*megides-hakhurbn*), "the stories of about the *khurbn*, the *khurbn* of our time." The "destruction of our time"—the Holocaust, a term Altman does not use—is clearly lined to the destructions of previous times. The preface introduces the transcendent biblical time frame by recalling the Genesis scene in the Garden of Eden, when God tells Adam and Eve to be fruitful and multiply (Altman gives the biblical Hebrew and provides a translation into Yiddish).

The narrator continues, "Today it's different" (*haynt iz anderish*) (320). What makes "today" different is only implied: God no longer talks to humans; humans, particularly Jews, can no longer multiply because so few remain. In spite of the rupture between the past and the present or, better, because of it, there are stories that must be told and transcribed, as the narrator concludes: "I wrote the story for the sake of memory" (*Hob ikh di geshikhte forshribn l'zikorn*) (332).

Altman's sense of the present, like Bergelson's, can best be described as an "aftereffect." "Now" comes after the great monumental events of history have already taken place, when all that remains are obligations to be fulfilled. "*Haynt iz anderish*" (today it is different) is also the refrain of his prewar literature. His prewar novel *Medresh Pinkhes* (1936) opens with a reference to the Book of Ruth and concludes the opening with the disclaimer "haynt iz anderish." In Altman's prewar literature the characters feel the gap between the present and the past and sense the necessity of living beyond the upheavals of their time. His postwar literature heightens the experience of catastrophic loss.

Altman's interest in associative memory is key to his style. The play of association, according to Altman, is crucial to Peretz, Sholem Aleichem, and Tolstoy. References to Tolstoy in Soviet literature of the middle of the twentieth century are not, of course, unusual; as we saw in Chapter Four, *War and Peace* was the model for nearly every Soviet war novel. What is unusual is that Altman chooses Tolstoy's late work "Hadji Murad" as his prime Tolstoy text. As Altman points out, the opening frame of this work is built on a series of associations: the narrator, walking along, sees a field that has just been mowed, and a thistle that refused to be chopped down, and the sight reminds him of a story from long ago about Hadji Murad. The lack of a panoramic overview, the absence of a single narrative voice and a linear and stable time frame, and their replacement by contingency, fluidity, and multiplicity—features of Tolstoy's style in "Hadji Murad"—also characterize Altman's own writing. Monumental destruction does not lead in Altman's case to a monumental writing style.

In one of his "Bletlekh" (Pages), published in the Warsaw Yiddish newspaper *Yidishe shriftn* (Yiddish writings) in 1957, Altman notes that unlike other Jewish writers who had only negative memories of heder, the Jewish elementary school, he values it as a particularly important source of literary associations. He adds that he not only learned portions of the Bible by heart (*gelernt*), but "experienced" (*ibergelebt*) them. One of the vignettes from "Skeynishe notitsn," called "Vos der zikorn farhit" (What memory keeps), demonstrates the multiple ramifications of the childhood experience.

"What Memory Keeps" opens on a tragicomic note to the effect that the author once wrote a major work on the activity of memory, a work which he lost and whose contents he forgot. He does recall, however, Verlaine's line "memory, memory, what do you want from me" (*zikorn, zikorn! vos vilst du fun mir?*) from "Nevermore" (Poèmes Saturniens: Mélancholia II). It is not he who makes demands on his memory; on the contrary, it is memory that makes demands on him. In the story "In tif funem shpigel" (In the mirror's depths), the protagonist distinguishes between "practical memory," which he defines as a "collection of information," and memory that "calls him to account" (*vos mont hezhbun*) (Altman 1980, 240). The past is not a storehouse of items to be used for the convenience of the present; on the contrary, the past, according to Altman, disrupts the smooth surface of the present with its own demands.

The vignette "What Memory Keeps" (from the late 1970s) acknowledges the active role of memory, which leads the author "through dozens of years and countries, without a passport or visa" (*iber tsenlike yorn un lender, on a pas un an vizes*). Each separate memory carries the seeds of a previous memory within its frame; the disparate time frames merge into a single, unbroken whole, as in Bergson's theory of the continuity of memory and the present (Bergson 1991, 133–77). "Forty years ago," the narrator says, in the "Elite" café in Bucharest, Altman's friend, the theater director and poet Yankev Shternberg, also from Lipkany, reminds him that he, Shternberg, was always "more revolutionary" than Altman. The memory of this scene provokes a memory of a scene in the heder, an episode from "eighty years ago," and the scene in the heder recalls an intergenerational conflict from biblical times (Altman 1980, 329).

The biblical reference is particularly important, because it highlights the theme of the obligations of the past, the burdens transmitted from one generation to the next. Gekht plays on a similar theme in his postwar stories, but without the overt biblical framework. Altman emphasizes the Joseph story, in particular the hidden drama of Joseph and his father, Jacob. Reunited with Joseph in Egypt, Jacob asks to be buried not there but with his ancestors in Canaan. Altman recalls his emotions as his teacher explained the scene of Jacob's farewell:

> I, the littlest, was greatly struck by the place where Jacob our father (Jacob from the Bible!) is parting with his son, the great minister in Egypt, and asks to be buried in Canaan, in the cave where his ancestors lie.
>
> *Mikh, dem klenstn, hot shtark farkhapt dos ort, vu Yankev avinu (Yankev fun khumesh!) gezegnt zikh mit zayn zun, dem groysn har in Mitsraim, un bet, me zol im, ven er vet shtarbn, apfirn brengen tsu kvure in Kanaan, in der heyl vu es lign zayne eltern.* (329)

Jacob makes this request in the knowledge that Joseph harbors "resentment" (Rashi) against him because of Rachel, whom Jacob buried, in Altman's account, "in an open field," even though it would have been a short journey to take her body to a city, where there would have been a proper grave site. Genesis only hints at the tension surrounding Jacob's request; the full discussion is found in Rashi's commentary, which is the explanatory text the children in heder learned.

The author recalls his otherwise despised teacher acting out the confrontation between Jacob and Joseph: "Suddenly the tone of the rebbe's chant changed—today I would call it tragic . . . he [Jacob] justifies himself before Joseph, explaining why he, Jacob, buried his, Joseph's mother, in an open field" (*Un plutsem tut zikh an ender der ton funem zingen baym rebn, haynt volt ikh es ongerufn: tragish . . . er farentfert zikh far Yoysefn, farvos er, Yankev, hot zayn, Yoysef's, muter gebrakht tsu kvure in ofenem feld*) (329). Jacob justifies his choice of Rachel's burial site, according to Rashi, on the grounds that he chose it not for convenience but on God's command, as the future would show. Rachel would later weep for her children as they walked to their captivity. Altman does not spell out all this explanation but merely hints at it by saying that "Jacob kept on justifying himself." Joseph bears resentment against his father on account of an offense that Rachel could not have felt while she was alive, because its cause was her burial site.

Just at the moment when the teacher shows the children how Jacob "justified himself," Altman's friend, appearing at the open window of the heder, shouts a curse at the teacher: "the devil take your father!" (*a ruekh in dayn tatn arayn!*) (329). The deviant, "revolutionary" act backfires, because the teacher at this moment is enacting a scene that plays powerfully on his students' emotions, especially the emotions of his littlest student, Altman.

The teacher's name is Jacob (Yankl); the friend's name is Jacob (Yankev), recalling the name of the biblical Jacob. The tension between friends, "brother-writers," so to speak, resonates with the rivalry between Joseph and his brothers; this conflict in turn resonates with the intergenerational tension between Joseph and his father Jacob on account of Rachel's grave. "What Memory Keeps" is not limited to warm, nostalgic shtetl idylls but instead to a kind of infinite regress of the past, spilling over into the present. In "What Memory Keeps," the café in Bucharest, the heder in Lipkany, and the scene between Joseph and his father in Egypt all mirror one another, and the pain of the past—even the legendary past recounted in Genesis—intrudes on the present, and the events of the more recent past, especially the Second World War and postwar Soviet history, ramify in turn with these prior moments.

The episode of Joseph and Jacob offers suggestive parallels to Maria Torok and Nicolas Abraham's theory of the carryover of wounds from one generation to the next. Torok and Abraham describe this injury as an intrapsychic haunting. The children bear in themselves the secrets of their parents. Abraham and Torok write, "What comes back to haunt are the tombs of others" (1994, 172). It is precisely Rachel's tomb that haunts Joseph. Traditional Jews had the habit of seeing ongoing reality through a biblical lens, as if the here and now were nothing but a metaphor for biblical history. Altman's use of the Bible, in contrast, far from obscuring the perception of ongoing events, serves instead to intensify their emotional weight. For Altman, writing after the war, Rachel's grave in the open field resonates with the Nazi destruction of the Jews and the Soviet government's failure to commemorate their deaths. He counters the historical amnesia and failure of memory of his own time by remembering—deeply and along multiple paths of association—a seemingly trivial and historically innocent moment from his heder days.

Altman returns to similar themes in another postwar story, "In the Mirror's Depths." A psychiatrist and his friend discuss the subject of trauma. The psychiatrist distrusts Freud's theory that sexuality is the basis for all psychological disease. He offers his own explanation instead, which he derives from two Yiddish folk expressions, including the saying "Parents sin and children suffer" (*tate-mame zindikn un kinder kumen op*) (Altman 1980, 239). In this story, as in "What Memory Keeps," the theme of intergenerational wounding is key. The psychiatrist's language is particularly striking, in light of both the Rachel story and Torok and Abraham's theory of trauma. The psychiatrist says: "The moral type of person withdraws from the world and bears his secret with him in a tomb [*keyver*], the cause of his trauma. A great many cases of psychic trauma stem from the parents. In a sensitive child, a coarse scene between the parents remains for an entire life" (240). Abraham and Torok define the psychic process of incorporation as an alternative to mourning. Instead of acknowledging loss, victims symbolically take lost objects of love into themselves, thereby threatening their own boundaries and creating a "secret tomb" inside themselves. Episodes of incorporation include, for example, Viktor Shtrum carrying his mother's letter in his pocket, and Vasilii Grossman's letter-writing to his mother after her death. Altman is thinking about trauma in similar terms. Catastrophic mass death takes root in an individual's psyche where it overlaps and builds upon already existing structures of loss.

In Altman's story "In an apru tog" (A day off), one of the characters says that in Moscow he feels increasingly more "rooted in today, in tomorrow" (*Un ot do fil ikh mikh mit yedn tog alts mer ayngevortslt inem haynt, inem morgn*) (257). In this line, "today" means the "today" of Zabare's novel, the today in which a new world is being born. This and other Soviet motifs in Altman's postwar writing, including, for example, hagiographic references to Lenin, do not undermine the absolute singularity of his artistic vision.

Altman definitively turns his back on the Soviet meaning of "today" in an important vignette, "Mayn tatn's nit opgeshikt kartl" (My father's unsent postcard), found in his autobiographical cycle *An Old Man's Notes*. The tiny, two-page story describes Altman's memory of his father's illiteracy. He could recite the prayers and follow along when the weekly Torah portion was read, but could not read or write Yiddish or Hebrew, or Russian, and had to rely on his young, literate nephews to do his correspondence for him. On one occasion they refused, and the five-year-old Moshe watched helplessly as his father sweated over his postcard, which he filled with miniscule handwriting (*pitsinke oysiyelekh*). The postcard was never sent, because the Russian-speaking nephew pronounced it illegible and would not address it. The story concludes with another unsent message, the son's address to his father:

> Father . . . your fool of a son writes and speaks and reads a half-dozen languages, and he is something of a Jewish writer. But I swear, your unsent postcard with its miniscule handwriting is in my eyes today more valuable than everything I write, except for what I lost . . .
>
> *Tate . . . dayn shlimazolner zun shraybt un redt un leyent af a halbn tuts leshoynes, un er is a shtikl shrayber bay yidn. Ober, ikh shver, dayn nit opgeshikt kartl mit di pitsinke oysiyelekh iz in mayne oygn haynt mer vert fun alts, vos ikh shrayb, akhuts dem, vos ikh hob farloyrn . . .* (ellipsis in original) (Altman 1980, 358)

In the story "A Day Off," "today" is linked to the present and the future, but in this piece, "today" looks back to the past, to the "father's unsent postcard" and to the author's lost manuscripts. The use of the second person (*dayn zun, dayn nit opgeshikt kartl*) is a form of speaking to the dead, a visit to the grave. The words that the writer addresses to his father are also addressed to the readers of the text, who become witnesses to the author's oath, his own last will and testament, in which he renounces the value of everything he has ever published in favor of his father's unsent postcard and his own lost works. The legacy that Altman leaves his readers, like the legacy he received from his father, is at once a gift and the imposition of a loss.

Altman's repeated use of the motif of the tomb (*keyver*) in both the heder story, with its references to Genesis, and the story of the psychiatrist, set during the Cold War, suggests his vision of the hidden linkages of Jewish history. His vision is tragic, but not hopeless. The submerged connections between events brought to life by the involuntary work of his memory take him along a pathway (without passports or visas, as he says) where events from the recent and remote past appear in achronological simultaneity. Reading his short works as a single text reveals a single pattern in a tapestry that stretches from Genesis to the 1960s. It is astounding that Altman constructed this profoundly Jewish narrative in the context of his own prior incarceration in the Gulag for the crime of Jewish nationalism. It is also remarkable that his work appeared in mainstream Soviet-approved publications, such as *Sovetish heymland*, whose editors and leading critics urged their readers forward to new acts of joyous socialist construction.

Memory, Cultural Space, and Material Culture: Rivke Rubin and Dina Kalinovskaia

Rubin's story "Aza min tog" (A day like this), published in a volume of her works in Yiddish in 1982, and in Russian translation in 1986 under the title "Strannyi den'" (Strange day), uses a single day in 1975 as a point of departure for the narrator's memories from previous decades. Of particular importance is the role of the literary intertexts the author uses to open out her own narrative to other times and places. Bakhtin's understanding of the function of language in prose fiction sheds light on Rubin's work. For Bakhtin, language in novels functions in a densely textured and cacophonous linguistic space full of what everyone is saying, "other people's words." In Rubin's hands, Yiddish is not confined to the Jewish Autonomous Region or the former Pale of Settlement as the language of the shtetl. In "Aza min tog" Yiddish also belongs to Moscow, as a modern urban Soviet space, with its bustling metro system and its impossible stores, where salespeople deny that goods are available even though they are staring you right in the face. Yiddish provides a space where the voices of other authors, both Yiddish and Russian, speak again.

Rubin (1906–87) was a literary scholar and critic in addition to being a fiction writer; she wrote the introduction to the collected works of Sholem Aleichem published in Russian in the mid-1950s, in addition to her studies of other classical Yiddish authors; she served on the staff of *Sovetish heymland* from the time of its appearance in 1961. Her husband,

Meir Akselrod, was a well-known painter of Jewish themes; "Aza min tog" quotes one of his paintings, so to speak. The visual image becomes yet another intertext of the story. Rubin's daughter, Elena Akselrod, is a Russian-language poet currently living in Israel. Elena Akselrod's poems appear in the Russian version of "Aza min tog."

In the story, the protagonist and first-person narrator is a middle-aged woman who senses herself as having been left behind by the death of her husband and the betrayal by her best friend. Although the story recounts major historical events of European history, including the First World War, the revolution and civil war, the so-called Great Patriotic War, and the Nazi destruction of the Jews, these events do not add up to the conventional Soviet narrative of victory achieved and happiness restored. The story avoids the conventional realist structure of beginning, middle, and ending, and proceeds instead through a series of flashbacks. The great events of history are laid over the narrator's memory of her own personal experiences: her childhood, her friendships, her marriage, her relationships with her family, and the emotions, conflicts, jealousies, joys, and pains of these experiences. Allusions to works by other authors suggest the meanings of these events, both personal, immediate, and monumental. Bergelson and Aleksandr Blok occupy a significant place as intertexts in their own way—bits of the past reanimated in Rubin's text, and acts of cultural restoration, similar to Gekht's.

The title, "Aza min tog," alludes to a key passage in Bergelson's story "Among Immigrants":

> a day, like a year, a day like a long, long road. On a day like this, looking back, you think to yourself that you've walked a tremendous distance. A day like this drives all the lonely eccentrics outdoors, and they haunt the streets like mute, restless ghosts. (Bergelson 2005, 23)

> *a tog, vi a yor, a tog, vi a langer veg, af aza min tog, az men kukt zikh um tsurik, dakht zikh: me iz durkhgegangen an umgeveynlekh groyse shtreke. Aza min tog traybt aroys ale eynzame 'chudakes' in gas aroys, un zey blonzhshen arum, vi shtume nogndike gayster.* (Bergelson 1930b, 177–78)

The key phrase "aza min tog" (a day like this) occurs twice in the passage. The day itself expands beyond its normal limits and assumes an active role, driving the "eccentrics" out onto the streets, where they roam about like ghosts, fragments of a past that cannot be assimilated into the present.

Bergelson's strange day takes place in Berlin in the 1920s; Rubin's occurs in Moscow in 1975, but Bergelson's Berlin invades Moscow:

> As if on the eve of a holiday, or after a holiday—a restless, preoccupied Saturday evening after Shabes. And I am at sixes and sevens, because the day plays a strange game with me: when I am lit up in joy, bits of shadows stick to me, when I am overcome by darkness, flecks of light dance over me.
>
> *A min erev yontev oder shoyn gor nokh yontev—an umetiklekh-fartrakhter motse-shabes. Un ikh bin intsvishn. Take derfar, vos intsvishn, firt mit mir der tog a modne shpil: ot ver ikh bahelt un dokh klepn zikh tsu mir flekn fun shotns, un ot ver ikh fartunklt un es tantsn iber mir pasiklekh shayn.* (Rubin 1982, 7)

The day itself, as in Bergelson's story, takes an active role, filling the heroine's present moment with shadows and reflections of the past. In Bergelson's story, it is the marginal, self-styled "Jewish terrorist" who lives apart from everyone else, but in Rubin's story, it is a mainstream middle-aged woman, the first-person narrator who feels separate from others. At a restaurant celebrating a birthday, the narrator sharply senses her estrangement from her friends and family. Her isolation is due to the weight of the past, as in the phrase she uses to describe herself: "my head is full of the past" (*mayner [kop] iz ful mitn amol*) (31). This sudden separation from the present corresponds to one of the key dimensions of Benjamin's aura: "the strange weave of space and time, a unique appearance of a distance."[13] The heroine's recollections do not create an integral, unbroken link between past and present but instead an altered and alienated perspective on the "joyous" present.

There is a linguistic dimension to the narrator's sense of her own separateness. Everyone around her is speaking in Russian; at the birthday party, when the guests attempt to sing a Yiddish song, the narrator is the only one who knows the words. The dual linguistic registers of the story are indicated by the various names the narrator is called: Rokhil Borisovne (when she is formally addressed by a Russian speaker), and Rokhtshe, Rokhl, Rokhe, depending on the circumstances, when she is addressed by Yiddish speakers. Some of the scenes the narrator recounts from her past took place in Yiddish; others, in Russian; the first-person account she gives of her experience of that very particular day on which memories overtake her is in Yiddish.

The narrator's reminiscences revolve around her relationship with her friend from childhood, Lina. It is of interest that Rubin's story of survival and death, "A noenter mentsh" (published in one of the last issues of the journal *Heymland* in 1948) also concerns a friendship between two women (Rubin 1948). In "Aza min tog" Lina first makes her appearance in the story as a Polish (Jewish) refugee from the time of the First World War. In a section of the story titled "Dos meydele mit der reyf" (The girl with a hoop), Lina shows up on the street one day playing with a pink hoop, which she drives in front of herself with a stick. Lina teaches the narrator how to appear older and bigger in order to gain entrance to a feeding station set up by the Poles, who have reappeared in the town. Only children age fourteen and older are permitted to enter the feeding station. Lina's solution to the problem is a simple trick: the narrator, physically small, is to walk on her tiptoes like a ballerina; hence, the title of the vignette, "Puantn" (en pointe). The friendship with Lina lasts from childhood through institute days and the Second World War, and comes to an abrupt end sometime in the early 1970s when Lina publishes a newspaper article implicating the narrator's husband in bribery. The image of the hoop reappears at the end of the narrative, when the narrator considers calling her old friend but decides not to, and sees again the pink hoop and the little girl driving it.

Among the episodes from the past recounted in the narrative, the section entitled "A shmues in metro" (A conversation in the metro) stands out because of its interweaving of multiple time frames, its texture of allusions to Bergelson and Blok, and its portrait of the isolated narrator herself. In the vignette, the narrator recalls the year 1950, when her husband would take his sketchbook onto the subway and draw quick studies of his fellow passengers. He was looking for models for his important picture "Baym rand" (At the edge), which was to depict the mass execution of Jews, focusing on the moment right before their deaths. The central figure of the portrait, however, was still missing, and one night, in the subway, he thought he found the right model, a woman wrapped up in a shawl, "enveloped" and "withdrawn into herself" (*a farrukte, a far-zikh-figur*) (Rubin 1982, 13). Sholem asks his wife, "do you remember the story 'A witness'?" (*gedenkst di dertseylung 'An eydes'?*).

The answer is important for what it reveals about the cultural politics of memory, testimony, and translation. In the Yiddish original of the story the answer is:

> Do I remember? Of course, Sholem and I read it together in *Eynikayt*: "the suffering was in Jewish, but you had to recount it in Russian."
>
> *Tsi ikh gedenk? Mir hobn dokh zi tsuzamen geleynt mit Sholemen in 'Eynikayt': 'az di tsores zaynen geven af yidish, un dertseyln vegn zey darf men af rusish.'* (Rubin 1982, 13)

Rubin's citation is not exact; in Bergelson's story, the nameless witness recounts what he saw in the death camp, and Dora, another character, transcribes and translates his words into Russian, often stopping to ask whether she has it right. The witness's response to this question was: "You're asking for my expertise? . . . What can I tell you? The suffering was in Jewish" (*Mikh fregt ir do mevines? . . . Vos ken ikh aykh deruf zogn? Di tsores zaynen geven af yidish*) (Bergelson 1961, 692). The difference between Bergelson's Yiddish text and Rubin's is not significant, but when it comes to the Russian translation of Rubin's and Bergelson's Yiddish into Russian, there is a great difference. Both the Russian version of "An eydes" (Svidetel') and the Russian version of "Aza min tog" (Strannyi den') omit the line "the suffering was in Jewish" (*di tsores zaynen geven af yidish*). This statement of the linguistic and historical particularity of the Jews could be published in a Yiddish text, but not in a Russian one, not in 1961 when "An eydes" was translated into Russian, and not in 1986 when "Aza min tog" was translated into Russian.

In "Aza min tog" the woman on the Moscow subway in 1950 evokes an episode in Bergelson's story. The witness, referred to only as *"der yid"* (the Jew), recounts many terrible events that he saw in the death camp, but the only episode that makes him cry is the story of a "great beauty": *"in eyn partey—dertseylt er, iz geven a yunge froy, zeyer a groyse sheynkayt—a krasavitse"* (in one group, he recounts, there was a young woman, a very great beauty, a belle) (Bergelson 1961, 693). The Germans make another Jew in her group paint her portrait, and the painter and the model think they will be spared; but when the painting is finished, they are sent to the gas chamber like the other Jews. In Bergelson's story, witnessing, couched as a translation across a boundary, is a kind of survival beyond death. In Rubin's text, the unknown woman on the subway (we are not told whether she is Jewish) does not know that she resembles the figure from Bergelson's story, and Sholem's interest in her as a model is an unbearable burden to her. She disappears. As the narrative informs us, however,

> but whether she wants it or not, she has one constant living space, in my apartment. She sits on a peaceful canvas, wrapped up in her shawl, with her fear, her anguish, and her nobility.
>
> *ober tsi zi vil, tsi zi vil nit, iz eyn voyn-ort ba ir a bashtendiks, ba mir in shtub. Zi zitst af a fridlekhn layvnt, an ayngekutete in ir shal, mit ir shrek, mit ir angst, mit ir virde.* (Rubin 1982, 15)

The unknown model lives on in the completed painting (which was titled "Old Men, Women, Children," 1969), performing an involuntary service in someone else's memory and history.

After describing the painting, the narrator recalls a student she had before the war, who recited Blok's poem "Na zheleznoi doroge" (At the railway, 1910). Rubin's text quotes only its final words, "vse bol'no" (everything hurts); the poem as a whole, however, resonates with Rubin's story and its intertext from Bergelson. The opening lines read:

> Under the embankment, in an unmowed ditch,
> She lies and looks as if she were alive,
> In a brightly colored kerchief thrown over her braids,
> Beautiful and young.
>
> *Pod nasyp'iu, vo rvu nekoshennom,*
> *Lezhit i smotrit, kak zhivaia,*
> *V tsvetnom platke, na kosy broshennom,*
> *Krasivaia i molodaia*
>
> (Blok 1997)

The kerchief echoes the shawl from the painting; her beauty parallels the beauty Bergelson's witness attributes to the woman in the death camp (Bergelson uses the Slavic term *krasavitse* for "beauty"). The ditch and the train are associated with the mass death of Jews during the war, and the train also parallels the Moscow subway. In adducing these points of comparison, I am not arguing that Blok's poem anticipates the Holocaust but rather showing the impact of the quotation of the poem in the context of Rubin's story. The quotation changes the meaning of the original text; the new context adds new meaning to the quoted work. The citation of another's language, whether Blok's or "Sholem's," expresses the narrator's own pain. The quoted passages are like the flecks of light and shadow from the past overwhelming her in the present.

In the Blok poem, as the train rushes by, the passengers stare at the body of the girl: "their steady glance encircled / The platform, the garden with its faded greenery, / Her body, and the policeman next to her." The girl's youth "rushed by" like the train, without bringing her the fulfillment of her dreams. Blok emphasizes the standpoint of the dead girl left behind:

> Don't approach her with questions.
> It's all the same to you, and she's had enough:
> By love, dirt, or the wheels
> She's been crushed, and everything hurts.

> *Ne podkhodite k nei s voprosami,*
> *Vam vse ravno, a ei—dovol'no:*
> *Liubov'iu, griaz'iu il' kolesami*
> *Ona razdavlena—vse bol'no*

(Blok 1997)

Like the girl "under the embankment," Rubin's narrator is left behind as "life passes through to its next destination like a train" (to use another quotation from Blok). While everyone else at the restaurant is celebrating a birthday, she is "filled" with the past. To be left behind on the platform is to hear the music from Bergelson's speeding train. Blok's and Bergelson's prewar motif fits the backward-looking sensibility of postwar Jewish writers such as Rubin.

Blok is part of the canon of modern Russian literature; the educated reading public from the Soviet times to the present day knows the poem

"Na zheleznoi doroge" by heart. Bergelson, a central figure in the Soviet and world Yiddish canon who was also known to Russian-language audiences through translation and through the stage performance of his works, did not have Blok's stature among the Russian-language audience. In creating a literary space in which Bergelson and Blok exchange words, Rubin suspends the boundaries between the high culture of the Russian Silver Age and Yiddish literature. Yiddish is not merely the language of the Jews, or the language of the shtetl, or of the past; it is a language that belongs to Moscow and to world culture (in addition to Blok, Rubin refers to Dante, Delacroix, and Van Gogh). Her vision of Yiddish as a language of world literature resembles Altman's.[14]

Like Rubin's "Aza min tog" Dina Kalinovskaia's novella *O subbota* (Oh, Saturday) uses a single day in 1975 as a point of departure for memories of the past. Kalinovskaia (1934–2008), a brilliant prose stylist, endured undeserved obscurity in Russia and in the West. *Oh, Saturday*, originally written in Russian, was first published in Yiddish translation in 1975, and then in Russian in 1980 (Kalinovskaia 1980); it appeared as a separate volume in 2008. Set in Kalinovskaia's native Odessa, it is the story of a reunion: Grisha Shteiman returns to Odessa to visit his former lover, Mariia Isaakovna (Mania), his brothers Monia and Ziunia, and his friend Saul Isaakovich, Mariia's brother. The anticipation of his visit fills the characters with memories of the time they shared. Saul Isaakovich remembers 1921. He and his two comrades, political agitators, looked forward to the speeches they were going to make to the assembled crowd. The crowd locked the three in a shed and attacked them: they beat the two young men and assaulted the woman, cutting off her long braid. Saul remained permanently injured from the blows he received; he never again slept with his wife and during the Second World War was not drafted because of his nervous illness. His wife, Rebekka, began an affair with his comrade Misha Izotov. Ever since that time, Saul has wanted to return to the scene of the violence, as if he were looking for a "forgotten grave, to stand at the grave of his happiness with Rebekka, the grave of her young love of laughter, the grave of his easy relations with his friends, equality among men" (Kalinovskaia 1980, 45). In Kalinovskaia as in Altman the grave figures not only as a marker of the injury suffered in the past but also as the inner site of the self's permanent haunting.

Misha Izotov eventually married Saul's sister, Mania, and the two sisters-in-law barely tolerate each other. Mania remained in love with Grisha, the brother who left, and it was her persistent efforts that led to his reappearance in their lives. The characters in Kalinovskaia's *Saturday*, like the heroine of Rubin's "Aza min tog," like the Jews in Bergelson's early stories, and like the heroine in Blok's "At the Railway," stayed behind. When she sees Grisha again, Mania cries because he left her all those years ago; she asks why he left, and he asks why she stayed:

> You really didn't understand that it was easier for you to stay than for me to go?
> What do you mean, easier, Manechka? Remember what was going on then! The fighting, pogroms, starvation, typhus, cholera [bandy, pogromy, golod, tif, kholera]!
> Of course, Grishenka, of course . . . For you it was fighting, and cholera, but for me it was the variety show "Beaumonde!" (55)

What is implied but unspoken in this exchange is that Mania had to go through the business of daily life during this time that Grisha names as one of "fighting, pogroms, starvation, typhus, cholera." Indeed, when Mania remembers the years she spent without Grisha, in a loveless marriage, then through the war, evacuation, her widowhood, and raising her daughter alone, one of the details she recalls was the pleasure of clean bedding after the Sunday washing. In this debate between the reunited lovers, Kalinovskaia asserts a gendered view of the meaning and weight of ordinary daily life against the overwhelming pressure of living in history.

Whereas Altman's biblical frame and choice of theme lend an Oedipal, archetypal weight to his writings, marking the epoch in which the lives of his characters unfold, Kalinovskaia's writing, which also alludes to the Bible, shifts emphasis away from the world-historical significance of events, transferring the narrative center of gravity from history to domesticity. The description of the reunion of the four brothers in the story, calling to mind the reunion of Joseph and his brothers, assumes biblical cadences, especially in the repeated use of the word "and" ("Then Grisha asked his middle brother how things were, and Zinovii answered, that everything was fine—his health, and his wife, and his wife's health, and his son, and his son's son, and his daughter-in-law, and the apartment, and the dacha") (67). Kalinovskaia's narrative, however, recalls episodes from the past not in terms of the language of Genesis but in an intimate family idiolect, including half-Yiddish and half-Russian expressions. For example, when the newly rediscovered Grisha is about to visit, the flurry of baking and cooking recalls a prior time, referred to as "the time of Misha Izotov."

The title "Oh, Saturday" is significant: Saturday, the Jewish Sabbath, as a religious holiday, is said to "recall" the creation and the exodus from Egypt, and is understood to anticipate the redemption that is to come, when time will end (Deut. 5:12).[15] Kalinovskaia alludes to this traditional threefold understanding of the Sabbath. At the end of the story Saul Isaakovich visits the synagogue, a place both located within the city and cut off from it, a place where "time itself" ends. Half asleep, he has a vision of forty pilgrims wandering in the desert for forty years. Mania senses that time is going back to the beginning, and finds it appropriate that Grisha calls her by the affectionate term "child" (*detochka*).

In *Oh, Saturday* the author uses a particularly marked form of language to describe Sabbath time:

> Saturday, Saturday! It seems endless—so slow are the thick drops of time as they mature, invisible to the eye, impalpable to the senses, filling out to their full weight, and not limited by anything save their own ripeness, then quietly melt away, and without a groan, without a splash fall from the transparent vessel of the day into the open throat of the vessel of night, dark and golden.
> Saturday, Saturday! A long web of twilights!
>
> *Subbota, subbota! Ona kazhetsia neskonchaemoi—tak medlennyi gustye kapli vremeni, tak nezametno glazu, neoshchutimo zreiut oni, nalivaiutsia polnovesnost'iu i, nichem ne podtalkivaemye, krome sobstvennoi spelosti, tikho otchuzhdaiutsia i bez stona, bez vspleska padaiut iz prozrachnogo sosuda dnia v razverstoe gorlo sosuda nochi, temnogo i zolotogo.*
> *Subbota, subbota! Dolgaia pautina sumerek!* (23)

The passage, with its emphasis on the viscous quality of time on the Sabbath, recalls both Mandelshtam and Babel. Mandelshtam's 1917 poem "Golden Honey Flowed So Thick and Slowly from the Bottle" (Zolotistogo meda struia iz butylki tekla), originally published in Odessa, refers to Odysseus' return. Kalinovskaia plays on the same theme in her story; her Penelope, however, does not survive.[16] In the *Red Cavalry* story "Gedali," Liutov is "tormented by the thick sadness of memories" (*gustaia pechal' vospominaniia*); in Gedali's shop the "warm air flows past us" as the "young Sabbath" (*iunaia subbota*) rises to ascend her throne (Babel 1990 2:29–31). Kalinovskaia, like Gekht and Rubin, uses hidden quotation to reanimate the language of authors repressed in the Stalin period. Her citation echoes and enhances their version of the "noise of time."

Babel's story describes, in a schematic way, the conflict between the revolution and the Sabbath, between the promise of utopia and the pull of memory. The narrator, traveling with Budenny's army, is constantly in motion, as the titles of the story cycle indicate: he "crosses the Zbruch"; he is "on the road to Brody." The narrative takes the form of a journey through space, a space that attracts and repulses the hero with its history of past entanglements and passions. In Kalinovskaia's writing, in contrast, the focus is not on a journey but on home, on living in a domestic space. Indeed, the narrator in *O, Saturday* refers to the story as a "construction" and a "building" or "house" (*stroitel'stvo, dom*) (Kalinovskaia 1980, 104).

In "Risunok na dne" (The drawing on the bottom) Kalinovskaia figures the embeddedness of history within a domestic space using the homey image of two women, a mother and a daughter, redecorating their apartment. Marusia's diligence over an epic twenty-year time span has finally led to the recovery of the apartment she shared with her husband and children before the war. As the daughter, Serafima, strips away the wallpaper left by the previous tenants, she finds newspapers from the 1940s pasted underneath. Theater announcements, official communications about the number of German planes destroyed, and finally warnings addressed to the Romanian soldiers occupying the city not to retreat, on pain of death. Unknown to her children, Marusia, the mother, finds a cache of letters from her lover, Grisha, from the early 1920s. This is the same Grisha from the novella, *O, Saturday*, and the same story of departure and staying behind.

A family dispute about a material object provokes a set of reflections on legacy and memory. The one remaining teacup from a collection of six, each with a different "picture on the bottom," is the occasion for a quarrel that carries over from Marusia and her sister to Marusia's two grown children. The unmarried Serafima claims it for her own, but her brother, who marries and has a child, takes possession of the cup on the grounds that he must tell his child the family's stories.

Altman's memory "keeps" scenes from heder and the scenes depicted in the biblical texts he learned in heder; Kalinovskaia's heroine, in contrast, has a memory for the minutiae of domesticity that the character could not possibly remember. Serafima magically remembers her great-grandmother's house in Warsaw, where she never was, where her mother was taken by her grandmother when her mother was a little girl. She remembers the veranda, the wicker furniture, the sunlight on the tablecloth with its embroidery and its monogram of her great-grandmother, "NG," and the "yellow, gray, and rose-patterned stripes" on the wallpaper (Kalinovskaia 1985, 65). It seems clear that the kinds of family stories she would tell and the kind her brother would tell would be quite distinct, and that gender plays a role in the formation of their memories. The "houses" Kalinovskaia creates in her writing are not isolated from history, but rather history is located within their confines: the events of the first part of the twentieth century are found within the experience of daily life, embedded in its passions, jealousies, conflicts—and in its crockery and wallpaper, objects suffused with meaning.[17]

The haunted places of Soviet Jewish memory are not actual burial sites or official monuments but reveal themselves without warning in the exigencies of the moment, at a restaurant in Moscow or in a café in Bucharest. Gekht, Gorshman, Altman, Rubin, and Kalinovskaia register when and where time stopped and started over again, the moment when the clock became the anniversary of a death. The intrusion of the past in the present, whether in the form of an uncanny silence, the reappearance of a text or an actual person, or the resurgence of memories, including memories that belong to others, and the citation of the literary works of others, challenges postwar prescriptions about happiness. This literary art, however, does not serve as a static verbal monument to the dead. Instead of a memorial that fixes the past, memory's disruptive force shatters the "joyous construction" of Soviet culture of the 1960s and 1970s, revealing the gaps and fissures left by the unmourned violence of the past.

Six Jewish Spaces and Retro-Shtetls

> I love houses. I love children. I love the inner warmth that emanates from people to things, and from things to people.
>
> *Ikh hob lib a shtub. Ikh hob lib kinder. Ikh hob lib di inveynikste varemkayt, vos git zikh iber fun mentshn tsu zakhn, fun zakhn tsu mentshn.*
> Itsik Kipnis, "No Matter When" (Ven-nit-ven) (1969, 216)

In the 1920s and 1930s the express train signified the epoch-making significance of socialist modernity. After the war, Itsik Kipnis published a short work using the homier image of the tram to suggest the return to normal life. In "Ven-nit-ven" (No matter when) two friends meet by accident in a grocery store in postwar Kiev and decide to visit the cemetery outside the city. Their journey engages the larger narrative of twentieth-century Jewish literature in Russia: the onward motion of history that leaves a landscape of wreckage in its wake. The two friends in Kipnis's story must walk to the cemetery because the tram is temporarily out of service. This is no ordinary visit but something approaching a religious obligation, as if the travelers were making a pilgrimage. Indeed, in his short work "Babi Yar" Kipnis urges his readers to mark the anniversary (the *yortsayt*) of the mass killing with a trip to the site, a journey that must be made on foot, in order to retrace the steps of the dead. In "No Matter When" the focus shifts. The dead must be remembered, and the living must continue to live. By the time the two friends finish their visit to the cemetery, tram service is once again in operation. The last line of the story reads, "The half-empty tram started on its way" (Kipnis 1969, 220). The war is over; Hitler is defeated; and the victory holds the promise of something positive (*zol undz zayn gut*). The tram is working again, and daily life resumes its course as the protagonists return to the city, with its houses, lights, and the warmth that the narrator so loves. The tram, the emblem of the round of daily life, is both half empty and, at the same time, back in service.

Kipnis, Shmuel Gordon, Shire Gorshman, Fridrikh Gorenshtein, Inna Lesovaia, and the other authors who are the subject of this chapter represent and imagine the survival and continuing existence of the Jewish body politic in Jewish places in Soviet and post-Soviet Russia after the massive destructions of the twentieth century. In these writers' work, Jewish characters are emphatically embodied: they eat, drink, have babies, talk, and argue. The ethnographic details of foods, objects, life cycle events, and customary observances are unabashedly Jewish, as if there were no other possibility. In some cases, the ethnographic detail is Soviet Jewish, especially when it comes to Gordon and Gorenshtein.[1]

Although my primary concern is not with history or demographics, a brief discussion of Jews in Jewish places in the postwar Soviet Union will clarify my argument. Consider Itsik Kipnis's native shtetl of Sloveshne (Slovechno). Located in Ukraine, Sloveshne was more than half Jewish before the war but had only a few dozen Jewish families afterwards, and as of 2007, had none.[2] Berdichev, well known in the popular imagination as a "Jewish" city, was the site of massive Jewish deaths during the war. The destruction of Jewish lives and Jewish culture, however, did not mean the absolute end of Jewish life in the region of the former Pale of Settlement. Jews returned to the places they once inhabited after military service and evacuation. As Mordechai Altshuler puts it in *Soviet Jewry Since the Second World War*, "a large majority" of Jews who survived the war "returned to their previous areas of residence after the war" (1987, 93). According to Altshuler, they tended to concentrate in particular neighborhoods in Soviet cities, and in Kiev in particular, in areas that historically had a higher Jewish population. Altshuler also provides important information about language use: according to the 1959 census, 21 percent of Soviet Jews "declared a Jewish language as their native tongue." Although this figure fell to 17 percent in the 1970 census, the overall picture suggests that writers such as Gordon, Gorshman, Gorenshtein, and Lesovaia are representing and not merely imagining an important stratum of Jewish life in postwar Russia.[3]

These interrelated sociological and literary phenomena have gone largely unnoticed. I have touched on the reasons in the introduction to Part II, but the argument is worth reiterating here. The dominant story runs something like this: the world of the shtetl was destroyed or at least transformed beyond recognition by the First World War, the Russian Revolution and Civil War, the Second World War, the ongoing dejudaization carried out by Soviet Jews themselves, and the anti-Jewish campaigns of the postwar period. The Arab-Israeli Six-Day War of 1967 provoked a resurgence of Jewish national consciousness, which had found its way in masked form into some Russian-language literature authored by Jews. The shift in Jewish self-awareness, combined with pressure from the United States, led to massive emigration in the 1970s, the so-called era of stagnation—also known as "mature socialism"—under Brezhnev. The collapse of the Soviet Union in 1991 added to the outpouring of Jews from the former Soviet empire. In this view, the only form of Jewish culture after the Second World War was an impoverished literature in a heavily Sovietized Yiddish, and anything resembling a Jewish literature or culture in Russian virtually disappeared. This chapter tells a different story—about the persistence of Russian-Jewish culture in both Yiddish and Russian in the postwar period.

Yuri Slezkine's revisionist view of Soviet Jewish life corrects some aspects of the narrative of Jewish oppression by pointing to the high number of success stories among Soviet Jews and their overrepresentation in the elite. The picture of an assimilated and professionalized Jewish population in the capital cities is, however, incomplete, because it leaves out the former Pale and furthermore avoids the question of Jewish culture altogether, arguing that the Yiddish writers murdered by Stalin "had dedicated most of their lives to promoting Stalin's 'socialist content' in Yiddish 'national form'"(Slezkine 2004, 298). Slezkine does not address postwar Jewish literature in either Russian or Yiddish.

Both the established wisdom and the revisionist view need some modification, because both neglect the continuity of a Jewish life world in the postwar Soviet Union.[4] The aspirations of the people who inhabited this world, as represented by Gordon, Gorenshtein, Gorshman, and Lesovaia, were not defined solely by the quest to leave for Moscow or Israel. When Gorenshtein left the Soviet Union, he went to Germany. Other writers to be discussed in this and later chapters made the same journey; Inna Lesovaia still lives in Ukraine. Postwar Soviet

Jewish literature radically reworks the traditional Jewish opposition of "diaspora versus Israel," adding new dimensions to what constitutes the Jewish notion of home.[5]

For these authors, the Jewish home is found in the former Pale of Settlement, where it is neither a wasteland nor the site of full plenitude and unbroken tradition, but rather something in between. Thus my focus in this chapter is on bodies, places, and objects as the site of negotiation between cataclysmic history and the continuity of the everyday, between (Soviet) modernization and globalization and the force of an intractable, local, and specific Jewish inheritance.[6] The relation between history and the everyday ought not to be seen as a simple opposition between the two but rather as a more complex process in which the literary work enfolds history into the quotidian, and into the spaces and objects of the quotidian.[7] Material objects, food, and the interior passages of the home receive the imprint of (imagined) histories, both personal and political. To use Kipnis's image, warmth emanates from people to objects and back from objects to people. Objects that circulate only within the domestic confines of the family retain the aura of past lives, often inaccessible to the tools of history but nonetheless caught up within it.

Chapter Five focused on inadvertent memory in unexpected places, the impossible elongation of time, disjointed from space. In contrast, this chapter explores a seemingly more natural relationship of Jewish space and time in continuity with the past, shifting from the uncanny, or "unhomely," to the familiar home. The uncanny and the familiar are, of course, species of one another, and the uncanny is not entirely absent from the pages that follow. The past is no mere memory in these spaces; rather, it assumes tangible form. For some writers the quintessential Jewish space of the shtetl remained legible within the confines of the Soviet framework.

Dan Miron's groundbreaking study of the literary imagination of the shtetl provides the point of departure for my readings of postwar Soviet Jewish literature of the home. Miron revises the prevalent view that the work of the classic Yiddish authors Sholem Aleichem and I. L. Peretz reflected, or had a metonymic relation to, historical reality. Readers typically understood classic Yiddish literary representations of the shtetl as if they were historically accurate accounts, because of their emotional need (particularly after the Holocaust) to reconnect with a past that had been utterly destroyed. Miron demonstrates that the dominant trope of this literature was not metonymy but metaphor. The literary shtetl from the 1870s to 1920 did not share the qualities of the people, things, and places that it represented. Instead, the literary imagination rendered the shtetl metaphorically as "a tiny, exiled Jerusalem . . . not only an earthly, mundane Jerusalem as opposed to the 'celestial' Jerusalem but also the low, downtrodden Jerusalem-in-exile as opposed to the lofty, royal, independent ancient capital graced by the presence of God in His Temple" (Miron 1995, 30). The shtetl was both the holy city and the place where the Jewish body politic had its existence, and as such it was also represented in earthy, bodily terms. The shtetl was an extension of the original Jewish polity; its foundation was linked to a transcendental intervention that vouchsafed its continuity with Jewish sacred history; and finally it was a temporary home for the Jewish people, who would ultimately be restored to Israel. Eventually, Yiddish authors tried to get their readers to see their immediate surroundings without the metaphorical lens of biblical history.

In contrast to the authors of classic Yiddish fiction, the authors who are the subject of this chapter do not, for the most part, depict Soviet Ukraine or Belorussia as versions of an exiled Jerusalem. Postwar Soviet Jewish writing about the shtetl and other Jewish places relies on metonymy and other devices associated with novelistic realism. Nevertheless, the authors imagine and represent ongoing reality in Jewish spaces dense with particular Jewish ways of doing things; they all show a sense of connection to the past, and some even suggest a link to a transcendent Jewish body politic. Kipnis's remarkable postwar publication about Sloveshne reveals the full range of possibilities. Fridrikh Gorenshtein uses a Yiddish-inflected Russian to outline the Jewish space of Berdichev, whose architecture resembles the chaotic spaces of Der Nister's magisterial novel of the 1930s, *The Family Mashber* (Mishpokhe Mashber). Grigorii Kanovich's shtetl centers on the cemetery, emphasizing the world beyond. Shmuel Gordon's Yiddish travelogues trace a journey through the *shtetlekh* of Ukraine, conjuring a virtual Jewish space out of the remnants of Jewish life found there. Shire Gorshman and Inna Lesovaia, a writer active in the early years of the twenty-first century, embody the relation between history and the everyday in interior, domestic spaces and family events.

Shtetl Time

Time and space can be used to suggest each other. In the shtetl and in observant Jewish communities to this day, the cyclical alternation between weekday (*vokhedik*) time and Sabbath/holiday (*shabesdik/yontevdik*) time organizes daily life. Bergelson's two-volume autobiographical novel *Baym Dnyeper* (At the Dnieper) stresses this model of ordered time and, correspondingly, the joy and coherence of everyday life. It provides a striking contrast to the rest of his work, which typically foregrounds discontinuity and rupture. *At the Dnieper* was published in the Soviet Union in the 1930s, a decade consumed by building a future in which the shtetl, as an unproductive Jewish urban center, and the village (non-Jewish and Jewish) would have no place.[8] The anti-shtetl campaigns carried out by Soviet Jewish activists in the 1920s and 1930s, reflected in the literature, film, and dramatic performances of the time, exploited the image of the moribund or dead shtetl that they inherited from the previous generation of writers.[9] Even though my emphasis here is on postwar writing and publication, I include Bergelson's novel because it illuminates the model of continuity that is key to the works in this chapter. Bergelson left the shtetl, but it stayed with him.

While the author had proclaimed in *Mides ha-din* (The harshness of the law, 1929) the advent of a "new, stronger world" and the death of the old Jewish way of life, *At the Dnieper* nonetheless returns to this old, outdated Jewish way of life and offers a positive view of its characteristic organization of time. The first volume of *At the Dnieper* describes the world of the shtetl through the perspective of Penek, the unloved youngest child of the wealthy Levin family, who live in the "white house." Penek's story is the story of his socialist education, as Susan Slotnick shows, his gradual rejection of his father and his father's world, and his eventual filiation with the servants and the poor workers from the "*hintergeslekh*," the back streets of the town (Slotnick 1978).[10] What this description of the novel misses, however, is the child's sense of joy, the magic that he sees in the world of the shtetl around him. In this regard, Penek resembles the boy hero of the early chapters of Sholem Aleichem's *From the Fair*. When we first meet the seven-year-old Penek, he has been jumping around the dining room atop chairs that he has overturned. Penek feels sorry for his overworked father, who does not know or has forgotten "how good it is to stamp, dance, and overturn worlds from great joy" (*vi gut iz tsu tupen, tanstn un iberkern veltn fun groys freyd*) (Bergelson 1932, 7). Penek feels this joy from meeting new people, absorbing their gestures and features, from summer weather, from a new suit he orders (the suit grows by itself, with a trunk, legs, and arms, like a Golem), from his dreams, in which he sees things upside down (*mitn kop arop un mit di fis aroyf, vi er hot lib*, "with his head down and his feet up, the way he likes things"), and from his father.

Bergelson describes Penek's attachment to his father as part of an instinctual, physical connection to the child's sense of home. Even though this attachment is threatened by the father's illness, by external forces, and by Penek's own dawning awareness of the great inequity in the shtetl, it is all the more precious while it is felt (57). Penek feels a deep desire (*glustenish*) to be with his father, to listen to his voice and see his face, and this feeling is "not only from love and not only from his heart, but from Penek's whole body, from each limb separately and from all his limbs together" (*nit bloyz fun libe un nit bloyz fun hartsn nor fun Peneks gantsn kerper, fun yedn eyver bazunder un fun ale eyvrim ineynem*) (54–55). Penek's desire for and pleasure in his father's every wrinkle and gesture extends to the whole shtetl and its inhabitants; each new meeting gives him "great pleasure" (*gvaldik fargenign*) (155). The young boy learns to accumulate the trivial events of his daily life, to store them up in his memory, which the author describes in corporeal terms. Penek's memory "demands to be filled, like a glutton's empty stomach" (*vi a leydikn mogn bay a freserl*) (153). This is a fleshy memory, a bodily organ: it wants to eat. Food is also a key motif in Gorshman's and Lesovaia's work. The displacement of memory from the mind to the stomach is characteristic of the downward, embodied turn of works that stress the continuity of life in the present.

Penek's deeply embodied receptivity and joy has its origin in the Jewish sense of time, the alternation of the weekdays with Sabbaths and holidays. Jewish time is built not only around the mournful calendar of remembrances but also around this continuous alternation of celebratory and workday time. It is not Penek's encounters with the river, woods, or any other part of the natural world, usually described as outside the boundaries of the shtetl, or his meetings with non-Jews that provide him with his joy. The source is Penek's own father, who embodies this alternating calendar of holiday joy and weekday work. Bergelson writes, "The oldest one in the house has a weekday beard, a big, dark-grey, almost a miser's beard, and his face is a holiday face" (*Der elster in 'hoyz' hot a vokhedike bord, a hipshe, a tunkl-groye—kimat a kaptsonishe bord—un a ponem iz bay im a yontevdiks*) (6). Penek receives the traditional Jewish alternation of weekdays and holidays in his own way. Their cyclical ups and downs become part of his own emotional and artistic ups and downs:

> To a greater extent than for other people, Penek experienced different times: there were whole weeks and months when he would observe people and see something very full, and he would bear within himself countless feelings; at that time he himself was festive and life around him was thoroughly festive, and there were again days, when he would look and look at people, but would see nothing, then he sensed with a sinking feeling his nothingness, his weekday good-for-nothingness.
>
> *Fil mer vi bay andere zaynen bay im, Penekn, di tsaytn farsheydn: faran gantse vokhn un khadoshim, ven, tsukukndik zikh tsu mentshn, derzet er epes zeyer fil, trogt in zikh inveynik on a shir gefiln, denstmol iz er aleyn a yontevdiker un dos lebn arum im iz durkhoys yontevdik, un faran vider teg, ven er kukt af mentshn, kukt un kukt un derzet gornisht, denstmol filt er mit gefalnkayt zayn nishtikayt, zayn vokhedikn pust-un-pas.* (303)

Penek's experience of "different times" corresponds to the alternation of weekdays and holidays.[11] The cycle of Jewish time encompasses the cycle of his own creativity and its cessation. When Penek feels artistic responsiveness and creativity, the feeling fills everything around him. The passage links the budding author's creativity with the divine creativity celebrated during Sabbaths and holidays, when God's creation of the world is recounted. Significantly, Bergelson does not assimilate the Soviet model of intellectual labor in this passage; he does not compare the young artist's joyous creative work to the proletarian labor of the mere weekday. The novel as a whole criticizes traditional Jewish institutions and celebrations (one of Penek's black moods comes over him the night before the Jewish New Year); it attacks the false piety of wealthy families such as Penek's and provides stark portraits of the terrible poverty of the shtetl's backstreets. As Dan Miron argues, the opening of the novel undermines the traditional biblical frame of reference in which the classic Yiddish authors situated their narratives. But Bergelson nonetheless uses the traditional alternation of holiday and weekday as a framework of meaning and coherence for the author. The place, the shtetl, gives the young boy a particular sensibility about time, not so much the content of time, for example, what happens or whom he sees, but the cyclical variation in his sense of time: his rush of joy at finding the world full (holiday time) and his despair at finding it empty (workday time).

Read autobiographically, *At the Dnieper* is not merely an anti-shtetl work, or a socialist Bildungsroman with emphasis on the hero's dawning awareness of class distinctions. The *yontevdik/vokhedik* (holiday/weekday) distinction that organizes time in the shtetl plays a vital role in the author's aesthetic *Bildung*. The notion of continuous, ordered time, both "empty" and "full" to use Bergelson's own language, is something concrete and particular that the hero—and the author—takes with him from the shtetl into the world beyond.

Itsik Kipnis: The Shtetl as Object of Desire

In 1967 the editors of *Sovetish heymland* sent Kipnis greetings on his seventieth birthday, praising him for "remaining true to the theme of the shtetl, into which life had brought so many remarkable changes" (Tsu Itsik Kipnises 70-yorikn iubiley 1967). This compliment must have grated on Kipnis's nerves, since Soviet literary officials had for most of his career attacked him for this very characteristic of "remaining true" to the shtetl and to a concept of Jewishness that had little to do with Soviet definitions of nationality or with the Soviet model of the friendship of nations. Kipnis (1896–1974) initially attracted critical attention for his work *Khadoshim un teg* (Months and days, 1926), a lyrical chronicle of the early days of his marriage and the pogrom that killed dozens of Jews in Sloveshne in 1919, including his first wife's family.[12] Bergelson saw the reincarnation of Sholem Aleichem in this work, but Bergelson, like other Yiddish critics, complained about its apolitical stance.[13] Some attacked the author's love for the shtetl itself and the atmosphere of the novel, which they saw as more suitable for a classic Yiddish author, such as Abramovitsh in the 1870s, than for a Soviet author writing in the 1920s. This criticism reached a fever pitch in the late 1940s. Kipnis, like Gekht and Altman, spent time in the Gulag for "anti-Soviet nationalist agitation." His provocative postwar essay "On khokhmes, on kheshboynes" (Without thinking, without calculation), published in Lodzh in *Naye lebn* (New life) in 1947, argued that the Jewish star should be a sign of pride: "I want all of the Jews who are now walking the streets of Berlin with firm and victorious steps to wear on their chest, next to their medals and decorations, a small and lovely star of David."[14] Needless to say, this message was not well received during the postwar anti-Jewish campaign. Among the other materials used to convict the author was a manuscript called *Nostalgia for Childhood, for Home*, written during the period 1946–49.[15] The Kiev censor, I. E. Aron, concluded that the work "idealized the patriarchal way of life, emphasizing ad nauseam the rituals and religious customs of the old days, while minimizing the class struggle."[16] Imprisoned in 1949, Kipnis was released in 1955 and allowed to return to Kiev in 1958. Kipnis revised *Nostalgia*, giving it a new title, *Mayn shtetele Sloveshne* (My *shtetele* Sloveshno), and published excerpts from it in the Warsaw Yiddish newspaper *Folks-shtime* (The people's voice) in 1959; the work in its entirety appeared in Tel Aviv in 1971. As the author writes in his preface, the book is "a gravestone, or, a sign for a gravestone to the city of my birth" (*a matseyve oder a simen fun a matseyve far mayn geburts-shtot*) (Kipnis 1971, 41). As befitting a monument, the writing is static, all the fissures of shtetl life smoothed over, in particular the author's near-constant conflict with his father, a point he emphasizes in his other writing.

Kipnis's autobiographical fiction *Untervegns* (On the road), completed before his arrest, also describes the author's native shtetl of Sloveshne in the early 1920s. It was first published in New York in 1960, with a second publication in Israel in 1977, and a third in Moscow in 1979.[17] Its appearance in the Soviet Union in the late 1970s is itself an extraordinary journey to a place and time that Soviet culture claimed to have left behind. *Untervegns* describes the social transformations taking place in the shtetl in the early Soviet years. The hero grows apart from "Jewishness" (*yidishkayt*), leaves the shtetl for Kiev, where he becomes acquainted with Soviet Yiddish literature, and publishes his first works in Yiddish. This part of the story is directly autobiographical: Kipnis himself made a similar journey in 1920, sponsored by the Leatherworkers' Union. He became a protégé of the Yiddish poet David Hofshteyn and began publishing in the early 1920s with a collection of poetry, *Oksn* (Oxen), then moving on to prose and stories for children.[18] Although *Untervegns* describes the hero's departure from the shtetl, it also dramatically departs from the conventional Soviet narrative of upward mobility.

In *Untervegns* Jewish tradition persists in spite of the ongoing reality of political and social change and violence. The novel begins ironically. In a tone of exasperation, the narrator describes how the shtetl inhabitants continue their normal routine:

> It happened to be a Friday in the shtetl. Sloveshne did not get very far away from itself. As long as it was Friday, it was Shabes; the two things came together. How could it occur to anyone that this particular Friday could tear itself away from its Shabes? And I, sunk in the atmosphere of a small shtetl, could hardly tear myself away from them both.
>
> *In shtetl iz akurat geven fraytik. Sloveshne iz vayt fun zikh nit avek. Vi bald fraytik, iz shoyn mit im in eynem gebundn shabes. Un farvos zol emetsn aynfaln, az der doziker fraytik kon zikh durkh abi velkhn opraysn fun zayn shabes. Un ikh, vos bin eyngetunken in kleynshtetldikayt, zol zikh durkh vos es iz opraysn fun zey beydn.* (Kipnis 1977, 213)

The shtetl, Friday, and the Sabbath are bound together, no matter what happens. The ambivalence of the narrator's attitude toward the shtetl chronotope—its particular linking of time and space—is especially apparent in the last line of the passage, in which he admits to his own immersion in "small-shtetlness." In Kipnis as in Bergelson, the terms used to describe the distinction between weekday (*vokhedik*) time and Sabbath/holiday (*shabesdik/yontevdik*) time also function to register emotion and mood. Even though he carries on the Sabbath and no longer prays with the other men, the terms from that world still have meaning for him. When the hero is at sixes and sevens, out of sorts, he is "*vokhedik.*"

Untervegns takes place in the aftermath of the violence that *Khadoshim un teg* describes; the hero, Ayzik, is a widower, whose first wife, Buzye, died before the story begins (Kipnis's first wife died in the aftermath of the Sloveshne pogrom of 1919). Ayzik, for his part, never recovers from the loss of Buzye: "I have a weakness, a kind of hump that grew onto my soul and the hump even has a pretty, beloved name: Buzye!" (*Ot hob ikh eyne a shvakhkayt, aza min hoykerl, vos iz angevoksn af mayn neshome un dos hoykerl heyst dafke mit a sheynem, mit a libn nomen:— Buzye!*) (318). The hero reflects that his second wife, Polye, would understand that his "weakness" was not the sort of problem one goes to a doctor for, but rather that "a hump like this should be treasured, adorned in silks and precious stuff" (*aza hoykerl darf men tayer haltn, men darf es tsirn in zaydns un in eydlste shtofn*) (318). In this poetic image of psychic introjection, similar to Altman's motif of the tomb, the hero keeps his dead wife alive as a beautiful and treasured object inside of himself.[19] Ayzik's ongoing love affair with his dead wife, Buzye, is the key to the story, transforming the image of the shtetl space into an object of desire, and reordering the boundaries separating the hero from the shtetl. He is in indeed immersed in the shtetl, because it is embedded in him.

In *Untervegns*, the narrator observes that everything in the shtetl is close by: "there was the valley and there was the hill with the cemetery . . . walking along the paving stones we had before our eyes both this world and the world to come" (*i di-velt, i yene-velt*) (384). As the novel unfolds, the qualities associated with "this world" (*di-velt*) and the "world to come" (*yene-velt*) change places. The cemetery where Buzye is buried is "homey," "familiar" (*heymlekh*); its orderly rows of tombs (*shtiblekh*) and gravestones are "tidy and nice" (*tsikhtik un lib*) (234, 401). In contrast to this language of pleasant domesticity, the language used to describe the hero's second marriage comes from the world of the dead. When the hero's sister hears of the marriage, she comments on its unsuitability by using the expression that literally means "two corpses are going dancing" (*tsvey meysim geyen tanstn*). Polye, the second wife, lives in a house that is so big and empty that the couple feels "strange" and "uncanny" (*unheymlekh*) (247). Polye's disquiet (*umet*) emanates from her whole body, even from her laughter (*di umet kukt bay ir aroys afile funem gelekhter*" (317).

The "hump" that grew on the hero's soul is fecund: the association between desire and death in his inner landscape appears in the external space of the shtetl and its environment, littered with the bodies of beautiful dead women; but unlike comparable civil war works, none of them are pogrom victims, and none produce a sense of horror or disgust in the hero. During a trip to a neighboring village, Ayzik meets a man whose wife has just died. He imagines using the episode in a scene for a story. It would be sunset, and the body of the dead woman would be lying on the floor. The glare of the setting sun would penetrate the windows of the room, but the light from the candles surrounding the body would emanate with equal strength from the windows. This meeting of the light from within with the light from without has mystical overtones.

The most shockingly erotic encounter with a dead woman comes near the end of the novel. By this time, the hero has already left the shtetl for Kiev and no longer observes Jewish practice. He dreams that he is in a shtetl during the second day of Rosh Hashanah, the Jewish New Year. Standing on the street, he sees a wagon in which someone is lying, covered in a cloth: "It is a woman. It is Polye, but she does not recognize me, because I am not myself" (*S'iz a froy. S'iz Polye nor mit mir ken zi zikh nit. Ikh bin dokh nit ikh*) (452). A man, similar to the hero's father but not his father, accompanies the wagon. The hero wants to drive the man away to take the woman for himself. He likes her face, which is "a reflection from a lot of suffering" (*an opshpiglung fun a sakh laydn*). It turns out that the couple are on their way to the maternity hospital: the woman is having a hard labor. The scene switches to the bathhouse, but the hero is ashamed, and does not undress. The woman has also been brought to the bathhouse from the hospital:

> She is so alive, young, and beautiful. I see her naked, although I know that she dead, it appears that the beautiful custom of bathing the corpse [in the bathhouse] remains . . . I . . . feel desire, male desire . . . A thought occurs to me to bathe myself together with her so that perhaps we will be buried together.
>
> *Zi iz azoy leybik, yung, un sheyn. Ikh ze zi a nakete, khotsh ikh veys, az zi iz toyt, veyzt zikh aroys, az s'iz geblibn a sheyner minheg tublen di toyte . . . ikh*

fil tsu ir glustung, mener-glustung . . . Mir falt ayn a gedank zikh tublen tsuzamen mit ir un men vet undz efsher tsuzamen mit ir bahaltn. (453)

The dream turns out to be prophetic: Polye dies after giving birth to their daughter. In the novel, the hero shows little emotional response to this event, makes little effort to return home for the birth or the funeral, and does not even meet his own child until many months later.[20] His desire for the dead woman outweighs his attachment to the living.

The hero has his dream of the shtetl and the woman who dies in childbirth in his room at the outskirts of the city (*ek shtot*). The place where he has his room reminds him of the shtetl and of the joys and grief that are particular to a small shtetl. His neighbor in the next room cries out in the middle of the night when her husband dies, and the hero hears in her sob desire, vitality, and the fullness of life. In *Untervegns*, the shtetl is broken off from Jewish sacred history, but the hero is not broken off from the shtetl, because he carries it with him, embedded in his psyche. This other, inner shtetl is no dead weight; it eroticizes everything around him. The present moment of the novel is a time when Soviet power has been triumphantly established, and the hero has relocated to the modern, urban, Soviet space of Kiev. This present moment and this space, however, also preserve a substrate of a prior time and another space, in an infinite regress in which womb and tomb, Ayzik and Buzye, desire and death, shtetl and Soviet city intertwine and overlap. The theme of failed natality, which I discuss in Chapter One in relation to Babel and Markish, resonates powerfully in Kipnis's work.

Soviet Berdichev: The Archeology of the Present

One of the greatest and most complex visions of a uniquely Jewish place is the portrait of Berdichev, the "city of N" in Der Nister's *Di mishpokhe Mashber* (The family Mashber), the first volume of which was published in the Soviet Union in the 1930s, the era of the five-year plans and the rush to the future. Chapters from both this work and Bergelson's *At the Dnieper* appeared in the same issue of the Soviet Yiddish literary journal *Sovetish* (Soviet) in 1935. The preface to *The Family Mashber* opens with the line "the world described in this book has disappeared without a trace" (*di velt, vos vert geshildert in dem dozikn bukh, iz shoyn shpurloz farshvundn*); the book, however, which consists of two lengthy volumes, with some indication of a planned third volume, is itself the trace. Using a different kind of space, not a small shtetl but an urban center—the city of Berdichev—and using the time frame of the 1870s, Der Nister constructs Jewish space as open, fluid, and vulnerable to cataclysmic change. Dedicating the second volume to his daughter, who died in the siege of Leningrad, Der Nister says that his broken heart is the monument to her unknown grave. There is, however, nothing fixed or rigid in the world created by *The Family Mashber*. Its key space is the threshold, the space of change. Indeed, the meaning of the family name in Der Nister's novel underscores the theme of change: "*mashber*" means "crisis" (Wisse 2000, 124). The family crisis revolves around the clash between two of the three Mashber brothers: Moshe, a financial leader in the city, who goes bankrupt, and Luzi, who becomes the leader of the marginal Bratslaver Hasidic sect in "the city of N."

In this work, the crisis in the Mashber family ripples throughout "N"—Berdichev—as a whole. The looming catastrophe threatens the city not only in its aspect as Jerusalem below but also in its cosmic, otherworldly aspect as Jerusalem above. To a far greater extent than Bergelson's *At the Dnieper*, Der Nister's *Family Mashber* interposes the "vertical, otherworldly" axis onto the plane of everyday, ordinary life of the Jewish body politic, especially in its carnivalized, intensely embodied form. Berdichev is a place where desire, eating, drinking, drunkenness, buying, selling, spiritual longing, mystical and apocalyptic visions, Jewish holiness and Jewish blasphemy, joy and despair, the grotesque and the sublime are never far apart. The cemetery caretaker sells his wares as avidly as any merchant at the market; the head of the burial society is an "aberration" with a shrunken face and a voice like a newborn kitten; the pallbearers are "half-Golems" (Der Nister 1948, 62). Moshe Mashber, an upright citizen and a good Jew, is surrounded by "hyenas," for whom the word "money" has a pathological effect. One of his assistants has a "pious, fox-like face" (*a frum-foksish poniml*) and can sniff out money like a dog. In contrast, Luzi Mashber speaks of the great joy that "lifts and purifies, creating wonder, that makes the old young, and transforms the crudest thing to that which can reach the greatest height" (*derheybt un laytert, shaft vunder—makht fun alt yung, un fun der grobster zakh—aza, vos kon biz der hekhter haykh aroyfderlangen*) (93).

As Mikhail Krutikov has shown, Jewish writers both before and after Der Nister represented Berdichev as an "in your face" Jewish city, a city that respected the marketplace above all and reveled in the life of the body (Krutikov 2000). Vasilii Grossman's sketch of Berdichev, "Berdichev Not As a Joke, but Seriously" (Berdichev ne v shutku, a vser'ez), published in *Ogonek* (The Flame) in 1929, attempts not without irony to clean up the city's image by tracing the history of its proletarian struggle. His own later work of fiction "In the City of Berdichev" (1934) returns to the more familiar image of Berdichev. The air inside the Jewish house where the pregnant commissar is billeted is so thick with human habitation, with the smells of "kerosene, garlic, sweat, goose fat, [and] unwashed bedding that she draws in as much oxygen as possible, as if she were about to dive into water" (Grossman 2005, 9). Gorenshtein uses similarly embodied imagery in his 1975 play "Berdichev."

Gorenshtein was born in Kiev in 1932; his father, a professor, was shot in Magadan when the author was a young child, and his mother died during the war in evacuation. Gorenshtein grew up in state-run orphanages and in the homes of relatives, a bitter experience reflected in "Berdichev." Aside from his writing for film (he did the screenplays for *The Slave of Love* [Raba liubvi], 1976, and *Solaris*, 1972), his only work of fiction to be published in the Soviet Union was a short story for the journal *Iunost'* (Youth) in 1964. Together with such writers as Bitov and Aksenov, Gorenshtein was a participant in 1979 in the banned literary almanac "Metropole," which was first published in Russia in 1991. Gorenshtein emigrated to Germany in 1980 and remained there until his death in 2002. His last novel, *Letit sebe aeroplan* (The airplane flies), based on the life of Marc Chagall, was published in Moscow in 2003 (Gorenshtein 2003).[21]

In the novel *The Psalm* (Psalom), Gorenshtein takes a dim view of Russia and Jews in Russia, using his reinvented Antichrist to curse both; in "Berdichev," in contrast, absolute and apocalyptic judgments are absent (Gorenshtein 1986).[22] Like Der Nister and other writers, he uses a grotesque image of the Jewish body. The foul-mouthed Rakhil' and her sister Zlota, the two protagonists, are querulous, greedy, and provincial; their view of the world is limited to what they read in Soviet newspapers. Their admiration for Stalin is sincere; they are fully at home in the very particular world that Anna Shternshis so aptly calls "Soviet and kosher." At a wedding they sing songs to Stalin in a mixture of Yiddish and Russian: *"loz libn khaver Stalin, far dem lebn, far dem nayem, far Oktober revoliutsii, far der Staline konstititutsii"* (Let's love comrade Stalin for our life, our new life, for the October revolution, for the Stalin constitution).[23] Later in the play, in a discussion of the Suez War of 1956, Gorenshtein's heroine approves of her Jewish son-in-law's application to fight against Israel. While their feelings about Zionism are distinctly Soviet, their almost visceral disgust towards non-Jews is traditionally Jewish (Shubinskii 2005, 38). In *Psalom*, Gorenshtein condemns such individuals; in "Berdichev," he affirms them and, what is more, celebrates their way of life. The historical events noted in the play, including the Second World War, the Hungarian uprising, and the Suez War, are seen from the confines of Rakhil's narrow horizon, embodied in her noisy, overstuffed, and ever-contested apartment with its sewing machine, record player, its series of television sets, its bust of Lenin, and its portrait of Stalin. The changing props, each closely linked to a particular decade (cans of American evaporated milk in 1946, for example), underscore the importance of material, daily life and the ongoing present.

In this world, the significance of historical events pales before the hustle and bustle of daily life. There is one exception, one moment of stillness in the general tumult. The otherwise contentious Rakhil' reflects: "But we could after all live quietly and peacefully . . . How few of us remain. My husband perished, your son too, our sister died, our younger brother Shloime perished, Papa and Mama died in Central Asia . . . How few of us remain" (Gorenshtein 1988). Rakhil' senses herself to be part of a small remnant of what once was a large and thriving community. This is the only moment in the entire work in which the Second World War casts a shadow over the characters. Unlike his novel *The Psalm* and unlike the work of Bergelson and Altman, in which the narrative "now" is unbearably burdened by the catastrophic events of twentieth-century history, the characters in Gorenshtein's "Berdichev," for the most part, live in the present without being haunted by the past. Gorenshtein contrasts his characters' lack of awareness with his own messianic perspective.

For Rakhil' and Zlota and the other people who inhabit "Berdichev," furniture, food, living space, status, and salaries, and all the other concrete details of daily life are what matter and are worth fighting over, as the play's subtitle reveals: "Drama v trekh deistviiakh, vos'mi kartiny, 92 skandalakh" (A drama in three acts, eight scenes, 92 quarrels). In this world, the past does not disturb the present so much as it takes sides in the quarrels found in nearly every scene. The dead serve to buttress the claims of the living. Rakhil' begins her speech in Act I with two facts that establish who she is: a party member since 1928 and a widow since 1943, when her husband was killed at the front (documents are pulled out of the buffet as evidence). She brings up these facts whenever her status and her claims to her belongings are challenged. During evacuation, Rakhil' explains, the Ukrainian woman who used to bring the milk took all the family furniture; but the NKVD provided her with substitutes. Having survived the war, returned to Berdichev at the invitation of the party, and regained her apartment with replacement furniture, she now faces a new threat: the tenant in the neighboring apartment, a certain *Bronfenmakher* (Yiddish for "liquor-maker"), wants to knock a wall down and use her kitchen as a back entrance to carry out his garbage. According to Rakhil', party membership and war widowhood grant her certain rights and should protect her against such indignities. She asks her sister's dressmaking client in an amusingly ungrammatical Russian, "*Chto vyi skazhete, tovarishch Vshivoldina, on imeet pravo ustroit' sebe chernyi khod cherez moia kukhnia i nosit' cherez menia svoi pomoi?*" (What do you say, comrade Vshivoldina, does he have the right to build himself a back entrance through my kitchen and carry out his garbage through me?) (117).

As Krutikov observes, Rakhil's language consists of Yiddish translated into Russian (and also Yiddish rendered in Cyrillic). In "Berdichev," Yiddish inhabits Russian, ignoring its rules and usages completely. Dominated by curses and abuse, this language draws attention to daily life in its most exaggerated and embodied form: "if you would swell up, that would be good"; "let him walk around with his head in the earth"; "every bone in your body should hurt"; "he should get a swelling in his brain"; "they should know that it's dark in my asshole"; and "May a car run you down and break you into pieces." The last curse on the list, which Rakhil' says to her neighbor, comes true. The language of invective reaches the status of a nearly autonomous presence in the work. Some of the non-Jewish characters also know Yiddish; in the courtyard, the following song, a mixture of Russian and Yiddish, can be heard: "*Otsem, drotsem, dvadtsat' vosem', ot a zekel beyner, az der tate kisht di mame, darf nit visn keyner*" (Knick-knack paddy whack, Give a dog a bone, when Papa kisses Mama, let no one know) (131). The slaps, punches, and kicks that accompany almost every scene add to the effect created by the language. Invective, as Bakhtin writes, overturns hierarchy, bringing the focus to the body, to eating, drinking, and diseases of the body, and moreover to the lower body, to defecation, to the body in death and in birth. The language of the marketplace and of the carnival transforms the organization of space along the vertical axis to the horizontal axis, to the horizontal line of ordinary time. Rakhil's speech exemplifies this downward thrust: her body becomes a metonym for her kitchen; the neighbor's plan to use her kitchen as a "back entrance" to carry out garbage suggests an eroticized and grotesque image of the lower body and its waste products. Berdichev as a Jewish space is filled to bursting with its own particular language, a low Yiddish of curses and abuse, which makes a mockery of the high seriousness of Soviet hierarchical culture.

At the end of the play another perspective on Berdichev emerges. The young boy Vilia, now a writer in Moscow, says:

> Berdichev is an ugly hovel, built out of the shards of the great Temple for protection against cold, rain, and heat . . . People always acted like this in times of catastrophe and shipwreck, when they built themselves shelters on the shore out of the wreckage of their ships, in times of earthquakes or fires, when they built huts out of the ruins of the buildings that had been destroyed or burned . . . The same thing takes place also at a time of historical catastrophe, when people need a place not in order to live, but in order to survive . . . This entire ugly hovel of a Berdichev seems like a heap of garbage to a person who comes from the capital, but once you take it apart you will find that the staircase,

spat upon, and covered with slops, leading to the crooked doors of this hovel, is made of the finest marble of the past, along which the prophets once walked, on which Jesus of Nazareth once stood ... (ellipses in original; 240)

The image of the filthy staircase in Gorenshtein's "Berdichev" resonates with the filthy windows of the synagogue in Der Nister's *Family Mashber*: "He is a wandering and exiled God. He demands little: no extra cleanliness, spaciousness, or airiness, no columns. Nothing fancy on the outside. He only asks that at night from inside his building a small flickering light from a cheap kerosene lamp should be visible through the unwashed windows; that it should be quiet, and that a broken spirit should find rest" (Der Nister 1948, 32). For both authors, exilic architecture is constructed out of the recycled and improvised bricolage of survival. Both authors create a link between the Jewish community of their times and the Jewish body politic that transcends time.

Kanovich's Haunted Shtetl

In Grigorii Kanovich's work from the 1970s, the same period in which Gorenshtein wrote "Berdichev," the mood is unfailingly bleak. The key metaphor is the graveyard: "The shtetl and the cemetery were my country" (*moim gosudarstvom byli mestechko i kladbishche*), the first-person narrator says in his shtetl trilogy (Kanovich 1974, 163). Kanovich, born in Kaunas, Lithuania, in 1929 into an observant family, studied literature at the university level and began publishing in the late 1940s in both Russian and Lithuanian. Active in Lithuanian Jewish communal affairs in the late 1980s, he was outspoken in his pessimism about the future of Jewish life in Eastern Europe, and departed for Israel in 1993. *Ptitsy nad kladbishchem* (Birds over the cemetery) and *Blagoslovi i list'ia i ogon'* (Bless the leaves and the flame), the first two volumes of the trilogy, imagine the shtetl as alive with its dead.

The hero of the work is an orphan, Danil, raised by his grandparents. His grandfather is preoccupied with his clocks; grandfathers are the keepers of a time that perpetually eludes them. In Bergelson, the grandfather's clocks signal the anniversaries of death, but in Kanovich, in contrast, the clocks have more to do with hope and longing. The grandfather stays up late at night taking his clocks apart and putting them back together, "resurrecting the dead," as the narrator puts it, and entrusting his clocks with his secrets and "his longing for something that passed, flitted by like a ray of sun in cloudy weather" (1974, 52). The grandmother never loved her husband and constantly broke the clocks he mended.

After the death of Danil's grandparents, everyone else in the shtetl—the refugee who repairs clocks, the barber, the wedding musician (who locks up his violin at night lest it run off to play without him), and the synagogue caretaker—is eager to take in the child. They seek heirs, not so much to carry their own work into the future as to carry their memories forward. The hero's orphanhood leaves him the task of caring for other people's pasts.

The one-legged cemetery caretaker finally adopts Danil, who grows up in the cemetery. In the second volume, life in the present is by and large absent. The cemetery caretaker sees his dead wife and children in the fire at night; even the horse cries as he remembers his previous owners; as is traditional, the dead rise from their graves to pray in the synagogue at night. The image of the shtetl as a cemetery points to its link with the world beyond. According to Miron, the cemetery is considered a holy place, not only because of the holy individuals and intercessors located there but also because of the link to the future coming of the Messiah and the resurrection of the dead, whose journey back to Jerusalem would begin from their gravesites. The grave, as Miron writes, "is the opening of an underground corridor that will eventually lead to Eretz-Yisroel and to resurrection" (Miron 1995, 35). In Kanovich's novel, the dead watch the hero learn to skate and see him fall in love; he hears their voices interrupting one another, speaking as they used to when they were alive; the hero sees his dead father and grandparents "float up to the surface of [his] memory . . . like drowned people floating on the surface of a river" (Kanovich 1977, 100). In the final volume of the work, describing the Nazi occupation, the hero's dead grandmother takes on the role of guardian angel and guides him along the path to survival. In Kanovich as in Kipnis, the cemetery is part of the continuing life of the shtetl.[24]

Kanovich's post-Soviet story "Park zabytykh evreev" (The park of forgotten Jews), published in 1997 in the Russian-language journal *Oktiabr'* (October) (after the author's immigration to Israel), returns to similar problems of place and memory as his earlier work. Kanovich asks: Who is the guardian of Jewish memory in the post-Soviet landscape? A group of elderly people meet in a square in Vilnius every day in order to indulge in the "sweetest and most bitter drink on earth—memories" (*samyi sladkii i samii gor'kii napitok na svete—vospominaniia*) (2007). The hero, a Jewish tailor who served in the Soviet army during the Second World War, finds that time doubles and triples as his thoughts take him from one decade to the next. He recalls, for example, returning to his shtetl after the war to find the synagogue transformed into a bakery. Kanovich's description of the synagogue space resembles, in a small but significant way, the description found in Der Nister's *The Family Mashber*. In Der Nister's novel, the air of the old synagogue is imbued with the prayers of the people who crowded into it. In Kanovich, similarly, the synagogue is "not as a place, but a receptacle—fleshless and palpable at the same time" (Kanovich 2007). Kanovich's hero, Itsik Malkin, remembers finding a tallis in the synagogue and saying Kaddish for the murdered Jews of his shtetl. At the same time, his friend sitting next to him in the "park of forgotten Jews" dreams of a similar postwar moment when his entire company of soldiers began reciting Kaddish for their dead Jewish comrades. The coincidence of dream and memory structured by the literary narrative transforms the placc, a public square in Vilnius, into a Jewish space.

In this post-Soviet work, Kanovich engages the problem of place and commemoration. He expresses skepticism about the appropriation of memory by the Soviet state. In the same scene above, the hero discovers that aside from a few prayer shawls, the synagogue contained only the caretaker's galoshes. He humorously and pointedly reflects on the kind of museum exhibit in which galoshes could be found: under thick glass with a caption that reads, "Footwear of the Jews in Bourgeois Lithuania" (*Obuv' evreev v burzhuaznoi Litve*). The imaginary museum exhibit indicts the Soviet failure to commemorate the murder of Jews on Soviet territory under the German occupation.

The Soviets, however, are not the only target of Kanovich's criticism of the misappropriation of memory. In another scene, an American professor arrives in Vilnius in order to shoot a film about the Jews of Eastern Europe. Itsik resists the entire enterprise of memory tourism. He does not believe that his life should be recorded on tape: "he did not believe in the use of testimony that could be bought and sold." He objects to the film shoot as well. The American visitor wants to juxtapose a photograph of Itsik as a young man visiting Paris with his wife and Itsik as an old man in Vilnius. Itsik refuses the idea of payment: "Who is going to pay me for refusing to permit the film? Or did you just come to me as if to a gravesite? To leave a flower on each grave and go back to New York?" Focusing on the beginning (the 1920s) and the end (the early twenty-first century) elides the entire Soviet period and its unique Jewish cultural formation. But Itsik does not want to be made a part of someone else's memory tourism. He does not want to become a place, as it were, along a well-trodden path that would include other privileged sites of memory in some sort of predictable package called "The Jews of Eastern Europe." Memory tourism offers a simulacrum of authentic experience for the tourist; it transforms the unique, irreplaceable contours of someone else's life into a commodified and ultimately dead object.[25] The confrontation between Kanovich and the visitor recalls a scene from I. L. Peretz's "Impression of a Journey Through the Tomaszow Region in 1890." Peretz attempted to gather information about Jews in the *shtetlekh* of Poland, and in the published work that resulted, the author recounts a moment when the tables were turned on him. His informant started asking him questions, probing Peretz's motivation for the journey. Peretz's interlocutor suggests that the trip itself serves the interviewer more than it does his subjects, as a form of Jewish compensation. He offers a fable in the way of explanation: when an assimilated German Jew observes the anniversary of his mother's death, he goes to a restaurant and orders kugel. "Kugel is his Judaism. Maybe your Judaism is stories. Is it the anniversary of a death for you?" (Peretz 2002, 78). The American visitor in Kanovich's story similarly travels to Vilnius as if marking the anniversary of a death. But Kanovich's hero refuses to play his part, and will not allow his life to become a destination on the visitor's mournful heritage tour, insisting instead on the unpredictable twists and turns of his own memory and his own narrative art.

Shmuel Gordon: Reading Soviet Space in Jewish

Originally published in the Yiddish journal *Sovetish heymland* in the 1960s, collected in the volume *Friling* (Spring; in Yiddish, 1970), and translated into Russian in 1976 under the title *In the Vineyard*, Shmuel Gordon's travel writings retrace the author's postwar search for signs of life in the *shtetlekh* of Podolia, Ukraine. Gordon (1909–98), born in Lithuania, spent his childhood in orphanages in Ukraine and graduated from the Yiddish department of Moscow Teachers' Training Institute.[26] He began his writing career with the publication of a few poems in the late 1920s, and became a well-known author of short stories and nonfiction prose in the next decade. Gordon served in the army during the war and worked for the newspaper of the Jewish Anti-Fascist Committee, which led to his arrest and imprisonment in the Gulag until 1953, the year of Stalin's death. As Gennady Estraikh points out, Gordon's postwar publication in Russian translation was significant, with over seven volumes in large print runs. For example, a 1976 collection of his stories, which included the travelogue series, had a print run of one hundred thousand (Gordon 1976). The most extraordinary accomplishment of his writing career took place after his death: the publication in Israel in 2003 of his novel *Yisker* (Memorial), a monumental work commemorating the Yiddish writers murdered in 1952. Gordon based the work on a document he wrote while he was still in the camps, which detailed the false accusations against him and other members of the Jewish Anti-Fascist Committee; he supplemented it with research he conducted during perestroika.[27]

Gordon's travelogue both idealizes the shtetl and affirms Soviet Jewish life in the postwar period.[28] His travelogues provide an itinerary of Jewish heritage in Russia by enfolding cataclysmic history into a framework of continuity and by emphasizing the qualities of faithfulness, sincerity, and sweetness. The stress on continuity and the affirmation of everyday life correspond to the values of Soviet postwar "culture 2" (Soviet historical consciousness; see Chapter Five) as described by Vladimir Papernyi: the joyous struggle to build socialism that pervades everyday life, the romance that any worker could become a hero of socialist labor and that any day could be a special day, including, for example, such holidays as the "Day of the Railroad Worker" (*den' zheleznodorozhnika*), which in Gordon's shtetl travelogues turns out to be a particularly special occasion. The alternation of weekday and holiday time unfolds in Gordon in a Soviet context.

The opening frame story "Medzhibozh" puts the narrator at a bus station, looking at the posted schedule on the wall; the narrator finds himself reading aloud the Slavic names of the *shtetlekh*, "which from childhood on I took for genuinely Jewish ones, and from these I now list the closest and most precious: Pogrebishtshe, Tetiyev, Polonye, Bratslav, Ostropolye, Lyubar, Shpolye" (Gordon 1970, 390). Indeed, the titles of the stories in the Yiddish original of Gordon's travelogue recreate a Jewish atlas out of Soviet geography: "Medzhibozh," "Derazhne," "Pogrebishtshe," "Der Umanier tsug" (The train to Uman), "Kazatin," and "In Toliati." Uman, where R. Nakhman of Bratslav is buried, has been a pilgrimage site from the nineteenth century to the present; in *The Family Mashber*, set in the 1870s, Der Nister has Luzi Mashber visit Uman. Medzhibozh was the headquarters of the eighteenth-century founder of Hasidism, R. Yisroel Ben Eliezer, the Baal Shem Tov (the Master of the Good Name), and it remains an important pilgrimage site to this day. Medzhibozh was also the home of the famous Jewish jester Hershele Ostropolier, who lived at the court of the Baal Shem Tov's grandson and functioned as "a countervoice within the revolutionary religious movement, the irrepressible and joyous skeptic who cannot be inhibited from telling the truth" (Wisse 2000, 103). Both the Baal Shem Tov and Hershele make their appearance in Gordon's stories. Gordon's narrator also imagines alternative itineraries that would link specific places with Jewish literary heritage, for example, Bergelson's birthplace, Okhrimove; in so doing, Gordon embeds Soviet history into his atlas of Jewish places and legacies. The Russian translation of Gordon's travelogue removes the place names from the titles; for example, instead of the title "Medzhibozh" the Russian gives "V razrushennoi kreposti" (In a ruined fortress).[29] The Russian translation makes illegible the very thing that Gordon seeks to write large: the continuity of Jewish life in Jewish places.

What is at stake for Gordon is nothing less than the shtetl itself, revived, transformed, and with a new lease on life. In the story "Medzhibozh" the narrator asks himself, "If I didn't know that this was Medzhibozh, would I guess that here there was once a Jewish shtetl?" (*a yidish shtetl*) (1970, 392).[30] Gordon receives his answer, he says, even before he talks to anyone in the town: the architecture itself speaks to him. One house in particular "answers" his question. Despite its bright blue paint (a sign of the countryside that invades the former shtetl) it "preserved something, which even if you moved it to the far north, you could nonetheless recognize its origin" (*farhit in zikh azoyns, vos ven me trogt es afile ariber fundanen afn ekstn tsofn, volt men sayvisay derkent, funvanen s'shtamt*) (393). The windows with their shutters, the cleanly raked little porch (*dos reyn-opgeshobene ganekl*), "and many other signs, which cannot be counted" would all speak to this undefined but recognizable quality.[31] The retro-shtetl is the product of the interaction between the tourist and the place. It is organized around questions and answers; it resembles a traditional Jewish text like the Passover Hagadah with its four ritualized questions, which define why this night is different from all other nights, just as Gordon's questions and answers determine what makes this house different from all other (non-Jewish) houses.

Reading the signs depends on a special form of insider knowledge. Gordon describes the day he spends with the unofficial tour guide of Medzhibozh, who shows him the gravesites of the Baal Shem Tov and Hershele Ostropolier. When Gordon points out that there is no marking on Hershele's gravestone, his guide points to a series of signs that identify it, including its low position relative to the Baal Shem Tov's. She then proceeds to tell him various Hershele stories, none of which Gordon recounts but only indicates by their first lines alone; for example, "once our Hershele went to Eliezer the rich man to borrow a gold wine cup" (*kumt er, undzer Hershele, eynmol areyn tsu Eliezern dem gevir antlayen a goldenem bekher*) (1970, 400). Those who have ears to hear, so to speak, will understand the referent. Recognition is key to the production of the (retro)shtetl. Gordon, in contrast to Bergelson and Kipnis, for example, is not interested in the creation of new artistic forms or the use of narrative devices such as estrangement that would disrupt readers' expectations about the shtetl. His point is rather to enfold Medzhibozh—both the story and the place—in an untroubled tradition that predates and continues through the twentieth century.[32]

One of the indicators of this unbroken continuity has to do with intercessionary notes. In Gordon's writing, the tour guide shows him "*kvitlekh*," the notes left by Jewish pilgrims seeking intercession at the gravesite of the Baal Shem Tov. This tradition was well established in Jewish communities. During the time between the Jewish New Year and Yom Kippur, as Gordon himself points out, Jews would visit the cemetery to ask their dead relatives to intercede for them and ask God to provide for such benefits as marriage and prosperity. Shire Gorshman's travel writing, published in 1981, also refers to the tradition of visiting the cemetery during the time leading up to the High Holidays ("*me geyt afn reynem ort, s'iz dokh bald di yontoyvim, geyt men*") (Gorshman 1981, 29).[33]

The story "Pogrebishtshe," for example, begins with a reflection on the parallel between an old railway timetable and an old calendar: both provoke memories; both function as souvenirs, not so much from other places as from other times. As he travels to Pogrebishtshe, the shtetl of his childhood, his accumulated memories make the town in its present guise difficult to see: "the old Pogrebishtshe will probably block out the new, which is soon going to be right under my nose, plain to see" (*dos alte Pogrebishtshe vet mistome far mir farshteln dos naye, vos s'shteyt mir bald far tsu derzen mit di eygene oygn*) (Gordon 1970, 416). The notable personages included in his journey through his birthplace—"Sholem the capmaker, Khaykel the tailor, and Arn the porter"—are not recorded on any heritage tour or in any Soviet history book. Wandering around the deserted lot that used to contain his parents' house, the author recalls a scene from childhood: men with rifles standing over his mother until she finds some Kerensky money that she had hidden in her women's prayer book to pay them off. The attempt at ransom fails, however, and his brother is led out and shot. These events, and the events of the Nazi genocide, have no memorial marker.

One set of encounters in Podolia reveals the spontaneous and episodic nature of memorialization. In the local registry office (ZAGS) Gordon meets a Jew whose family was killed during the Nazi genocide and who cannot find a record of their existence. His son would have been forty this summer, he tells Gordon. The Jew creates his own memorial space by reading other names in the metrical records out loud, adding "may he rest in peace" for those who died a natural death and "eternal memory" for those who were killed (422). The narrative does not explain how the survivor knew the difference. Later, Gordon meets the same man on the train going to Uman. Every summer he travels to the places where his family was killed during the Second World War: "When summer begins, there begin for me the anniversaries of deaths. Five memorials a year" (*Heybt zikh on der zumer, heybn zikh bay mir on di yortsaytn. Finf yizkers a yor*) (438). Gordon rewrites the speeding express train of modernity as a mobile gravestone. Instead of racing toward the future, his train serves as a vehicle for memorialization.

On the whole, Gordon emphasizes the continuity and legibility of Jewish life in Podolia and other places in the former Pale of Settlement. The shtetl that he finds is not the same shtetl that existed before the war, however ("*s'iz nokh nit oys shtetl*," the shtetl is not finished yet) (429). Gordon embeds his descriptions of postwar Jewish life in an unbroken tradition that runs from the eighteenth century (the twin gravesites of the Baal Shem Tov and Hershele) through the Second World War and beyond. Motifs from Jewish life and Soviet Jewish life saturate his text. The caretaker at the cemetery in Pogrebishtshe reminds him of a character from Sholem Aleichem; other moments call to mind the work of the Soviet-era Yiddish poet Shmuel Halkin. A grandmother supervising her grandson's morning calisthenics compares the exercise to the prayer said on awakening—the "*mode ani*." The old, prerevolutionary shtetl is gone, but the new shtetl, with its cinemas, parks, full hotels, and summer vacationers, has taken its place, and new customs replace the old. The past reasserts itself in this place, not to haunt visitors but to charm them. For example, a grandmother scolding her grandson starts out by calling him "Pavlik" but soon reverts to the child's Yiddish name, "Fayvele." This special, Jewish place casts a sweet, restorative Jewish spell on its tourists.

Music plays an especially important role in this special Jewish charm. The author sings along with a group of schoolchildren as they sing Leyb Kvitko's popular song "Khayzerlikh" (Porosatia, Piglets). Originally written in Yiddish in 1935 as part of the campaign to settle Jews on the land, rid them of their traditions (such as the dietary laws prohibiting pork), and transform them into agricultural workers, the song was translated into Russian and became known to generations of Soviet schoolchildren.[34] Gordon comes across a little boy, Dovid, who plays

Yiddish songs on his accordion, including both traditional wedding songs and "Zog nit keynmol, az du geyst dem letstn veg" (Never say that you are going on your last way).[35] With lyrics written by Hirsh Glik in 1943 and set to music by Dmitrii Pokrass, this song was sung by the partisans of the Vilna ghetto uprising and became internationally known as a Holocaust song. Gordon also finds an old-style *"badkhen"* (wedding jester—a Yiddish rap artist) who sings song after song and addresses everyone he meets in joking rhymed couplets, as a real-life reanimation of the jokester Hershele Ostropolier. The *badkhen* sings a wedding song that registers both the Soviet "peace to the world" campaign of the 1960s and a specifically Jewish curse about "enemies who should burst from envy, / like, may their names be blotted out, Hitler's country" (*platsn zoln zey fun kine / vi es hot geplatst, yimakh-shmoy, Hitler's medine*) (464).

The episode in which Gordon the old Yiddish writer meets Dovid the young musician underscores the author's emphasis on the unbroken flow of tradition in this Jewish place:

> How does an eight or nine year-old boy get the melodies from Jewish weddings of long ago, from wandering bands, the songs about unlucky loves and unlucky lives, pain, and trouble? . . . Dovidke, however, doesn't play the tunes the way we used to play them . . . Every generation sings in its own way. And the path that a melody cuts from generation to generation is like the path made by a spring that suddenly runs dry, so that no memory of it seems to remain, and all at once it shows itself again, often in the place where one did not expect it.

> *Vi kumen tsu dem akht-naynyorikn yingele di nigunim fun amolike yidishe khasenes, lider fun de amolike yidishe vander-trupes, lider vegn umgliklekhe libes un umgliklekhe lebns, payn un tsorn? . . . Di yidishe nigunim shpilt ober Dovidke epes nit azoy, vi me flegt zey amol bay undz shpilin . . . Yeder dor zingt af zayn oyfn. Un der veg, vos es makht durkh a nign fun dor tsu dor, iz vi der veg fun a kval, vos vert plutsem oysgetrinkt, keyn zeykher, dakht zikh, fun im nit farblibn, un mitamol bavayzt er zikh vider, aftmol dort, vu me hot zikh nit gerikht af im.* (424)

"From generation to generation" (*fun dor tsu dor*) is a phrase that in its original Hebrew occurs in liturgy, where it signifies each generation's obligation to praise God. Gordon uses the phrase in a secular Jewish context to highlight the persistence of Jewish culture in the Soviet Union across the generations.

In his own time, Gordon's heritage narrative provided an alternative to mainstream Soviet accounts of the recent past, but his fundamental grammar derives from the forward-looking history enshrined in "culture 2" and corresponds to the more predictable aspects of heritage tours in the post-Soviet era. The choreographed sentiment that ranges from the tragedy of the Jewish mourner to the sweetness of the little boy playing Yiddish songs on his accordion provides the reassurance of a future life for the shtetl in the postwar Soviet environment. Gordon's nostalgic shtetl narratives do not disrupt the present by means of their view of the past but rather serve to confirm the rightness of Jewish participation in Soviet life. His nostalgia, however, does not deny history or disavow loss; reading the signs of shtetl life in the Sovietized towns and villages of Podolia restores Jewish history to places that would otherwise make their Jewish past invisible.[36]

Gendered Jewish Spaces: Gorshman and Lesovaia

Shire Gorshman, a contemporary of Gordon, offers a contrasting view of the Jewish world that they both describe. Her autobiographical writings encompass places traditionally associated with Jewish life, including the *shtetlekh* and cities of Lithuania and Belarus, but they also describe agricultural settlements and communes, new Jewish spaces created in Palestine in the 1920s and in the Soviet Union in the 1930s. The shtetl in Gorshman's writing, while far from romanticized, is not merely a place of obsolete traditions to be overcome, its inhabitants to be turned into proletarians or agricultural laborers (like Gorshman herself). The shtetl still has something to offer; its gifts, however, are riddled with ambivalence.

Unlike Gordon, who finds signs of Jewish life in the *shtetlekh* of Podolia, Gorshman's postwar travels back to Lithuania yield utterly no traces of the Jewish places of her childhood: "we drive through the shtetl; no sign whatsoever remains of what was there" (*mir forn durkh shtetl, keyn shum simen fun dem, vos do iz geven*) (Gorshman 1984, 271).

When she returns to Krok (Krakes), her native shtetl, the sight of the empty field that Germans used as a killing place during the war devastates her. A concrete memorial marker is all but illegible, the letters scraped away, apparently by vandals. Gorshman writes, "the Jewish letters have been as if pecked asunder by iron beaks" (*di yidishe oysyes zaynen vi tsepikt mit ayzerne shnoblen*) (272). Wherever and whenever her stories are set—in Palestine, the commune in Crimea, or Moscow, before the war or after—the shtetl's connection to today preserves the texture of a complex, lived experience, including the experience of loss that cannot be redeemed.

This living connection between life in the shtetl and life in the present is not the warm, sweet emotion of kitsch, the evocation of the stable values of a traditional world. Gorshman's writing reveals deep fissures of conflict, destruction, and violent change, enmeshed in the fabric of daily life. The 1948 collection *Der koyekh fun lebn* (The power of life) contains several stories set in the prewar shtetl, narrated from the perspective of a young girl. "Mayn ershte libe" (My first love) describes a girl's crush on a young woman, a customer in her mother's bakery. The young woman, elegant and ethereal in her beautiful striped silk blouse, comes every day to buy a snack, and hates it when the child's mother shouts after her that her baking is tasty. When the younger girl learns that the young woman is engaged, she imagines the groom as the embodiment of perfection. She is outraged to see the groom shouting at his bride, and refuses to eat. In preparation for the wedding celebrations, the mother bakes "*kitkes*," braided pastries, coating them with an egg wash, which leaves them golden brown and perfect after they have baked. The girl takes a nail and scrapes off the crust from all the loaves as an act of revenge against the coarse, rude groom. The mother, undaunted, reapplies the egg wash, and returns the loaves to the oven. Satisfied with her work, she announces that no sign of the damage remains, but the little girl, unconvinced, sees in the ruined loaves the clear traces of her own displeasure. In this story, the motif of food does not serve the purposes of nostalgia. The *kitkes*—the festive braided loaves—do not work to evoke the abundance of the past, but rather, their damaged perfection speaks of the tiny, private world of a child, who has no other language to express her desires or her anger.

"Der driter dor" (The third generation) conveys the complexities of the author's attitude toward the shtetl. In this story, as in others, food—and the lack of food—is a central motif, but it means something very different from the "kugel Judaism" mocked by Peretz's interlocutor in "Impression of a Journey Through the Tomaszow Region in 1890." Gorshman did not get along with her stepfather, and grew up in the house of her maternal grandparents. Gorshman's grandmother, a physically powerful woman, worked as a dyer. In the brief autobiography that opens *33 noveln*, the author describes her grandmother's skill at collecting mushrooms, herbs, and berries from the woods adjacent to Krok, and gives an example of her illiterate grandmother's provocative sayings: "A man understands nothing. You can tell him that half the goose is out feeding herself while the other half is boiling on the stove, and he'll consider the matter closed" (*A man farshteyt go—o—o—ornisht! Zog im—a halbe gandz fitert zikh, di andere helft—kokht zikh,—un pazhaluiste!*) (Gorshman 1961, 7). Gullible men will accept all sorts of inane stories as the truth, but women know better.

Gordon uses the theme of the succession of generations to suggest the unbroken chain of Jewish tradition; Gorshman's "Third Generation," in contrast, depicts the sharp conflicts that separate generations. The grandparents receive a letter from their granddaughter, who has just given birth and is now sick and miserable in a hospital in Vilna. She has mastitis and is unable to feed her child; she and her "friend" (*khaver*), who are not married, have no money and share a room in an unheated house. Her appeal to her mother was fruitless; her mother answered by saying that she and her baby could "lie in the hospital or in another place" (*in bikur-kholim oder in an ander ort*), implying that she could be dead and in the cemetery for all she cared (18). The grandmother bakes butter rolls and buns with gooseberries, packs them in a basket together with butter and honey, takes a wagon to the station, rides the train to Vilna, feeds her granddaughter and great-granddaughter, and brings everyone, including the young man, back to Krok, where she cares for them until they are back on their feet. The older generation, not the parents but the grandparents, save the "third generation," the generation of new Jews, who leave the shtetl, abandon its traditions, but remain nonetheless dependent on it to survive.

Gorshman returns to this episode in a subsequent autobiographical work, "Khanes shof un rinder" (Khane's sheep and cattle), which describes her life from the 1930s through the end of the war, including her participation in the "Voyo Nova" commune. The heroine's marriage brings an end to her life on the commune. She moves to Moscow with her three children and her second husband in 1931. The transition is difficult. The poverty, overcrowding, the enmity of her neighbors in the communal apartment, and the long commute to work on the tram (which frightens Khane at first because she cannot believe that it really stays on its rails) are a stark contrast to the freedom of life on the commune and to the intimacy of life in the shtetl, where women talked about "what you cooked yesterday and what you were going to cook today" (*vos nekhtn hot men gekokht un vos me hot bedeye tsu kokhn haynt*) (1984, 99).

Ten years later, in June 1941, Khane takes her youngest daughter to visit her mother and stepfather in Lithuania, ending their twenty-year estrangement. Gitl, the mother, prepares an extravagant spread:

> The sponge cakes were done, high as top-hats. The *babkes*, rich in egg yolks and cream, were glazed and sprinkled with chopped nuts, cinnamon and sugar. The fruit flans, smooth and fluffy, were frosted over with powdered sugar. Gitl had decorated the honey-cake with a goose and goslings made of cloves . . . Gitl put the chopped liver on large platters, added a garnish of green onions, dill and the odd radish rose and sprinkled it with grated hard-boiled egg. A ladle-full of unstrained goose fat, cracklings included, went over it all . . . The large, translucent gooseberries were whole, yellow like polished amber; the dark red strawberries lay in their reddish syrup as if just picked. (1994, 146–48)[38]

All this abundance, this conspicuous display of maternal nurture, however, has a dark underlining: the memory of Gitl's previous rejection of her daughter, which Gorshman describes in "The Third Generation." In "Khane's Sheep and Cattle," in contrast to the earlier story, the rejection is framed in harsher language. Gitl remembers what she wrote: "For all I care, you can lie in Kovno's public ward and may your bastard be left an orphan" (1994, 148). The detailed description of traditional foods does not serve to embed the moment in a chain of unbroken tradition or to evoke warm memories of the past. On the contrary, the glistening cakes and fruits and the layers of embellishments cannot cover up but only heighten the unspoken and unresolved animosity between mother and daughter.

This intergenerational animosity around the theme of nurture continues forward into the next generation in a terrible new form. The visit to the shtetl in June 1941 ends abruptly as the sound of guns begins to be heard, and Khane and her daughter quickly leave Krok and make the perilous trip back to Moscow and then further east, having left her parents behind in Lithuania (Khane's grandparents are already dead). Rayzele, the heroine's daughter, blames her mother for Gitl's death at the hands of the Nazis. She refuses to let Khane approach her and screams at her to go to the war to fight the fascists: "do you remember that we left Grandma?" (*du gedenkst, vi mir zaynen geforn fun der boben?*) (1984, 148). Diagnosed with a psychiatric illness that is the result of the trauma of the prewar visit to Lithuania, the child is hospitalized when the family returns to Moscow, and despite efforts to feed her artificially, starves herself to death in 1942.

In writings describing the numerous dislocations that shaped Gorshman's own life, including the departure from the shtetl to the city, to Palestine, to the commune in Crimea, and then to Moscow, the shtetl and its abundance are preserved in memory as a place of "longing" (*benkshaft*). At the same time, the image of the shtetl is riven by the violence of intergenerational conflict and war, and the foods linked with memories of the shtetl speak of irrevocable loss passed along, as a bitter inheritance, from generation to generation. Cataclysmic history and family history overlap, as in Der Nister's "Heshl Ansheles," but in Gorshman, unlike Der Nister, the violence is turned inward.

Inna Lesovaia's stories also imagine Jews living in an unabashedly Jewish space into which politics and history have been enfolded. Lesovaia describes apartments crowded with Jewish relatives, memories, photographs, food, and stories. Unlike many post-Soviet writers and artists, whose celebration of the collapse of the Soviet Union quickly turned to nostalgia and an embrace of kitsch, Lesovaia creates a continuity with the past without retracing the monumental landmarks of (Soviet) history, and neither denying nor disappearing into traumatic history.³⁹ Lesovaia's interwoven narratives take us from the Kishiniev pogroms of 1903 to the Soviet war in Afghanistan, but the meanings of historical events in her work never collapse into predictable narratives of emancipation achieved or progress won, whether by the approach of Soviet troops or by "repatriation" to Israel. Immigration to Israel does not resolve Soviet Jewish fates in Lesovaia's writing. As in Gorshman's and Kipnis's narratives, in Lesovaia's work the cataclysmic events of history intertwine with the conflicts and disasters of private family life.

Born in 1947 in Kiev, Lesovaia worked as a painter until the early 1990s, when she suffered a devastating loss of vision and began publishing prose fiction. Her first collection of stories was published under the title *Dama sdavala v bagazh* (A lady left her luggage) (Lesovaia 2003). A later novel, *Bessarabskii romans* (A Bessarabian romance) traces the fates of a Jewish family through Romanian and Soviet history in the first half of the twentieth century, culminating in a young actress's performances with Solomon Mikhoels (Lesovaia 2008). The narratives in *Dama sdavala v bagazh* focus on groups of Jewish families and friends, and characters from one narrative appear in other works from later eras, with different personalities and different fates, creating the impression of a world populated almost entirely by relatives—a bounded Jewish world, a shtetl. For example, Manechka, the hardworking and long-suffering sister in "Manechka i Fridochka" (Manechka and Fridochka), whose childhood takes place in the early years of the twentieth century, appears as a spoiled and untalented child, and later as an American émigré in "Vverkh po Frolovskomu spusku" (Up Frolov Street).

The catastrophic events of the past leave their mark on the lives of the characters in Lesovaia's Jewish world, but without destroying the ongoing life of the present. In one of the stories, the narrator's mother attends the synagogue on Yom Kippur and reads the prayers from the memorial service to honor the memory of her sister, killed by the Nazis. The family continues to accept the man who was once married to her, and his new wife, as their own. What united the new family with the old, the narrator remarks, was their common dead. In Lesovaia's writing, the past is not enshrined in the form of sacred memories; it is, on the contrary, contested and quarreled over, and thereby drawn into the present or, in one story, into the eternal future. In "Manechka i Fridochka," the two sisters challenge each other's versions of their past, and Fridochka blames her older sister for the deaths of her own children during wartime evacuation. The ever-successful Manechka, the object of her sister's envy, dies first, but her surviving sister Fridochka is jealous nonetheless, because Manechka will see her own unborn children before her sister does (in accordance with folk belief about life in the hereafter). The significance of the epic rivalry between the two sisters swallows up even the Nazi genocide and extends into life beyond the grave.

In Lesovaia's stories the juxtaposition of different timeframes produces the effect of a multilayered intersection of the past and the present. In "Manechka and Fridochka," for example, the narrator points to the moments in the story that later become the source for the two sisters' subsequent competing memories. Time shifts forwards and backwards with such passages as "This became one of Manechka's favorite stories" (Lesovaia 2003, 26). In the opening scene of "I Love Everyone, of Course," as a family gathers for a party, a little boy remarks to his grandfather, "Look, grandfather, who is coming!" A blank space on the page follows this line and introduces the next: "It was us" (2003, 107). With the shift from third to first person, the present is sutured into the past. Lesovaia's narratives produce a deep sense of the givenness of the community: everyone is already assembled, and you take up your place among them. Other people came before and made the crucial decisions; this situatedness, however, reaffirms the continuity of life in the present and is distinguished from the catastrophic perspective of "now" as aftereffect, a perspective characteristic of Bergelson.

"Ia liubliu, koneshno, vsekh" (I love everyone, of course), the story in which this time-shifting takes place, is organized around three celebrations: a birthday set in the 1950s, a wedding that takes place fifteen years later, and an anniversary at some time in the late 1970s. The first-person narrator is a child in the opening scenes; she is a married woman with a child in the concluding section. The heroine, however, is Musia—a tall, fat woman and an excellent cook and housewife—who dominates the narration of each of these events. We first meet her returning from the market with a huge pumpkin, from which she extracts cup after cup of seeds. We part from her at the end of the story as she stuffs ducks with raisins, rice, and the birds' own livers. In the opening of the story, at the first celebration, Musia's elderly mother participates only reluctantly: for her the losses she suffered during the war overshadow all present joys. But Musia's attitude is different: "what could be done? Musia did not know how to resurrect the dead" (*chto delat'? Musia ne umeet voskreshat' mertvykh*) (100). What Musia does know how to do is to live, to prepare food, to clean (even the communal staircase that no one else is willing to touch), to bathe an elderly relative without embarrassing him, to wash a pile of dirty diapers, and to put a cranky baby to sleep so that he stays asleep the whole night, as if this were the most important act in the world. And in Lesovaia's writing, and perhaps after all in reality, it is.

In "I Love Everyone, of Course," pregnancy, the body, birth, violence, and death are all intertwined. The opening of the story juxtaposes images of the preparation of sausages and pastry with pictures of the high, rounded stomachs of the pregnant women at the party, the filthy toilet in the courtyard, and the men's stories of lovers they had during the war. Here is the "Jewish body politic" in its lowly form. These images correspond to Bakhtin's description of the open, carnival body (Chapter One). There is, however, a significant difference between Bakhtin and Lesovaia. For all the emphasis that Bakhtin places on bodily processes and products, the body remains depersonalized and abstract. The "joyous relativism" of carnival and its constant cycle of birth and death swallow up individual memory, leaving no trace behind. In Lesovaia, in contrast to Bakhtin, the body is always *someone's* body, and the particular someone lives on, carrying history and memory into the future.

An example from the story highlights Lesovaia's unique treatment of this question. At the birthday party, Fima, one of the uncles, remembers returning to the destroyed city of Kiev after the war: "it seemed to Fima that he was also destroyed on the inside, as if he were eighty years old." The feeling never left him, and Fima blames the problem on his macabre profession, connected with the dead: Fima takes the photographs that mark non-Jewish gravesites ("*eti goishe pokhorony . . . tsvetnye portretiki na keramicheskikh ovalakh*," these goyish funerals . . . color portraits on ceramic ovals) (128–29). This grim line of work, Fima reasons, made it possible for him to feed four children. Fima's work also leaves its mark on all the family's portraits; as one character complains, all of Fima's photographs make their subjects look dead. Tragic history leaves its imprint on the artifacts of domestic life but also enables life to continue.

Gekht, Gorshman, Altman, Rubin, and Kalinovskaia each register the moment and the place when time stopped and started over again, the moment when the clock became the anniversary of a death, as in the line from Bergelson's story, "*yeder zeyger a yortsayt*" (every clock is the anniversary of a death). "I Love Everyone, of Course" incorporates the *yortsayt*—the anniversary of a death—into the cycle of family holidays. The birthday boy boasts to one of his guests that he has two birthdays, the eighth of July and the first of August. One is the day of his birth, and the other is the anniversary of mass death: "It's because on the eighth of July they killed Papa's old wife and children" (112). The family keeps its own calendar of remembrances without living completely in its shadow. The anniversary of the deaths is recontextualized as a child's second birthday and becomes part of the alternation of weekday and holiday time, and each occasion is marked, remembered, accompanied by eating, drinking, and guests. Lesovaia does not use the Yiddish words *vokhedik* and *yontevdik*, but she describes the practices associated with them.

As a writer born after the war, whose work includes events from the end of the twentieth century, Lesovaia's vision of the historical canvas takes her in new directions, in contrast to the older generation of writers. At the end of "I Love Everyone, of Course," the little Jewish boy who has two birthdays has grown into a career military officer about to depart for Afghanistan. The war in Afghanistan, the last war of the Soviet empire—in many ways the Soviet equivalent of the American war in Vietnam—left its soldiers disgraced, disenfranchised, and in many cases, mutilated. The Second World War created official monuments and days of commemoration; the war in Afghanistan did not. By the end of "I Love Everyone, of Course," other family members have left for Canada and Israel, where new tragedy befalls them. One of the relatives murders his entire family. Horrific violence repeats throughout the story, but the emotion it provokes is never simply horror.

Violence, however, even on a mass scale, never means the end in Lesovaia's writing, as it does for Bergelson and Babel. One small but telling detail makes this point clear. In Babel's story "Gedali," set during the Russian Civil War, the narrator wanders around a nearly deserted Zhitomir: *"Vot predo mnoiu bazar i smert' bazar. Ubitaia zhirnaia dusha izobiliia"* (Here in front of me is the bazaar and the death of the bazaar. The fat soul of abundance is dead) (Babel 1990, 29). In Lesovaia, in contrast, the "fat soul of abundance" came back to life, as is evident not only from her copious descriptions of food but in her allusion to this very line. In "Vverkh po Frolovskomu spusku" the description of the bazaar begins with the words *"Neistovoe, gordoe izobilie bazara! Tugoi krugovorot tolpy!"* (The frenzied, proud abundance of the bazaar! The slow movement of the densely packed crowd!) (Lesovaia 2003, 342). The cadence comes from Babel; unlike Babel, however, what Lesovaia observes is not the end of the Jewish community but its continuity and full life.

Jewish authors working in both Yiddish and Russian before and after the Second World War "remained true to the shtetl" despite its destruction. The literary imagination of a stable Jewish life world in the twentieth century is a surprising feature of Jewish literature in Soviet and post-Soviet Russia and Ukraine. The contours of this world are already given; here things are done in a Jewish way; time unfolds in an orderly alternation of holidays and weekdays; cataclysmic events intrude, but do not destroy it. Place and time adhere to one another; as Kipnis remarks, his shtetl of Sloveshne could not tear itself from Shabes on a Friday, no matter what happened. Individuals are embedded in this closed Jewish world, and even when they leave, its rhythms follow them. This image of the provincial Jew contrasts sharply with the more well-known picture of the mobile, cosmopolitan Jew, at home everywhere and nowhere. The Jew's social position as intermediary, negotiator, and agent, and the stereotypes associated with these roles, were well established in tsarist Russia. The establishment of Soviet power in the 1920s opened new doors for Jews among a newly constituted elite. Chapter Seven explores the multiple ways that they inhabited their roles as translators and cultural go-betweens in the Soviet empire. Soviet society exploited the cosmopolitan potential of the Jews (who took full advantage of the new opportunities) and at the same time demonized Jews for their creation and participation in cosmopolitan culture.

Seven Translating Empire

> Oh, Eastern translations,
> How my head aches from you.
>
> Arsenii Tarkovskii, "Perevodchik" (The translator) (1983, 135–36)

The Bolshevik revolution gave new life to Russian literary translation. As early as 1918, the new government launched a massive project called *Vsemirnaia literatura* (World literature) with the goal of translating the major works of European literature into Russian. Translation continued to be important throughout the Soviet period: Maurice Friedberg estimates that 70 percent of Russian-language literary works published in the Soviet Union in the 1970s were translations (1997, 5). In the 1920s and 1930s translation was fundamentally tied to the revolutionary reform of Russian language and culture and the remaking of the national languages and cultures that had formerly been part of the tsarist empire.[1] The enterprise of translation as both a government-supported industry and a form of cultural politics assumed distinct contours in an environment in which the conceptualization, creation, and management of "national" difference changed dramatically over the decades, revealing a fundamental set of tensions at its core between cultivating and controlling minority cultures, and between sociological and biological models of difference. The so-called friendship of nations and the institutions and enterprises it created had a long and productive life, extending well beyond the 1930s into the postwar and late Soviet period. Translation played a key part in the state's project of developing the cultures of the national minorities and, moreover, in the creation of a "unified socialist culture" (Shveitser 1987, 9).

The Soviet nationality regime created unique possibilities for the *Kulturträger* (culture-bearer) and the translator. Yuri Slezkine has shown how Jews became model Soviets, used by the government as "missionaries, surrogates, eager converts, and incorruptible officials"

(2004, 237). This chapter focuses on one dimension of this phenomenon, namely, Jews as translators, both literally and figuratively, and concentrates on the role of Jews in the implementation of the policy known as the "friendship of nations." Jews transmitted Soviet cultural values to the so-called national minorities and translated their works into Russian. Not all Jews were translators and cultural emissaries, and not all who served in this role were Jews, but Jews were disproportionately represented among the ranks of writers, literary researchers, journalists, professors, and translators throughout the Soviet years, even though their relative numbers in these fields were higher in urban centers and before the war than outside of urban centers and after the war.[2] Jews served as "enlighteners" in the Soviet imperial mission by working as educators and translators for minority peoples in Central Asia, the Caucasus, and Siberia; as ambassadors for the new socialist way of life; and as emissaries of Soviet humanism, in which Russian culture, the Russian language, and the Russian literary canon played a key role. Translation also provided income for otherwise hard-pressed writers: most of the authors I have discussed thus far also served as translators, and in the course of their work reflected on its broad implications. David Vygodskii, Osip Mandelshtam, Iurii Karabchieveksii, Felix Roziner, Semen Lipkin, Dina Rubina, and Liudmila Ulitskaia probe the possibilities, pleasures, and dangers that accompanied the Jews' niche as Russian cultural producers, emissaries, and translators in the Soviet empire.[3]

Two broad perspectives, one theoretical and the other historical, frame the discussion that follows. Translation theory no longer accepts the view that language is a transparent vessel of meaning, or that translation provides a neutral space for the transfer of content from one language to another—as Mandelshtam put it, "pouring grain from one sack into another" (1979, 284). Proponents of postcolonial studies argue that the presumption of universalizing neutrality in translation masks the imposition of power by a dominant culture over a weaker one, ignoring the gaps and heterogeneity between cultures and languages. As Talal Asad wrote, "there are asymmetrical tendencies and pressures in the languages of dominated and dominant societies" (1986, 164). The problem of rendering a statement in one language into another becomes more difficult if the relations of power between the two languages are uneven. In this context, the something that is invariably lost in translation is more than just a nuance of meaning. Translations into a so-called weaker language may also undermine and invert the original meaning of a text, shifting the balance of power in an unforeseen direction. Mikhail Bakhtin's work on hybrid speech, and Homi Bhabha's arguments about the subversive force of colonial mimicry, raise provocative questions about the Jews' role as cultural emissaries and translators in the Soviet empire.[4] Jews who became Soviet cultural emissaries in Central Asia and the Caucasus were both colonial agents and colonial subjects at the same time: they not only translated the languages of the national minorities, including Yiddish, into Russian, and vice versa, but also translated themselves into Soviets.[5] How they regarded their own otherness and the otherness of the languages they translated is a key concern of this chapter. Significantly, the critical language that I am using occurs in the speech of my native informants, including David Vygodskii, Dina Rubina, and other writers, as I will show.

Soviet cultural politics and nationality policies inform these theoretical issues. The premise of the "empire of nations," as Francine Hirsch argues, rested on the sociological premise that cultural characteristics were not immutable, and that therefore the human condition could be improved (2005). Cultural emissaries exploit their own and others' capacity for change, just as translators take advantage of the malleability of language. The eminent Soviet translator Kornei Chukovskii, who prior to the revolution had written about Russian-Jewish literature, compared the art of translation to the art of acting: "the translator must learn to imitate another's gestures, intonation, poses, and manners" (1941, 194). The plasticity of self and language were necessary for the revolutionary enterprise of remaking the world.

Self-invention in the Soviet regime had its limits, however. Beginning in the 1930s, but particularly in the war years, Soviet nationality policy decisively shifted from the sociological to the biological model. Amir Weiner observes that "Soviet policy towards its Jewish minority" revealed, more than anything else, the tension between the biological and sociological models of national difference (1999, 1141). Even though Jews served as emissaries of Soviet culture and Russian literature, their allegedly intractable difference made them both vulnerable and threatening to the system. Jews as translators and guardians of Russian culture were agents of an enterprise that could and did turn against them, transforming them into double agents whose contacts with Western and Eastern Others and whose own otherness were suspect.

The Friendship of Nations and Its Afterlife

The 1930s saw a turn away from revolutionary internationalism and the encouragement of nativist difference (as embodied, for example, in non-Cyrillic alphabets) toward an emphasis on the importance of Russian and the cultural dominance of the Russian people. The preface of the first issue of the literary almanac *Druzhba narodov* (Friendship of nations), published in 1939, makes this clear by explicitly linking political power and the promotion of so-called cultural development: "Only a victorious nation can create and nurture all the conditions for the flowering of culture . . . It discovers them, forces them to sound in a new way and to give birth to new feelings" (6). The discordant image of forced song and forced birth unwittingly suggests torture and rape, the dimension of terror that was part and parcel of the "friendship of nations." The language of the passage uncannily echoes Psalm 137, in which the Babylonian captors demand a song from their prisoners, the Jews. In the Soviet Union, the cultivation of national minority culture was indeed violent: alphabets, print cultures, and people were destroyed in the process of creating national languages and literary traditions.[6]

The preface to the first issue of *Friendship of Nations* goes on to say that the cultural accomplishment of the various peoples of the USSR became available only after 1917, when the works of the great national Russian poet, Pushkin, were translated into the languages of the national minorities, and when their works were translated into Russian. The list of national writers includes: Shevchenko; Sholem Aleichem; the Armenian poet and translator Hovannes Tumanian (1869–1923); Ganjavi Nizami, the twelfth-century Persian writer touted as an Azerbaijani writer in the Stalin period; and Novai, the fifteenth-century poet and philosopher who lived in what is now Afghanistan.[7] The translation of the national literatures of the Soviet Union promoted the Russocentrism of Soviet cultural politics, because official recognition of the importance of a national literary tradition came only when the works were translated into Russian. Which works "deserved" translation was up to the Kremlin. As Shimon Markish put it, the Soviet Union created an "imperial *Russian* culture which continually absorbs the best (by whatever standard) that is created in the provinces" (1994, 202). Russian did not only make or break national minority literature. The *Friendship of Nations* authors went on to assert that Russian literature "set forth the principle of universal literature" (*nachalo obshchelovecheskoi literatury*). Russian is not like all other particular, concrete languages but rather constitutes a universal value. Russian literature is a model for the other national literature because it participates in universal human culture, serves as a necessary antidote to the ever-present danger of national particularism, and overcomes the barriers between the historical past and contemporary modernity. In this context translation served the ideological goal of remaking and delimiting the so-called minority national cultures of the Soviet Union, marking them as comparable to Russian culture, but not quite equal to it.

The 1930s also saw an explicit shift in the practice of translation. Fidelity to the original was denounced as literalism and formalism, and was replaced by the doctrine of "socialist realism," which fostered Marxist rewritings of the original text. Yet even in the Russocentric framework of this time, prominent theoreticians of translation insisted on the importance of preserving national difference in Russian-language versions of national minority literature. Kornei Chukovskii insisted on the "maximally exact reproduction of the original" and attacked what he called the "chauvinism" of Russifying the text—at a moment when "Russian chauvinism" was no longer a sin but had become a virtue instead.[8]

Translators on Trial

In "National Poetry in Russian Translation," published in 1934, David Vygodskii strenuously objected to the homogenization of Russian translations of the Yiddish poet Perets Markish, whose unique creative personality and rich literary language were lost in the Russian versions of his work. Vygodskii captured the corporeal and conflicting nature of Markish's writing: the poet "tore the past from himself, piece by piece, flesh and all" (Vygodskii 1934). Vygodskii (1893–1943) was a poet, literary scholar, critic, and translator. Born in Gomel, he received a gymnasium education and later completed a degree in literature in St. Petersburg. He knew over a dozen languages, including Hebrew and Yiddish, and was particularly interested in the developments in Hebrew and Yiddish poetry of his time. His archive contains drafts of several lengthy anthologies of Jewish literature that never saw the light of day. The best Hebrew poets, Vygodskii noted, "attempted to unite European and Jewish" principles in their writing (Vygodskii 1920s). Vygodskii's profound knowledge of European literature made him a "culture-bearer," but not in the sense that he was a Soviet cultural functionary. His vision exceeded the Russocentric cultural template that emerged in the 1930s. For Vygodskii, literature meant "world literature," in which Jewish literature—from the Hebrew poets of Golden Age Spain to the twentieth-century writer Markish and the Hebrew poet Saul Chernikhovksii—played a prominent role.

Among many other works, Vygodskii translated Heine into Esperanto, but he was best known for his translations of the work of Latin American and Spanish authors into Russian. He was part of a circle that included Akhmatova, Mandelshtam, Mikhail Zoshchenko, the Formalist critics Viktor Shklovskii and Iurii Tynianov, and his cousin, Lev Vygotskii, the eminent developmental psychologist (who changed the spelling of his name so as not to be confused with David). Vygodskii was arrested in 1938 together with numerous Leningrad authors and translators, including, for example, Benedikt Lifshits, V. A. Zorgenfrei, and N. A. Zabolotskii; the mass arrests came to be known as "*delo literaturov*" (the case of the writers) and "*delo perevodchikov*" (the case of the translators).[9] The government's fabricated charges, however, had little to do with the content of their literary work. Nonetheless, Vygodskii's links with Latin American, French, Spanish, and American authors, publishers, and private individuals (some wrote to him in Esperanto), and with the Hispanic-American Society, which he helped to found, were used to convict him of conducting counterrevolutionary activities. His contact with the Western Other—a crucial part of his translation work—made him dangerous to a regime that was building socialism in one country. David Vygodskii died in a camp in Kazakhstan in 1943.[10]

In the 1930s, Vygodskii served as a staff writer for the journal *Zvezda* (The star), writing frequently about translation and the Soviet minority literatures. He planned a special issue devoted to Jewish literature. Vygodskii insisted that the concept of Soviet literature had to emphasize its multilingual diversity. Soviet poetry, Vygodskii wrote, did not consist merely of the work of Russian writers but was rather the work of Russian, Armenian, Georgian, and Yiddish writers, among others (1934). Vygodskii developed the idea of a multiplicity of voices by invoking the notion of the literary "hybrid" (*gibrid*) and singled out the Ukrainian poet Ivan Kulik for his use of the "Negro-Ukrainian hybrid" (*negritiansko-ukrainskii gibrid*) in his poem "Chernaia epopeia" (Black epic) (Vygodskii 1934, 165). Babel, Gekht, Veniamin Kaverin, and Il'ia Sel'vinskii, among others, also used literary hybrids in their work by combining Yiddish and Russian, and by creating a linguistic space between the two.[11] According to Vygodskii's contemporary, Bakhtin, a hybrid construction is a single utterance that contains two styles, languages, and belief systems. Hybrid utterances decentralize language by pulling against its unifying force.[12] The politics of translation at this time laid great stress on a unified Russocentric and socialist realist literature. Given this framework, Vygodskii's praise for the use of the hybrid is all the more significant. It reflects what Lawrence Venuti calls a "translation ethics of difference," a practice that respects the foreignness of the translated work by inserting that strangeness into the target language (1998, 81–87).

Mandelshtam, like Vygodskii, also objected to the uniform, colorless quality of Russian translations of his time. "Even the most inattentive reader," Mandelshtam wrote, "will notice that virtually all foreign writers from Anatole France to the latest dime novelist—speak the same clumsy language in Russian translation" (1979, 283). Translation was supposed to be a conduit that "united the brain of the average Soviet reader with the creative life of East and West," but the conduit, Mandelshtam concluded, was polluted by hackwork. The poet himself was embroiled in a major controversy involving translation work he had done for the "Land and Factory" publishing house. The publisher failed to give credit to A. G. Gornfel'd and V. N. Koriakin, the two prior Russian translators of Charles de Coster's *Til Eulenspiegel*, making it seem as if Mandelshtam, who had revised their translations, was instead their sole author. Gornfel'd and David Zaslavskii accused him of plagiarism; Mandelshtam wrote a blistering attack on Gornfel'd in 1929–30 in an essay that became known as the "Fourth Prose."

The essay weaves together the themes of Jewishness, writing, and translation. Gregory Freidin writes that in this work Mandelshtam names himself "an heir of biblical shepherds, patriarchs, and kings," takes great pride in the "honorable title of Jew," and also attacks Gornfel'd in "strangely anti-Semitic" language.[13] Mandelshtam tells Gornfel'd, "you would have fared better bearing your woes to your banker with his sciatica, potato kugel, and *talesim*" (Mandelshtam 1979, 319). Clare Cavanagh argues that the plagiarism controversy enabled Mandelshtam to create a new identity, which united the image of the Jew as outsider with that of the poet as outsider (1991). The noble Jew of biblical lineage "is not necessarily Jewish: the 'honorable calling of Jew' becomes a blanket title for all who refuse to do business with the official culture of an oppressive state" (321). As Cavanagh puts it, "foreignness, disruption, incoherence become the essence of an art and a culture that are made, like Mandelshtam himself, of 'air, perforations and truancy'" (323).[14]

Cavanagh's emphasis on the disembodied, non-Jewish Jew requires further discussion. The term Mandelshtam used to describe his experience of the Gornfel'd controversy was "literary circumcision" (*literaturnoe obrezanie*). It was only by means of this ritual that he acquired the "honorable calling of Jew." As Mandelshtam himself put it, he was subjected to a "hideous and repugnant ritual . . . the name of this ritual is literary circumcision and dishonoring, and it is performed in accordance with tradition and the calendar needs of the writers' tribe, the sacrificial victim being selected by the Elders" (Mandelshtam 1979, 321).[15] It was this wounding, no matter how "hideous" (Mandelshtam describes it as near "castration"), that gave birth to his new poetics of criminality, placelessness, and "air"—the space between the threads of the Brussels lace or the hole in the doughnut, which is Mandelshtam's favorite part. Mandelshtam uses another image in "Fourth Prose" to suggest the connection between circumcision and naming: "It's as if I have been punched full of holes with a conductor's steel punch and stamped with my own surname" (1979, 324). In Genesis, circumcision gives Abram his new identity as Abraham; it is the covenant in the flesh by which God promises to make the Jews fertile and make kings of them (Gen. 17:6, 14).

By being stamped with his own surname and punched full of holes, Mandelshtam becomes the poet of the "Fourth Prose," who travels painfully back and forth between "the body of literalness"—the unique unrepeatable utterance—and the elusive spin of meaning. Derrida defines translation as the passage between the two (2001). For Mandelshtam, a word is a material thing, produced by a fleshy organ, the mouth. It leaves a physical trace in the mouth; the corporeal weight of the spoken word is a central theme of "Nashedshii podkovu" (Horseshoe finder). The emphasis on the body, however, does not necessarily suggest literality; there is no one-to-one correspondence between authors and words, or between words and meanings. Meanings shift. Mandelshtam ends "Fourth Prose" with the Talmudic image of two Jews, "an inseparable pair, one forever asking, the other—forever evading, evading [in Russian, *krutitsia*, literally, 'spinning']" (1979, 325). Mandelshtam is both of these characters at once: in "Fourth Prose" he narrates his own recircumcision as the Jew who overcomes the old Pauline dichotomy between Jewish carnality and literality, on the one side, and Christian spirituality, on the other. He occupies both positions at the same time: he is fleshy and spiritual.

At the same time that Mandelshtam was writing "Fourth Prose," Perets Markish and David Bergelson were also reworking the biblical trope of circumcision to suggest the Jews' painful passage to the Soviet promised land, as discussed in Chapter Two. Markish used the figure of the stamp on the heart and the scars on the body as forms of wounding that the new and terrible Soviet covenant continually reinflicted. It is not surprising that this configuration of pain, promise, community, and productivity should have provided a compelling trope for male Jewish writers searching for a way to describe both the production of normative Soviet culture and subjectivity with its illicit alternatives. Mandelshtam was arrested in the same year as Vygodskii, in 1938. Gornfel'd died in 1941, a few months before Hitler invaded the Soviet Union.[16]

Postwar Anti-Jewish Campaigns

The immediate postwar period marked a clear turning point in relation to Jews. The key events include: the murder of Mikhoels in 1948; the arrest of members of the Jewish Anti-Fascist Committee, and their subsequent murder; the anti-Jewish turn of the anticosmopolitan campaign in 1949; and the 1952 "doctors' plot." The "core message," according to Amir Weiner, of the anti-Jewish campaigns of the late 1940s was that "the Jew remained an eternal alien to the body national" (1999, 1143). The anticosmopolitan campaign is particularly significant in relation to the Jews' role as Russian cultural emissaries, because it branded Jews as dangerous interlopers in Soviet society.

In 1945 Stalin said that "Russia was the most preeminent nation of all the nations that make up the Soviet Union," and from that time "cosmopolitan" as a term of opprobrium was practically synonymous with anything that was not Russian, including Western culture, technology, and science. The Soviet Union launched a campaign that demonized cosmopolitanism as a "reactionary bourgeois ideology advocating the refusal of national traditions and culture, patriotism, and rejecting governmental and national sovereignty" (from the *Bol'shaia sovetskaia entsiklopediia*, 1969–78). Cosmopolitanism was linked with "kowtowing to the West" (*nizkopoklonstvo pered zapadom*). Literary journals, theatrical performances, individual works and authors, including Anna Akhmatova and Mikhail Zoshchenko, that were not sufficiently pro-Russian became the target of attacks in the propaganda campaign that became known as the "*zhdanovshchina*" after its spokesman, Andrei Zhdanov. Finally, "cosmopolitan" began to circulate as a specific term of abuse against Jews, seen as particularly dangerous cosmopolitans because of their links to the worldwide Jewish community and their allegedly insufficient devotion to Russian culture. The author and critic Alexandr Fadeev denounced Isaak Nusinov, a prominent scholar of Yiddish and Russian literature, because Nusinov's analysis of Pushkin (in his 1941 book *Pushkin and World Literature*) attributed too much importance to the European dimension of the poet's greatness.[17] Nusinov, arrested in 1949, died in prison.

The Jew as outsider—the fundamental message of the late 1940s—

reappeared in the literary trials of the 1960s. In 1964, the poet Joseph Brodsky was tried and convicted on the charge of "parasitism" (*tuneiadstvo*), that is, the failure to maintain steady employment in an officially recognized institution. The basis for laws against parasitism was the Marxist credo that those who do not work do not eat. Brodsky, employed at a geographic institute, received no higher education in literature or any other field, was not a member of the Writers' Union, had not served in the army, and had limited contracts for his translation work. He could not prove that his poetry was officially sanctioned; the judge asked him, "Who identified you as a poet? Who ranked you as a poet?"[18] The issue of translation and the problem of defining authorship emerged at the trial: Brodsky was accused of appropriating another's labor, because he used someone else's word-for-word translations (*podstrochniki*) of Serbian and Polish works that he then reworked into his own Russian texts. The trial transformed Brodsky's use of interlinear translations, a standard practice, into something resembling plagiarism. Brodsky was convicted of "parasitism" and was sentenced to five years of exile "in a remote location," where he performed agricultural labor on a collective farm. As David Bethea explains, Brodsky himself understood the motivation behind his arrest in terms of his own position as an outsider: "I just happened to combine the most inviting characteristics in that I was writing poetry and that I was a Jew."[19]

Two years later, in 1966, Iulii Daniel', a translator and fiction writer (the son of the Yiddish author and playwright Mark Daniel'), and Andrei Siniavsky, who used the Jewish-sounding pseudonym "Abram Terts," were convicted for crimes of slandering the Russian government. The prosecution made much of the fact that Siniavky's pseudonym came from the Jewish criminal world of Odessa. The newspaper campaign against Daniel' and Siniavsky recycled rhetoric from Stalin's "doctors' plot": both the Jewish doctors in the 1950s and the writers in the 1960s were compared to "werewolves." At the trial, the prosecutors' language suggested that what Daniel' and Siniavsky were really being charged with was the crime of imposture. One of the prosecutors, referring to Siniavsky, said that "for a time, he gave himself out as a Soviet literary critic." According to the prosecution, Siniavsky turned out to be the hoodlum Terts, who betrayed his country with anti-Soviet literature published abroad. As Siniavsky put it in a novel he wrote about his trial and incarceration, "he must understand that he is neither Andrei nor Donatovich, but the proven and inveterate traitor, Abram Terts."[20] The language used against Daniel' and Siniavsky code the putative dangers of the Jews' role in the Soviet system: their abnormal power, their capacity to mask their true identity, and their dangerous plasticity.

Anti-Jewish attacks of the late 1940s also served as the template for subsequent anti-Jewish campaigns challenging the Jews' capacity to serve as translators (in the broad sense), emissaries, and producers of Russian culture. The 1977 controversy known as "The Classics and Us" (*Klassika i my*) reanimated the ideology of the anticosmopolitan campaign. "The Classics and Us" was the name of a forum held by writers, theater directors, and literary critics in the Central Writers' Club (Tsentral'nyi Dom literatorov) in Moscow. The literary organ of the Writers' Union, the journal *Moskva* (Moscow), published the stenographic transcript of the event in 1990. The controversy has occupied the central stage of the Russian literary scene for decades, and writers all over the political spectrum have returned to the provocative debate in the post-Soviet period.[21] During the 1977 forum, Stanislav Kuniaev, a writer and critic, insinuated that blood and not language or talent determined who could be considered an author of a Russian classic. His discussion of the poems of Eduard Bagritskii painted a picture of Bagritskii the Jew as the enemy of Russian culture.[22] Just as in the anticosmopolitan campaign of the 1940s, participants in the 1977 forum attacked Abram Efros's ability to direct Russian plays on the grounds of his non-Russian nationality. Approximately two decades later, in an elaboration of his position, Kuniaev introduced the distinction between Russian authors who produced (real) Russian literature and Russian authors of Jewish (or other non-Russian) descent whose works could only be termed "Russophone" (*russkoiazychnyi*).[23] Along similar lines, Vladimir Bondarenko distinguished between Russian literature, cosmopolitan literature written in Russian, and Russophone literature (2002). In an interview from 2007, Kuniaev agreed that ordinary textbooks of Russian literature contained only Russophone authors, such as Joseph Brodsky, Tatiana Bek, and Vasilii Grossman, while lacking works written by Russian authors. Russia had lost the Second World War on the front called "Russian literature."²⁴ According to these views, "Russophone" and "cosmopolitan" are pejorative terms.²⁵

Yiddish and the Language of Tolstoy

This history of suspicion profoundly influenced the Jews' trajectory as Russian cultural producers, translators, and emissaries in the late and post-Soviet period. Slezkine argues that Jewish prominence in elite cultural professions hinged on the absolute rejection of Jewishness and Yiddish, what he calls the transformation of shtetl Jews into "Pushkin Jews" (only in Soviet Russia, as the case of Nusinov shows, could allegedly getting Pushkin wrong have fatal consequences). Iurii Karabchievskii's autobiographical fiction captures what this process of self-transformation felt like from the inside. He shows that the loss of Yiddish and the loss of the Jewish past were fraught with ambivalence.

Trained as an electrical engineer, Karabchievskii started publishing poetry in the Soviet Union in the early 1960s; he participated in the banned literary almanac *Metropol'* (Metropolis) in 1979, but first gained attention in literary circles with his controversial book on the poet Vladimir Mayakovsky.²⁶ Karabchievskii's "Life of Aleksandr Zil'ber" was written in the mid-1970s and initially published abroad; it was published in Russia in the journal *Druzhba narodov* (Friendship of nations) in 1990, in a collection of other works by the author in 1991 (the year the Soviet Union collapsed), and republished in 2004.

"The Life of Aleksandr Zil'ber" opens with a reflection on the multiple associations of the word "camp" (*lager'*):

> Words do not live their own, separate lives—words live only in combination with other words, both spoken and unspoken. We say "camp" and the gloomy apparitions surround this word from all sides, crowding together and flapping their black wings. But when we say "camp" and add "pioneer," it works like a charm. The ghosts disappear into the netherworld, the bugle blares and the drum beats, happy games, soccer and volley ball, river and woods, berries and flowers . . . But each person, no matter how his life turns out, has his own camp theme—let my words not sound blasphemous or offend anyone's sufferings. For me the terms even coincide, what can I do, that's the way it is. (Karabchievskii 1991, 5)

In the story, the young boy's unpleasant experiences of the Soviet pioneer camp included regular beatings doled out by a fellow camper with anti-Semitic inclinations. The victim insisted that his father died at the front; the bully insisted that Jews did not serve on the front. The word "camp" thus functions as a hybrid in and of itself, bringing together and splitting apart the horrific, joyous, and humiliating associations that its utterance provokes. The utterance of the word "camp" sets in motion a coincidence of conflicting meanings, differently accentuated for each speaker.

The misery of the hero's childhood in the "Life of Aleksandr Zil'ber," including his version of "camp" life, stems in part from the oppressive conditions for Jews created by the "doctors' plot." The usual cruelty and bullying that schoolchildren practiced on other schoolchildren intensified to an intolerable degree during that time, made worse by anti-Semitic pronouncements from the government and school officials. The unhappiness of the hero's childhood, however, stems just as much from the oppressive conditions of his home life as it does from the political conditions of the time in which he grew up. The source of his misery is his miserly, uneducated, all too Jewish stepfather, always muttering in Yiddish, his fingers and lips always moist in order to count and recount his money. The portrait of the stepfather shares features of the stereotypical Jewish capitalist found in both nineteenth- and twentieth-century Russian literature. The world of the Jewish past, as mediated by the stepfather, is a narrow, paranoid place, devoid of art, literature, and culture and dominated by the all-encompassing pressure to survive. In the course of the story, the stepfather spends time in prison for some unspecified economic crime involving the possible embezzlement of government property.[27]

The stepfather's Yiddish is as limited and uninspiring as his outlook on life. It is only a "language of parody" (*parodiinyi iazyk*):

> Here's a language for you, a language like any other language: sounds, words, sentences. It has everything that a real language has, as is usual among people. Live, speak, count, curse. You want to write your wife—take the old Phoenician letters, they are just the thing, like a saddle on a cow. Write, don't be afraid, no matter what stories you told, you won't succeed in writing poems, and as for novels—it's out of the question. (43)

This passage reflects the feelings of the character, Aleksandr Zil'ber.[28] The attitudes of the author, Iurii Karabchievskii, are more complex. The question of the virtues of Yiddish as a literary language resurfaces later in the text in relation to the child's grandfather. The grandfather spoke a remarkable mixture of languages, consisting of Russian, Yiddish, Hebrew, Ukrainian, and Polish, and in this "prodigious kasha . . . there was nonetheless a definite regularity, and undoubted naturalness, I would even say, a harmony" (113). No one else, of course, could understand it, and the author would be required to include, for every half-page of the grandfather's language, a half-page of translation, "as if it was not a half-literate old Jew speaking, but someone like Madam Scherer" (113). The reference is to the opening scenes of *War and Peace*, which take place in the salon of a Petersburg aristocrat who speaks only French; Tolstoy's text contains long passages of French. The idea of parallel roles for the fashionable French of a nineteenth-century aristocrat and the pastiche of Yiddish and other languages spoken by the "old Jew" seems absurd.

At the same time that the character Aleksandr Zil'ber derides Yiddish, the author inserts Yiddish into his Russian text. Karabchievskii transliterates Yiddish into Russian characters in the original and provides a Russian translation in the footnotes. In the story, the hero's grandfather was able to leave Zhitomir before the German invasion; his wife, left behind, was killed. Whenever the grandfather became ill, he became delirious and saw his wife being buried alive. The grandfather would cry out in the language he considered Russian that her arms were still moving, and plead with the people around him (in his delirium) to dig her out. Then he would argue with God—in Yiddish: "*Neyn gotenyu, ikh vil nit leybn. Far vos, gotenyu? Far vos tust mir azelkhe tsores?*" (No, God, I don't want to live. Why, God? Why do you give me such pain?) (106).

The grandfather's defiance would usually give way to remorse and an admission of his own guilt before God: "*Yo, gotenyu, du bist gerekht. Ikh bin shuldik*" (Yes, God, you are right. I am guilty). The author registers the emotional associations of the grandmother's death through the juxtaposition of languages, Russian and Yiddish, adding depth to his own earlier observation that words live only in combination with other words.

In the world of Karabchievskii's story, Yiddish remains confined to characters whose value emerges only later, as in the case of the stepfather and especially the grandfather.[29] The fictitious character Aleksandr Zil'ber cannot entertain the possibility of Yiddish as a literary language, but the story, "The Life of Aleksandr Zil'ber," puts the possibility into practice. The first-person narrative describing Aleksandr Zil'ber's coming-of-age as a Russian-language writer performs a double gesture of erasing and reinscribing Yiddish into a Russian literary environment, echoing similar gestures in Russian-language works from the 1920s and 1930s. The suffering that the grandfather describes only in Yiddish corresponds to what Karabchievskii characterizes elsewhere as the "little, tiny remainder that demands another form of expression."[30] Bergelson's 1946 "A Witness" provides an apt context for Karabchievskii's model of the "remainder." The story (see Chapters Four and Five) speaks to the suffering of the Jew's body and its resistance to abstraction and universalization by framing the problem of Jewish memory in terms of the necessary failure of translation.

Translation, whether of a text into another language or of a person into another identity, is not a clean, complete process; something is always left behind from the prior language or identity, and this something haunts the new text or remade person.[31] Karabchievskii's remark about the "remainder" resonates with Walter Benjamin's model of translation as coming from the "afterlife" of the original. Yiddish, the original language, was killed off but somehow remains and, as spoken by the grandfather, exceeds the limits imposed by the proper, legitimate, "cultured" Russian of his grandson.

Ghostwriting National Difference

The pressure to produce national minority literature in Russian translation led to the use of interlinear cheat sheets in translation work. To put it bluntly, Soviet translators produced Russian versions of works they did not and could not read, from cultures they knew nothing about. The problem was not limited to the early years of the "friendship of nations." As E. G. Etkind, one of the leading figures of the Soviet translation establishment, wryly observed in 1962, the "universal translator," relying on an interlinear translation, produces Russian translations from "Bengali, Swedish, Polish, Chinese, Rumanian, and the Bantu language of the Negroes" without any knowledge of these languages or the literature, culture, and history of the people who write in them (Etkind 1962, 133).[32] The ordinary and widely acknowledged nature of this practice did not prevent it from becoming a crime in the case against Joseph Brodsky, however. The use of interlinear translation in the absence of linguistic and cultural knowledge enhanced the withering away of national differences, and the trivialization of the national minority literatures. It created employment possibilities for many literary writers who did not know languages other than Russian. It also led to Felix Roziner's novel *A Certain Finkel'maier*.

The eponymous hero, the Jewish poet Aaron-Khaim Mendelevich Finkel'maier (the name is supposed to sound "too Jewish"), officially employed as a low-level bureaucrat in the fishing industry, is, as Alice Nakhimovsky puts it, "a closet poet," who cannot publish his own poetry under his own name (Nakhimovsky 1992, 182).[33] He calls his poetry "an intimate detail of my personal life" (*intimnaia podrobnost' moei chastnoi zhizni*) (Roziner 1981, 117). On one of his journeys to Siberia, Finkel'maier encounters the huntsman Manakin, a member of the tiny minority group the "Tongor."[34] Manakin divides his time between hunting, oral poetry, and drinking. Finkel'maier adapts the huntsman's words to the conventions of Russian poetry and agrees to pay him half of everything he earns as the supposed translator of "Aion Neprigen," the lyrical Siberian huntsman. Finkel'maier produces his best poetry in the guise of translations of the work of "Aion Neprigen"; and Aion Neprigen, the literary persona realized in the person of Manakin, becomes the leading national poet of the Tongor people. He is enrolled in adult education courses, stops hunting, and ultimately receives a high position in the local party. The idyllic "friendship of nations" embodied in the relation between the Jew and the Tongor, however, leads to disaster. Manakin contrives to have the first volume of "Aion Neprigen"'s poetry, authored by Finkel'maier, published under his own name, severing the connection between Finkel'maier and his own writing. Finkel'maier's spotty work record, his ties to a group of unofficial artists, and in general his irregular life make him the ideal target of the government's campaign against "parasitism," and in a fictitious reworking of the 1964 Brodsky trial, the Soviet government convicts Finkel'maier and sends him to Siberia.

The Jew as the "national poet" of the Tongor is the fundamental conceit of the novel, its Jewish joke. The novel carefully establishes Finkel'maier's Jewishness. Finkel'maier's name, body, speech, sexuality, and personal history are all stereotypically Jewish. Finkel'maier's nose is hooked, his eyes large and moist, his expression ironic; he is grotesquely tall and clumsy. He grew up in a region of Moscow that he calls a "shtetl" (*mestechko* in Russian); he speaks "*zhargon*" (Yiddish) and speaks Russian improperly, with Jewish intonations. His father worked in the garment industry and was imprisoned for the trade in women's clothing that he conducted on the side. The childhoods of Finkel'maier and Karabchievskii's Zil'ber have much in common.

Finkel'maier the too-Jewish Jew does not, however, produce literature that reflects his Jewishness but rather his Jewish role as intermediary, visible and invisible at the same time. His brilliance at this role is what gets him into trouble. In one of the comic high points of Roziner's novel, Finkel'maier sits for university entrance exams but fails, charged with cheating because the copious citations he gave from Pushkin's *Eugene Onegin* contained orthographic idiosyncrasies unique to the great author, evidence, to quote the administrator, that "The book lay open on your lap" (63). Finkel'maier's defense—that he knows the work by heart—leads nowhere. As he attempts to justify himself, he slips into nonstandard Russian, and he is told to "learn to speak properly." As Finkel'maier is dragged from the room, he quotes the famous section of Pushkin's novel in which Tatiana writes a letter to Onegin. Tatiana writes her letter in French, and Pushkin's narrator apologizes for her poor knowledge of Russian. I give the passage in Walter Arndt's translation:

> I'll have to furnish a translation
> Of Tanya's letter in the end,
> She knew our language only barely,
> Read Russian magazines but rarely;
> In her own language she was slow
> To make her meaning clear, and so
>
> (Pushkin 1963, 73)

Finkel'maier's quotation of Pushkin's apology for Tatiana is a great comeback line, with a long trajectory in Russian literature. The topos of the Jew's poor Russian and more general failure to possess a native language goes at least as far back as nineteenth-century Russian and European literature, and can be found in the work of the best-known Russian-Jewish writers of the twentieth century, including Mandelshtam, who characterized his father's language as, "anything you like, only not a language" (*vse chto ugodno, no ne iazyk*) (Mandelshtam 1990, 1:19–20). The Jew, denied admission to the university because of his Jewishness and his incapacity to speak Russian properly, quotes and claims an affinity with Russia's greatest national writer and with his heroine, who also fails to speak Russian properly. Finkel'maier uses Pushkin's text to defend himself, refracting his feeling through the medium of someone else's language. The reader's knowledge of who Pushkin is, and who Finkel'maier is, and the gap between the two, makes the scene funny.

What is comic here, however, turns tragic later in the novel, when Finkel'maier renounces his own work. Manakin, the Tongor huntsman, outsmarts his so-called translator and succeeds in publishing Finkel'maier's poetry under his own name, Danila Manakin, without any protest from the actual author. The absence of material proof of his own work as an author will land Finkel'maier in the courtroom on trial for "parasitism" and, ultimately, in Siberia. The irony is that Finkel'maier's model of literary creativity is indeed parasitic, in the direct sense that it depends on what has already been said in another's language.

Finkel'maier is a fiction but a fiction that depends on and reflects the actual phenomenon of translators ghostwriting, coauthoring, and even authoring their own work in the guise of translations from the national minority literatures of the Soviet Union. The particular historical configuration of law, ideology, literature, and politics, together with an overarching system of enforcement in the Soviet Union, enabled a specific type of cultural production that was at the same time fractured by its own products. In *A Certain Finkel'maier* as in the real world of the Soviet Union, Jews occupied positions all over the disciplinary regime, defining, regulating, censoring, and reproducing Soviet culture in its official and unofficial forms. This system created an opening in which *Finkel'maier* the novel and Finkel'maier the phenomenon could emerge.

The oeuvre of the poet and translator Semen Israilevich Lipkin (1911–2003) provides an extraordinary example of this phenomenon. Born in Odessa, Lipkin was an early protégé of Eduard Bagritskii. Some of Lipkin's poems were published in the early 1930s, but for most of the Soviet century only his translations saw the light of day. Among the members of his circle were the poet, painter, and translator Arkadii Shteinberg, the poet Boris Slutskii, and the writer Vasilii Grossman. Shimon Markish somewhat unfairly writes that Lipkin, at least until 1968 when he published a controversial poem, "Soiuz" (Union), with allusions to Israel, "was generally considered a dependable member of the literary 'establishment' who knew his place and valued it" (S. Markish 1991, 210). In 1979 Lipkin left the Soviet Writers' Union, to which he had belonged since its inception in 1934, to protest the expulsion of young authors who had contributed to the unofficial literary almanac *Metropol'*.[35] The theme of the Nazi genocide ran throughout his poetry, including work he wrote during and after the Soviet time.[36] Like Grossman, his unpublished work compared Nazi camps with Soviet camps.

For most of his career, Lipkin worked for the state enterprise that translated "the literature of the peoples of the USSR." Among the Yiddish authors whom he translated into Russian were Perets Markish and Shmuel Halkin. Working from interlinear translations, Lipkin created Russian-language versions of the literatures of Central Asia, including the boilerplate praise-to-Stalin literature of the 1930s. In his memoirs, published in 1997, Lipkin describes his experience translating a Kirgiz poem titled "To Comrade Stalin." The interlinear translation was "semi-literate," and he was given only a few hours to render the eight-page work into Russian. The party officials who assigned him the task told him that they wanted to "encourage the author" and that he, Lipkin, could shorten the work as he wished. Lipkin recounts that he set himself the task of imitating the Kirgiz folk style of multiple rhyme schemes in his writing. It seems clear that Lipkin Finkel'maiered the poem, which was published in the newspapers and later anthologized, bringing Lipkin immediate success.

Among the Central Asian epics that Lipkin translated were the Kalmyk "Dzhangar" and the Kirgiz "Manas." Kirgiz is a Turkic language spoken by the predominantly Moslem inhabitants of present-day Kyrgyzstan, formerly part of the Soviet Union and located on the border with China. The epic recounts the resistance of the Kirgiz people against the Chinese and Mongol overlords and the attempts of a dispersed people to be reunited in their native land under the leadership of the hero, Manas. Lipkin sees in "Manas" the influence of the Exodus story via the Koran. Lipkin recounts a conversation with Mukhtar Auezov, the preeminent Soviet-era scholar of the epic, in which Auezov asked Lipkin how he, a city dweller, "conveyed the poetry of a nomadic people, the odors of the smoke-filled yurt." Lipkin's reply was, "I remembered" (1997, 445). He had studied the Hebrew Bible in the original as a boy, and used it in his own poetry. His interpretation of the influence of Exodus on "Manas" reveals his own affiliation with the Zionist ideal, and yet at the same time it is precisely as a Jew that he articulates an affinity with the Kirgiz epic. Translating "Manas" into Russian was one way of translating his own Jewish concerns into the literary form that was available to him. Lipkin attempts, within the limits of Soviet national politics, to engage a hybrid translation of the other that is also a self-translation. Lipkin's own ethics of difference can be found in a poem he wrote in 1984, titled "Dvuedinstvo." The title corresponds to something like "dyadicity," a trinity with two terms instead of three. The poet explicitly rejects the Soviet state's linking of religion and nation, and reaches for an inclusive religious vision in multiple vernaculars. The poem ends with the lines "We will keep silence with the Buddhists in the mosque / And in the synagogue remember Christ" (*Budem v mecheti molchat' s bodisatami / I o Khriste vspominat' v sinagoge*) (Lipkin 2008, 320). Dislocating religious practice, community, and sacred space—for example, Jews in synagogues remembering Christ, and orchestrating the juxtaposition of the Russian and non-Russian words for mosque, Buddhist, and synagogue—Lipkin creates a palpable sense of difference.

His translation work raises other questions, however. Lipkin's reading of the epic via the biblical Exodus and his own Zionism may have changed the Islamic and Koranic elements of the original. Lipkin's position as a translator of the Kirgiz epic is necessarily ambiguous. He imagines his translation as a form of "writing back," that is, appropriating the language of the center and using it for purposes directly opposed to its political ideology. In writing back to the Soviet Union as a

Jew, however, he may have written over and altered other voices in the original text.[37]

Lipkin, however, was aware of the complexities of his role as a translator in the Soviet imperial context and was engaged with the fundamental problems it posed. In 1979–80 he wrote a short novel called *Dekada* (The festival), which was first published in New York in 1983. The title refers to the ten-day celebrations of the art and literature of the national minorities, which included literary readings, concerts, and art exhibits and were held on a regular basis in Moscow from the 1930s through the 1960s.[38] In the midst of these demonstrations of the "friendship of nations," the Soviets also practiced ethnic cleansing. In 1943 Stalin expelled the entire Kalmyk population from its homeland, sending them thousands of miles east to Kazakhstan. Some Kalmyks had allegedly collaborated with the German occupiers, which provided a pretext for punishing an entire people. Households were given one to two hours to prepare, and the cattle cars used for the transport, the lack of hygiene, and the deliberate withholding of drinking water meant that many died en route. The Stalinist government disestablished the Kalmyk Autonomous Soviet Socialist Republic, which was subsequently restored in 1958. This is one of many cases of large-scale, ethnically based punitive action of the time; the 1944 expulsion of the Balkars is another example.[39]

The hero of *The Festival* is a fictitious version of Lipkin himself, a poet-translator named Stanislav Bodorskii, who while not Jewish, has problems with another dimension of his identity, his father's noble origins. He establishes himself as a translator of Central Asian epics, and struggles with his own complicity in the destruction of native culture that his work necessarily entails: the rewriting of history, the distortion of the cadences of the original to suit the devices of socialist realism, and the compulsory introduction of the figure of the Russian "friend" who solves native problems. Bodorskii encourages a young author and budding painter named Alim Safarov, who is a member of the punished ethnic group; Lipkin's close friend, the poet and painter Arkadii Shteinberg, who served time in the Gulag, is one of the prototypes for this character. The insertion of fragments of "Manas" and fragments from the Kirgiz creation narrative, as well as lengthy quotations from Alim's notebooks, disrupts the conventional realist style of the work.

Soviet humanism and the Soviet "friendship of nations" were designed to raise Russian above the status of being simply one of the languages of the peoples of the USSR to the rank of universal signifier. The Russian language was the gateway to universal culture. Lipkin's novel reveals the cultural destruction that this policy left in its wake: the transformation of an ancient epic tradition into a hackneyed set of clichés, and the substitution of its exalted "metaphysical allegory" with the conventions of socialist realism. Lipkin's work challenges the alleged superiority of Russian and Russian literary conventions. Using his position as a Jew and as a translator of Kirgiz and other Eastern languages, he manages to unsettle the relation between the center and the periphery.

Agonized deliberations about language choice between the major and the minor "national" language, reflected in *The Festival*, also appear in Lipkin's poetry. In "Imenam na plitakh" (To the names on the stones), published in 1998, the poet says that he would like to be buried "between Rachel and Shmuel" (*posredi Rakhilei i Shmulei*). He will tell the dead, "I wrote not in Yiddish, and not in Hebrew / But I wrote about you" (*Ne na idishe, ne na ivrite / Ia pisal, no pisal o vas*) (Lipkin 1998, 4). The poem suggests that all of Lipkin's poetry is a translation of sorts from the languages he did not write in: Hebrew, which was banned in 1921, and Yiddish, which in the words of his fellow poet Boris Slutskii was "killed, like a person" (*tot iazyk, kak chelovek, ubityi*) during the Second World War.[40] Lipkin did not write in Hebrew or Yiddish, but he was nonetheless addressing the "names on the stones," the dead Jews. The enunciation of the choice (in both the novel and the poem) suggests the real presence of the space between languages, the traces left in one language by the afterlife of another (the "remainder"), and the possibility of an altered space, be it Muslim or Jewish, in the framework of Russian.

No Getting Away: Dina Rubina in Uzbekistan

Like Lipkin's, Dina Rubina's Soviet-era work exposes the contradictions of the Jews' role as cultural emissaries among the national minorities. Rubina, currently living in Israel, is a prolific and popular writer who began publishing in the 1970s in the Soviet Union at a remarkably young age.[41] She is the author of dozens of stories and novellas, composed for the most part in a realist, semiautobiographical style with a characteristically dark sense of humor. Bookshops in Moscow in the early years of the twenty-first century have stocked dozens of volumes of her works. Rubina did indeed serve as a cultural emissary: her *Syndicate (A Comic-Book Novel)* (2004) recounts the fantastic, absurd, and sometimes moving adventures of the author's three years as an Israeli cultural representative in Moscow, working for a large organization, the "Syndicate" of the title (the Sakhnut in reality), whose mission is to encourage Russian Jews to emigrate to Israel.

Rubina's autobiographical "Kamera naezzhaet" (The camera zooms in), written in the 1990s and published in a collection of stories in 2001, tells the hilarious and grotesque tale of a young author whose detective story is made into a film by Uzbekstudio.[42] In 1984 Dina Rubina's "Zavtra, kak obychno" (Tomorrow, as usual) was indeed adapted for film and produced by Uzbekfil'm as *Nash vnuk rabotaet v militsii* (Our nephew works for the police). "Kamera naezzhaet" is located at the end point of a trajectory that was set in motion many decades earlier. The heroine's conflicts with the director of the film, and her difficulties teaching music to Uzbek shepherds at an "Institute of Culture" in Tashkent, reveal the deep ethnic, religious, and political tensions that are the fallout of prior Soviet cultural politics. As a cultural emissary, the Jew both bears and transmits European and so-called universal culture to the "backward peoples," but in relation to Russia, the Jew embodies a dangerous national particularism that can never be effaced.

"Kamera naezzhaet" takes its heroine from Tashkent to Moscow and finally to Jerusalem, reflecting the geographical displacements that characterize Rubina's own life and that of other Soviet Jews. Her parents grew up in Ukraine, and wartime evacuation took them to Tashkent, where the author was born and grew up. In an interview given in 1999 in Jerusalem, Rubina describes herself as "a basically colonial person . . . From childhood on my consciousness has been instructed in a constant mimicry, a patient, intelligent watchfulness" (Golovanov 1999, 273–74). Postcolonial theory views mimicry not merely as a tool of oppression but as a potentially subversive gesture, because the mimicry of the colonized questions the stability and integrity of the colonizer's identity. But in the Soviet Jewish context, the question arises as to what position the Jew occupies. Rubina's protagonists in "Kamera naezzhaet" (The camera zooms in) and "Uroki muzyka" (Music lessons) are neither and both the colonizer and the colonized. The distinctions between these positions blur beyond recognition. As a native of Uzbekistan who is not Uzbek, as a Soviet whose nationality is not listed as Russian but as Jew, and as a cultural emissary—a music teacher who instructs Uzbeks in the music of Schubert—the heroine embodies multiple positions in a highly charged Soviet colonial environment. This multiplicity presents a danger to a system that seeks to fix identity, language, nationality, and national territory in a totalized grid of relations.

In the story, few traces of Uzbek culture remain: the filmmakers speak Russian, and although the actors are Uzbek, a pair of experts from Moscow dub the sound. The Uzbek actors are just faces and bodies, puppets who mouth meaningless phrases as they go through their moves during the shoot. In one comical scene, the hapless author learns that the best text for dubbing is Russian cursing, *mat*, because it fits the cadences of any speech. "Kamera" zooms in on the absurdity of Soviet language policy in its parodic treatment of the theme of the greatness of the Russian language. Russian is the pathway to the cultural riches of world civilization because it is so rich and musical in its curses.

Rubina's heroine teaches music to Uzbeks at an "Institute of Culture" in Tashkent. The institute is the child of the "friendship of nations" policy that brought enlightenment to the "backward nations" in the form of world culture. As Rubina's narrator explains: "According to the intention of the bureaucrats at the Ministry these shepherds, enriched by the spiritual wealth of world culture, were supposed to return to the places of their birth in order to take positions as artistic directors in local cultural centers and facilitate the enlightenment of the masses" (Rubina 2001, 93). The language of the original Russian is deliberately stilted to mimic Soviet officialese. Contrary to expectations, the enlightened shepherds end up taking positions as salespeople in the city, without returning home. In the story, a problem arises when the sexual norms of the culture of the "unenlightened masses" conflict with the norms implicit in the subject of the music lesson, namely, romantic love. Rubina's heroine cannot force her Uzbek student to understand that a serenade is a love song, because as the student says, "We don't love!" (*My ne liubim!*); that is, there is no culture of romantic love as in the serenade. The heroine concludes that it would be better for "the universal cultural system . . . if the shepherd's song existed separately and Schubert separately, and in that case it would not even be desirable for the performer of the shepherd's song to study Schubert, otherwise the final outcome would be Khamsa Khakimzade Niazi's 'Khoi, ishchilar!'" (98). As the narrator explains earlier, Niazi is "the founder of Soviet Uzbek culture," and the song title means "Hey, workers!" (Ei, rabochie!) (93). The writers of the 1939 literary almanac *Druzhba narodov* (Friendship of nations) touted the triumph of Soviet nationality policy as the elevation of the "backward peoples," who after 1917 could read Shakespeare in their own language. But the Rubina story calls into question the wisdom of mixing Schubert with the musical traditions of Central Asia by showing that the Soviet education campaign helped to destroy, rather than promote, the development of traditional cultures.

From the perspective of the Soviet cultural establishment, the Jew's capacity to serve as cultural intermediary to the "backward peoples" is risky, because the Jew's universalism is suspect. It is an impostor universalism that masks Jewish clannishness. In "Kamera naezzhaet" this problem comes to a head in an episode around a figure that the narrator names "the Loyal Jew" (*Vernopodannyi Evrei*). Government control of the film script rests in the hands of one Fania Moiseevna, who approves of the script as a whole but objects to the national identity of its hero: "*Neplokho, neplokho . . . Tol'ko vot geroi na 'Uzbekfil'me' ne dolzhen byt' evreem*" (Not bad, not bad . . . Only the hero in an Uzbekfilm production cannot be a Jew) (83). The heroine's response is worth quoting at length:

> "Where did you get that he is a Jew?" I finally asked, in a friendly way.
>
> It is curious that she and I both pronounced this word identically, this name, this taboo, softening its pronunciation, approximately like this—*ivre* as if this could in some way conceal the essence of the concept, defend, soften and even unobtrusively assimilate it. (Rubina 1990, 83)

The word "Jew" in Russian is *evrei*, accented on the second syllable. The Jewish censor discovers that the hero of the film is a Jew by the way his grandmother urges him to eat. The Uzbek director of the film protests that the author has made the film into a "synagogue." The very term "Jew" bespeaks the Jew's role as a dangerous particular, who must be assimilated without drawing attention to the process. The tiniest trace of Jewishness threatens to contaminate the whole enterprise of the "friendship of nations."

As the scene continues, the government official Fania Moiseevna distributes the national identities of the characters in the film according to a tried-and-true formula that goes back to the "*druzhba narodov*" days of the 1930s: one of the characters, Grigorii, is to remain as the "Russian friend" (of the "backward people," the Uzbeks), and the criminal world is to be divided evenly between Russians and Uzbeks, and not Ossetians and Koreans as in the original script, because as Fania puts it, the national feelings of the minorities must not be offended (86). There is a particular irony in the constellation of ethnic relations as Rubina describes them: the Jew is both the gatekeeper of the entire system, manipulating who gets to stand in what position, and at the same time a dangerous, unpredictable element inside the system, whose neutrality masks a suspect particularity. The Jew writes the script and censors the script, but cannot take a role in the script as one of the players, as a Jewish actor. *A Certain Finkel'maier* makes the same point but in different terms. The Jew is everywhere and nowhere simultaneously, all-powerful but also despised and dangerous, the invisible insider/outsider par excellence.

The Translator as Christ: Liudmila Ulitskaia

Mandelshtam, Karabchievskii, Roziner, Lipkin, and Rubina reveal the paradoxes of the Jew as translator and cultural producer in the Soviet context. In contrast, in her 2006 novel *Daniel' Shtain, perevodchik* (Daniel Shtain, the translator) Liudmila Ulitskaia not only remains blind to these contradictions, embracing the Soviet "friendship of nations," but goes as far as to apotheosize the translator as convert, while demonizing the Jew. Her previous works represent Jews far more sympathetically. The 2006 novel is a strange mixture, combining Soviet definitions of the Jew left over from the 1930s with conservative Christian perspectives on Judaism. The Jew remains marginalized as a dangerous particularity, hostile to the universality that Christianity proffers. In remarks made in 2004, Ulitskaia said, "Having encountered Christianity in the 60s, for several decades I've been living with the happy sensation that in my hands is a universal key that opens all locks."[43] My criticism of *Daniel Shtain, the Translator* is not directed against those Soviet Jews who, like Ulitskaia, converted to Christianity. My remarks are limited to her novel, which in the name of something larger, something transcendent, remains nonetheless confined to a particular and narrow vision, a product of the Soviet nationality grid.

Daniel Shtain is based on the real-life story of Daniel (Oswald) Rufeisen, a Polish Jew who passed for a Christian during the Nazi occupation. While working as a translator for the Gestapo, he managed to save three hundred Jews from the town of Mir, in Belorussia. Even though his true identity was discovered, Rufeisen found protection at a convent, where he converted to Catholicism. After the war, he became a priest in Poland and subsequently left for Israel as a Jew seeking repatriation in his national homeland. The Israeli government denied him the right of return, but he remained in Israel, serving mass in Hebrew, and died of a heart attack in 1998. My discussion is not concerned with Rufeisen the historical person but only with the novel, which as Ulitskaia herself emphasizes, is a fiction made up of bits and pieces of her own life.[44]

The work is stylized as a documentary compendium and consists of fictitious letters, transcriptions of talks, lectures, and interviews, notes, police archives, and other personal papers. It spans the years 1939–2006, and its cast of characters numbers almost two dozen individuals, all of whose lives were touched in some way by Daniel' Shtain. Among them are included, for example, a monk in Kraków, who knew him after the war, Pope John Paul II, an Arab gardener, a German woman, Daniel's assistant in Haifa, his brother and sister-in-law, an Israeli scholar of Jewish studies, a former Stalinist and partisan who accepts Jesus while living in an old-age home in Israel, her estranged daughter, a fanatical right-wing Russian-Jewish settler in Israel, a former inmate of the Gulag, and Liudmila Ulitskaia herself. All these characters sound remarkably alike: Ulitskaia's Russian remains unaccented by all the other languages that her characters speak. As Iurii Maletskii put it in his 2007 review of the novel, "practically everyone, both the Arab and the German, and others—speak and write in a unified Esperanto—in the literary Russian on the level of a composition written for school" (Maletskii 2007, 174). Here there are no linguistic mixtures or hybrids, of the type that David Vygodskii envisioned in the 1930s, against the grain of Soviet translation. Everyone in the novel articulates the truth of Christianity.

In Israel, Daniel' Shtain conducts a modified Catholic mass in Hebrew, reconciles Jews and Arabs, offers counsel to a married couple (a converted Jew and a Lithuanian convert from Catholicism to Russian Orthodox Christianity), helps the runaway son of the fanatical Jewish settler, and visits his old friend John Paul II, who subsequently establishes relations between the Vatican and Israel. As one reviewer, Galina Rebel', writes, "the Jewish-Polish-Catholic Israeli Daniel' Shtain is a translator, intermediary, liaison, travel guide, and builder" (Rebel' 2007, 207). Daniel' Shtain is the ultimate Jewish go-between. Ulitskaia puts it this way: "Daniel' closed the impassable gap between Judaism and Christianity with his own body" (Ulitskaia 2008, 500).

Daniel' says that by profession he is a priest, but by nationality he is a Jew ("*professiia moia—sviashchennik, a natsional'nost'—evrei*") (82). The reason that Daniel' Shtain can be a Jew and a Catholic priest is that he wants to take Christianity back to the time of Jesus, to disregard, as Rufeisen himself said, the subsequent two thousand years of Jewish and Christian history.[45] However, in Nechama Tec's biography of Oswald Rufeisen, the priest does not say that he is "by nationality" a Jew. He does not define his Jewishness in terms of nationality. The use of this term in the novel is Ulitskaia's own invention. In the novel, Ulitskaia adapts Rufeisen's position to her own Soviet-informed views of Jews and Judaism. The Soviet nationality system did not define Jews as practitioners of the religion called Judaism but rather as members of a particular national/ethnic group. While Semen Lipkin explicitly rejects this dual-purpose definition in favor of a more open-ended view, Ulitskaia sticks to the more rigid categorization. Judaism is obsolete, and its continuing evolution in belief, practice, and institutions is irrelevant. In an earlier work, for example, she describes the Passover preparations of an old Jewish woman named Genele as follows: "All of the complex beliefs of her ancestors, all the numerous restrictions and prohibitions that over the millennia had lost their rational sense, were linked in Genele's mind to this brainless, clean little bird symbolizing the paschal lamb."[46] If "Genele the Purse Lady" accurately reflects the loss of Jewish knowledge among Soviet Jews, by the time *Daniel Shtain* was published, in 2006, new knowledge had become accessible (in new publications, websites, and other sources), but Ulitskaia chose not to avail herself of it. From the viewpoint of the novel, Jews share no common memories and have no meaningful history except their persecution, which Ulitskaia refers to as the "hateful Jewish question" (*gnusnyi evreiskii vopros*).

Soviet models of Judaism merge with the novel's limited theology to produce a simplistic image of the Jew as the enemy of Christianity. Daniel' describes the emergence of Christianity as follows: "For the apostles the resurrection of Jesus was an eschatological event, which the prophets of Israel foresaw. Therefore Christ's disciples called upon all Jews to acknowledge that they [the disciples] were the true Israel, the community of the New Testament. And here they collided with the stubborn, unceasing enmity of official Judaism" (Ulitskaia 2008, 157–58). "Official" Judaism as a belief system came to a stop with the advent of Christianity, which superseded it. According to this view, denying the truth of Christianity is tantamount to becoming Christianity's enemy.

Jews who rejected the New Testament rejected the true Israel, the new universal community. In so doing, they cut themselves off from the spiritual realm offered by Christianity and remained confined to the literal and the carnal. More than one character in the novel express some version of this view, including Jewish characters, as if to make it approximate a truth generally agreed upon, even by Jews themselves. For example, Avigdor Shtain, Daniel's brother, who did not convert, dislikes the rite of circumcision: "Why cut, when the same thing can be done symbolically? Baptism is better" (488). Sometimes Jewish carnality is positive; Daniel', for example, says that for Jews, unlike Christians, "conception is not associated with sin, but is one of God's blessings" (283). In other instances Jewish carnality takes on a collective character. The character named "Ulitskaia" writes in one of her letters that it is difficult to live in Israel: "the brew is too dense, the air is thick" (500). The Jewish body politic imbues the very atmosphere of Israel with its heavy, overbearing weight. Isaak Gantman, married to a woman rescued by Daniel', writes that "Jewry [*evreistvo*, not Judaism] is obtrusive and authoritarian, an accursed hump on the back and a beautiful gift . . . which cannot be removed, like gender" (19). He goes on to say that the Jewish dedication to the Torah, a form of ideology, shapes the Jews' "exclusivity and their isolation in Christian or any other society" (215). Daniel' says that the novelty of Jesus' teaching was to put "love above law," and the former Stalinist, Rita Kovach, converts because Jesus taught her love.

This negative picture of the Jew is as old as the New Testament. As David Nirenberg explains it, Paul appropriated ideas from both the Greek philosophical tradition and the Hebrew Bible to create a Christian model of "an idealized brotherhood in the spirit." Paul directed his universalism against one adversary, the Jews. Nirenberg writes, "to the extent that Jews refused to surrender their ancestors, their lineage, and their identity, they became emblematic of the particular, of stubborn adherence to the conditions of the flesh, enemies of universalism, of the spirit, and of God."[47] It is all the more striking that Ulitskaia should recycle this old canard about the carnal, particularistic, and literal-minded Jew after the collapse of the Soviet Union, a time of relative freedom. In contrast, during the Terror, writers such as Mandelshtam and Vygodskii explored new ways of articulating the relation between the particular and the universal. Vygodskii, for example, stressed the importance of cultural hybridity, in which Jewish literature would play a role in the canon of world literature.

In the passage I quoted earlier, Daniel' Shtain says that when Christ's disciples proclaimed themselves to be the new Israel, they encountered the enmity of "official Judaism," suggesting that "unofficial," ordinary Jews embraced the new teaching. Indeed, Jewish characters in the novel express Christian viewpoints. However, it is not merely in the time of Christ that Judaism showed itself to be the enemy of Christianity. In the world of the novel, Jews living in the 1990s are the enemies of the figure who represents Christ—Daniel' Shtain, the translator. Nothing is made explicit, but all the hints point in one direction. The fanatical settler, Geshon Shimes, whose son Daniel' helps, disables the brakes of the car Daniel' drives. The author also suggests that extremist Jews called upon supernatural forces to destroy the hero. It was rumored that shortly before his assassination in 1995, Yitzhak Rabin was the target of a kabbalistic curse known as the "*pulsa dinura*" (lashes of fire). The differences between the real-life story and Ulitskaia's fiction are important. Rufeisen died in 1998, but in the novel Daniel' Shtain dies in 1995. Some critics of the work argue that the difference in the dates is irrelevant, but clearly the author is trying to link the rumored curse with her hero's death. In the novel, she creates a fictitious newspaper article that describes the ritual, identifies Shimes as the owner of the vehicle who drove the kabbalists to the sacred spot where they issued their curse against Rabin, and has the article end with the hint, "Who knows who will be the next victim of 'the lash of fire'?" (Ulitskaia 2008, 494). The article is dated December 1, 1995, and in the novel, Daniel' dies in a fiery car crash later that month. The Jews' access to secret, magical knowledge, their personal vengefulness, and their refusal to acknowledge the eschatological significance of Christ drive them to their new act of hatred.[48]

For all its pretensions to a post-Soviet, postmodern, ecumenical "friendship of nations," Ulitskaia's vision of Christianity looks back to the time before Vatican II, which declared in 1965 that Jews are not to be held responsible for Christ's Passion. The staging of the kabbalistic curse that kills Daniel' Shtain jars against the novel's rhetoric about a new relationship between Christians and Jews, especially in light of the Holocaust. The scene of the curse belongs to a much earlier era of Jewish-Christian discourse. As Sander Gilman writes, "whenever Jews appear in medieval Christian religious drama, they are shown conjuring up the spirits of darkness with mock Hebrew oaths" (Gilman 1986, 24). Ulitskaia reproduces traditional anti-Jewish dogma.

The novel's conservative Christian views of the limitations of Judaism and the harmfulness of Jews, and its repetition, in the post-Soviet era, of Soviet nationality policy that eviscerates difference, go hand in hand with its homogenizing linguistic practice and implicit model of translation. The interchangeability of languages, the universal truth of Christianity, and the universal truth of Soviet socialism all share a disregard for the concrete particularity of any one specific language or nation for the sake of something that transcends them. The Russocentric turn of Soviet cultural policy in the 1930s held that Russian is not like all other particular, concrete languages but rather constitutes a universal value (like Christianity in contrast to other religions).

Even though Daniel' Shtain uses his work as a translator for the Nazis to save Jews, the larger thrust of the novel *Daniel Shtain, the Translator* is, minimally, to show the limitations and harmfulness of Judaism and, maximally, the benefits of conversion. The claim that Jewish-Christian identity is possible, and even desirable, is completely equivocal in light of the novel's demonstration of the enmity of fleshly, literal-minded Jews, who circumcise rather than baptize and who use their secret, magical language to kill (the letter kills, but the spirit brings life). Translation and conversion are related etymologically in English, as many critics have pointed out.[49]

Working as translators of Western European and national minority literatures, including their own, Jews faithfully served as producers of Soviet imperial culture. However, their skill in that role left them vulnerable to the charge of disloyalty to Russia; their authenticity as Russian literary artists has been attacked from the 1940s to the present day. Even in the Soviet empire, translation as a literary act could and did serve the ethical goal of animating difference. Vygodskii's cosmopolitan vision of world culture, for example, defined a place for Hebrew and Soviet Yiddish within its framework. The embrace of a universal and inclusive perspective does not necessarily lead to the evisceration of concrete specificity. Mandelshtam, Chukovskii, and Vygodskii protested the homogenization of language in Russian literary translations. Mandelshtam insisted on both the elusive spin of meaning and the fleshy, carnal specificity of the individual word. Karabchievskii, and Lipkin, attempted a hybrid gesture that leaves one language open to another, honoring the remainder that resists translation, and thereby making possible multiple and contested meanings. The open-ended view of translation, of language, and of literary production of these writers escapes the zero-sum game that forces art into the service of monocultural politics. Sadly, this phenomenon has gained strength in the twenty years since the collapse of the Soviet Union. Ulitskaia's transformation of Oswald Rufeisen into a Christ figure, however flawed, is an attempt to mitigate religious and ethnic tensions in post-Soviet Russia by reverting back to the arbitrary imperial universalism of Soviet times.

Eight Afterwards

> Those forces which put Soviet literature in motion ceased long ago. What remains are only the ruins of words.
> Aleksandr Genis, "A View from the Cul-de-Sac"

> In reflecting on the literature of the recent period, one wants to pause precisely on the category of the 'last.' . . . The last cannot be defined in terms of the category of time: it is after time . . . The new literature is last, not because of the moment of its appearance, but because of its makeup, its essential 'beyondness.'
> Mikhail Epshtein,
> "After the Future: On the New Consciousness in Literature"

Jewish authors, artists, and theorists contributed to the development of socialist realism as a literary and artistic practice; their writing shaped the narrative of the Second World War; they helped to formulate the version of Soviet universalism that gave them a major role as culture bearers and translators of Soviet civilization, in which the Russian artistic canon was key. At the same time, Jews also kept the backward-glancing calendar of remembrance; their work marked the destruction that piled up on the way to the ever-deferred bright future. The end of the Soviet Union made it possible for those who had been Soviet subjects to talk about, among many other things, the central role of Jews in Soviet civilization. These concluding pages provide an overview of responses to the collapse of the Soviet Union and its grand narratives, noting the parallels with earlier moments in Soviet history. I discuss how prominent writers, both Jews and non-Jews, interpret the end of Soviet history in philosophical terms; how they experienced the events of August 1991; and how literary and visual artists reacted to the collapse and the possibility of a new relation to the past. Three figures illustrate the range of responses: Alexandr Melikhov, a St. Petersburg writer; the visual artist Ilya Kabakov, who left Soviet Russia in 1988; and the poet and novelist Oleg Iur'ev, currently living in Germany. Melikhov reveals a deep and melancholic attachment to the Soviet Jewish story; Kabakov and Iur'ev in different ways provide alternative histories and temporalities.[1] Iur'ev highlights the ways in which Jews and Jewish history are at once strangely present and absent in late Soviet culture. What these and many other artists share in the post-Soviet period is the burden of an impossible past. Revolutionary culture destroyed memory; post-Soviet culture, in contrast, is obsessed with it. In 2010, bookstore shelves bulge with memoirs and diaries.[2] Yet the question remains as to how the past functions in the current moment, whether it serves to estrange the present or snuggle up more closely with it, thereby confirming the rightness and inevitability of contemporary culture and politics.

The Big Picture

After the end of the Soviet Union not everyone embraced the idea of renegotiating the relation to Soviet culture. The period of the dissolution of the Soviet Union also saw the reconfiguration of its foundational myths. Some writers, both Jewish and non-Jewish, published new totalizing accounts of Russian-Jewish life in the twentieth century. Solzhenitsyn's *Dvesti let vmeste* (Two hundred years together), a two-volume narrative of Russian-Jewish life, published in 2001, is an example of this tendency.[3] According to Solzhenitsyn, ever since Jews gained their viselike hold of the Russian intelligentsia in the late nineteenth century, they dominated every aspect of Soviet life, all the while maintaining their own clannish loyalty to one another and their fundamental enmity toward Russian culture. Fridrikh Gorenshtein's *Psalom* (The psalm), written in the 1970s and first published serially in Russia in 1991, paints the events of Soviet history from the 1930s to the 1970s, including the famine, the war, the anticosmopolitan campaign, and the Brezhnev "era of stagnation," as under a divine curse. The supernatural hero, Dan, the Jewish Antichrist, draws the individual lives of the human characters into a divine plan of judgment and punishment. Unlike Solzhenitsyn and others in the late and post-Soviet period, Gorenshtein does not blame the suffering caused by the Soviet regime on the Jews. However, as in his earlier work, the play "Berdichev," he describes modern Jewry as debased. For example, the greedy, effete, lazy, and obese art historian Alexandr Ivolgin (born Kats) writes articles attacking the great Yiddish actor Mikhoels. Centuries of crowding in shtetls gave rise to a weak people. Only in the era of the Hebrew Bible were the Jews free from the "degeneration" that subsequently plagued them. Solzhenitsyn's and Gorenshtein's perspectives, notwithstanding their differences about the role of the Jews in Russia, mirror one another in their attempt to recapture a pure, homogeneous ethnic community, located in a mythologized past.

Other writers also see an overlap between Jewish history and Soviet history but without the mythologizing, Soviet-style framework used by Solzhenitsyn and Gorenshtein. Vasilii Grossman was the first to argue for the parallel between Hitler's and Stalin's murderous regimes; it was Grossman who in *Life and Fate* wrote that the camp is the fastest-growing city in Europe. Beginning in the 1990s, Grossman's theoretical heirs began to link the *aftereffect* of the massive destruction of human life under communism with the Nazi genocide of the Jews. The trauma of Soviet history is the delay in seeing and knowing its overwhelming injury. The catastrophe that was Soviet life already took place, wrote Mark Kharitonov in 1990, in an article titled "Literatura posle katastrofy" (Literature after catastrophe) (Kharitonov 1990). The terminology is significant: the word *katastrofa* was used in the Soviet time instead of the term Holocaust. Kharitonov is an award-winning fiction writer and essayist, who was born in Zhitomir in 1937. In this essay, he raises Theodor Adorno's famous question about the possibility of writing poetry after Auschwitz, only in relation to the Soviet collapse. How can Russian literature after 1991 represent and address Soviet history? Alexandr Barash, a literary critic and author now living in Israel, made a similar comparison in 2004. He argues that Hebrew authors writing after the Holocaust, and Russian-language authors writing "after the communist anti-utopia," have to contend with Adorno's question, which addresses the problem of writing after massive destruction. This destruction is the central experience of the entire twentieth century, according to Barash (2004, 255).

Mark Lipovetsky and Alexander Etkind also link the Holocaust and the "Soviet catastrophe," embodied in the Gulag (Lipovetsky 2008; Etkind 2009). The Gulag was as monumentally death-dealing as Hitler's regime; it caused massive trauma not yet resolved in the post-

Soviet period, and it has significance beyond its temporal boundaries. Etkind argues that post-Soviet literature is haunted by the undead of the Soviet past; using the Holocaust work of Dominick LaCapra, Eric Santner, and others, he claims that post-Soviet writing shows a failure to work through the loss that was suffered (Etkind 2009).[4] The mythically pure prerevolutionary past—the Russia imagined by Solzhenitsyn and others—cannot be redeemed by yet more symbolic exclusions, according to this reading of Soviet history.

The attempt to understand the Soviet catastrophe in light of the Holocaust shows how far post-Soviet theorists have departed from what used to be official Soviet historiography, which denounced the discussion of the specificity of Jewish victimization under the Nazis as nationalistic. Russian was the universal signifier: only in terms of the "Russian" experience could universal meanings be attained; "Jewish," especially after the war, was automatically particularistic and "too Jewish." In a similar vein, Solzhenitsyn in *Two Hundred Years Together* laments the excess of Jewish memory in relation to the Holocaust, objecting to the worldwide significance of Babi Yar "as a symbol" in contrast to the lack of attention to the murder of thousands of Soviet prisoners of war at the Darnitskii camp, located a short distance from the scene of the massacre (Solzhenitsyn 2001 2:380).[5] In this larger context, addressing the aftereffect of the Soviet "catastrophe" in light of the aftereffect of the Holocaust reflects a polemic against the right; it also reflects a post-Soviet and Western-oriented alignment with the most significant currents of Jewish thought in the twentieth century.

The perception and theorization of "now" as "after"—this preoccupation with the aftereffect—do not belong uniquely to the post-Soviet moment or to "after Auschwitz." The post-Soviet temporal disorientation has an even earlier precedent. For Jewish authors the massive destruction of Jewish life during the Russian Civil War heightened the rupture created by the First World War. The undead of the Ukrainian pogroms haunt Bergelson's Berlin stories of the 1920s, in which "now" means only "after," after monumental loss. In the same time period, Mandelshtam figured himself as the apparition haunting contemporaneity. The beginning of the Soviet epoch and the end of the Soviet epoch echo one another.

The legacy of destruction has important implications for the general picture of Jewish culture in post-Soviet Russia. Characterizing the post-Soviet moment in terms of renewal—or the rediscovery of "roots" and the resurrection of traditions, as if they continued without change from before 1917 to the present—is misguided. The past is not a fixed object that can be retrieved as if by opening a chest of drawers. Russian-Jewish memories and "roots" are woven into the fabric of Soviet civilization, which collapsed.[6] The death of Iurii Karabchievskii tragically reveals this intimate connection. Karabchievskii made several trips to Israel attempting to live there as an immigrant, but kept on returning to Russia. In one of his last interviews, he said that "Russian Jewry was coming to an end," and that for him there was nowhere else to spend the last days of this epoch except Russia. In 1992 he committed suicide.[7] His death came in the wake of the end of the Soviet empire.[8]

Coping with Collapse

It was precisely at this time that Russians experienced an overwhelming sense of upheaval. Boris Vasil'ev, a staff writer for the mainstream journal *Oktiabr'* (October), described his sense in October 1991 that time itself no longer accommodated the enormous changes taking place: "events no longer fit into time but protrude from every passing hour" (Vasil'ev 1992, 4). On August 19 of the same year, a self-declared governmental committee declared a state of emergency, and citing the allegedly imminent national and international political crisis, and the "apathy and despair" supposedly created by Mikhail Gorbachev's reforms, it took power.[9] Tanks entered Moscow, and Boris Yeltsin and tens of thousands of Muscovites barricaded themselves at the "White House" (the building that housed the Supreme Soviet). Yeltsin proclaimed that the takeover was illegal. In a few days the putsch failed, and Gorbachev returned to Moscow. In December 1991 the Soviet Union officially abolished itself. The political upheaval that had taken place in 1989 through Eastern Europe generally, the end of communism in Czechoslovakia, Poland, Hungary, and East Germany, the secession of Lithuania and the other Baltic states, the conflict between Armenians and Azerbaijanis, the Chernobyl explosion, food shortages, and a multitude of other factors contributed to its end.

The collapse of the grounding narratives of the Soviet Union was felt throughout this period; for example, the literary critic A. Bocharov published an article titled "Myths Are Swarming, Myths Are Shattering" (Mchatsia mify, b'iutsia mify) in January 1990; he wrote that the myth that children were the only privileged class in Soviet Russia was one among many that had lost its power (Bocharov 1990). He was not the only one to declare the end of Soviet myths. Natal'ia Ivanova, a prominent literary critic and journalist, similarly wrote that the utopian myth of building a "bright future" was over (Ivanova 1990). Gorbachev's own policy of glasnost facilitated this narrative about the end of Soviet foundational narratives. The publication of numerous works that had been previously banned, including Vasilii Grossman's *Life and Fate*, his essays on the Nazi genocide (for example, "The Murder of the Jews of Berdichev"), Solzhenitsyn's *Gulag Archipelago*, and a host of other works written throughout the Soviet years, contributed to the reevaluation of Soviet culture and society. In 2007 Vasilii Grossman's *Life and Fate* (Zhizn' i sud'ba) was staged as a play at the Maly Theater in St. Petersburg under the direction of the renowned Lev Dodin. The theatrical production visualized Grossman's provocative comparison between Hitler's murder of the Jews and Stalin's Gulag by using a volleyball net as the outer periphery of both the Soviet and the German camps. The volleyball net remained on stage throughout the entire production, the Nazi camp and the Gulag thus forming an integral part of the domestic space of the Shtrum household in Moscow.[10] Dodin spent two years before staging the play teaching his students about the events it describes.

The proliferation of old/new authors so characteristic of the late and post-Soviet period had the positive impact of revealing previously hidden knowledge; however, it also deepened the prevailing sense of temporal disorientation. The barrage of resurrected publications, according to Katerina Clark, "made somewhat elusive even pinpointing the moment *Now* in the evolution of Soviet culture" (Clark 1993, 299). Galina Belaia saw no reason for rejoicing over the reentry of previously repressed works. Soviet civilization had "crashed," and the proliferation of essays, novels, poems, and artworks from the past, which might seem to be a form of cultural "wealth[,] were in reality only the fragments of various cultural worlds which accidentally coincided with one another" (Belaia 1990, 141).

Roman Jakobson's theories of language shed light on the phenomenon of cultural fragmentation in the late Soviet era. In his essay "Two Aspects of Language and Two Types of Aphasic Disturbance," Jakobson distinguishes between "contiguity disorder," in which speakers fail to make connections between verbal units, and "substitutability disorder," in which speakers cannot substitute one word for another, giving instead nothing but links between units. The lack of context and link in contiguity disorder leads to the "degeneration of the sentence into a mere word-heap" (Jakobson 1987, 106). Contiguity disorder is the inability to tell a story. The collapse of the grand narrative of Soviet culture meant that everyone began to suffer from contiguity disorder, so to speak, because the story they had been hearing for seventy years no longer made sense. The words lay "in ruins," as Aleksandr Genis said in 1990. The heap—of words, bodies, waste products, and things—is the leitmotif of Soviet work of the 1980s and 1990s. Push the clock forward a decade or so to the early years of the twenty-first century, and the other type of language disturbance, the substitutability disorder, appears: words appear in prefabricated stories, devoid of content. Post-Soviet culture also revels in the comforting embrace of stories that have already been told but now reappear severed from their original context and "reframed."[11]

The trajectory from the word heap to fixed narrative characterizes the transition from the late to the post-Soviet period; the work of the St. Petersburg author Aleksandr Melikhov exemplifies this trend. Melikhov's provocative novella *Izgnanie iz Edema: ispoved' evreia* (Exile from Eden: The confession of a Jew) (1994) expresses an ironic and melancholic longing for the Soviet Union, the homeland that never accepted him as a Jew; in contrast, his work *Krasnyi sion* (Red Zion), published ten years later in 2004, while not free of ironic displacements, creates nonetheless a sense of national belonging lacking in the earlier work. In the first novella, Leningrad is the site of the narrator's yearning for the Soviet Union; in the second, Birobidzhan fulfils his wish for a homeland. The first novella vividly portrays the collapse of Soviet civilization into a trash heap of things and words; the second, in contrast, self-consciously embraces the security of already given, fixed narrative.

Melikhov, born in 1947, holds a doctorate in math and physics. He is a journalist, serving on the editorial board of the St. Petersburg literary journal *Neva*, a critic, and a fiction writer. *Exile from Eden*, which received the Nabokov Prize from the St. Petersburg Union of Writers, is the fictitious autobiography of a Jewish writer with the resonant name of "Katzenelenbogen." The hero, the son of a Jewish father and a Russian mother, spends his childhood years in the late Stalin period in Kazakhstan, the border area between Russia and Central Asia. The critic Andrei Nemzer disparagingly sums up the work's disparate contents as including "the Jewish question, and also the problems of the nation, creativity, the individual and society, childrearing, democracy, the younger generations, the market, Soviet history [*sovka*], the floors, the ceiling, and the toilet" (Nemzer 1998).

The work opens with a challenge. "Tell me," the narrator asks, "is it possible to live with the name Katzenelenbogen?" (Melikhov 1994, 3). This name, uttered out loud in the "portals of the Soviet leviathan," has the same effect as the word "syphilis," because "Katzenelenbogen" is synonymous with—(and here the text gives only the first two letters, "*ev*," of the Russian word for "Jew," *evrei*). The narrator comments, "it is easier even physically to spit at myself in the face" than to read this word. Of course, Melikhov has forced us to do just that—read the word "Jew"—in the subtitle, "Confession of a Jew." Indeed, a review of Melikhov's work, published in 2000, notes that the subtitle "Confession of a Jew" "still grated on the nerves" when the work was published in 1994. Readers of this text are implicated in the scandal caused by the very word "Jew," contaminated in the disease, and partnered in the crime being confessed to.

Nemzer's review also points to a complicity between Melikhov's text and its post-Soviet audience, which ceased believing in political authority and in the authority of culture. The work and its audience are well suited to one another because the "malicious," "melancholic," and "resentful" reading public requires precisely the "ironic, irresponsible, formless, tired, and anemic writing" that Melikhov offers them. Both the work and its audience suffer from the same post-Soviet malaise of love, hate, and longing, now turned against the external world, now turned in on the self. This is a form of nostalgia laden with the ambivalence of melancholy; nostalgia that carries a wound.

In *Exile from Eden* anti-Semitism causes the hero's melancholia. Anti-Semitism has the all-penetrating glare of an x-ray, which reveals the truth underneath the assimilated Jew's professed loyalty; the Jew's interiority is always suspect. Under the pressure to assimilate and the gaze of the "x-ray," the hero destroys his own heritage. This memoir about remembering is also about the deliberate destruction of memory. The hero describes how his Jewish father would dive lower and lower into the river of forgetfulness until the blood ran from his ears in order to "wave before his offspring" a scrap of the *peyes* (sidelocks) of some "unknown" Ruvim. The son's all-consuming need to become "one of us" drives him to destroy the scraps of memory that the father rescues. Stung by his schoolmates' mockery of the stories he tells about his uncle Moishe and his uncle Ziamia, he describes himself drowning their memories and admits that an old chipped chamber pot had more of a chance to rise to the surface of memory than the members of his father's family. The narrator describes the process as a struggle to the death: "if I permitted him to emerge on the surface only once I would have to sink to the depths." In a domestic enactment of the official Soviet campaign of "dejudaicization," the son kills off his father's memories, transforming him into "a person without childhood games and friends, without brothers and sisters, without first precious games and memories" (Melikhov 1994, 21).

The child's violence has consequences for the adult, whose grownup image of his ancestors' past is nothing more than an absurd and fragmented mosaic:

> And now I carefully grope with my hands in the underwater gloom, where I drowned everything that my father wanted to share with me, (now when he doesn't compromise me, I love him a thousand times more, perhaps when all the Jews disappear they can find forgiveness?), but I only stumble on the senseless broken pieces, which I don't know where to put—the *tsimmeses* [cooked dish of carrots], *lekakhs* [honey-cakes], Purims . . . I try to assemble a panel a thousand kilometers wide, matching together tens of fragments the size of a

> hand span, but the pictures that result are all different . . . Now a dead world appears—a shtetl . . . a half-darkened heder, where children are brought either from the age of five, or from the age of two, to be taught exclusively the rules of Talmud (a seven-year old boy memorizes the judgments of seventy three wise men about the nuances of the divorce process), and a rebbe with a goat-like beard, whom I guess at only through the Paris dreams of Chagall, beats the guilty ones on the palms of their hands. (21)

The picture becomes increasingly unclear as the narrator describes the rebbe's wife kneading dough, which he says she will have to bury in a sacred place, spitting to the left and the right, if she omits even one of the "666 ritual intricacies"—mistaking the number of the Beast in the Apocalypse of John for the 613 *mitzvot*.

The hero's memory is not involuntary but the product of hard labor, not integral but fragmented, and finally, not his own memory but borrowed from others. The use of quotation, whether verbal or visual, heightens the loss of individual memory, emphasizing mediation, transfer, and substitution. Chagall's paintings, to which the narrator refers, have been reproduced in the popular media to the point of commodification: the rebbe in the passage above is not part of an integral, living memory but rather resembles a logo or a brand. The hero's nostalgia is the result of bricolage, which as we know from Lévi-Strauss, is an assemblage of contingent, heterogeneous, and recycled materials "that come from other constructions and destructions" (Lévi-Strauss 1966, 19).

In *Exile from Eden* whatever access to the past may be had comes only in the form of scraps and fragments. In one telling episode, the son finds a library slip (*kontrol'nyi listok*) issued in his father's name for an album of photographs from the civil war–era pogroms, and interprets the tiny, faded piece of paper as the father's testament to him. *The Jewish Pogroms of 1918–1921* was published in Moscow in 1926 under the auspices of the "Jewish section" of the commissariat for nationalities. Melikhov's narrative contains a long, excerpted passage from this book describing the rapes, torture, and shootings that took place in the Pale of Settlement during the Russian Civil War.

Melikhov's work filters the past through a triple lens of loss—the exclusion from the "unity" of the nation, membership in which required the destruction of the father's memory, and subsequently, the loss of Soviet Russia: "My Homeland is not Russia, but the USSR, that is, Soviet Russia, the typical picture of my childhood, which makes my heart contract . . . is not a weeping willow and not the curving bank along a pond, but a rusty motor in an oily stream, faded malachite green foliage, shifting heaps of crushed stone, the deafeningly loud dance space of the city park" (Melikhov 1994, 104). The author goes on to say that when the "longing for his Homeland" (*toska po Rodine*) becomes completely unbearable, he makes his way to a garbage heap outside St. Petersburg. There he feels at home: "Among broken pieces of brick, smashed concrete, old logs, rusted caterpillar tires, carburetors, among the twisted pipes, the worn out accordions of steam heating, ruined toilet tanks, flattened tin cans, canisters, jars from imported Vietnamese fish, varnish, insecticide, there along the whole miles of garbage along the sea gates of Petersburg, once again I feel calm. That is, indifferent. That is, happy" (104).

The past is fragmentary, discarded, and outmoded; it is found in the trash heap, the incoherent list of objects that no longer have any use in the material culture of daily life but function only as signs of a civilization that is destroyed. Walter Benjamin's angel, his wings clipped, finds himself amidst the garbage left behind by the Soviet experiment.

The contrast between Melikhov's *Confession of a Jew* and *Red Zion* (Krasnyi sion), published ten years later, in 2004, is striking. The central motif of the work is return: the implied author, Melikhov returns to Jewishness. Language, having degenerated to the word heap, returns to contexture, to story, to myth and fairy tale; indeed, the term "fairy tale" (*skazka*) is a significant repeating element of the text. On the front cover of *Red Zion* the author's original and more Jewish surname, "Meilakhs," replaces the Russified pseudonym "Melikhov."[12] In *Confession* the term "Jew" is a source of shame, denoting "the social role of an outsider" and "a nation that practically does not exist." In *Red Zion*, in contrast, "Jew" means something more than a term of abuse, and this positive meaning has emotional resonance, presumably not only for the implied author but for the implied reader as well. *Red Zion* overcomes the pain of nostalgia by textually and fictively creating a return to the past, and at the same time indulging the pleasure of imaginary national belonging. The hero returns to Birobidzhan, the Soviet Jewish national homeland. The return is not complete, but the emphasis, nonetheless, is on the value of restoration, the importance of myth, and the fullness of memory.

The hero of *Red Zion*, Bentsion Shamir, is a generation older than Lev Katzenelenbogen. He is a well-established Israeli writer, and *Red Zion* is both his autobiography and the story of how he wrote it. As a young boy living in a town on the border of Poland and Russia in the 1930s, he had an ideally happy childhood with his brother and sisters, his mother, and his father, a doctor: "everything that surrounded him was not simply unique in its own way, but was the only possible way it could be" (*ne prosto edinstvennym v svoem rode, no dazhe edinstvenno vozmozhnym*) (Meilakhs 2005, 25). The symptom of "substitutability disorder" is the dominant artistic device of the work as a whole. The experience of a happy childhood is the belief that there could be no other childhood. Contrast what Melikhov said ten years earlier in *Confession of a Jew*: "reminiscences of one's barefoot childhood are one of the most intolerable genres of Soviet official nationality" (Melikhov 1994, 15). In *Red Zion*, however, the idyllic childhood does not last long. The Germans invade Poland, and Bentsion and his family flee eastward to the country of the Soviets. One sister is shot by the Germans; one dies from conditions on the transport train; the Soviet-imposed forced labor leads to the father's suicide; the brother is arrested for thieving; but Bentsion survives because his mother hits on the idea of abandoning him in an orphanage soon after their arrival in Central Asia.

As a boy, Bentsion befriends a hunchbacked Jewish shoemaker Berl, an ardent Stalinist, whose only desire is to go to Birobidzhan. Berl, who cannot quite pronounce the word "Birobidzhan," recites from Kalinin's speeches by rote and declares, "in ten years Bori ... Beri ... Birobidzhan will be the most important, if not the only custodian of Jewish socialist national culture" (*let cherez desiat' 'Bori . . . Beri . . . Birobidzhan budet vazhneishim, esli ne edinstvennym khranitelem evreiskoi sotsialisticheskoi national'noi kul'tury*) (Meilakhs 2005, 11). Berl's use of language, both here and in other instances—he calls himself *"rabotnik tyla"* (a rearguard worker), and describes camels as *"vazhnoe transportnoe sredstvo"* (an important means of transport)—typifies Jakobson's substitution disorder. To use Jakobson's terms, though in a different sense, words only function in "prefixed, bound blocks," and what they are bound to is the Soviet ideology of the idealized workers' state, the bright socialist tomorrow, and in the case of Birobidzhan the bright national tomorrow for Soviet Jews.

In the text of Meilakhs's novella Birobidzhan exercises its allure, not as a beacon from the future but as a remnant of the past, whose reality is never realized except as a museum to what has been destroyed. "Jews in Birobidzhan played the same role as Indians in America: the exoticism of those who have perished" (146).

The destruction of Birobidzhan as a living community, and the destruction brought by the Second World War, makes the hero's nostalgic return to Birobidzhan possible. After the war, Bentsion makes his way to Israel, where, the narrator says, he "composes if not a heroic, then a completely respectable biography for himself": he serves as a young officer in the Israeli war of independence; he earns his Ph.D., marries, becomes a well-respected author of fiction, and finally a cultural representative to post-Soviet Russia. Along the way to his success, however, he loses his sense of purpose; there is no one around him with whom he could share his "myth." Only in Moscow, after suffering a heart attack, does he experience a turning point. Berl had bequeathed to him a silver cigarette case containing his portrait, and Bentsion decides to take Berl's gift to Birobidzhan. The decision transforms his routinized life into a meaningful "drama," and everyone around him becomes, knowingly or not, a participant in the "mass spectacle" (*massovka*).

In Birobidzhan, Bentsion accomplishes his goal. He discovers a tiny museum to a (fictitious) Soviet Yiddish writer, Meilekh Terlitskii, whose first name, of course, calls to mind the author's own original name of Meilakhs; the last name, "Terlitskii," is in homage to Aleksandr Melikhov's real-life father, who came from the shtetl of Terlits. The famous Yiddish author in the novella is a fictionalized version of the real-life Yiddish author Boris Izrailovich (Buzi) Miller, 1913–88, who lived in Birobidzhan and served as the main editor of *Birobidzhaner shtern* (The Birobidzhan star). Convicted on the charge of nationalism in 1949, during the outbreak of the anti-Jewish campaign of the postwar years, he spent seven years in the Gulag. In the novella, the so-called museum to the Yiddish writer is located in his apartment, lovingly maintained by his widow. Her poverty and her thickly accented speech (*Zdkhkhavstvyite, chto vam intekhkh'esuet*—she cannot pronounce "*r*") touch the hero to the quick, taking him back to his childhood in Poland. The writer's widow gives the hero her late husband's stories to read, and the last twenty-five pages of Meilakhs's novella are given over to lengthy excerpts from Buzi Miller's Birobidzhan stories, translated from Yiddish into Russian (Russian-language translations appeared, for example, in 1974). These are stories about the last holdout in a shtetl, who hides gold from the communists and dies a disgraceful death (the story "Zoloto"); and about a heroic son who goes off to be a builder in Birobidzhan and then a frontline soldier in the Second World War ("Synov'ia"). Miller's works typify the Soviet Jewish narrative in its heroic mode.

The reading scene in *Red Zion* accomplishes several things at once. Meilakhs gives us descriptions of Birobidzhan as it is today, including a restaurant that provides its customers with Soviet kitsch, an example of more nostalgia. The scene suspends the forward motion of time in the novel at the same time that it allows the past and the present to merge. The lengthy excerpts from Buzi Miller's stories render Birobidzhan a "prefixed bound block of language," the kind of language symptomatic of the substitution disorder. We cannot read a summary of Buzi Miller's works; we have to read his words in the order in which he wrote them, to get the full effect. The words cannot be substituted; they can appear only as a bound block of language. Meilakhs explicitly describes the Yiddish writer's style as "consisting of ready made blocks" (*sostoiashchii iz gotovykh blokov*) (222).

If in *Confession of a Jew* readers were made complicit in the shame of Jewishness, here they are made complicit in the sentiment of nostalgia. At first Bentsion finds the famous Yiddish writer's prose unbearable in its ordinariness and its colorlessness, but he gradually finds it more and more appealing: "the more schematic, colorless and sickly-sweet the story, the more cozily Bentsi fit into it. He took pleasure in its ordinariness, as if he were in a warm bath" (223). Bentsion decides finally to imitate the Yiddish writer, to write something simple and noble, just as he did, and to call it *Red Zion*. The hero "would be re-embodied as Meilekh Terletskii," and he "would create a piercingly sad and noble tale [*skazka*] of an unrealized Jewish homeland, similar to a *matreshka* [nesting doll], placed inside another, mighty and universal fatherland" (225).

Whereas the hero of the 1994 *Confession* by Aleksandr Melikhov "gropes in the underwater gloom" only to emerge with an incoherent bricolage of recycled Jewish memory, the hero of the 2004 *Red Zion* by Aleksandr Meilakhs slips comfortably into a warm bath of Birobidzhan prose. The imagined pleasure of nostalgic return resonates with childhood, with motherhood (the *matreshka*), and with the fairy tale of the bright socialist future for Jews in their own Soviet homeland. In the 1970s, Shmuel Gordon's Yiddish travelogue through the former Pale of Settlement used sentimentality to assure readers of the Soviet Jewish future. The difference between Soviet Jewish kitsch of the 1970s and Soviet Jewish kitsch in 2004 is that the post-Soviet author knows the fairy tale is dead. *Red Zion* is a myth from the past.

Quoting Soviet Yiddish writers in the pages of a post-Soviet novel is not merely recycling old, dead material, however. The insertion of bound blocks of language does not necessarily signify that all meaningful engagement with the quoted text is impossible. Alexei Yurchak's work suggests the ways that the quotation of fixed passages also creates a more dynamic and dialogic possibility. In his study of late Soviet culture, *Everything Was Forever, Until It Was No More: The Last Soviet Generation*, Yurchak argues that the formation of prefabricated bound blocks of official discourse was both a stabilizing and a destabilizing force in Soviet culture. Their meaning became less important as their performative range increased. The same text could have multiple meanings, depending on the contexts in which it was introduced and the uses to which it was put (Yurchak 2006, 53). In the novel *Red Zion* the quoted texts can perform a similarly open-ended function. Putting Russian translations of Yiddish works before the reading audience again offers the possibility of creating a new relation to Soviet Yiddish, creating new literary value in the post-Soviet world.

The Trash Heap: Ilya Kabakov

Melikhov's garbage heap is not unique in the late and post-Soviet period. Literature in the era of glasnost was filled with grotesque bodies and the formerly hidden wastelands of Soviet daily life, that is, the so-called *chernukha*, which described the hospital, the abortion clinic, and the prison.[13] The devastated landscape of *Exile from Eden* resonates with the history of Jewish literature in twentieth-century Russia, particularly but not only in work written in the aftermath of the Russian Civil War. In Markish's 1921 poem "Di kupe" (The mound), a pogrom leaves a pile of corpses that reach to the heavens, darkening the day with blood and pus. In Babel's *Red Cavalry*, Gedali's curiosity shop is full of the refuse of the past; the catacomb and the morgue replace normal human habitation. Gorenshtein's play "Berdichev," written in the 1970s, also uses the image of the garbage heap as a metaphor for the city itself, which was built out of the ruins of "historical catastrophe." The difference between the earlier and later periods has to do with the precipitating event and the artist's capacity to respond to it. Markish and Babel were reacting to the deaths that had just taken place. Markish, Bergelson, Kvitko, Gekht, and others confronted the destruction of a way of life that they knew intimately. Historical amnesia had not yet set in. Melikhov and other artists and authors of the later period, in contrast, do not confront mass Jewish death but rather the destruction of late Soviet civilization, in which Jewish culture was submerged nearly to the point of invisibility. The difference is between the eyewitness and the archeologist.

If there is one artist of the late Soviet period who made art out of the flotsam and jetsam of Soviet civilization, it is Ilya Kabakov.[14] In his piece "Box with Garbage" (Iashchik s musorom, 1981), for example, broken shoes, old pans, and other discarded objects lie on copies of the Soviet-era newspaper *Izvestiia*. Another piece, called "The Garbage Man," consists of scraps of garbage from daily life with precise documentation about where and how each item was obtained and used before it became refuse. The assemblage of scraps and fragments from Soviet daily life lacks an overarching framework of meaning, since the "myths" of the past, such as "life has become more joyous," no longer hold. Another installation from 1992, "The Toilet," offended viewers with its depiction of three Soviet-style toilets (stalls with holes in the ground) contiguous with the dining room, living room, and bedroom typical of a Soviet-era apartment. In a talk he gave on Kabakov in 2004, Boris Groys showed that Kabakov's method in using the waste products of Soviet civilization more resembles archeology than history. Groys argued that in the wake of the destruction of history and the destruction of institutions that could have developed historical memory, the only guarantor of historical memory is the dustbin. The archeological artist evacuates bits and pieces from it without providing an account of the relation between the objects. There is no recuperation of historical narrative (Groys 2004). Kabakov's garbage installations, like Melikhov's *Exile from Eden*, transform Jakobson's "contiguity disorder" into an artistic medium designed to reflect historical truth. Indeed, Kabakov's theorization of conceptualism, the art movement that he helped to found in Russia, directly addresses the problem of the absent narrative and the central importance of random "things."[15]

Kabakov's more recent installations, in contrast, reflect the reverse swing of the pendulum, back to contexture and linear progression. The shift from the 1980s and 1990s to 2004–05 is from the trash heap as artistic medium to a narrative of origins and heirs, a genealogy that is fictitious but nonetheless embeds Kabakov in a story of fathers and sons. His 2004–05 exhibit at the Museum of Contemporary Art in Cleveland, "The Teacher and the Student: Charles Rosenthal and Ilya Kabakov," constructs an account of his fictitious forerunner, Rosenthal, and also provides a story about Kabakov's fictitious artistic descendent, another invention named Igor Spivak. The exhibit also showed in the Melnikov Bus Garage in Moscow in 2008. Kabakov himself created the work exhibited under the names Rosenthal and Spivak, as well as supplying alleged photographs of his "teacher" and his "student." According to the information provided by Kabakov, Charles (Sholom) Rosenthal was born in Kherson in 1898, helped out in his father's photography studio, and studied in St. Petersburg and Vitebsk in the famous art school run by Chagall and later by Malevich; he left for Paris in 1922 and died there in 1933. In his paintings allegedly dating from the 1920s through the early 1930s (all done later by Kabakov), the blank geometrical spaces and white light of Suprematism invade the heroic daily life scenes and monumental bodies of socialist realism. In the work by Kabakov's fictitious heir Spivak (dating from the 1990s), the white space dominates the canvas, leaving fragmentary remainders of typical Soviet images.[16]

Kabakov, his fictitious teacher and student—Rosenthal and Spivak—and his alter ego, "the garbage man," are Jewish. Instead of displaying explicit Jewish content, the installations allude to the destroyed Jewish past.[17] Kabakov as the garbage man writes about his project on Sholem Aleichem's novel *The Wandering Stars*, and notes that he showed the work to the artist Robert Falk (who also plays a role in Kabakov/Rosenthal's development). Falk designed sets for various Jewish theaters in the 1910s; "Wandering Stars" was performed at the Moscow State Yiddish Theater in 1941. As befitting an archeologist, the garbage man journeys to the field, as he writes in his commentary to "A Garbage Novel," "in search of preserved Jewish places," only to find "half-residences, half-ruins, quiet and petrified melancholy, despair" (Kabakov 1996, 89). The sorrow of Babel, Markish, and other writers of the 1920s echo in these words. The art critic Robert Storr sees an allusion to Jewish history in Kabakov's description of Rosenthal: the phrase "born in Kherson" with the given name Sholom calls to mind the great scholar of Jewish mysticism Gershon Sholem, a friend of Walter Benjamin (Storr 2005, 143).

Leonid Katsis, in contrast, criticizes Kabakov for avoiding Jewish content, observing that giving Rosenthal the death date 1933 enables Kabakov to skirt the Nazi destruction of the Jews of Europe (Katsis 2008). This is not entirely accurate. Kabakov was born in 1933 and experienced, as he himself reports it, a terrifying evacuation from Dnepropetrovsk in 1941 (Wallach 1996, 17–18). His accompanying text to his 1990 installation "The Corridor/My Mother's Album" references the "perpetual cataclysm" hinted at in his biography of Rosenthal: "revolution, civil war, famine, social upheaval, repressions, the Second World War, again famine" (Wallach 1996, 193). Every image from the Rosenthal, Kabakov, and Spivak series graphically marks loss, as opposed to other alternative histories of the post-Soviet period that saturate every space with meaning and in so doing create the fantasy of intactness and completeness. The striking white and black spaces of the Rosenthal series disrupt the illusion of the possibility of full disclosure and the myths of perfection central to socialist realist visual narrative. And yet in Kabakov's art there is some strange repetition of what is visible but cannot be acknowledged, as if hearkening back to the Soviet time when the word "Jew" could not be uttered aloud.

Alternative History and Geography: Oleg Iur'ev

Building their fragments and narratives around the crash and retrofitting of Soviet life—and Soviet Jewish life under erasure—Kabakov and Melikhov reflect the larger trends of late and post-Soviet culture. Oleg Iur'ev, like Kabakov and Melikhov, uses scraps of Soviet and Soviet Jewish life in his prose, but the identities, worlds, and histories that he imagines are free from the glare of the Soviet x-ray and nostalgia for the trash heap of Soviet civilization. His novel *Poluostrov zhidtiatin* (Zhidtiatin Peninsula), published in 2000, narrates the beginning of the end of Soviet history from a Jewish perspective and through a lens that elongates and fractures time.[18] His use of language produces the experience of the crash of the Soviet Union as an effect of reading.

Iur'ev, a poet, playwright, and fiction author, was born in 1959 in Leningrad and has lived in Frankfurt am Main since 1991. His critically acclaimed play "Miriam" (1984) tells the story of a heroine who foils the advances of a White officer, a Ukrainian leader, and a Bolshevik during the Russian Civil War.[19] In the 1980s, Iur'ev cofounded an unofficial literary group in Leningrad called "Kamera khraneniia" (The Checkroom); later, the group started a publishing house, and its subsequent incarnation as a website, "Kamera khraneniia," is one of the most important venues for new literary works.

In an interview, Iur'ev said that for him the "Jewish theme" has no particular meaning, because as a writer he does not work thematically. He went on to say that given his origins and biography, however, he has an overabundance of what he calls "Jewish building material" (*evreiskii stroitel'nyi material*). His prose refers to specific events in Jewish history, including the pogroms in the early part of the twentieth century (his play "A Little Pogrom at a Train Station Buffet"), the destruction of Jewish towns during the civil war, the Holocaust, Jewish life in postwar Soviet Russia, and he also alludes to such Jewish texts as the Talmud, Jewish mystical literature, and Jewish legends (for example, his novel *The New Golem* [Novyi golem]).[20] Iur'ev is not rejecting Jewish themes but rather the reified image of the Jewish past in Soviet Russia.

In 1991 Iur'ev wrote a short piece for *Strana i mir* (Our country and the world) in which he discussed the history of Jews in Russia as the history of their disappearance. In his essay "An Absent Place," Iur'ev discusses the post-Soviet renaming of Leningrad to St. Petersburg, comparing the fate of St. Petersburg after the revolution to the fate of the Jews. "History is conducting an experiment, as it were: what remains if you take everything away? Neither the structure of life, nor the social, national, and religious structure of relations which constituted the body of culture—nothing or almost nothing remains" (Iur'ev 1991, 131). These remarks should be taken in the polemical spirit in which they were made. To call Leningrad St. Petersburg will not bring back prerevolutionary St. Petersburg. In terms of Jewish life, the point is the impossibility of retrieving what once was in the forms in which it once existed, not the impossibility of producing new works in which Jewish "building material" is central. Jewishness and Jewish culture are a source of anguish to Melikhov's hero in *Exile from Eden*; for Iur'ev, in contrast, Jewish culture is a source of literary creativity, separate and distinct from the Soviet framework.

Zhidtiatin Peninsula does not provide a socialist realist or a realist depiction of a recognizably Jewish life world but rather a dense texture of allusions in which history, language, and identity are destabilized and estranged.[21] Its two narratives and commentaries offer competing visions of the past. The work focuses on the night of Chernenko's death in April 1985 from two parallel perspectives: a thirteen-year-old boy from an assimilated Soviet Jewish family, and his double, a thirteen-year-old boy from a group of crypto-Jews. Both families live in the same building, one upstairs and one down. The crypto-Jewish family is named "Zhidtiatin," which means something like "Yidl"; the area where the novel is set, the border zone between Russia and Finland, is named for them. The "normal" Soviet Jewish family bears the name "Iazychnyk," which suggests "pagan."

The Zhidtiatins, the crypto-Jews, trace their origins to a Jew who fled Queen Isabella in the sixteenth century and was rescued by Novgorodian merchants. Their strange, not-quite-Jewish practices and beliefs keep them at a forty-five degree angle from the surrounding world. The Zhidtiatin narrative begins with a chapter titled "And There Will Be Blood for a Sign on Our Houses," taken from Exodus 12:13, in which God warns the Jews that he will kill the firstborn of the Egyptians, but "pass over" those houses marked with blood. The thirteen-year-old boy, the future prince of the clan, lies in bed, drugged and bound, recovering from his circumcision. The first voice we hear in the crypto-Jewish narrative belongs to the young hero's grandmother, who exhorts him to sleep and not to wake until he remembers "everything as it was, as it is. Where are you? Who are you? Where everything is—above, below, to the right, to the left. Where Rome is, where Jerusalem (Iur'ev 2000, 8). The grandmother's injunction points to the failure of knowledge, the historical amnesia characteristic of Soviet society.[22] Rome, in the alternate sacred geography of the crypto-Jews, means Leningrad, and Jerusalem corresponds to Helsinki. The child says, "we keep our faith from ancient times and in secret Sabbaths . . . we go to the priest Egor to church and to the 'Baltic Float' club to the movies so as to avert the eyes of others" (30–31). The crypto-Jews believe that the Roma are descendents of Pharaoh's soldiers who escaped drowning, and that the fates of Jews and Gypsies are therefore linked. They refer to Russians as *"zababony"* and find the Russian language only partly comprehensible. They believe that prerevolutionary orthography is their own secret Jewish writing, and the young boy, who reads *Pionerskaia pravda* (the youth version of *Pravda*) in secret from his grandmother, reads in his own special, secret way, first every second letter, then every third. The only point of contact between the crypto-Jews and the "simple Soviet people" among whom they live is the messianic ideology that they share. The communist paradise that the boy learns about in school seems to him to be the same dogma he learns in secret from his grandmother.

In the mirror narrative, the other thirteen-year-old, named Iazychnik, also lies in bed, suffering from tonsillitis. The narrative consists of his feverish free-floating associations triggered by the reality around him—the scraps of anxious conversations he overhears about the political events of the time, including most significantly the death of Chernenko. The boy's uncle, for example, worries about what he calls the "interregnum" (*mezhdutsarstvie*) and mutters about "the possibility, God forbid, of some Beilis-Shmeilis, and maybe with it, another Dreyfus-Shmeyfus." The narrative of the "normal" Soviet family grotesquely recapitulates Russian-Jewish and Soviet Jewish history: the young boy's ancestor Naftali-Ber ben Iaakov was known as the silent *Iazychenskii tsadik* (holy man); the boy's grandfather on his father's side was the chairman of the Committee on Jewish Poverty, and "during the cult of personality he was illegally repressed" by a distant relative, whom the boy's grandmother refers to as "*a zokhn vey* a relative!" (suggesting the kind of relative who makes you lament, "woe is me!"). The boy's father, divorced from his mother, remarried a non-Jew and emigrated to Israel, where the non-Jewish wife becomes an announcer for an Orthodox radio program. References to Soviet-era realia dominate the narrative; these include the names of typical Soviet stores ("Kul'ttovary, Kerosin, Produkty," Stationary, Kerosin, Groceries), texts (an aircraft carrier bears the name "The Story of a Real Man," referring to Boris Polevoi's Second World War–era novel about a double-amputee pilot), songs and singers ("A Million Crimson Roses," and Alla Pugacheva), and a popular movie imported from the West (the 1959 *Some Like It Hot*, with Marilyn Monroe).

The double commentaries that form a physical, graphical border between the two narratives are the work of a fictitious professor of Slavistics, Iakov Gol'dstein. The commentaries provide useful dates, definitions, identifications, translations of Yiddish, Finnish, and Tartar expressions, supplementary texts such as the words to the song "A Million Crimson Roses," and references to fictitious scholarly works on pertinent topics. The commentaries offer a sociological portrait of Soviet Jews, describing their migration from the Pale of Settlement to major urban areas; their successful professionalization, useful for the development of the Soviet economy; the anti-Jewish campaign of the late 1940s; and limitations on Jewish access to higher education in the 1960s.

The author's difficult language enhances the peculiar temporality of the work, the time of in-between, an island of time, free from progress toward the bright future but lacking a stable point of reference. Here is a passage that describes how the boy feels when his arms and legs have "fallen asleep":

> The insides of my arms and legs have become so light and so sourish and tasteless, and also ticklish, as if there had been poured into me from all four sides "Poliustrovo" mineral water, whose dark-green bottles with dust on their sloping shoulders (their name is legion) stand

in slightly rusty, flat, finely spoked cases along all the lower shelves of the store "Stationary, Produce, Kerosene," and this half-swamp water silently and imperceptibly bursts its bubbles (that run into each other as they lie massed against the inside of my skin). (Iur'ev 2000, 31)

The vantage point continually shifts along the fresh chains of associations that begin with the physical sensation, jump ahead to the taste of the mineral water, shift to the bottles in which it is sold, to the store, and back again to the interior of the body. The metonymic chains do not add up to anything larger but burst under their own weight, like the bubbles of the mineral water. Iur'ev is not reframing the present in the obsolete narratives of the past; instead, he stops narrative in order to stop time. This narrative technology defeats the purpose of conventional realist narrative: there's no actor and no action but rather the total stasis of the interregnum—a time *in between*. At the beginning of the twenty-first century, we encounter once again the time of the interval, the intermission, a redeployment of the same temporality used by authors in the 1920s.

Iur'ev inscribes one orientation in space and time, the fictitious mythico-religious framework of his not-quite-Jewish crypto-Jews, onto the scientific history of his fictitious professor. His crypto-Jews perform strange rites in expectation of their Messiah, and his modern, acculturated Soviet Jews wait to see what the outcome of Chernenko's death will be, mindful of Jewish history at similar moments of transition. *Zhidtiatin Peninsula* creates an alternative history of the present without remythologizing the past. The theme of deferred redemption, however, resounds throughout the writing of twentieth-century Jewish authors, particularly those who lived in the bright future.

Even those such as Iur'ev who argue that the revolution and the establishment of Soviet power completely destroyed Jewish culture in Russia are themselves creatively engaged in renegotiating a relation to the past, and thereby opening up the possibilities for new art, literature, and scholarship in the present and future. The era of perestroika and glasnost, the 1990s, and the subsequent decade have seen the production of new works of Jewish culture, new theatrical and musical events, as well as the emergence of new institutions and new publications devoted to the study of Jewish life and expression in many forms.[23] A series of Russian-Jewish journals, which aim at comprehensive coverage of religion, history, politics, and the arts, have had varying degrees of success. Some, such as *Paralleli* (Parallels), which began publication in 2002, were short-lived; others, including *Le-Khaim* (To life) and the Kiev journal *Egupets* (Yehupetz) continue to flourish in the first part of the twenty-first century. *Le-Khaim*, an online journal that began publication in 1999, contains religious literature, literary criticism, book reviews, and original works of fiction and poetry. *Narod knig v mire knig* (The people of the book in the world of the book; produced in St. Petersburg) provides scholarly articles as well as an ongoing survey of publications and writing about Jews in new monographs and the periodical press.

Departments and institutes of Jewish studies have been established in St. Petersburg, Moscow, Kiev, Minsk, and Kharkov. The Russian State Humanities University (RGGU) instituted a program for the study of East European and Russian Judaica in 1991. In 2009 the Jewish Theological Seminary and RGGU jointly published a bilingual Yiddish and Russian volume of essays on Yiddish literature and culture in the Soviet Union.[24] The institute Petersburg Judaica at the European University in St. Petersburg, directed by Valerii Dymshits, conducts ethnographic research in the former Pale of Settlement; and its publications, exhibits, and web pages have shed much light on the continuity of Jewish life in Russia in the Soviet period and beyond. In 2009, plans were under way for a museum of Russian-Jewish history to open in the Melnikov Bus Garage (where Kabakov showed his "alternative history") in Moscow. At the end of the first decade of the twenty first century, however, increased Russian nationalism, decreased funding opportunities, and new threats to academic and personal freedom make the future of Jewish studies in Russia uncertain.

The 1990s saw one of the largest migrations out of Russia to the United States, Germany, and Israel (Tolts 2007). The turn of the twenty-first century, however, has seen a completely new phenomenon; as Caryn Aviv and David Shneer write, "more Russian Jews now migrate to Russia from Israel than the other way around" (2005, 49). Unlike other immigrants, Russians in Israel have continued to write in Russian and have created Russian-language literary and art journals, such as *Ierusalimskii zhurnal* (The Jerusalem literary review) and *Zerkalo* (The mirror; published in Tel Aviv). Many of these authors, including, for example, Dina Rubina and Iuliia Viner, retain their popularity in Russia. In Viner's writing, Yiddish and Hebrew provide a counterpoint to the Russian text.[25] The three languages that Jewish authors living in Russia worked in at the beginning of the twentieth century once again appear on the same page, after a long hiatus.

Jewish-related sites in Russian on the Internet have proliferated, with topics ranging from religious practice (toldot.ru) to literary criticism, authors' pages, online Jewish encyclopedias in Russian, poetry, fiction, and polemical prose. In addition, most journals have a virtual existence. The websites originate in Russia, Ukraine, Germany, Israel, and the United States, but their reach, of course, is global, contributing to what Zvi Gitelman calls the "global shtetl" (Gitelman 1998b, 127). The broad array of literary, artistic, and scholarly production shows the continuing importance of Jewish culture in Russian, both within and beyond the geographical boundaries of Russia and beyond the life of the Soviet Union.

Reference Matter

Notes

Introduction

1. For other uses of Benjamin's theses on history in relation to Jewish history and memory, see, for example, Boyarin (1992, 32–51).
2. See Veidlinger (2000); Estraikh (2005a); Shneer (2004); Krutikov (1999); and Shternshis (2006).
3. See Sicher (1995); for a recent collection of essays that includes Babel's Jewish context, see Freidin (2009).
4. Liberman explicitly mentions Bergelson and other Yiddish writers as part of a comparative analysis necessary for the proper understanding of Babel (Liberman 1996, 10). Ruth Wisse includes both Yiddish and Russian-language writers in her chapter "Literature of the Russian Revolution: From Isaac Babel to Vasily Grossman" (Wisse 2000, 99–129). Yuri Slezkine's chapter "Babel's First Love: The Jews and the Russian Revolution" briefly touches on Markish's *Brothers* in a wide-ranging discussion of the role of Russian Jews in the new revolutionary culture (Slezkine 2004, 104–203).
5. He went on to say that their response is "easy to understand: both were innovators, revolutionaries of writing in Yiddish, and Babel's innovation, which was strongly imbued with Jewish imagery (which was both traditional, derived from the Bible, and everyday, worldly) could not help but please them" (Markish 1994, 169).
6. See his essay of 1926, "Mikhoels," in (Mandelshtam 1979, 260–63).
7. For a discussion, see also Roskies (1984) and Yerushalmi (1989).
8. On this point and Soviet time generally, see Brooks (2000, 77–82).
9. For other approaches to Mandelshtam and Judaism, see, for example, Freidin (1987); Cavanagh (1995); Katsis (2002); and Vinokur (2008).
10. See Shternshis (2006) and Gitelman (2003).
11. Aleksandr L'vov also challenges this conclusion (2008).
12. The Russian Formalists and Mikhail Bakhtin provide what can be termed an "indigenous" theory for this corpus; the best overview of Russian formalism

can be found in Eichenbaum (1965). For a critical overview of "new formalism," see Levinson (2007).

13. Joseph Sherman's brilliant translation of Bergelson's *Opgang* (Bergelson 1999) and his translation of *Nokh alemen* are examples (Bergelson 2009). For an anthology of works of Russian Jewish authors in English, see Shrayer (2007b).

14. I was surprised to find a variant of this line used by Benjamin Harshav and Barbara Harshav in the introduction to their magisterial anthology of American Yiddish poetry (1986, 20).

15. I base this conclusion on statistics provided by Martin (2001, 424–26). Pinkus calls 1939–53 the "years of destruction"; the 1930s, the years of the Terror, are not included in this designation (1988). For a succinct discussion that compares Jewish life and culture with other nationalities designated as non-Russian, see Smith (2006).

16. For a discussion of the arrest and deaths of the members of the Jewish Anti-Fascist Committee, see Rubenstein and Naumov (2001).

17. See, for example, Slezkine (2004) and Pinkus (1988).

18. The argument that Markish and Bergelson were dedicated communists whose work was aimed at promoting "Stalin's socialist content in national form" has been made most recently by Slezkine (2004, 298).

19. For an introduction to Yiddish, see Harshav (1990). A history of Yiddish literature from its inception through the 1970s, including Soviet Yiddish, may be found in Liptzin (1985). For an introduction to the three foundational figures, see Frieden (1995). The most complete discussion of Abramovitsh is found in Miron (1996). An innovative study that bridges the gap between the classics and later developments may be found in Garrett (2003). For a reassessment of the relation between Hebrew and Yiddish literature, see Miron (2010). Articles on Yiddish literature and criticism, and on individual authors, may be found in *YIVO Encyclopedia of Jews in Eastern Europe*, http://www.yivoencyclopedia.org.

20. For discussions of nineteenth-century Jewish authors who wrote in Russian, see Murav (2003) and Safran (2000).

21. For the essay "Evrei i russkaia literatura" and responses to it, see Ivanova (2004).

22. On his goal of overcoming "assimilation from the cradle," see An-sky (1910); for studies of the author, see Safran and Zipperstein (2006) and Safran (2010); and for the photographs, Avrutin, Dymshits, Ivanov, Lvov, Murav, and Sokolova (2009).

23. See Hofsheyn's "Ikh gleyb s'iz mir bashert" and Markish's "Veys ikh nit, tsi kh'bin in dr'heym," both in Shmeruk (1964, 224, 375).

24. For a discussion, see Estraikh (2005, 6–36).

25. For an illustrated album of Kultur-Lige artists with discussions in English and Ukrainian, see Kazovsky (2007).

26. See Shneer (2004, 40) and Moss (2009, 217–52).

27. See Estraikh (1999). The Introspectivists in New York also used phonetic spelling for Hebrew words.

28. A discussion of the issue of language change may be found in Smith (1998).

29. For a discussion, see Estraikh (2003).

30. For discussions of Kafka's writing as Jewish literature, see Robertson (1985) and Miron (2010, 303–402). In an essay first published in 1956, Clement Greenberg made the fascinating argument that Kafka's Jewishness inhered in the temporal structure of his works, namely that everything has already been decided and we wait uncertainly for the outcome (1961, 266–73). I make a similar claim about temporality in Bergelson.

31. For a discussion of cultural hybridity in the sphere of visual culture, see Wolitz (1995).

32. See, for example, Wirth-Nesher (1994); Wisse (2000); Kramer (2001); and Miron (2010, 303–13).

33. For more on Litvakov, see Estraikh (2005, 57, 130, 169); Krutikov (2001); and Moss (2009, 108–9, 116–17, 233–41).

34. First All-Union Congress of Soviet Writers, 1934, p. 716, cited by Tertz [Siniavsky] (1960, 148). Siniavsky emphasizes the teleology of socialist realism and compares it to eighteenth-century classicism.

35. Meir Viner, "O nekotorykh voprosakh sotsialisticheskogo realizma," cited by Estraikh (1998, 25). For a study of Viner, see Krutikov (2010).

36. For a collection of essays exploring new approaches to socialist realism, see Lahusen and Dobrenko (1997).

37. Yael Chaver argues for a Zionist version of socialist realism (2007).

38. For a discussion of the song in the context of Stalinist culture, see Boym (1997). Clement Greenberg first connected Norman Rockwell and socialist realism in an essay from 1939, "Avant-Garde and Kitsch" (1961, 3–21).

39. For discussions of temporality, see Clark (1985, 136–55).

40. Another key Yiddish historical novel from this time is Der Nister's *Di mishpokhe Mashber* (The family Mashber), discussed in Chapter Six.

41. See the discussion of this issue in Blok in Hackel (1978).

Chapter 1

1. Based on a text by Petr Lavrov written in 1875, the song was the Russian national anthem during the time of the Provisional Government in 1917. For the text, see "Workers' Marseillaise," available from www.marxists.org/history/ussr/sounds/index.htm- 28k.

2. I take my account from Khazan (2006).

3. For a discussion, see Shneer (2004, 134–214) and Estraikh (2005).

4. See Budnitskii (2005, 7); for a documentary history, see Miliakova (2007).

5. I am modifying Bergelson's language from "Tvey rotskhim" (Two murder-

ers). The protagonist, Anton Zarembo, is "the leader of a small group that plundered and murdered Jewish shtetls in Ukraine" (*ataman fun a kleyner bande, vos hot barabevet un gekoylet yidishe shtetlekh in Ukrayne*) (Bergelson 1930b, 6:206).

6. See Bakhtin (1965); for a discussion, see Emerson (1997, 162–206).

7. For a discussion of Bakhtin's distinction between the closed-off body in contrast to the grotesque body, see Morson and Emerson (1990, 449).

8. According to some critics, Levinson is a Jew only according to his passport, but for others, he is a "living Jewish warrior." For the negative view of Levinson's Jewishness, see Khazan (2001, 201); for the positive view, see Kleinman (1928, 164). See also Slezkine (2004, 192–94).

9. A. Lezhnev was the pseudonym of Abram Gorelik (1893–1938), a prominent literary critic who was associated with the "Pereval" writers' group, and who advocated a literary humanism that was out of touch with the trends of the 1930s. He was arrested and shot in 1938. His writings about the shtetls of Belarus reveal a harsh attitude toward Jewish traditional life. Lezhnev also participated in Jewish educational politics. In an inspection trip to a Yiddish school in Belarus, Lezhnev wrote that Jewish parents consider Yiddish obsolete and prefer to speak with their children in Russian.

10. This language is from Aleksandr Voronskii's recapitulation of the criticism of *Red Cavalry* from his "Literary Portrait" of Babel, first published in 1928 (Voronskii 1928, 190).

11. See "Ikh zegn zikh mit dir" in Shmeruk (1964, 375). Unless otherwise noted, translations are my own. For an analysis of Markish's early work that emphasizes linguistic and physical freedom, see Kronfeld (1996, 202–8). An analysis of his temporal poetics may be found in Finkin (2008).

12. See Markish (1935) and Markish (1969).

13. I am grateful to Lazar Fleishman for pointing this source out to me.

14. I am modifying the translation in Babel (2002, 332).

15. I am using Leonard Wolf's translation of an excerpt of the poem and my own translation of the material that does not appear in the excerpt.

16. Amelia Glaser argues for a more pro-revolutionary response in Babel and Markish (Glaser 2004).

17. Vsevolod Ivanov's train in "Armored Train" (Bronepoezd, 14–69) is as swollen with disease as the armored train in Markish's *Brothers*. For an English translation, see Proffer, Proffer, Meyer, and Szporluk (1987, 152–215).

18. In 1931, Litvakov modified his stand about *Brider*, conceding that although Markish had succumbed to "nationalist deviation," the work was an example of a large-scale "revolutionary canvas" and in general served as evidence that Markish was "growing toward us" (1931, 34).

19. For more on Kvitko, see Estraikh (2005, 132–34) and Shneer (2004).

20. The term also resonates with the title of the Berlin journal *In shpan* (In

harness), which was, as Gennady Estraikh writes, pro-Soviet and in which David Bergelson played a leading role (2005, 69).

21. "A Cloud in Trousers" (Oblako v shtanakh) is a particularly vivid example. See Maguire (1987, 432–49); for a discussion of Mayakovsky's self-mythologizing and his suicide, see Jakobson (1987, 273–300).

22. For the analysis, see Borenstein (2000, 73–124).

23. Gregory Freidin argues for the importance of Nietzsche among Babel's contemporaries and sees a Nietzschean flavor in Babel's depiction of the rabbi in *Red Cavalry* (1994).

24. See Voronskii (1928, 166) for a discussion.

25. Other critics have discussed the timeless quality of the *Red Cavalry* stories; Judith Kornblatt, for example, has aptly noted that the work "forces the reader into a reading act that, in total, suspends linear time and causal expectations" (1992, 117). Ehre also emphasizes the timeless, static quality of Babel's description of both Polish and Jewish sites in *Red Cavalry* (1986, 72).

26. For another discussion of "The Palace of Motherhood," see Belaia, Dobrenko, and Esaulov (1993, 10).

27. For example, in "Chelovek, kotoryi zabyl svoiu zhizn'," the narrator described parents who adore their child with the expression "*smotreli emu v glaza*" (literally, "looked at him straight in the eye"). The parallel Yiddish expression is "*kukn in di oygn*" (also literally, "to look in the eyes"), but which means to be devoted to someone.

28. Gekht fuses elements of the Esther story with the Christian legend according to which the Jews are forced to wander for their sin of killing Christ. Ahasveros is the name given to this accursed Jewish figure.

29. For a translation of *Nokh alemen*, see Bergelson (1977) and Bergelson (2009); for *Opgang*, see Bergelson (1999).

30. For a new collection of essays on Bergelson, which includes a biography and a bibliography, see Sherman and Estraikh (2007).

31. For the Kultur-Lige, see Kazovksy (2003).

32. In 1926, Shlomo Shvartsbard assassinated Semen Petliura in Paris, and was acquitted at his trial. I have been unable to determine when Bergelson composed "Among Immigrants," which was first published in 1927, but he doubtless knew of these events. For a discussion, see Schur (2007).

33. In his fifteenth thesis on the philosophy of history, Benjamin writes that calendars do not measure time the way clocks do, because calendars register holidays, which are days of remembrance (1969, 261). Bergelson's clocks work like Benjamin's calendars.

34. In "Old Age" (Altvarg)—which is comparable to Babel's "Old Shloyme"— Bergelson uses the biblical story of Nineveh to frame the experience of a pious refugee in Berlin. The old man, racked with guilt over his divorce, and in mourning

for the destruction of his home in Ukraine, sees Berlin as a modern-day Nineveh. For an English translation, see Bergelson (2005, 9–19).

35. The story has been translated into English, with some omissions, but nonetheless remains neglected in the critical literature. See Howe and Greenberg (1977, 84–123).

36. For a discussion of Nusinov on Bergelson, see Estraikh (2005, 89); for a discussion of cubism in Pasternak, see Jakobson (1987, 311).

37. The translation of the story that appears in Howe (1977, 84–123) by Seth Wolitz omits this passage, possibly because of the version of the original that was used.

38. A discussion may be found in Freidin (1978).

39. Cavanagh 1991, 336, n. 11. For the fragment, see Mandelshtam (1991, 3–4:514). An alternative discussion of Mandelshtam's relation to Judaism and Christianity may be found in Freidin (1987, 21–22, 126–45).

40. I adapt the phrase from *"A tut zhe putalsia prizrak"* in "Shum vremeni" (Mandelshtam 1990, 2:13).

41. Susan Slotnick argues similarly that Bergelson promotes the revolution as the consequence of historical necessity, which the individual has no choice but to recognize and obey (1978, 233, 330). As Gennady Estraikh points out, the phrase refers to the messianic doctrine of two messiahs, one who comes to inflict punishment and one who comes to administer mercy. *"Mides-hadin,"* the strict messiah, is half a couplet, so to speak; the other half is *"mides rakhmones"* or *"mides khesed,"* the idea of mercy. Also see Jeffrey Veidlinger's argument about Hasidic belief in two forms of judgment, the strict and the merciful. By use of the term, according to Veidlinger, "Bergelson equates Soviet power with the evil of . . . exilic oppression" (2000, 135).

42. For a discussion of *Mides-hadin* that does justice to its complexities, see Krutikov (2007).

43. For a discussion, see Beiner (1984) and Buck-Morss (1986).

44. For the significance of the dreamy state in Benjamin, see Buck-Morss (1986, 106).

Chapter 2

1. For discussions of gender and sexuality in relation to the image of the Jew, see, for example, Biale (1997) and Boyarin (1997).

2. See Slezkine (1994) and Martin (2001).

3. For a discussion of the choice of the Jewish national language as Yiddish and not Hebrew or other Jewish languages, see Shneer (2004, 30–59) and Gitelman (1972, 276–85).

4. For more on Dimanshtein, see Shneer (2004, 28–29).

5. For a discussion, see Gilman (1991).

6. For a discussion of Nordau along these lines, see Mosse (1992).
7. Mikhail Kalinin, cited by Weinberg (1998, 46).
8. For the aesthetic of socialist realism, see Robin (1992). An alternative view of the whole, integral body of the socialist realist hero may be found in Nadtochii (1989). On the one hand, the hero must abandon his individual body in order to join the collective, but on the other, he remains an individual, and as such must suffer. The socialist realist hero is drowned, burned, maimed, and frozen; the socialist realist text masks these punishments under the guise of self-sacrifice. Lilya Kaganovsky also shows that notwithstanding the stereotype of the clear-headed, party-minded, healthy, and strong hero of the 1930s and 1940s, closer inspection of literature and film of the time reveals an abundance of mangled, wounded bodies (Kaganovsky 2008).
9. See Howe (1977, 25).
10. See, for example, Zel'tser (2006).
11. All biblical citations taken from May and Metzger (1973).
12. For another translation, see Howe, Wisse, and Shmeruk (1987, 546–48). I have used John Hollander's translation of the opening line.
13. Itsik Fefer, "Nu, iz vos, az m'hot mikh gemalet," cited in Niger (1958, 347–48).
14. The controversy is discussed in Shmeruk (1964, 751–52).
15. For a discussion of Gastev, see Steinberg (2002, 195–96).
16. For a discussion of the Golem, see Idel (1990).
17. For this phrase and its meaning, see Kaganovsky (2008).
18. See Markish (1938); for the Russian translation, see Markish (1938).
19. "Konets bogadel'ni" (The end of the old age home), first published in 1932, is an example. See Sicher (1985, 20).
20. I am grateful to William Nickell, whose talk on "Karl-Yankel" at the University of California at Santa Cruz in May 2008 spurred my thinking about this work. Babel's story is not unique in Russian-language work of the time in addressing circumcision; David Khait's novella *Alagarnaia ulitsa* (Alagarnaia Street) also features a grandmother who insists that her grandson be circumcised.
21. For a discussion of this story in the context of *Red Cavalry*, see Hyman (1956, 622).
22. William Nickell, Santa Cruz, May 4, 2008. For a discussion of this phenomenon, see Bemporad (2006, 147–60).
23. For an English translation, see Babel (2002, 621).
24. His first story to be published, "Old Shloyme," appeared in a Kiev journal in 1913. A discussion of the circumstances can be found in Van De Stadt (2007).
25. Efraim Sicher confirms that Babel read Rozanov but does not provide specific titles (1985, 110). Gabriella Safran does not see a link between Rozanov's image of effeminized and sexualized Jewish men and similar images in Babel (Safran 2002, 264 n. 32).

26. For a discussion of this article, see Murav (2000). Laura Engelstein discusses the homoerotic overtones of Rozanov's description (1992, 322–24).

27. *Chernaia kozha* (Black skin, 1931) is another example of a film touting Soviet tolerance.

28. It is listed both with an English title, as *The Return of Nathan Becker*, and with the Yiddish title, *Nosn Becker fort aheym*. Available from http://www.brandeis.edu/jewishfilm/Catalogue/films/returnofnathanbecker.htm. For a discussion of the reception of the Yiddish film at the time of its release, see Gennady Estraikh, "A film mit a klang," *Der forverts*, December 18, 2009.

29. For more on the film, see Veidlinger (2000, 132) and Chernenko (2003). Kador Ben-Salim also starred in the 1923 *Krasnye diavoliata* (Red devils).

30. For more on Mikhoels, see Gordon (1999).

31. Mikhoels also played in the 1935 *Lunnyi kamen'* (Moonstone), about a geological expedition. The film was directed by A. Minkin and I. Sorokhtin. See Widdis (2003, 226).

32. For more on the significance of the *nigun* as a form of prayer, see Belcove-Shalin (1995, 99).

33. Cited in Zuskina-Perel'man (2002, 430).

34. Zuskin's own published remarks about the role connect to a childhood memory of a real-life daydreamer who wanted to get rich by selling rare postage stamps.

35. For a discussion of this and other aspects of the role, see Ivanov (2007, 326) and Zuskina-Perel'man (2002, 101). An overview of Zuskin's theatrical performances can be found in Lyubomirski (1976, 185–239).

36. For more on the commune, see Dekel-Chen (2005, 101). Estraikh briefly discusses Gorshman's participation (2005, 84).

37. See Gorshman (1961); the author's first name appears as "Shirke." For the Russian, see Gorshman (1963).

38. See Gorshman (1984, 6–154). It was translated into Russian as "Stada i otary Khany" and published in Gorshman (1979).

39. For a discussion of Yiddish women's rewriting of the opposition, see Shreiber (1998).

40. Libkes was the pseudonym of Kipnis-Shapiro, the sister of Itsik Kipnis. She was born in Sloveshno, Ukraine, in 1900, received her education in Kiev, and started publishing in the 1920s. An English translation of a love poem by Libkes may be found in Burstin (2006).

Chapter 3

1. I base my account on Arad (2008 and 2009); see also Dobroszycki and Gurock (1993); Al'tman (2002 and 2009).

2. For a discussion of the inadequacy of Auschwitz as a symbol of the Holo-

caust, see Snyder (2009). Snyder compares the mass killings carried out by the Nazis with those carried out by the Soviets. For a discussion that anticipates some of Snyder's arguments about the distinctive nature of the Holocaust on Soviet territory, see Garrard (1995).

3. Yuri Slezkine argues that Jews made particularly good Soviets because they were good service nomads, go-betweens, and Mercurians. The war brought about the "nationalization of ethnic Jews" (2004, 286–97).

4. "Ikh bin a yid" was first published in *Eynikayt* on December 27, 1942. For an English translation, see Leftwich (1961, 162–65). For the Yiddish, see Fefer (1943, 121–25). For a discussion of "So what," see Chapter Two.

5. Jeffrey Brooks discusses the complexities facing Ortenberg, Erenburg, and Grossman (Brooks 2000, 170–75). For a study of the role of Soviet Jewish photojournalists during the Second World War, see Shneer (2011).

6. As the title indicates, the poem uses the motif of a dream of a death camp, similar to Sel'vinskii's in "Kandava," which I discuss in Chapter Four (Slutskii 1999, 9). Slutskii's poem was published after his teacher's (Slutskii 1969).

7. Unless otherwise noted, translations are my own. I am grateful to Marat Grinberg for directing me to this source.

8. Slutskii did not date his poems, but thematic similarities between this and other poems suggest the date of its composition during the "Doctors' Affair" (Slutskii 1999, 121).

9. For studies of Erenburg, see Rubenstein (1996), Sarnov (2004), and Altshuler, Arad, and Krakowski (1993, 9–105).

10. See Altshuler, Arad, and Krakowski (1993, 158).

11. I am grateful to Joshua Rubenstein for sharing these materials.

12. "*Bud' ty prokliat, and semia tvoe, i dom tvoi, i put' tvoi*" (Erenburg 1960, 239).

13. For a discussion of this episode in light of the censorship of Jewish authors and Jewish themes in Soviet literature, see Blium (2006).

14. It is likely that German, born in Riga, came from a family that had converted in previous generations. His father, Pavel Nikolaevich German, received the title of nobleman from the tsar and served as an officer in the army in the First World War. His mother, Nadezhda Konstantinova née Ignat'eva, taught Russian at a gymnasium (Fainberg 1970, 37). German's son, Aleksei, the noted film director, has said in interviews that his father was not Jewish and that his mother was, even though she subsequently converted. German does not appear, for example, in two important bibliographical reference works dedicated to Russian-Jewish writers (*Rossiiskaia evreiskaia entsiklopediia*, published in Moscow in 1994; and N. I. Rutberg and I. N. Pidevich, *Evrei i evreiskii vopros v literature sovetskogo perioda. Khronologicheski-tematicheskii ukazatel' literatury, izdannoi za 1917–1991gg na russkom iazyke*, published in Moscow in 2000). Online discussion websites from Russia visited in the summer of 2006 reveal a curious split. Some participants include German among other Jewish writers such as Grossman and Kazakevich, while others

say that the government "made him into a Jew" during the anticosmopolitan campaign. The well-known scholar of Soviet Jewish literature Maurice Friedberg told me in a personal conversation that German was Jewish (June 27, 2006, University of Illinois at Urbana-Champaign).

15. See Branover (1994–2000, Vol. 1, 530) and Kazakevich (1990).

16. By the editor of *Znamia*, Vsevelod Vishnevskii. See Kazakevich (1990, 294 n. 1). The novel became the basis of a film made in 2002.

17. The translation is presumably by the author himself. See Kazakevich (1954).

18. For the text of An-sky's "Oath," see http://www.stanford.edu/class/hebrew/yiddish/resources/shvue.html.

19. "Opravdanie nenavisti" appeared in *Pravda* on May 26, 1942; "Im ne zhit'," in *Krasnaia zvezda* on April 5, 1942; and "Ubei!" on July 24, 1941.

20. For a discussion of the connections between the trial testimony and the novella, see Murav (2008).

21. David Shneer explicates the link between the theme of blood and revenge in "Literalizing a Metaphor: Perets Markish, Jewish Nationalism, and Spilling Blood," unpublished manuscript. I am grateful to David for sharing his work with me.

22. According to Seidman, the Yiddish *Un di velt hot geshvign* describes a scene in which surviving young men go to Weimar to steal food and clothing and to "rape German girls," but the narrator indicts them for their failure to fulfill "the historical commandment of revenge" (Seidman 2006, 221). Seidman does not specify a textual source for this commandment, but a good candidate is Psalm 137.

23. For a discussion of the debate surrounding the film, see Walters (2009).

24. Cited by Joshua Rubenstein and Ilya Altman (2008, 22).

25. The Russian omits the final word of the original Yiddish text, "amen," but otherwise preserves the legal and religious sense of what Fefer explicitly calls his "oath" (*shvue*) and his "vow" (*neyder*). The Russian renders these two terms as "*kliatva*" and "*zavet*."

26. For an overview of Der Nister, see Shmeruk (1964, 737–41). For an essay that includes some discussion of the war stories, see Cholawski (1997).

27. See Boyarin (1997).

28. Jean-François Lyotard raises the question of the victim's testimony (1988).

29. I am grateful to Hillel Halkin for discussing this poem with me during his visit to the University of Illinois in 2006. The Yiddish text of the excerpt:

An altn, a farbitenem,
Tserisenem, tseshlisenem,
A hundert mol gelitenem
Arumnemen, bagrisn im.
Bruder du umshuldiker
Un hundert mol gelayterter,
Di tsayt—zi makht geduldiker,

Nor keynmol nit dervayterter.
Zog, velkhn kleyd dir onton itst?
Un velkhe freyd farshapn dir?
Nokh umglikn farplanterte
Zol zayn mayn shtub a hafn dir.
Nit traystn dikh, nit orev zayn
Mit vos dayn brokh dir lindern?
Vest in dayn nest der khorever
Nit trefn shoyn di kinder mer.
Dayn nakhle nit fartrunkenen iz,
Keyn odlers nit fartrogn zey:
Inmitn veg a "yunkers" iz
Arop af tsu dershlogn zey.
Zol afzindn dos blut in dir,
Un oysbrekhn a fayer zol
Af ontsindn dem mut in dir,
Di kraft di umgehayere,
Vos nemt ayn shtet un gegntn
Un festungen fartilikt zi,
Un mindste gob bagegnte
Fun tifn harts bavilikt zi.

30. The article is also found in Shmeruk (1964, 218–19).

Chapter 4

1. The poem may also be found in Shmeruk (1964, 487–89). A translated excerpt from this poem appears in Howe, Irving, Wisse, and Shmeruk (1987, 376), translated by Leonard Wolf. The translation that appears as the epigraph to this chapter is mine.

2. For a discussion of this problem, see, for example, Shneer (2010).

3. For general discussions of officially published Soviet literature about the destruction of the Jews, see Friedberg (1970) and Hirzowicz (1993).

4. For an argument that Rybakov's novel deracinates Jewish identity, see Rosenshield (1996). James Young discusses the documentary obsession in Kuznetsov's novel as well as D. M. Thomas's reliance on Kuznetsov in *The White Hotel* (Young 1988, 53–63). Sicher analyzes Kuznetsov's discussion of the parallel between the Nazi and the Soviet systems (2005, 117).

5. See Novick (1999).

6. For a study that challenges the notion that American Jews failed to respond before the trial, see Diner (2009); for the Eichmann trial as formative, see Levy and Rothberg (2003, 2–5).

7. For a discussion, see Young (1988), Novick (1999), and Levy and Rothberg

(2003). Levy and Rothberg provide an excellent starting point for the significant body of theory that has arisen in relation to the Holocaust.

8. "Prosthetic memories" are memories that are not the result of personal experience but are created instead by technology that functions to supplement the actual event. See Landsberg (1997). Marianne Hirsch defines "postmemory" as memory mediated "through an imaginative investment and creation" (2003, 416).

9. For an overview of the historiography of the Holocaust in the former Soviet Union that includes a discussion of terminology, see Gitelman (1997). For a post-Soviet example of the new type of scholarship on the Holocaust, see Shubinskii (1994) and Arad (1992).

10. Der Nister (Pinye/Pinkhes Kahanovitsh/Kaganovich) published a collection of short stories titled *Karbones* (Sacrificial victims) in Moscow in 1943. I discuss "Heshl Ansheles" in Chapter Three. An example of the journalistic use of the term appears in an article on the history of the Yiddish novel by Y. Okrutny that appeared in *Yidishe shriftn*, published in Lodzh in 1947. The author remarks that "until the Hitler-khurbn our literature wandered circuitously between the small shtetl and the wider world" (Okrutny 1947, 14). For a discussion of the appearance of the term "Holocaust" and a critique of "khurbn," see Roskies (1984, 261).

11. I am relying on Roskies for my model of what constitutes traditional responses (1984). For a discussion of terminology used to describe what is now known as the Holocaust, see Young (1988, 83–98).

12. David Shneer, lecture, "From the Pale to Moscow: Russian-Jewish and Soviet-Yiddish Studies," Russian-Jewish Studies Training Workshop for Junior Scholars, University of Illinois, Urbana-Champaign, June 2006.

13. See chapter 4, "Memory of Excision, Excisionary Memory," in Weiner (2001, 191–235).

14. I take the term "unprecedented" from an exhibit about Soviet and German war propaganda at the State Museum of Political History in St. Petersburg, which I visited in May 2010. The English language introduction to the exhibit described the war as "unprecedented in the history of mankind."

15. For an informative discussion that includes a wide range of works, see Friedberg (1970, 31–50). In his essay "The Holocaust and the Armed Struggle in Belorussia," Sholom Cholawski offers a typology of nine different ways that Russian and Belorussian documentary and artistic literature "disregarded the Jewish aspect of the Holocaust or even the involvement of Jews in the war" (1997, 215). These strategies include, for example, "complete estrangement," "reference by implication," and "obfuscation by balancing." The author finds that in contrast to the Soviet Russian template of diminishing and erasing the Jewish dimensions of the Nazi war, Soviet literature in Yiddish shows a tendency "to give expression to the unique Jewish aspect of the Holocaust and to a sense of the increasing Jewish awareness of these authors" (Cholawski 1997, 228). Ephraim Sicher's 2005 study *The Holocaust Novel* reasserts that the Soviets

repressed knowledge about the destruction of the Jews in the Final Solution (2005, 115–19).

16. In addressing this question, I do not mean to deny or minimize other suffering that the war brought, including the brutality of the victorious Soviet army. For a discussion of the aftermath of the Soviet liberation of Budapest, for example, see Erickson (1983, 508).

17. I take my account of Sel'vinskii's biography from Farber (1971) and Voskresenskaia (1984).

18. The edition published in *Krasnaia zvezda* speaks of "Russian grief" (*russkoe gore*); subsequent rewordings in 1964 and 1971 omit this phrase and introduce other variations. I use the version found in Sel'vinskii (1971). Unless otherwise noted, all translations from this and other works are my own. For information about the poem's publication, see Zakharenko and Khanukaeva (2000, 40–41). The text of the poem may also be found in Sel'vinskii (1985, 96–100). For a discussion of the impact of the poem, see Anninskii (2003). For an excerpt from the Soviet government's investigation into the murder of the Jews of Kerch', see Arad (1992, 183–85).

19. Catherine Merridale characterizes the mass killing at Kerch' as providing the first evidence of the German policy of such killings (2006, 291). For a discussion of the Kerch' mass killing, see Al'tman (2002) and Arad (1992, 183–85). Photographs of the Kerch' mass killing, captioned "Hitlerite Atrocities at Kerch," were sent to Britain from Moscow. See Struk (2004, 47). For a discussion of the photography, Sel'vinskii, and knowledge about the identity of the victims, see Shneer (2011, 100–108). I am grateful to Kiril Feferman, who in 2009 at Yad Vashem helped me understand what Sel'vinskii saw at Kerch'.

20. It is instructive to compare Sel'vinskii's response to an article that appeared in the *New York Times* on January 7, 1942, reporting that "Soviet Foreign Commissar Vyacheslaff M. Molotoff . . . charged that the Germans shot 8,000 in Kamenetz and Podolsk, 3,000 in Mariupol, several thousand in Kerch" (Molotoff Accuses Nazis of Atrocities; Note Detailing "Crimes" Handed to All Foreign Diplomats 1942). Molotov's description of the mass killing in Kiev conforms to the narrative of the universality of suffering by identifying the victims as "Russians, Ukrainians, Jews," even though he uses the phrase "a large number of Jews."

21. For a discussion of pain and language, see Scarry (1985, 42–45, 60–61).

22. See, for example, Derrida (2005, 65–96); Sidra DeKoven Ezrahi, "Representing Auschwitz," in Levy and Rothberg (2003); and Lyotard (1988, 9).

23. A discussion of this and other Soviet war crimes trials may be found in Prusin (2003) and in Bourtman (2008).

24. A discussion of the killings in Krasnodar may be found in Arad (2009, 291–92, 375). For a history of the Holocaust in Crimea, see Feferman (2007).

25. For an overview of Sel'vinskii's participation in the war and a selection of his letters and diary entries from this time, see Voskresenskaia (1984).

26. For the text of the story, see Gekht (1963, 48–88).

27. For a discussion of the film and its reception, see Zuskina-Perel'man (2002, 262–63). I am grateful to Sasha Prokhurov for directing me to the film. For a discussion of the typical Soviet film that deemphasized the hardships of German occupation, see Youngblood (2001).

28. See Der Nister (1946 and 1969). The 1969 edition is abbreviated. Also translated as "New Growth," the title looks back to a Yiddish literary movement of 1922 of the same name. See Estraikh (2005, 111–12).

29. An excerpt from the second volume appeared in the New York Yiddish publication *Yidishe kultur* (Markish 1946).

30. A review of the English version of the novel by the noted Slavicist Edward Brown briefly discusses the reception of the novel in the West as marred by the socialist realist style of writing (1986).

31. In his memoirs, the poet Semen Lipkin, who was a friend of Grossman's, argues that *For a Just Cause* is not merely a conventional Soviet novel of the war (1997, 529–32).

32. The novel first came out in 1952 in the journal *Novyi mir*, edited by Andrei Tvardovskii. For a discussion of his demands for revision, see Lipkin (1997, 533), and for a discussion of the differences between the 1952 and the 1959 editions, see Nakhimovsky (1992, 120–29).

33. See, for example, Nakhimovsky's argument that "Grossman does not ask whether it was worthwhile for a Jew to freely identify with other Jews, to continue or reestablish a group identity not totally bound up with the Holocaust or Soviet state anti-Semitism." She finds that for Grossman, "beyond the Holocaust there is very little" (1992, 151).

34. Grossman seems to be attributing the first use of the name "Patriotic War" to Stalin, even though it was Molotov who first introduced the reference in a speech he had made the month before.

35. The literary use of a blank space is significant in Holocaust literature. For a discussion of the ellipsis in Primo Levi, see Druker (2004). Aharon Appelfeld uses a blank page between the two books of his novel *The Age of Wonders* to signify the events of the Holocaust (Schwartz 2001).

36. For another discussion of the letters written by Vasilii Grossman to his father, see Garrard and Garrard (1996, 174–76).

37. Grossman's letter of September 15, 1950, cited by Garrard and Garrard (1996, 352–53).

38. Cited by Garrard and Garrard (1996, 353).

39. There is, to be sure, the French prison camp in *War and Peace*, but it is a place of renewal, not mass destruction. Pierre discovers the meaning of life as embodied in Platon Karataev.

40. David Rousset, *Universe Concentrationnaire*, cited by Arendt (1973, 451).

41. For a discussion that emphasizes the Christian iconography of this scene, see Nakhimovsky (1992).

42. The translation by Robert Chandler, published in 1985, omits the troubling "you" (Grossman 1985a). His new translation restores it (Grossman 2006, 554).

43. For another discussion of this story, see Sherman (2007).

44. Shoshana Felman's discussion of the problem of testimony has directly inspired my approach. See Felman and Laub (1992). For an English translation of the story, see Bergelson (1974).

45. I take the phrase from *Civilization and Its Discontents*: "In the photographic camera [man] has created an instrument, which retains the fleeting visual impressions, just as a gramophone disc retains the equally fleeting auditory ones; both are at bottom materializations of the power he possesses of recollection, his memory . . . Writing was in its origin the voice of an absent person" (Freud 1961, 37–38).

46. I have condensed and vastly simplified the arguments of Elaine Scarry (1985) and Emmanuel Levinas, specifically, Levinas's discussion of "useless suffering" (1988).

Introduction to Part II

1. This narrative is implicit in Shimon Markish's "The Role of Officially Published Russian-Jewish Literature in the Reawakening of Jewish National Consciousness (1953–1970)" (1991).

2. For a discussion, see Estraikh (2008).

3. For an overview, see Shmeruk (1991) and S. Markish (1991).

4. The dating of this poem has not been determined. It was published in *God za godom*, the Russian-language supplement to *Sovetish heymland* in 1988. The version published in the anthology *Menora* in 1993 differs from the *Sovetish heymland* edition and the manuscript version published by Marat Grinberg in *Slovo/Word* in 2006 (Slutskii 2006a). I am using the *Sovetish heymland* / Grinberg version, because it makes more sense to say that the world of the Jewish village was "told about" (*raskazan*) by Bergelson as opposed to "searched for" (*razyskan*), as in the *Menora* version.

Chapter 5

1. For a discussion of the play, see Veidlinger (2007). Dovid Katz lists it as one of the major Yiddish works published in the Soviet Union (2007, 305).

2. For a discussion of attitudes toward the past in *Sovetish heymland*, see Estraikh (2000).

3. A discussion may be found in Nemzer (2008, 719).

4. See Miriam Hansen's discussion of Benjamin's concept of aura (2008).

5. For discussions of these events, see Vaksberg (1994).

6. For a discussion of the novel's honest representation of the emotions, see Gibian (1960, 82–85).

7. Gekht made this problem the center of an earlier postwar work, the story cycle *Budka solov'ia*, published in Moscow in 1957. Set in a timber-felling settlement in Siberia, and reflecting Gekht's own experience in the Gulag, the stories center on the consequences of a wartime love affair. A woman who gave birth to a child out of wedlock reunites the child with his father, who is happily married. The ethical dilemma is whether she herself may remarry and introduce the child to a new father figure.

8. For a discussion of this concept, see Roskies (1984, 261).

9. For the letters, see Iavorskoi (2004). I am grateful to Leonid Katsis for directing me to this source.

10. RGALI, f 1234, #17, ed. khr. 286.

11. I base my discussion on Shul'man (2006).

12. There are several variants of his name, including Moisei Elevich and Moisei Il'ich Al'tman. I am indebted to Mikhail Krutikov for directing me to this writer. I base my account of his life on Niger and Shatzsky (1956, 92–93); for an overview of Altman's work and a brief discussion of his life, see Shraybman (2005).

13. Cited in Hansen (2008, 339).

14. Erenburg's treatment of Babel offers interesting contrasts. For Erenburg, Babel was a writer of international acclaim, of the same stature as Thomas Mann, James Joyce, and Hemmingway (Babel 1966, 5). Erenburg does not publically recognize Babel as a Jewish writer.

15. "You shall remember that you were a servant in the land of Egypt, and the Lord your God brought you out thence" (Deut. 5:12). The Kiddush recited on the Sabbath includes language about the day as a reminder of the creation and the Exodus.

16. For the English translation, see Mandelstam (1973, 93–94); for the original Russian, see Mandelshtam (1991, 1:63). I am grateful to Stephanie Sandler for directing me to the poem.

17. For a discussion of the gendering of "historical imaginaries," see Burton (2003).

Chapter 6

1. Most of the writers to be discussed in this chapter do not, however, make it into the canon of Jewish or Yiddish literature, because they are "too Soviet."

2. For a discussion of Sloveshne, see Altshuler (2004).

3. Among those who migrated to the capital centers after the war were a significant number who were far less assimilated than their counterparts who had migrated earlier. There were neighborhoods in Moscow, including Ostankino, Cherkizovo, Malakhovke, and others, inhabited by Yiddish speakers without

higher education, who did not participate in the elite professions. I will return to this issue in the next chapter in my discussion of Karabchievskii and Roziner.

4. For a discussion of the shtetl that engages recent revisions of Soviet Jewish culture, see L'vov (2008).

5. A useful discussion of the limitations of this opposition may be found in Fonrobert and Shemtov (2005).

6. Ruth Gruber uses the term "Jewish space" to convey the sense of a virtual Jewish environment reinvented in Europe after the fall of the Berlin Wall in the absence of Jews (2002). Her study omits significant discussion of the former Soviet Union except as a place from which Jews emigrated. While some authors distinguish "space" as a generic term from the more specific "place," I am using the two terms interchangeably; see Bender (2006).

7. J. Moran discusses the false opposition between history and the everyday (2004). For a study that explores how a literary work sets up a complex relation between a private obsession around a thing and the political economy of a particular time, see Brown (1999). I am grateful to Bruce Rosenstock for directing me to this article.

8. Two out of a projected five volumes of this work were published: the first, subtitled *Penek*, in 1932, and the second, subtitled *Yunge yorn* (Early years), in 1940 (Bergelson 1940). Chapters from the work were published earlier in both Yiddish and Russian. The work as a whole went through multiple editions in Yiddish and in Russian translation. See Slotnick (1978, 455) and Estraikh (2005, 143).

9. According to Jeffrey Veidlinger, the theater's production of Sholem Aleichem's "Menachem Mendl" stressed rigid body movements, "individual feelings concealed behind painted expressions," and an overall impression of pantomime or "marionettes controlled by an offstage puppeteer" (2000, 39). The staging of Peretz's "Night in the Old Market" emphasized that the world of the shtetl and the God of the shtetl was dead. However, Anna Shternshis argues that Jewish audiences often viewed the antireligious and anti-shtetl images with sympathy. Instead of attending to the antireligious message, audiences viewed the object of the theatrical satire in positive terms. The Yiddish theater's production of anti-shtetl works, according to Shternshis, offered audiences a fleeting return to prerevolutionary life (2006, 70–105).

10. The second volume of *At the Dnieper*, published in 1940, picks up the action around ten years after the first. Penek is eighteen, living in Kiev around the time of the Kishiniev pogrom of 1903. For a discussion of the end of the first volume, see the Introduction to this study.

11. Yakov Shternberg discusses this concept in relation to Bergelson's style (1987).

12. For an eyewitness account, see Miliakova (2007, 172–76).

13. See Mayzel (1960, 13–14). For discussions of *Khadoshim un teg* in English, see Roskies (1984, 183–85), Roskies (1999, 52–53), and Krutikov (2007).

14. Cited by Altshuler (2004, 80).
15. I base my account on Altshuler (2004).
16. Aron is likely to have been a Jew, although I have not been able to find more information about him. Cited in Altshuler (2004, 149).
17. In his introduction to the New York edition, Nakhman Mayzel writes that he is publishing the work from a manuscript dated 1947–48, when the author finished writing it (1960).
18. A discussion may be found in Goldberg (1993).
19. For a discussion of how introjection preserves alterity, see Deutscher (1998).
20. Brokha (Bella) Kipnis, the author's daughter, devoted much of her life to preserving her father's legacy. See Lenchovskii (1999).
21. For English translations of his stories, see "Bag in Hand" in Perova and Turnbull (2005); and for one of his novels, see Gorenshtein (1991).
22. For a discussion of *Psalom* and "Berdichev," see Shubinskii (2005).
23. The original Russian contains a mixture of Yiddish and Russian.
24. A darker view may be seen in Parnell (2008); for a general discussion of Kanovich, see Krutikov (2003); an overview plus a translated excerpt may be found in Shrayer (2007b, vol. 2, 862–74); see also Terpitz (2008, 204–57).
25. For a discussion of the role of distance and separation in the production of "authentic" souvenirs, see Stewart(1993, 132–69).
26. For a study of Gordon, on which I base my account of his life, see Estraikh (2005).
27. See Gordon (2003). The documentary novel was serialized in *Sovetish heymland* prior to its Israeli publication. I am grateful to Mikhail Krutikov for directing my attention to this work.
28. For a discussion of Gordon's shtetl writings, see Estraikh (2008, 94–99).
29. I am grateful to Valerii Dymshits of the Interdisciplinary Center for Judaica at the European University in St. Petersburg for directing me to this story.
30. The Yiddish original is more emphatic than the Russian translation: the Yiddish redundantly states, "Jewish shtetl" (*a yidish shtetl*), whereas the Russian omits the adjective, using only the word for "shtetl" (*mestechko*) (Gordon 1976, 402).
31. Alla Sokolova includes the "*ganek*" (translated as porch, balcony, or gallery) as one of the characteristic architectural features of houses built by Jews in Podolia (2000).
32. For the Enlightenment-era writer Yisroel Aksenfeld, in contrast, Medzhibozh was a locus of controversy regarding Hasidism in the early part of the nineteenth century. Medzhibozh in 1813 signified a *break*, not continuity, with the past.
33. Research conducted in Podolia by the Interdisciplinary Center for Judaica led by Valery Dymshits shows that the custom persists through the turn of the twenty-first century. According to Gennady Estraikh, what distinguishes Gor-

don's description of his visit in the mid-1960s is a particularly Soviet feature of the requests for intercession: all the notes ask for peace in the world ("*zol zayn sholem af der velt*"), which corresponds to the Soviet slogan of the time, "*miru mir*" (peace for the world) (Estraikh 2005, 144).

34.
Anna-Vanna, nash otriad
Khochet videt' porosiat!
My ikh ne obidim:
Pogliadim i vydem!

Anna-Vanna, our group
Wants to see the piglets!
We wont hurt their feelings:
We'll pet them and leave them!

In the Yiddish original the opening lines read:

Ana Vana brigadir,
Efn uf fun shtal di tir!
Vayz di naye sheyne,
Khazerlekh di kleyne

Anna-Vanna Brigadier
Open the door of the stall!
Show us the piglets itty-bitty
So fine and pretty!

35. Aaron Kramer's translation of the first stanza reads:

Never say that you are going on your last way
Though leaden clouds may be concealing skies of blue
Because the hour we have hungered for is near;
And our marching steps will thunder: We are here!
Because the hour we have hungered for is near;
And our marching steps will thunder: We are here!" (Glik and Kramer 2007)

36. For a discussion of nostalgia's potential to provide an alternative optics, see Fritzsche (2002).

37. I am grateful to Olga Litvak for explaining this expression to me.

38. The introductory note to the excerpt from *Khanes shof un rinder* from which this passage is taken mistakenly sets the story generally between 1917 and the Second World War, but the larger work clearly identifies the summer of 1941 as the time when the author and her youngest daughter went to visit Gorshman's parents.

39. For discussions of post-Soviet nostalgia, see Oushakine (2007) and Boym (2001).

Chapter 7

1. A discussion of the Soviet remaking of Russian can be found in Gorham (2003). For a discussion of the reform of Yiddish, see Estraikh (1999). For studies of translation in Russia, in addition to Friedberg, see Wachtel (1999) and Leighton (1991).

2. According to Slezkine, in Leningrad in 1939, Jews "made up 31.3 percent of all writers, journalists, and editors . . . 18.5 percent of all librarians; 18.4 percent of all scientists and university professors" (2004, 224). In 1979 Jews were 0.7 percent of the population of the Soviet Union, and in 1978 they represented 6.5 percent of professionals in the fields of writing, literary work, and journalism. See Altshuler (1987, 21, 167–70).

3. The list of prominent Russian-Jewish translators also includes Adalina Adalis and Naum Grebnev; Vasilii Grossman translated, as did Babel and Gekht. For a collection of Adalis's original poetry, see Adalis (2002).

4. See Bakhtin (1981), Bhabha (1994), Niranjana (1992), and also Spivak (1993, 179–200).

5. For a discussion focused on the interwar period, see Shternshis (2006, 148–58).

6. See Smith (1998).

7. For Nizami's adoption, so to speak, by the people of Azerbaijan, see Lipkin (1997, 448).

8. See Chukovskii (1941, 33, 74).

9. I am grateful to Anatolii Iakovlevich Razumov, the compiler and editor of *Knigi pamiati zhertv politicheskikh repressii "Leningradskii martirolog,"* for discussing these cases with me.

10. For more on Vygodskii, see Kel'ner (2003, 172–83), Fatkhullina (1992), and Shoshin (1993). I am grateful to Viktor Kel'ner for sharing his knowledge with me.

11. In *Konets khazy* (The end of the gang) the gang boss, Baraban, a former rabbinical student, injects Yiddish expressions into his Russian speech; see Kaverin (1926, 47).

12. See Bakhtin's explanation of the hybrid (1981, 304–8); for a discussion of the parallels between Bakhtin and Lev Vygotskii, see Morson and Emerson (1990, 210–14).

13. See Freidin (1987, 292, n. 151).

14. Cavanagh is citing "Fourth Prose" (Mandelshtam 1979, 324).

15. Jane Gary Harris and Constance Link omit the term "circumcision." I have modified their translation accordingly (Mandelshtam 1979, 321).

16. Gornfel'd was not such a literalist as Mandelshtam makes him out to be. In his essay "Muki slova" (Torments of language; which Mandelshtam praises), Gornfel'd says that "people do not convey [*peredaiut*] anything to one another, they only provoke thought in another." This rejection of language as a vessel into

which meaning is contained is similar to Mandelshtam's rejection of translation as the act of pouring grain from one sack to another.

17. For a discussion, see Pinkus (1988, 150–61) and Fitzpatrick (2005, 289–94). On Nusinov's role in Yiddish literature in the 1930s, see Estraikh (2005, 125–26, 134–35).

18. Frida Vigdorova, "Pervyi sud nad Iosofom Brodskim," cited in Murav (1998, 193). Vigdorova, a journalist, took notes during the trial despite the judge's repeated admonitions to stop; her transcript was circulated in *samizdat'* and published more than twenty years after the trial took place.

19. James Atlas, "A Poetic Triumph," cited by Bethea (1994, 141–42). A discussion of Brodsky and Jewishness is in Bethea (1994, 140–73).

20. For a longer discussion, see Murav (1998, 196–208).

21. For a justification of Kuniaev, see, for example, Pavlov (2007) and Kuniaev (2008).

22. For a discussion of the way nationalist writers used the state's apparatus to critique literature written by Jews in the "Metropol'" affair, see Mitrokhin (2006). I am grateful to Il'ia Kukulin for directing me to this article.

23. See, for example, Simenenko (2001).

24. These remarks can be found in Kuniaev (2007).

25. Il'ia Kukulin discusses these issues (2008).

26. For a response to the Mayakovsky book, see Boym (1991, 185–86).

27. For a discussion of Jews charged with economic crime in the era of the postwar anti-Jewish campaigns, see Pinkus (1988, 177–78).

28. Karabchievskii's characterization of Yiddish resembles Mandelshtam's description of his father's language as *"vse chto ugodno, no ne iazyk"* (Mandelshtam 1990, vol. 1, 19–20).

29. A contrasting view of these roles can be found in Krutikov (2003).

30. The Russian reads, *"ma-alen'kogo kakogo-nibud' ostatochka, trebuiushchego inogo sposoba vyrazheniia."* See "Toska po Armenii" in Karabchievskii (1991, 214).

31. I argued for this complex picture of self-transformation in Murav (2003).

32. The entry for "literary translation" found in a Soviet encyclopedia of 1968 also complained about the lack of "qualified cadres who knew languages."

33. Roziner wrote the novel in the period 1971–75, in Moscow; it was circulated in *samizdat'*, published in Russian in London in 1981 (the edition I am using), and translated into English by Michael Heim and published by W. W. Norton in 1991. See Roziner (1981).

34. As Alice Nakhimovsky points out, the "made-up name Tongor sounds similar enough to that of a small Siberian nation, the Tongus (or Tungus)" (1992, 245 n. 6).

35. Karabchievskii, as I mentioned earlier, was among the participants, but Lipkin's protest was specifically directed against the expulsion of Evgenii Popov and Viktor Erofeev. See Lipkin (2005).

36. See, for example, "Imenem na plitakh," "Mertvym" (about Babi Yar), "Moisei," and "Zola."

37. I take the term "writing back" from Ashcroft, Griffiths, and Tiffin (1989).

38. For a discussion of the festivals and "officially sanctioned non-Russian national identity," see Brooks (2000, 93–97).

39. A discussion can be found in Pohl (1999, 64–68).

40. The Slutskii poem "Ia osvobozhdal Ukrainu" was published in *God za godom*, the Russian-language supplement to *Sovetish heymland*, in 1988. See also the introduction to Part II of the present study, and Marat Grinberg, "Foreshadowing the Holocaust: Boris Slutsky's Jewish Poetic Cycle of 1940/41," unpublished paper.

41. For a discussion of her post-immigration writings, see Ronell (2008).

42. A review of the collection can be found in Dmitriev (2002).

43. Liudmila Ulitskaia, cited in Shrayer (2007a, 1104). For a discussion of the phenomenon of Russian-Jewish conversion to various denominations of Christianity, see Kornblatt (2004).

44. For a biography of Rufeisen, see Tec (1990).

45. For an extensive quotation of Rufeisen's model of Christianity as an extension of Judaism, see Tec (1990, 167).

46. See "Genele the Purse Lady" in Shrayer (2007b, 1110).

47. David Nirenberg, *Christian Sovereignty and Jewish Flesh* (paper presented to the Program in Medieval Studies, University of Illinois, November 14, 2003).

48. For an article that make a similar point, see Martynova (2009).

49. For example, Naomi Seidman, who shows that in medieval Europe translation and conversion were "closely allied if not parallel operations" (2006, 141).

Chapter 8

1. For a discussion of magical realism as an important new genre in post-Soviet fiction, see Etkind (2009). Etkind argues that the vast majority of these works remythologize the present.

2. During a trip to St. Petersburg in May 2010, I found that most mainstream bookstores I visited displayed, for example, the previously unpublished diaries of the poet Ol'ga Berggol'ts, *Zapretnyi dnevnik* (Forbidden diary) (2010); a memoir of the prize-winning poet and researcher of the Leningrad blockade Daniil Granin, titled *Vse bylo ne sovsem tak* (It wasn't entirely like that) (2010); and a memoir by the noted translator Lilianna Lungina, titled *Podstrochnik* (The interlinear) (Lungina 2009). The book was transcribed from a popular television film by Oleg Dorman by the same title, featuring Lungina narrating her life.

3. Solzhenitsyn (2001). For discussions, see Moskvin (2001), Katsis (2001), Mahoney (2002), and Klier (2002). For a discussion of the demonization of the Jew in post-Soviet literature, see Mondry (2009, 244–70).

4. For a comparable analysis based on art in postcommunist Germany and Poland, see Scribner (2003).

5. Carolyn J. Dean analyzes the controversy in France around the crimes of Stalin and Hitler, and addresses the mentality of the zero-sum game that underlies the charge of excessive memory (2006).

6. The Winter 2004 issue of *Reform Judaism*, for example, proclaims that in Eastern Europe and the former Soviet Union "thousands of young adults—including those with hidden Jewish ancestry—are reclaiming a heritage nearly destroyed by the Nazis and the communists" (A Phoenix Rises in the East 2004).

7. A son living in Israel published a short novel in Russian called *The Translator*. The most complete list of his published works is found at http://magazines.russ.ru/novyi_mi/arhiv/karab/. For the interview, see http://magazines.russ.ru/novyi_mi/arhiv/karab/interv.html.

8. For a discussion of Soviet writers' attachment to the Soviet empire and their fictions of suicide, see Ivanova (1998).

9. A detailed eyewitness account of August 19 and the subsequent few days may be found in Liubarskii (1991).

10. "Ubiistvo evreev v Berdicheve" was published in *Znamia* 1990 (June):144–52. The production stumbled, however, in its use of a vaguely Hasidic dance to enhance the Jewishness of Viktor Shtrum. Neither Shtrum, a nuclear physicist, nor his mother, an eye doctor, had anything remotely to do with Hasidism.

11. See Boym's distinction between ironic and restorative nostalgia (2001, 48–51). The discussion of "reframing" is found in Oushakine (2007).

12. In a personal communication, the author states that this replacement was made without his knowledge, and further explains that he took on the Russified surname to begin with because an editor told him he had little chance of getting his work published otherwise. The interview was conducted September 7, 2006, in St. Petersburg. The twists and turns of Judeophobia and Judeophilia in the Russian publishing world are a separate story.

13. An analysis can be found in Lipovetsky (2002). For a discussion of this phenomenon in the work of women writers, see Goscilo (1993) and Murav (1995).

14. For discussions of Kabakov, see Boym (1998) and Groys (2006).

15. See Lipovetsky (2001) for a discussion.

16. See Kabakov (2005) for images and commentary.

17. For a definition of Jewish identification among late Soviet Jewish artists in terms of the structure of their relationship to mainstream Russian culture, see Misiano (1995). Misiano argues that the Jewish identity of these artists was given both by their sense of being enclosed and separate and by their longing to go beyond these limits.

18. The novel is the first in a trilogy; the second volume is *Novyi golem* (2004), and the third, *Vineta*, was published in *Znamia* in 2007.

19. The play has been performed in Moscow, Tel Aviv, Prague, and Berlin, and was also broadcast on German television. For the text, see Iur'ev (1990).

20. For a discussion of *Noyi Golem*, see Krutikov (2004).

21. Iur'ev may be compared to Leonid Girshovich, also living in Germany, whose works *Prais* and *Vij* also imagine alternative histories in which Jewish identity is estranged. For a discussion, see Lipovetsky (2008, 388–417). I am grateful to Mark Lipovetsky for sharing his work with me.

22. Andrei Bitov engages this question in his fiction; for a discussion, see Spieker (1996).

23. See Gitelman (2003); Aviv and Shneer (2005, 26–49); and Gitelman and Ro'i (2007, 221–330).

24. I am grateful to Leonid Katsis for presenting me with the volume. See Katsis, Kaspina, and Fishman (2009).

25. See, for example, her story "Mir forn" (We're going), in which the Yiddish phrase of the title is the leitmotif of the work. The story was published in *Druzhba narodov* in 2006.

Works Cited

A Phoenix Rises in the East. 2004. *Reform Judaism* 33(2):63.
Abraham, Nicholas, and Maria Torok. 1994. *The Shell and the Kernel: Renewals of Psychoanalysis*, translated by N. T. Rand. Chicago: University of Chicago Press.
Adalis, Adalina. 2002. *Bessonitsa*. St. Petersburg: Limbus Press.
Al'tman, I. A. 2002. *Zhertvy nenavisti: Kholokost v SSSR 1941–1945 gg*. Moscow: Kovcheg.
———, ed. 2009. Kholokost na territorii SSSR: Entsiklopediia. Moscow: Rosspen.
Altman, Moshe. 1936. *Medresh Pinkhes: Nokh Motl Umru's bletlekh*. Bucharest: Sholem-Aleichem farlag.
———. 1948. Der vorstl. *Heymland* 5:41–50.
———. 1957. Bletlekh. *Yidishe shriftn* 4:5.
———. 1959. *Korni: Rasskazy*, translated by O. Liubomirskii. Moscow: Sovetskii pisatel'.
———. 1974. *Oysgeveylte shriftn*. Bucharest: Kriterion.
———. 1980. *Di viner karete: Roman, dertseylungen, noveln*. Moscow: Sovetskii pisatel'.
Altshuler, Mordechai. 1987. *Soviet Jewry Since the Second World War: Population and Social Structure*. New York: Greenwood Press.
———. 2004. Itsik Kipnis: The "White Crow" of Soviet Yiddish Literature. *Jews in Russia and Eastern Europe* 52/53:68–167.
Altshuler, Mordechai, Yitshak Arad, and Shmuel Krakowski, eds. 1993. *Sovetskie evrei pishut Il'e Erenburgu*. Jerusalem: Prisma Press.
An-sky, S. 1910. Kolybel'naia assimiliatsiia. *Evreiskii mir* 23/24:14–21.
Anninskii, Lev. 2003. Il'ia Sel'vinskii: Etot stikh . . . "kak stakan okeana." Available from http://zavtra.ru/cgi/veil//data/denlit/085/81.html.
Arad, Yitzhak, ed. 1992. *Unichtozhenie evreev SSSR v gody nemetskoi okkupatsii (1941–1944)*. Jerusalem: Yad Vashem.
———. 2008. The Destruction of the Jews in German-Occupied Territories of the Soviet Union. In *The Unknown Black Book: The Holocaust in the German*

Occupied Soviet Territories, edited by J. Rubenstein and I. Altman. Bloomington: Indiana University Press.

———. 2009. *The Holocaust in the Soviet Union*, translated by O. Cumings. Lincoln: University of Nebraska Press, and Jerusalem: Yad Vashem.

Arendt, Hannah. 1973. *The Origins of Totalitarianism*. New York: Harcourt Brace Jovanovich.

Asad, Talal. 1986. The Concept of Cultural Translation in British Social Anthropology. In *Writing Culture: The Poetics and Politics of Ethnography*, edited by J. Clifford and G. E. Marcus. Berkeley: University of California Press.

Ashcroft, Bill, Gareth Griffiths, and Helen Tiffin. 1989. *The Empire Writes Back: Theory and Practice in Post-Colonial Literatures*. London: Routledge.

Avins, Carol. 1994. Kinship and Concealment in Red Cavalry and Babel's 1920 Diary. *Slavic Review* 53(3):694–710.

Aviv, Caryn, and David Shneer. 2005. *New Jews: The End of the Jewish Diaspora*. New York: New York University Press.

Avrutin, Eugune M., Valerii Dymshits, Alexander Ivanov, Alexander Lvov, Harriet Murav, and Alla Sokolova, eds. 2009. *Photographing the Jewish Nation: Pictures from S. An-sky's Ethnographic Expeditions*. Waltham, MA: Brandeis University Press.

Babel, Isaac. 1966. *Izbrannoe*. Moscow: Kemerovskoe knizhnoe izdatel'stvo.

———. 1990. *Sochineniia*. 2 vols. Moscow: Khudozhestvennaia literatura.

———. 2002. *Complete Works*, translated by P. Constantine. New York: Norton.

Bakhtin, Mikhail. 1965. *Rabelais and His World*, translated by Helene Iswolsky. Cambridge, MA: MIT Press.

———. 1981. *The Dialogic Imagination*, translated by C. Emerson and M. Holquist. Austin: University of Texas Press.

Barash, Aleksandr. 2004. Russko-ivritskie literaturnye sviazi v rezhime real time. *NLO* 68(4):252–59.

Beider, Chaim, ed. 1980. *Native Land: A Selection of Soviet Jewish Writers*. Moscow: Progress.

Beiner, Ronald. 1984. Walter Benjamin's Philosophy of History. *Political Theory* 12(3):423–34.

Belaia, Galina. 1990. Iskusstvo epokhi bezvremen'e. *Strana i mir* 3(57):141–47.

———. 1999. "I rechka, veroiatno, ele bilas', zatverdevaia v kamennom grobu: 'Ottepel': Sluchainost' ili neizbezhnost'?" *Nezavisimaia gazeta*, September 29, pp. 1, 10.

Belaia, Galina, E. I. Dobrenko, and I. A. Esaulov. 1993. *Konarmiia Isaaka Babelia*. Moscow: Rossiiskii universitet.

Belcove-Shalin, Janet. 1995. *New World Hasidism*. Albany: State University of New York Press.

Bemporad, Elissa. 2006. Red Star on the Jewish Street: The Reshaping of Jewish Life in Soviet Minsk, 1917–1939. Ph.D. diss., Stanford University.

Bender, Barbara. 2006. Place and Landscape. In *Handbook of Material Culture*, edited by C. Tilley, W. K. Keane, S. M. Rowlands, and P. Spyer. London: Sage.
Benjamin, Walter. 1969. *Illuminations*, translated by H. Zohn. New York: Schocken Books.
Bergelson, David. 1926. Dray tsentern. *In sphan* 1 (April):84–96.
———. 1929. *Mides-hadin*. Vilno: B. Kletskin.
———. 1930a. *Burnye dni*, translated by M. Bruk and S. A. Sapozhnikovoi. *Seriia evreiskoi literatury*. Moscow: Gosudarstvennoe izdatel'stvo.
———. 1930b. *Geklibene verk*, vol. 5. Vilno: B. Kletskin.
———. 1930c. Problemen fun der yidisher literatur. *Literarishe bleter* (24):437–39.
———. 1932. *Baym Dnyepr: Penek*, vol. 1 (2 vols.). Moscow: Der emes.
———. 1936a. Barg-aruf. *Forpost* :37–70.
———. 1936b. *The Jewish Autonomous Region*. Moscow: Foreign Language Publishing House.
———. 1940. *Bam Dnyepr: Yunge yorn*, vol. 2 (2 vols.). Moscow: Der emes.
———. 1943. *Geven iz nakht un gevorn iz tog*. Moscow: Der emes.
———. 1946. *Prints Ruveni*. New York: Yidisher kultur farband.
———. 1957. *Izbrannoe*. Moscow: Sovetskii pisatel'.
———. 1961. *Oysgevaylte verk*. Moscow: Melukhe-farlag fun kinstlerisher literatur.
———. 1974. The Witness. In *An Anthology of Modern Yiddish Literature*, edited by J. Leftwich. The Hague: Mouton.
———. 1977. *When All Is Said and Done*, translated by B. Martin. Athens: Ohio University Press.
———. 1999. *Descent*, translated by J. Sherman. New York: Modern Language Association of America.
———. 2005. *The Shadows of Berlin: The Berlin Stories of Dovid Bergelson*, translated by J. Neugroschel. San Francisco: City Lights.
———. 2009. *The End of Everything*. New Haven, CT: Yale University Press.
Berggol'ts, Ol'ga. 2010. *Ol'ga: Zapretnyi dnevnik*. St. Petersburg: Azbuka-klassika.
Bergson, Henri. 1991. *Matter and Memory*, translated by N. W. Paul and W. S. Palmer. New York: Zone Books.
Bethea, David. 1994. *Joseph Brodsky and the Creation of Exile*. Princeton, NJ: Princeton University Press.
Bhabha, Homi. 1994. *The Location of Culture*. London: Routledge.
Biale, David. 1997. *Eros and the Jews: From Biblical Israel to Contemporary America*. Berkeley: University of California Press.
Blium, A. E. 2006. Evreiskii vopros pod Sovetskoi tsenzuroi: 1917–1991. Otkrytyi tekst. Available from http://www.opentextnn.ru/censorship/russia/sov/libraries/books/blium/?id=537.
Blok, A. A. 1997. *Polnoe sobranie sochinenii i pisem v 20-ti tomakh*, vol. 3. Moscow: Nauka.
Bocharov, A. 1990. Mchatsia mify, b'iutsia mify. *Oktiabr'* 1:180–91.

Bondarenko, Vladimir. 2002. Russkost' i russkoiazychnost'. *Zavtra* 7.
Borenstein, Eliot. 2000. *Men Without Women: Masculinity and Revolution in Russian Fiction, 1917–1929*. Durham (NC) and London: Duke University Press.
Bourtman, Ilya. 2008. "Blood for Blood, Death for Death": The Soviet Military Tribunal in Krasnodar, 1943. *Holocaust and Genocide Studies* 22(2):246–65.
Boyarin, Daniel. 1997. *Unheroic Conduct: The Rise of Heterosexuality and the Invention of the Jewish Man*. Berkeley: University of California Press.
Boyarin, Jonathan. 1992. *Storm from Paradise and the Politics of Jewish Memory*. Minneapolis: University of Minnesota Press.
Boym, Svetlana. 1991. *Death in Quotation Marks: Cultural Myths of the Modern Poet*. Cambridge, MA: Harvard University Press.
———. 1997. Paradoxes of Unified Culture: From Stalin's Fairy Tale to Molotov's Laquer Box. In *Socialist Realism Without Shores*, edited by T. Lahusen and E. Dobrenko. Durham, NC: Duke University Press.
———. 1998. On Diasporic Intimacy: Ilya Kabakov's Installations and Immigrant Homes. *Critical Inquiry* 24(2):498–524.
———. 2001. *The Future of Nostalgia*. New York: Basic Books.
Branover, G. G., ed. 1994–2000. Rossiiskaia evreiskaia entsiklopediia, vol. 1 (4 vols.). Moscow: Epos.
Brooks, Jeffrey. 2000. *Thank You, Comrade Stalin!: Soviet Public Culture from Revolution to Civil War*. Princeton, NJ: Princeton University Press.
Brown, Bill. 1999. The Secret Life of Things (Virginia Woolf and the Matter of Modernism). *Modernism/Modernity* 5(2):1–28.
Brown, Edward. 1986. Review of Life and Fate. *Boston Globe*, April 13.
Buck-Morss, Susan. 1986. The Flaneur, the Sandwichman and the Whore: The Politics of Loitering. *New German Critique* 39:99–140.
Budnitskii, Oleg. 2005. *Rossiiskie evrei mezhdu krasnymi i belymi*. Moscow: Rosspen.
Burstin, Hinde Ena. 2006. *From the Other Side of the Wall*. Available from http://www.brandcis.cdu/hbi/614/archives/volume3/VIII,%2014/article4a.html (accessed August 2, 2010).
Burton, Antoinette. 2003. *Dwelling in the Archive: Women Writing House, Home, and History in Late Colonial India*. Oxford: Oxford University Press.
Cavanagh, Claire. 1991. The Poetics of Jewishness: Mandel'stam, Dante and the "Honorable Calling of Jew." *Slavic and East European Journal* 35(3):317–38.
———. 1995. *Osip Mandelstam and the Modernist Creation of Tradition*. Princeton, NJ: Princeton University Press.
Chaver, Yael. 2007. Outcasts Within: Zionist Yiddish Literature in Pre-State Palestine. *Jewish Social Studies* 7(2/Winter):39–66.
Chernenko, Miron. 2003. *Krasnaia zvezda, zheltaia zvezda: Kinematograficheskaia istoriia evreistva v Rossii 1919–1999*. Vinnitsa: Globus-Press.
Cholawski, Sholom. 1997. The Holocaust and the Armed Struggle in Belorussia as Reflected in Soviet Literature and Works by Emigres in the West. In

Bitter Legacy: Confronting the Holocaust in the USSR, edited by Z. Gitelman. Bloomington: Indiana University Press.

Choseed, Bernard. 1968. Categorizing Soviet Yiddish Writers. *Slavic Review* 27(1):102–8.

Chukovskii, Kornei. 1941. *Vysokoe iskusstvo*. Moscow: Khudozhestvennaia literatura.

Clark, Katerina. 1985. *The Soviet Novel: History as Ritual*. Chicago: University of Chicago Press.

———. 1993. Changing Historical Paradigms in Soviet Culture. In *Late Soviet Culture: From Perestroika to Novostroika*, edited by T. Lahusen and G. Kuperman. Durham, NC: Duke University Press.

Dean, Carolyn J. 2006. Recent French Discourses on Stalinism, Nazism and "Exorbitant" Jewish Memory. *History and Memory* 18(1):43–85.

Dekel-Chen, Jonathan. 2005. *Farming the Red Land: Jewish Agricultural Colonization and Local Soviet Power, 1924–1941*. New Haven, CT: Yale University Press.

Der Nister. 1943. Heshl Ansheles (Vegn eynem a fal inem itstikin okupirtn poyln). In *Heymland: Literarisher zamlbukh*. Moscow: Der emes.

———. 1944. Has. *Eynikayt*, June 29, p. 3.

———. 1946. Vidervuks. *Yidishe kultur* 6:42–47, 7:33–39.

———. 1948. *Di mishpokhe Mashper*, vol. 1 (2 vols.). New York: Ikuf.

———. 1969. *Vidervuks*. Moscow: Sovetskii pisatel'.

Derrida, Jacques. 2001. What Is a "Relevant" Translation? *Critical Inquiry* 27(2):174–200.

———. 2005. *Sovereignties in Question: The Poetics of Paul Celan*, edited by J. D. Caputo. Perspectives in Continental Philosophy. New York: Fordham University Press.

Deutscher, Penelope. 1998. Mourning the Other, Cultural Cannibalism, and the Politics of Friendship (Jacques Derrida and Luce Irigaray). *Differences: A Journal of Feminist Cultural Studies* 10(3):159–84.

diaspore, Assotsiatsiia po izucheniiu evreiskikh obshchin v. 2005. *Russko-evreiskaia literatura*. Elektronnaia evreiskaia entsiklopediia (accessed April 18, 2007).

Dimanshtein, Semen. 1934. *Di yidishe avtonome gegnt—a kind fun der oktober revolutsye*. Moscow: Der emes.

Diner, Hasia. 2009. *We Remember with Reverence and Love: American Jews and the Myth of Silence After the Holocaust, 1945–1962*. New York: New York University Press.

Dmitriev, Dmitrii. 2002. Neser'eznyi pisatel'. *Znamia* 3:218–20.

Dobrenko, E. I. 1993. *Metafora vlasti: Literatura Stalinskoi epokhi v istoricheskom osveshchenii*. Munich: Verlag Otto Sagner.

———. 2001. *The Making of the State Writer: Social and Aesthetic Origins of Soviet Literary Culture*. Stanford, CA: Stanford University Press.

———. 2004. Socialism as Will and Representation, or What Legacy Are We Rejecting? *Kritika: Explorations in Russian and Eurasian History* 5(4):675–709.

Dobroszycki, Lucjan, and Jeffrey S. Gurock, eds. 1993. *The Holocaust in the Soviet*

Union: Studies and Sources on the Destruction of the Jews in the Nazi-Occupied Territories of the USSR, 1941–1945. Armonk, NY: M. E. Sharpe.
Druker, Jonathan. 2004. The Shadowed Violence of Culture: Fascism and the Figure of Ulysses in Primo Levi's Survival in Auschwitz. *Clio* 33(2):143–62.
Efros, Abram. 2001. Lampa Aladdina. In *Al'bom evreiskoi khudozhestvennoi stariny Semena An-skogo*, edited by A. Kantsedikas and I. Sergeeva. Moscow: Mosty kultury.
Ehre, Milton. 1986. *Isaac Babel*. Boston: Twayne.
Eichenbaum, Boris. 1965. The Theory of the "Formal Method." In *Russian Formalist Criticism: Four Essays*, edited by L. T. Lemon and M. J. Reis. Lincoln: University of Nebraska Press.
Emerson, Caryl. 1997. *The First Hundred Years of Mikhail Bakhtin*. Princeton, NJ: Princeton University Press.
Engelstein, Laura. 1992. *The Keys to Happiness: Sex and the Search for Modernity in Fin-de-Siècle Russia*. Ithaca, NY: Cornell University Press.
Erenburg, Il'ia. 1942. Evrei. Krasnaia zvezda, November 1, p. 3.
———. 1943. Voina. Moscow: Ogiz.
———. 1944. Torzhestvo cheloveka. *Pravda*, April 29, p. 4.
———. 1954. *Ottepel'*. Moscow: Sovetskii pisatel'.
———. 1960. *Buria*. Moscow: Khudozhestvennaia literatura.
———. 1990. *Liudi, gody, zhizn': Vospominaniia v trekh tomakh*, vol. 2 (3 vols.). Moscow: Sovetskii pisatel'.
Erickson, John. 1983. *The Road to Berlin*. Boulder, CO: Westview Press.
Estraikh, Gennady. 1995. The Era of Sovetish Heymland: Readership of the Yiddish Press in the Former Soviet Union. *East European Jewish Affairs* 25(1):17–22.
———. 1998. A Touchstone of Socialist Realism. *Jews in Eastern Europe* 3(37):24–37.
———. 1999. *Soviet Yiddish: Language Planning and Linguistic Development*. Oxford: Clarendon Press.
———. 2000. The Shtetl Theme in *Sovetish heymland*. In *The Shtetl: Image and Reality*, edited by G. Estraikh and M. Krutikov. Oxford: Legenda.
———. 2003. Pig-Breeding, Shiksas, and Other Goyish Themes in Soviet Yiddish Literature and Life. *Symposium* (Fall):157–74.
———. 2005a. *In Harness: Yiddish Writers' Romance with Communism*. Syracuse, NY: Syracuse University Press.
———. 2005b. Shmuel Gordon: A Yiddish Writer In "The Ocean of Russian Literature." In *The Yiddish Presence in European Literature: Inspiration and Interaction*, edited by J. Sherman and R. Robertson. Oxford: Legenda.
———. 2006. From "Green Fields" to "Red Fields": Peretz Hirshchbein's Soviet Sojourn, 1928–1929. *Jews in Russia and Eastern Europe* 56(1/Summer):60–81.
———. 2008. *Yiddish in the Cold War*. London: Legenda.
Etkind, Alexander. 2009. Stories of the Undead in the Land of the Unburied: Magical Historicism in Contemporary Russian Fiction. *Slavic Review* 68(3):631–58.

Etkind, E. G. 1962. O poeticheskoi vernosti. In *Mastersvto perevoda*, edited by M. I. Malkhazova. Moscow: Sovetskii pisatel'.

Fadeev, Aleksandr. 1947. *Razgrom. Molodaia gvardiia*. Moscow: Sovetskii pisatel'.

Fainberg, Rakhil. 1970. *Iurii German: Kritiko-biograficheskii ocherk*. Leningrad: Sovetskii pisatel'.

Farber, L. M. 1971. Sel'vinskii. In *Kratkaia literaturnaia entsiklopediia*, edited by A. A. Surkov. Moscow: Sovetskaia entsiklopediia.

Fatkhullina, Rimma. 1992. Materialy k biografii Davida Vygodskogo. In *Litsa: Biograficheskii al'manakh*, edited by A. V. Lavrov. St. Petersburg: Feniks/Atheneum.

Fefer, Itsik. 1943. *Roytarmeyish*. New York: Alveltlekher Yidisher Kultur Farband.

———. 1967. *Lider, balades, poemes*. Moscow: Sovetskii pisatel'.

Feferman, Kiril. 2007. *The Holocaust in the Crimea and the Caucasus*. Jerusalem: Yad Vashem (in Hebrew).

Felman, Shoshana, and Dori Laub. 1992. *Testimony: Crises of Witnessing in Literature, Psychoanalysis, and History*. New York: Routledge.

Finkin, Jordan. 2008. Markish, Trakl, and the Temporaesthetic. *Modernism/Modernity* 15(4):783–801.

Fitzpatrick, Sheila. 2005. *Tear Off the Masks: Identity and Imposture in Twentieth-Century Russia*. Princeton, NJ: Princeton University Press.

Fonrobert, Charlotte Elisheva, and Vered Shemtov. 2005. Introduction: Jewish Conceptions and Practices of Space. *Jewish Social Studies* 11(3):1–8.

Freidin, Gregory. 1978. The Whisper of History and the Noise of Time in the Writings of Osip Mandel'shtam. *Russian Review* 37(4):421–37.

———. 1987. *A Coat of Many Colors: Osip Mandelstam and His Mythologies of Self-Presentation*. Berkeley: University of California Press.

———. 1994. Revolution as Esthetic Phenomenon: Nietzsche's Spectacles on the Nose and Autumn in the Heart of Isaac Babel's Russian Readers (1923–1932). In *Nietzsche in Soviet Culture*. Oxford: Oxford University Press.

———. 2009. *The Enigma of Isaac Babel: Biography, History, Context*. Stanford, CA: Stanford University Press.

Freud, Sigmund. 1961. *Civilization and Its Discontents*, translated by J. Strachey. Standard ed. New York: Norton.

Friedberg, Maurice. 1970. *The Jews in Post-Stalin Soviet Literature*. Washington, DC: B'nai B'rith International Council.

———. 1997. *Literary Translation in Russia: A Cultural History*. University Park: Pennsylvania State University Press.

Frieden, Ken. 1995. *Classic Yiddish Fiction: Abramovitsh, Sholem Aleichem, and Peretz*. Albany: State University of New York Press.

Friedlander, Saul. 1998. The Shoah Between Memory and History. In *Breaking Crystal: Writing and Memory After Auschwitz*, edited by E. Sicher. Urbana: University of Illinois Press.

Fritzsche, Peter. 2002. How Nostalgia Narrates Modernity. In *The Work of Memory:*

New Directions in the Study of German Society and Culture, edited by A. Confino and P. Fritzsche. Urbana and Chicago: University of Illinois Press.

Garrard, John. 1995. The Nazi Holocaust in the Soviet Union: Interpreting Newly Opened Russian Archives. *East European Jewish Affairs* 25(2):3–40.

Garrard, John, and Carol Garrard. 1996. *The Bones of Berdichev: The Life and Fate of Vasily Grossman*. New York: Free Press.

Garrett, Leah. 2003. *Journeys Beyond the Pale: Yiddish Travel Writing in the Modern World*. Madison: University of Wisconsin Press.

Gekht, Semen Grigorevich. 1923. Stariki—Evreiskaia bednota na Podole. *Ogonek* 25:13–14.

———. 1925. *Rasskazy*. Moscow: Ogonek.

———. 1939. *Pouchitel'naia istoriia*. Moscow: Izd-vo detskoi lit-ry.

———. 1959. V Moskve i Odesse. *Nash sovremennik* 4:226–34.

———. 1963. *Dolgi serdtsa*. Moscow: Sovetskii pisatel'.

———. 1983. *Prostoi rasskaz o mertvetsakh i drugie proizvedeniia*. Jerusalem: M. Wainstein.

German, Iurii. 1949. Pis'mo. *Zvezda* 3(March):207.

———. 1976. *Sobranie sochinenii v shesti tomakh*, vol. 4 (6 vols.). Leningrad: Khudozhestvennaia literatura.

Gibian, George. 1960. *Interval of Freedom: Soviet Literature During the Thaw, 1954–1957*. Minneapolis: University of Minnesota Press.

Gilman, Sander. 1986. *Jewish Self-Hatred: Anti-Semitism and the Hidden Language of the Jews*. Baltimore: Johns Hopkins University Press.

———. 1991. *The Jew's Body*. New York: Routledge.

Gitelman, Zvi. 1972. *Jewish Nationality and Soviet Politics: The Jewish Sections of the CPSU, 1917–1930*. Princeton, NJ: Princeton University Press.

———. 1997. Politics and the Historiography of the Holocaust in the Soviet Union. In *Bitter Legacy: Confronting the Holocaust in the USSR*, edited by Z. Gitelman. Bloomington: Indiana University Press.

———. 1998a. Introduction. In *Stalin's Forgotten Zion: Birobidzhan and the Making of a Soviet Jewish Homeland*. Berkeley: University of California Press.

———. 1998b. The Decline of the Diaspora Jewish Nation: Boundaries, Content, and Jewish Identity. *Jewish Social Studies* 4(2):112–32.

———. 2003. Thinking About Being Jewish in Russia and Ukraine. In *Jewish Life After the USSR*, edited by Z. Gitelman, M. Glants, and M. I. Goldman. Bloomington: Indiana University Press.

Gitelman, Zvi, and Yaacov Ro'i. 2007. *Revolution, Repression, and Revival: The Soviet Jewish Experience*. Lanham, MD: Rowman & Littlefield.

Glaser, Amelia. 2004. The End of the Bazaar: Revolutionary Eschatology in Isaac Babel's Konarmiia and Peretz Markish's Di Kupe. *Jews in Russia and Eastern Europe* 52/53:5–32.

Glik, Hirsh, and Aaron Kramer. 2005. *Zog nit keynmol*. Available from http://

savethemusic.com/yiddish/bin/music.cgi?Page=zognitkeynmol&English =zog_english (accessed June 2, 2007).
Goldberg, David. 1993. Fantasy, Realism, and National Identity in Soviet Yiddish Juvenile Literature: Itsik Kipnis's Books for Children. In *The Field of Yiddish: Studies in Language, Folklore, and Literature*, edited by D. Goldberg. Evanston, IL: Northwestern University Press and YIVO.
Golovanov, D. 1999. Ni zhesta, ni slova. *Voprosy literatury* 3:271–87.
Gorbatov, Boris. 1987. *Nepokorennye*. Donetsk: Donbas.
Gordon, Mel. 1999. Mikhoels in America. *Slavic and East European Performance* 19(2):58–68.
Gordon, Shmuel. 1970. *Friling*. Moscow: Sovetskii pisatel'.
———. 1976. *U vinogradnika*. Moscow: Sovetskii pisatel'.
———. 2003. *Yizkor: Di farmishpete shrayber*. Jerusalem: World Council for Yiddish Culture.
Gorenshtein, Fridrikh. 1986. *Psalom*. Munich: Strana i mir.
———. 1988. *Tri p'esy*. New York: Slovo.
———. 1991. *Travelling Companions*. San Diego: Harcourt Brace Jovanovich.
———. 2003. *Letit sebe aeroplan*. Moscow: Slovo.
Gorham, Michael S. 2003. *Speaking in Soviet Tongues: Language Culture and the Politics of Voice in Revolutionary Russia*. DeKalb: Northern Illinois University Press.
Gorkii, Maxim. 1930. O literature. *Nashi dostizheniia* 12.
Gorkii, M. A., and L. Z. Mekhlis, eds. 1937. *Tvorchestvo narodov SSST: 20 let velikoi oktiabr'skoi sotsialisticheskoi revoliutsii v SSSR 1917–1937*. Moscow: Pravda.
Gorshman, Shire. 1948. *Der koyekh fun lebn*. Moscow: Ogiz.
———. 1961. *33 noveln*. Warsaw: Farlag yidish bukh.
———. 1963. *Tret'e pokolenie: novelly i rasskazy*, translated by S. Rodov. Moscow: Sovetskii pisatel'.
———. 1979. *Zhizn' i svet*. Moscow: Sovetskii pisatel'.
———. 1981. *Ikh hob lib arumforn*. Moscow: Sovetish heymland.
———. 1984. *Yontev inmitn vokh*. Moscow: Sovetskii pisatel'.
———. 1994. Unspoken Hearts. In *Found Treasures: Stories by Yiddish Women Writers*, edited by F. Forman, E. Raicus, S. Silberstein Swartz, and M. Wolfe. Toronto: Second Story Press.
Goscilo, Helena. 1993. Monsters Monomaniacal, Marital, and Medical. In *Sexuality and the Body in Russian Culture*, edited by J. Costlow, S. Sandler, and J. Vowles. Stanford, CA: Stanford University Press.
Granin, Daniiil. 2010. *Vse bylo ne sovsem tak*. Moscow: OLMA Media Group.
Greenberg, Clement. 1961. *Art and Culture: Critical Essays*. Boston: Beacon Press.
Grossman, Vasilii. 1943. Der alter lerer. In *Heymland: Literarisher zamlbukh*, edited by P. Markish. Moscow: Der emes.
———. 1956. *Za pravoe delo*. Moscow: Sovetskii pisatel'.

———. 1980. *Zhizn' i sud'ba*, edited by S. Markish and E. G. Etkind. Lausanne: L'Age d'Homme.
———. 1985a. *Life and Fate*, translated by R. Chandler. London: Collins Harvill.
———. 1985b. Staryi uchitel'. In *Na evreiskie temy*. Jerusalem: Aliia.
———. 1985c. Treblinskii ad. In *Na evreiskie temy*. Jerusalem: Aliia.
———. 1985d. Ukraina bez evreev. In *Na evreiskie temy*, edited by S. Markish. Jerusalem: Aliia.
———. 1993. Ubiistvo evreev v Berdicheve. In *Chernaia kniga*, edited by V. Grossman and I. Erenburg. Vilnius: Yad Vashem.
———. 2005. *V gorode Berdicheve*. Ekaterinberg: U-Faktoriia.
———. 2006. *Life and Fate*. New York: New York Review of Books.
———. 2010. *The Road: Stories, Journalism, and Essays*, edited by R. Chandler, translated by R. Chandler and E. Chandler, with O. Mukovnikova. New York: New York Review of Books.
———. n.d. John and Carol Garrard Collection of Vasilii Semenovich Grossman Papers, 1925–1994. Harvard University, Houghton Library.
Groys, Boris. 2006. *Ilya Kabakov: The Man Who Flew into Space from His Apartment*. London: Afterall Books.
———. 2004. *Il'ia Kabakov: Zdes' i tam*. Available from http://plucer.livejournal.com/69848.html (accessed December 7, 2009).
Gruber, Ruth Ellen. 2002. *Virtually Jewish: Reinventing Jewish Culture in Europe*. Berkeley: University of California Press.
Hackel, Sergei. 1978. *The Poet and the Revolutionary: Alexander Blok's "The Twelve."* Oxford: Clarendon Press.
Halkin, Shmuel. 1943. Zol zayn mayn shtub a hafn dir. In *Heymland*, edited by P. Markish. Moscow: Der emes.
———. 1987. "Of Things Past." In *The Penguin Book of Modern Yiddish Verse*, edited by I. Howe, R. R. Wisse, and K. Shmeruk. New York: Viking.
Hansen, Miriam Bratu. 2008. Benjamin's Aura. *Critical Inquiry* (Winter):336–75.
Harshav, Benjamin. 1990. *The Meaning of Yiddish*. Stanford, CA: Stanford University Press.
Harshav, Benjamin, and Barbara Harshav, eds. 1986. *American Yiddish Poetry*. Berkeley: University of California Press.
Hellebust, Rolf. 2003. *Flesh to Metal: Soviet Literature and the Alchemy of Revolution*. Ithaca (NY) and London: Cornell University Press.
Hirsch, Francine. 2002. Race Without the Practice of Racial Politics. *Slavic Review* 61(1):30–43.
———. 2005. *Empire of Nations: Ethnographic Knowledge and the Making of the Soviet Union*. Ithaca, NY: Cornell University Press.
Hirsch, Marianne. 2003. Mourning and Postmemory. In *The Holocaust: Theoretical Readings*, edited by N. Levi and M. Rothberg. New Brunswick, NJ: Rutgers University Press.

Hirzowicz, Lukasz. 1993. The Holocaust in the Soviet Mirror. In *The Holocaust in the Soviet Union: Studies and Sources on the Destruction of the Jews in the Nazi-Occupied Territories of the USSR, 1941–1945*, edited by L. Dobroszycki and J. S. Gurock. Armonk, NY: M. E. Sharpe.

Hoffman, David L. 2003. *Stalinist Values: The Cultural Norms of Soviet Modernity, 1917–1941*. Ithaca (NY) and London: Cornell University Press.

Hofshteyn, David. 1922. *Troyer*. Kiev: Kultur-Lige.

———. 1987. Ikh gleyb s'iz mir bashert. In *A sphigl af a shteyn*, edited by K. Shmeruk. Jerusalem: Magnes Press.

Holquist, Peter. 2001. To Count, to Extract, and to Exterminate. In *A State of Nations*, edited by R. G. Suny. Oxford: Oxford University Press.

———. 2002. *Making War, Forging Revolution: Russia's Continuum of Crisis, 1914–1921*. Cambridge, MA: Harvard University Press.

Howe, Irving, and Eliezer Greenberg. 1977. *Ashes Out of Hope: Fiction by Soviet-Yiddish Writers*. New York: Schocken Books.

Howe, Irving, Ruth R. Wisse, and Khone Shmeruk, eds. 1987. *Penguin Book of Modern Yiddish Verse*. New York: Viking.

Hyman, Stanley Edgar. 1956. Identities of Isaac Babel. *Hudson Review* 8(4):620–27.

Iampol'skii, Boris. 1964. Povesti. Moscow: Sovetskii pisatel'.

Iavorskoi, A. L. 2004. Pis'ma Semena Gekhta v fondakh OLM. In *Dom kniaznia Gagarina: Sbornik nauchnykh statei i publikatsii*, edited by O. L. Muzei. Odessa: ZAO Plaske.

Idel, Moshe. 1990. *Golem: Jewish Magical and Mystical Traditions on the Artificial Anthropoid*, edited by M. Fishbane, R. Goldenberg, and A. Green. Albany: State University of New York Press.

Ionov, P. 1926. I. Babel'. Konarmiia. *Pravda*, June 27.

Iur'ev, Oleg. 1990. Miriam. In *Vosem' nekhoroshikh p'es*, edited by Z. K. Abdullaeva and A. D. Mikhaleva. Moscow: V/O Soiuzteatr STD SSSR.

———. 1991. Otsutstvennoe mesto. *Strana i mir* 4(64):131–36.

———. 2000. *Poluostrov zhidtiatin*. Moscow and Jerusalem: Gesharim.

Ivanov, Vladislav. 2007. *Goset: Politika i iskusstvo, 1919–1928*. Moscow: GITIS.

Ivanova, Evgeniia, ed. 2004. *Chukovskii i Zhabotinskii: Istoriia vzaimootnoshenii v tekstakh i kommentariiakh*. Moscow: Mosty kul'tury.

Ivanova, Natal'ia. 1990. Farewell to Utopia, or, a Subject for an Unwritten Novel. *Literaturnaia gazeta*, July 18, p. 4.

———. 1998. Afterward. *Russian Social Science Review* 39(4):75–97.

Jakobson, Roman. 1987. *Language in Literature*, edited by K. Pomorska and S. Rudy. Cambridge, MA: Harvard University Press.

Kabakov, Ilya. 1996. *The Garbage Man*. Oslo: National Museum of Contemporary Art.

Kabakov, Ilya/Emilia. 2005. *An Alternative History of Art: Rosenthal, Kabakov, Spivak*. Bielefeld: Kerber.

Kaganovsky, Lilya. 2008. *How the Soviet Man Was Unmade: Cultural Fantasy and Male Subjectivity Under Stalin*. Pittsburgh, PA: University of Pittsburgh Press.

Kalinovskaia, Dina. 1980. "O Subbota!" *Druzhba narodov* 8: 22–105.

———. 1985. "Risunok na dne." In *God za godom*, edited by A. Tverskoi. Moscow: Sovetskii pisatel', 49–75.

Kanovich, Grigorii. 1974. *Ptitsy nad kladbishchem*. Vilnius: Vaga.

———. 1977. *Blagoslovi i list'ia i ogon'*. Vilnius: Vaga.

———. 2007. *Park zabytykh evreev*. Available from http://www.lib.ru/NEWPROZA/KANOVICH/ (accessed June 3, 2007).

Karabchievskii, Iurii. 1991. *Toska po domu*. Moscow: S. P. Slovo.

Katsis, Leonid. 2001. Evreiskaia entsiklopediia—organ antisemitskoi mysli? *Ex libirs* 25:1–3.

———. 2002. *Osip Mandel'shtam: Muskus iudeistva*. Moscow and Jerusalem: Gesharim.

———. 2008. Il'ia Kabakov kak al'ternativa aktual'noi istorii. *Lekhaim*. Available from http://www.lechaim.ru/ARHIV/200/aktual.htm.

Katsis, Leonid, M. Kaspina, and David Fishman, eds. 2009. *Idish: Iazyk i kul'tura v sovetskom soiuze/Yidish: Shprakh un kultur in Sovetn-Farband*. Moscow: Rossiiskii gosudarstvennyi gumanitarnyi universitet.

Katz, Dovid. 2007. *Words on Fire: The Unfinished Story of Yiddish*. New York: Basic Books.

Kaverin, Veniamin. 1926. *Konets khazy: Povesti*. Leningrad: Zhizn' iskusstva.

Kazakevich, Emmanuel. 1941. *Sholem un Khave: Roman in ferzn*, edited by A. Kushnirov. Moscow: Der emes.

———. 1954. *Grine shotns*. Warsaw: Yidish bukh.

———. 1984. Zvezda. In *Voennye povesti*, edited by M. P. Shevchenko. Moscow: Sovetskaia rossiia.

———. 1990. *Slushaia vremia: Dnevniki, zapisnye knizhki, pis'ma*. Moscow: Sovetskii pisatel'.

Kazovsky, Hillel. 2003. *The Artists of the Kultur-Lige*. Jerusalem: Gesharim.

———, ed. 2007. *Kultur-Lige: Artistic Avant-Garde of the 1910s and the 1920s*. Kiev: Dukh i litera.

Kel'ner, Viktor. 2003. *Ocherki po istorii russko-evreiskogo knizhnogo dela vo vtoroi polovine XIX-nachale XX v*. St. Petersburg: Rossiiskaia national'naia biblioteka.

———. 2009. *K istorii nesbyvshikhsia nadezhd: Neopublikovannye knigi v fonde Davida Vygodskogo v otdele rukopisei Rossiiskoi natsional'noi biblioteki*. Peterburgskaia iudaika. Available from http://judaica.spb.ru/artcl/a12/vygotsky_r.shtml (accessed September 22, 2009).

Kharitonov, Mark. 1990. Literatura posle katastrofy. *Strana i mir* 3(57):148–52.

Khazan, Vladimir. 2001. *Osobennyi evreisko-russkii vozdukh: k problematike i poetike russko-evreiskogo literaturnogo dialoga v XX veke*. Moscow/Jerusalem: Mosty kul'tury/Gesharim.

———. 2006. *Mne nuzhno, khot' by na vremia, drugaia zhizn'.* L'chaim.ru. Available from http://www.lechaim.ru/ARHIV/174/hazan.htm#_ftn1 (accessed October 19, 2006).
Kheytov, L. 1935. Kempfn kegn altn shteyger: Mile-ritual. *Der apikoyres* 1:11–12.
Kipnis, Itsik. 1969. *Tsum lebn*. Moscow: Sovetskii pisatel'.
———. 1971. *Mayn shtetele Sloveshne*. 2 vols. Tel Aviv: I. L. Peretz.
———. 1977. *Di shtub un untervegns*. Tel Aviv: I. L. Peretz.
Kleinman, I. A. 1928. Evrei v noveishei russkoi literature. In *Evreiskii vestnik: nauchno-literaturnyi sbornk*, edited by S. M. Ginzburg. Leningrad.
Klier, J. 2002. No Prize for History: John Klier Reviews Aleksandr Solzhenitsyn's Recent Venture into the History of His Native Country. *History Today* 52(11):60.
Korman, E., ed. 1928. *Yidishe dikhterins: Antologye*. Chicago: L. M. Shteyn.
Kornblatt, Judith Deutsch. 1992. *The Cossack Hero in Russian Literature*. Madison: University of Wisconsin Press.
———. 2004. *Doubly Chosen: Jewish Identity, the Soviet Intelligentsia, and the Russian Orthodox Church*. Madison: University of Wisconsin Press.
Kramer, Michael. 2001. Race, Literary History, and the "Jewish" Question. *Prooftexts* 21(3):287–349.
Kristeva, Julia. 1982. *Powers of Horror: An Essay on Abjection*, translated by L. S. Roudiez. New York: Columbia University Press.
Kronfeld, Chana. 1996. *On the Margins of Modernism: Decentering Literary Dynamics*. Berkeley: University of California Press.
Krutikov, Mikhail. 1999. Soviet Yiddish Literature of the 1960s–1980s and Its Russian Translations. In *Yiddish in the Contemporary World: Papers of the First Mendel Friedman International Conference on Yiddish*, edited by G. Estraikh and M. Krutikov. Oxford: Legenda.
———. 2000. Berdichev in the Russian Jewish Literary Imagination: From Israel Aksenfeld to Friedrikh Gorenshtein. In *The Shtetl: Image and Reality*, edited by G. Estraikh and M. Krutikov. Oxford: Legenda.
———. 2001. Soviet Literary Theory in the Search for a Yiddish Canon: The Case of Moshe Litvakov. In *Yiddish and the Left*, edited by G. Estraikh and M. Krutikov. Oxford: Legenda.
———. 2003. Constructing Jewish Identity in Contemporary Russian Fiction. In *Jewish Life After the USSR*, edited by Z. Gitelman, M. Glants, and M. I. Goldman. Bloomington: Indiana University Press.
———. 2004. An Invisible Decade: The 1990s in the Russian-Jewish Imagination. *East European Jewish Affairs* 34.
———. 2007. Narrating the Revolution: From "Tsugvintn" (1922) to "Mides-hadin" (1929). In *David Bergelson: From Modernism to Socialist Realism*, edited by J. Sherman and G. Estraikh. Oxford: Legenda.

———. 2007. Rediscovering the Shtetl as a New Reality. In *The Shtetl: New Evaluations*, edited by S. T. Katz. New York: New York University Press.

———. 2010. *From Kabbalah to Class Struggle: Expressionism, Marxism, and Yiddish Literature in the Life and Work of Meir Viner*. Stanford, CA: Stanford University Press.

Kukulin, Il'ia. 2008. Reakstii dissotsiatsii: Legitimitsatsiia ul'trapravogo diskursa v sovremennoi rossiiskoi literature. In *Russkii natsionalizm: Sotsial'nyi i kul'turnyi kontekst*, edited by M. Lariuel'. Moscow: NLO.

Kuniaev, Sergei. 2008. "Klassika i my": tridtsat' let spustia. *Literaturnaia gazeta*, January 23, p. 6.

Kuniaev, Stanislav. 2007. "U menia svoia liniia fronta": Iz besedy s Iuriem Pavlovym. *Zavtra* 47(11):7.

Kuznetsov, Anatolii. 2001. *Babii iar*. Moscow: Zakharov.

Kvitko, Leyb. 1929. *Gerangl 1917–1929*. Kharkov: Tsentrfarlag-Kharkov.

L'vov, Aleksandr. 2008. Predislovie: Shtetl v XXI v. i etnografiia postsovetskogo evreistva. In *Shtetl XXI vek: Polevye issledovaniia*, edited by V. Dymshits, A. L'vov, and A. Sokolova. St. Petersburg: Evropeiskii universitet v Sankt-Peterburge.

LaCapra, Dominick. 1999. Trauma, Absence, Loss. *Critical Inquiry* 25(4/Summer):696–727.

Lahusen, Thomas, and Evgeny Dobrenko, eds. 1997. *Socialist Realism Without Shores*. Durham, NC: Duke University Press.

Landsberg, Alison. 1997. America, the Holocaust, and the Mass Culture of Memory: Toward a Radical Politics of Empathy. *New German Critique* 71(Spring–Summer):63–86.

Leftwich, Joseph, ed. 1961. *The Golden Peacock*. New York: Thomas Yoseloff.

Leighton, Lauren. 1991. *Two Worlds, One Art: Literary Translation in Russia and America*. DeKalb: Northern Illinois University Press.

Lenchovskii, R. I. 1999. Interview with Bella Kipnis. Kiev: Institut iudaiki, Proekt evreiskie sud'by Ukraini XX veka.

Lesovaia, Inna. 2003. *Dama sdavala v bagazh*. Kiev: Dukh i litera.

———. 2008. *Bessarabskii romans*. Kiev: Dukh i litera.

Lévi-Strauss, Claude. 1966. *The Savage Mind*. Chicago: University of Chicago Press.

Levinas, Emmanuel. 1988. Useless Suffering. In *The Provocation of Levinas: Rethinking the Other*, edited by R. Bernasconi and D. Wood. New York: Routledge.

Levinson, Marjorie. 2007. What Is New Formalism? *PMLA* (Publications of the Modern Language Association of America) 122(2):558–69.

Levman, S. 1936. Epos grazhdanskoi voiny. *Literaturnaia gazeta*, no. 59, p. 4.

Levy, Neil, and Michael Rothberg. 2003. *The Holocaust: Theoretical Readings*. New Brunswick, NJ: Rutgers University Press.

Leytes, A. 1934. A gesheft-firer—a shoykhet-moyel. *Der apikoyres* 3:17.

Lezhnev, Abram. 1929. *Literaturnye budni*. Moscow: Federatsiia.

Libedinskii, Iurii. 1958. *Izbrannye proizvedeniia*, vol. 1 (2 vols.). Moscow: Gosudarstvennoe izdatel'stvo khudozhestvennoi literatury.
Liberman, Ia. L. 1996. *Isaak Babel' glazami evreia*. Ekaterinburg: Ural'skii gosudarstvennyi universitet.
Lipkin, Semen. 1997. *Kvadriga*. Moscow: Knizhnyi sad.
———. 1998. Stikhi iz naidennogo bloknota. *Druzhba narodov* 9:3–7.
———. 2005. Tri zemnykh pory. *Znamia* 2:127–41.
———. 2008. *Ochevidets*. Moscow: Vremia.
Lipovetsky, Mark. 2001. Russian Literary Postmodernism in the 1990s. *Slavonic and East European Review* 79(1):31–50.
———. 2002. Strategies of Wastefulness, or the Metamorphoses of Chernukha. *Russian Studies in Literature* 38(2):58–84.
———. 2008. *Paralogii: Transformatsii (post)modernistskogo diskursa v russkoi kul'ture 1920–2000 godov*. Moscow: NLO.
Liptzin, Sol. 1985. *A History of Yiddish Literature*. Middle Village, NY: Jonathan David.
Litvakov, Moshe. 1929. Afn literarishn avnt vegn Markishes tsvey naye verk. *Der emes*, May 30.
———. 1931. *Af tsvey frontn*. Moscow: Tsentraler felker-farlag fun P. S. S. R.
Liubarskii, K. 1991. Avgustovskaia revoliutsiia. *Strana i mir* 5(65):1–89.
Lohr, Eric. 2001. The Russian Army and the Jews: Mass Deportation, Hostages, and Violence During World War I. *Russian Review* 60(3):404–19.
Lungina, Lilianna. 2009. *Podstrochnik*. Moscow: Astrel'.
Lunts, Lev. 1981. *Rodina i drugie proizvedeniia*, edited by M. Vainshtein. Jerusalem: Pamiat'.
Luppol, I. K., M. M. Rozental', and S. M. Tretiakov. 1934. *Pervyi vsesoiuznyi s"ezd sovetskikh pisatelei: stenograficheskii otchet*. Moscow: Sovetskii pisatel'.
Lyotard, Jean-François. 1988. *The Differend: Phrases in Dispute*, translated by G. Van Den Abbeele. Minneapolis: University of Minnesota Press.
Lyubomirski, Yeshue. 1976. *Af di lebnsvegn*. Moscow: Sovetskii pisatel'.
Maguire, Robert A., ed. 1987. *Russian Literature of the Twenties: An Anthology*. Ann Arbor, MI: Ardis.
Mahoney, D. J. 2002. Solzhenitsyn on Russia's Jewish Question. *Society* 40(1):104.
Maletskii, Iurii. 2007. Roman Ulitskoi kak zerkalo russkoi intelligentsii. *Novyi mir* 5:173–90.
Mandelshtam, Osip. 1973. *Complete Poetry of Osip Emelevich Mandelstam*, translated by B. Raffel and A. Burago. Albany: State University of New York Press.
———. 1979. *The Complete Critical Prose and Letters*, translated by J. G. Harris and C. Link. Ann Arbor, MI: Ardis.
———. 1990. *Sochineniia v dvukh tomakh*. 2 vols. Moscow: Khudozhestvennaia literatura.
———. 1991. *Sobranie sochinenii v chetyrekh tomakh*. Moscow: Terra.

Markish, Perets. 1921. *Di kupe*. Warsaw: Kultur-Lige.
———. 1929. *Brider*. Kiev: Kultur-lige.
———. 1934. *Eyns af eyns*. Kharkov and Kiev: Melukhe farlag far di natsionale minderhaytn in usr'r.
———. 1935. *Brat'ia*, translated by D. Brodskii, V. Bugaevskii, S. Lipkin, M. Petrovykh, A. Tarkovskii, and A. Shirt. Moscow: Khudozhestvennaia literatura.
———. 1938. *Mishpokhe Ovadis, Sovetish literarisher almanakh 6*. Moscow: Der emes.
———. 1938. *Sem'ia Ovadis*, translated by M. A. Shambadal. Moscow and Leningrad: Iskusstvo.
———. 1943a. *Far folk un heymland*. Moscow: Der emes.
———. 1943b. *Heymland: Literarishe zamlbukh*. Moscow: Der emes.
———. 1946. Gur arye. *Yidishe kultur* 6:26–29.
———. 1948. *Milkhome*. Moscow: Der emes.
———. 1956. *Milkhome*. 2 vols. New York: Yikuf.
———. 1969. *Stikhotvoreniia i poemy*, edited by V. N. Orlov. 2nd ed., *Biblioteka poeta*. Leningrad: Sovetskii pisatel'.
———. 1987. Say di. In *A Shpigl af a shteyn*, edited by K. Shmeruk. Jerusalem: Magness Press.
———. 1987. The Mound. In *The Penguin Book of Modern Yiddish Verse*, edited by I. Howe, R. R. Wisse, and K. Shmeruk. New York: Viking.
Markish, Shimon. 1985. Primer Vasilia Grossmana. In *Na evreiskie temy*. Jerusalem: Aliia.
———. 1991. The Role of Officially Published Russian Literature in the Reawakening of Jewish National Consciousness (1953–1970). In *Jewish Culture and Identity in the Soviet Union*, edited by Y. Ro'i and A. Beker. New York: New York University Press, 208–31.
———. 1994. Babel' i oni (Glazami otshchepentsa). *Znamia* 7:165–70.
Martin, Terry. 2001. *The Affirmative Action Empire: Nations and Nationalism in the Soviet Union, 1923–1939*. Ithaca, NY: Cornell University Press.
Martynova, Ol'ga. 2009. *Zagrobnaia pobeda sotsrealizma*. Available from http://www.openspace.ru/literature/events/details/12295/ (accessed October 19, 2009).
May, Herbert G., and Bruce M. Metzger, eds. 1973. *The Holy Bible: Revised Standard Version*. New York: Oxford University Press.
Mayzel, Nakhman. 1956. Tsum leyener. In *Milkhome*. New York: Yikuf.
———. 1960. Itsik Kipnis. In *Untervegns un andere dertseylungen*. New York: Yikuf.
Meilakhs, Aleksandr. 2005. *Krasnyi sion*. St. Petersburg: Limbus Press.
Melikhov, Aleksandr. 1994. Izgnanie iz Edema: Ispoved' evreia. *Novyi mir* 1:3–104.
Merridale, Catherine. 2006. *Ivan's War: Life and Death in the Red Army, 1939–1945*. 1st ed. New York: Metropolitan Books.
Miliakova, L. B., ed. 2007. *Kniga pogromov: Pogromy na Ukraine, v Belorussii, i evropeiskoi chasti Rossii v period grazhdanskoi voiny 1918–1922 gg*. Moscow: Rosspen.

Miron, Dan. 1995. The Literary Image of the Shtetl. *Jewish Social Studies: History, Culture, Society* 1(3):1–43.
———. 1996. *A Traveler Disguised: The Rise of Modern Yiddish Fiction in the Nineteenth Century*. Syracuse, NY: Syracuse University Press.
———. 2000. *The Image of the Shtetl and Other Studies of Modern Jewish Literary Imagination*. Syracuse, NY: Syracuse University Press.
———. 2010. *From Continuity to Contiguity: Toward a New Jewish Literary Thinking*. Stanford, CA: Stanford University Press.
Misiano, Viktor. 1995. Choosing to Be Jewish. In *Russian Jewish Artists in a Century of Change 1890–1990*, edited by S. T. Goodman. New York: Prestel.
Mitrokhin, Nikolai. 2006. Sanitary sovetskoi literatury. *Novoe literaturnoe obozrenie* 6:282–90.
Molotoff Accuses Nazis of Atrocities; Note Detailing "Crimes" Handed to All Foreign Diplomats. 1942. *New York Times*, January 7, p. 8.
Mondry, Henrietta. 2009. *Exemplary Bodies: Constructing the Jew in Russian Culture Since the 1880s*. Boston: Academic Studies Press.
Moran, J. 2004. History, Memory, and the Everyday. *Rethinking History* 8:51–68.
Morson, Gary Saul, and Caryl Emerson. 1990. *Mikhail Bakhtin: Creation of a Prosaics*. Stanford, CA: Stanford University Press.
Moskvin, V. A. 2001. V istoricheskom prostranstve khvatit mesto dlia vsekh. *Moskva* 9:198–231.
Moss, Kenneth B. 2009. *Jewish Renaissance in the Russian Revolution*. Cambridge, MA: Harvard University Press.
Mosse, George. 1992. Max Nordau, Liberalism and the Jew. *Journal of Contemporary History* 27(4):565–81.
Murav, Harriet. 1995. Engendering the Russian Body Politic. *Genders* 22:32–53.
———. 1998. *Russia's Legal Fictions*. Ann Arbor: University of Michigan Press.
———. 2000. The Beilis Ritual Murder Trial and the Culture of Apocalypse. *Cardozo Studies in Law and Literature* 12(2):243–63.
———. 2003. *Identity Theft: The Jew in Imperial Russia and the Case of Avraam Uri Kovner*. Stanford, CA: Stanford University Press.
———. 2008. Real Men and Phantom Stories: Violence and Prosthesis in Soviet War Literature. *Ab Imperio* 4:521–37.
Nadtochii, Eduard. 1989. Druk, tovarishch, i Bart (neskol'ko predvaritel'nykh zamechanii k voprosheniiu o meste sotsialisticheskogo realizma v iskusstve XX veka). *Daugava* (8):114–20.
Nakhimovsky, Alice Stone. 1992. *Russian-Jewish Literature and Identity: Jabotinsky, Babel, Grossman, Galich, Roziner, Markish*. Baltimore: Johns Hopkins University Press.
Nedogonov, Aleksei. 1977. *Izbrannoe*. Moscow: Khudozhestvennaia literatura.
Nekrasov, Viktor. 1954. "V rodnom gorode." *Novyi mir* 10: 1–65, 11:97–178.
Nemzer, Andrei. 1998. *Literaturnoe segodnia*. Moscow: Novoe literaturnoe obozrenie.

———. 2008. Odin iz nemnogikh schastlivtsev. In *Semen Lipkin: Ochevidets*, edited by T. I. Timiakova. Moscow: Vremia.

Niger, Shmuel. 1958. *Yidishe shrayber in Sovet-Rusland*. New York: S. Niger Book Committee of the Congress for Jewish Culture.

Niger, Shmuel, and Jacob Shatzsky, eds. 1956. *Leksikon fun der nayer yidisher literatur*, vol. 1 (2 vols.). New York: Congress for Jewish Culture.

Niranjana, Tejaswini. 1992. *Siting Translation. History, Post-Structuralism, and the Colonial Context*. Berkeley: University of California Press.

Notovitsh, Moshe. 1961. Tsu naye yidish-kinstlerishe haykhn. *Sovetish heymland* (2).

Novick, Peter. 1999. *The Holocaust in American Life*. New York: Houghton Mifflin.

Okrutny, Y. 1947. Di yidishe novele lebt iber a krizis. *Yidishe shriftn* 10:14.

Oushakine, Serguei. 2007. "We're nostalgic but we're not crazy": Retrofitting the Past in Russia. *Russian Review* 66(July):451–82.

Palmer, Scott. 2009. How Memory Was Made: The Construction of the Memorial to the Heroes of the Battle of Stalingrad. *Russian Review* 68(July):373–407.

Papernyi, Vladimir. 2006. *Kul'tura dva*. Moscow: Novoe literaturnoe obozrenie.

Parnell, Christina. 2008. Images of Jewish Identities in Lithuanian Literature of the Twentieth Century: Grigorii Kanovich and Markas Zingeris. *East European Jewish Affairs* 38(2):169–83.

Paustovskii, Konstantin. 1939. Pouchitel'naia istoriia. *Literaturnaia gazeta*, June 26, p. 4.

Pavlov, Iurii. 2007. "Klassika i my": Tridtsat' let spustia. *Nash sovremennik* 12:270–78.

Peredovaia. 1939. *Druzhba narodov: Al'manakh khudozhestvennoi literatury narodov SSSR* 1:5–10.

Peretz, I. L. 2002. *The I. L. Peretz Reader*. New Haven, CT: Yale University Press.

Perova, Natasha, and Joanne Turnbull, eds. 2005. *Captives: Contemporary Russian Stories*. Vol. 38, *Glas New Russian Writing*. Moscow: GLAS.

Petrovsky-Shtern, Yohanan. 2006. An-sky and the Paradigm of No Return. In *The Worlds of S. An-sky: A Russian-Jewish Intellectual at the Turn of the Century*, edited by G. Safran and S. Zipperstein. Stanford, CA: Stanford University Press.

Pinkus, Benjamin. 1988. *The Jews of the Soviet Union: The History of a National Minority*. Cambridge: Cambridge University Press.

Pohl, J. Otto. 1999. *Ethnic Cleansing in the USSR, 1937–1949*. Westport, CT: Greenwood Press.

Proffer, Carl R., Ellendea Proffer, Ronald Meyer, and Mary Ann Szporluk, eds. 1987. *Russian Literature of the Twenties*, edited by R. A. Maguire. Ann Arbor, MI: Ardis.

Prusin, Alexander. 2003. "Fascist Criminals to the Gallows!": The Holocaust and Soviet War Crimes Trials, December 1945–February 1946. *Holocaust and Genocide Studies* 17(1):1–30.

Pushkin, Alexander. 1963. *Eugene Onegin*, translated by W. Arndt. New York: E. P. Dutton.
Raskin, Arn. 1976. "Di hayntsaytike yidishe sovetishe novele." *Sovetish heymland* 8:95–104.
Rebel', Galina. 2007. Liudmila Ulitskaia: Evreiskii vopros? *Druzhba narodov* 7:207–11.
Redlich, Shimon, ed. 1995. *War, Holocaust and Stalinism: A Documented Study of the Jewish Anti-Fascist Committee in the USSR*, edited by H. Shukman. Vol. 1, New History of Russia. Oxford: Harwood Academic.
Rendall, Steven. 1997. The Translator's Task: Walter Benjamin. *Traduction, terminologie, redaction: etudes sur le texte es ses transformations* 10(2):151–205.
Reznik, O. 1945. Khudozhestvennaia publitsistika v gody voiny. *Novyi mir* 11/12:286–306.
Robertson, Ritchie. 1985. *Kafka: Judaism, Politics, and Literature*. Oxford: Clarendon Press.
Robin, Régine. 1992. *Socialist Realism: An Impossible Aesthetic*, translated by C. Porter. Stanford, CA: Stanford University Press.
Ronell, Anna. 2008. Some Thoughts on Russian-Language Israeli Fiction: Introducing Dina Rubina. *Prooftexts* 28(2):197–231.
Rosenshield, Gary. 1996. Socialist Realism and the Holocaust: Jewish Life and Death in Anatoly Rybakov's Heavy Sand. *PMLA* 111(2):240–55.
Roskies, David. 1984. *Against the Apocalypse: Responses to Catastrophe in Modern Jewish Culture*. Cambridge, MA: Harvard University Press.
——. 1999. *The Jewish Search for a Usable Past*. Bloomington: Indiana University Press.
Rozanov, Vasilii. 1932. *Oboniatel'noe i osiazatel'noe otnoshenie evreev k krovi*. Stockholm.
Roziner, Felix. 1981. *Nekto Finkel'maier*. London: Overseas Publication Interchange.
Rubenstein, Joshua. 1996. *Tangled Loyalties: The Life and Times of Ilya Ehrenburg*. Tuscaloosa: University of Alabama Press.
Rubenstein, Joshua, and Ilya Altman, eds. 2008. *The Unknown Black Book: The Holocaust in the German-Occupied Soviet Territories*. Bloomington: University of Indiana Press.
Rubenstein, Joshua, and Vladimir Naumov, eds. 2001. *Stalin's Secret Pogrom: The Postwar Inquisition of the Jewish Anti-Fascist Committee*. New Haven, CT: Yale University Press.
Rubin, Rivke. 1948. "A noenter mentsh." *Heymland* 3:67–74.
——. 1982. *Aza min tog: Roman, dertseylungen, etiudn*. Moscow: Sovetskii pisatel'.
Rubina, Dina. 1990. *Dvoinaia familiia: povesti, rasskazy*. Moscow: Sovetskii pisatel'.
——. 2001. *Vysokaia voda venetsiantsev: povesti, rasskazy*. Moscow: Vagrius.
Rudnitskii, K. L., ed. 1981. *Mikhoels: Stat'i, besedy, rechi*. Moscow: Iskusstvo.
Safran, Gabriella. 2000. *Rewriting the Jew: Assimilation Narratives in the Russian Empire*. Stanford, CA: Stanford University Press.

———. 2002. Isaak Babel's El'ia Isaakovich as a New Jewish Type. *Slavic Review* 61(2):253–72.

———. 2010. *Wandering Soul: The Dybbuk's Creator, S. An-sky*. Cambridge, MA: Harvard University Press.

Safran, Gabriella, and Steven Zipperstein, eds. 2006. *The Worlds of S. An-sky: A Russian Jewish Intellectual at the Turn of the Century*. Stanford, CA: Stanford University Press.

Santner, Eric L. 1992. History Beyond the Pleasure Principle: Some Thoughts on the Representation of Trauma. In *Probing the Limits of Representation: Nazism and the Final Solution*, edited by S. Friedlander. Cambridge, MA: Harvard University Press.

Sarnov, Benedikt. 2004. *Sluchai Erenburga*. Moscow: Tekst.

Sartre, Jean-Paul. 1948. *Anti-Semite and Jew*, translated by G. J. Becker. New York: Schocken Books.

Scarry, Elaine. 1985. *The Body in Pain: The Making and Unmaking of the World*. New York: Oxford University Press.

Schur, Anna. 2007. Shades of Justice: The Trial of Sholom Schwartzbard and Dovid Bergelson's Among Refugees. *Law and Literature* 19(1):15–43.

Schwartz, Yigal. 2001. *Aharon Appelfeld: From Individual Lament to Tribal Eternity*, translated by J. M. Green. Hanover (NH) and London: University Press of New England.

Scribner, Charity. 2003. *Requiem for Communism*. Cambridge, MA: MIT Press.

Seidman, Naomi. 2006. *Faithful Renderings: Jewish-Christian Difference and the Politics of Translation*. Chicago: University of Chicago Press.

Sel'vinskii, Il'ia. 1947. *Krym, Kavkaz, Kuban'*. Moscow: Sovetskii pisatel'.

———. 1971. *Sobranie sochinenii v shesti tomakh*. 6 vols. Moscow: Khudozhestvennaia literatura.

———. 1985. *Ia eto videl: Stikhotvoreniia i poemy*. Moscow: Sovetskaia Rossiia.

Sherman, Joseph. 2007. "Jewish Nationalism" in Bergelson's Last Book. In *David Bergelson: From Modernism to Socialist Realism*, edited by J. Sherman and G. Estraikh. Oxford: Legenda.

Sherman, Joseph, and Gennady Estraikh, eds. 2007. *David Bergelson: From Modernism to Socialist Realism*. Oxford: Legenda.

Shmeruk, Khone, ed. 1964. *A shpigl af a shteyn*. Jerusalem: Magnes Press.

———. 1991. Twenty-five Years of Sovetish heymland: Impressions and Criticism. In *Jewish Culture and Identity in the Soviet Union*, edited by Y. Ro'i and A. Beker. New York: New York University Press.

Shneer, David. 2004. *Yiddish and the Creation of Soviet Jewish Culture*. Cambridge: Cambridge University Press.

———. 2007. From Mourning to Vengeance: Bergelson's Holocaust Journalism (1941–1945). In *David Bergelson: From Modernism to Socialist Realism*, edited by J. Sherman and G. Estraikh. Oxford: Legenda.

———. 2010. Picturing Grief: Soviet Holocaust Photography at the Intersection of History and Memory. *American Historical Review* 115(1):28–52.

———. 2011. *Through Soviet Jewish Eyes: Photography, War, and the Holocaust*. New Brunswick, NJ: Rutgers University Press.

Shoshin, Vladislav. 1993. David Isaakovich Vygodskii. In *Raspiatye: Pisateli-Zhertvy politicheskikh repressii*, edited by Z. Dicharov. St. Petersburg: Istoriko-memorial'naia komissiia soiuz pisatelei Sankt-Peterburga.

Shraybman, Yekhiel. 2005. "Der groyser shrayber un denker Moshe Altman." *Forverts*, December 16, p. 11.

Shrayer, Maxim. 2007a. Ludmila Ulitskaya. In *An Anthology of Jewish-Russian Literature*, edited by M. Shrayer. Armonk, NY: M. E. Sharpe.

———, ed. 2007b. *An Anthology of Jewish-Russian Literature: Two Centuries of Dual Identity in Prose and Poetry*. 2 vols. Armonk, NY: M. E. Sharpe.

Shreiber, Maeera. 1998. The End of Exile: Jewish Identity and Its Diasporic Poetics. *PMLA* 113(2):273–87.

Shternberg, Yakov. 1987. *Vegn literatur un teater*. Tel-Aviv: H. Leyvik.

Shternshis, Anna. 2006. *Soviet and Kosher: Jewish Popular Culture in the Soviet Union, 1923–1939*. Bloomington: University of Indiana Press.

Shubinskii, Valerii. 1994. Sobytiia kholokosta v materialakh Gaisinskogo gorodskogo arkhiva. In *Trudy po iudaike: istoriia evreev na Ukraine i v Belorussii*, edited by V. M. Lukin, B. N. Khaimovich, and V. A. Dymshits. St. Petersburg: Peterburgskii evreiskii universitet.

———. 2005. Messianskii virus. Fridrikh Gorenshtein, Rossiia i evreistvo: Popytka vvedeniia v temu. In *Khronika evreiskikh somnenii*, edited by A. Frenkel'. St. Petersburg: Narod knigi v mire knig.

Shul'man, E. 2006. "Opasnost', ili pouchitel'naia istoriia." *Voprosy literatury* 2.

Shveitser, A. 1987. Sovetskaia teoriia perevoda za 70 let. *Voprosy iazykoznaniia* 36(5):9–17.

Sicher, Efraim. 1985. *Style and Structure in the Prose of Isaak Babel'*. Columbus, OH: Slavica.

———. 1995. *Jews in Russian Literature After the October Revolution: Writers and Artists Between Hope and Apostasy*. Cambridge: Cambridge University Press.

———. 2005. *The Holocaust Novel: Genres in Context*. New York: Routledge.

Silverman, Morris. 1984. *High Holiday Prayer Book*. New York: Prayer Book Press.

Simenenko, Aleksandr. 2001. Nashe interv'iu. Stanislav Kuniaev. Byt' russkoi literature. *Molodaia gvardiia* 3:171–74.

Simonov, Konstantin. 1954. "Novaia povest' Il'i Erenburga." *Literaturnaia gazeta* July 17, 20, pp. 2–3.

———. 1960. *Zhivye i mertvye*. Moscow: Sovetskii pisatel'.

Slezkine, Yuri. 1994. The USSR as a Communal Apartment, or How a Socialist State Promoted Ethnic Particularism. *Slavic Review* 53(2):414–52.

———. 2004. *The Jewish Century*. Princeton, NJ: Princeton University Press.

Slonim, Marc. 1949. Soviet Prose After the War. *Annals of the American Academy of Political and Social Science* 263:101–13.
Slotnick, Susan. 1978. The Novel Form in the Works of David Bergelson. Ph.D. diss., Columbia University.
Slutskii, Boris. 1969. *Sovremennye istorii*. Moscow: Molodaia gvardiia.
———. 1993. Ia osvobozhdal Ukrainu. In *Menora*, edited by A. Kolganova. Moscow and Jerusalem: Gesharim.
———. 1999. *Teper' Osventsim chasto snitsia mne*. St. Petersburg: Neva.
———. 2006a. Stikhi. Edited by M. Grinberg. *Slovo/Word* 50:93–97.
———. 2006b. *Zapiski o voine*. St. Petersburg: Logos.
Smith, Jeremy. 2006. Non-Russians in the Soviet Union and After. In *The Cambridge History of Russia*, edited by R. Suny. Cambridge: Cambridge University Press.
Smith, Michael G. 1998. *Language and Power in the Creation of the USSR, 1917–1953*. Berlin: Mouton de Gruyter.
Snyder, Timothy. 2009. Holocaust: The Ignored Reality. *New York Review of Books* (12). Availabe from http://www.nybooks.com/articles/22875.
Sokolova, Alla. 2000. The Podolian Shtetl as Architectural Phenomenon. In *The Shtetl: Image and Reality*, edited by G. Estraikh and M. Krutikov. Oxford: Legenda.
Sollors, Werner. 1995. Ethnicity. In *Critical Terms for Literary Study*, edited by F. Lentricchia and T. McLaughlin. Chicago: University of Chicago Press.
Solzhenitsyn, Aleksandr Isaevich. 2001. *Dvesti let vmeste (1795–1995)*. 2 vols. *Issledovaniia noveishei russkoi istorii*. Moscow: Russkii put'.
Spieker, Sven. 1996. *Figures of Memory and Forgetting in Andrej Bitov's Prose: Postmodernism and the Quest for History*. Frankfurt am Main: Peter Lang.
Spivak, Gayatri 1993. *Outside in the Teaching Machine*. New York: Routledge.
Steinberg, Mark. 2002. *Proletarian Imagination: Self, Modernity, and the Sacred in Russia, 1910–1925*. Ithaca (NY) and London: Cornell University Press.
Stewart, Susan. 1993. *On Longing: Narratives of the Miniature, the Gigantic, the Souvenir, the Collection*. Durham, NC: Duke University Press.
Storr, Robert. 2005. Blinded by the Light. In *An Alternative History of Art: Rosenthal, Kabakov, Spivak*, edited by I. E. Kabakov. Bielefeld: Kerber.
Struk, Janina. 2004. *Photographing the Holocaust*. London: I. B. Tauris.
Tarkovskii, Arsenii. 1983. *Stikhi raznykh let*. Moscow: Sovremennik.
Tec, Nechama. 1990. *In the Lion's Den: The Life of Oswald Rufeisen*. New York: Oxford University Press.
Terpitz, Olaf. 2008. *Die Ruckkehr des Stetl: Russisch-judische Literatur der spaten Sowjetzeit, Schriften des Simon-Dubnow-Instituts Herausgegeben von Dan Diner*. Gottingen: Vandenhoeck & Ruprecht.
Tertz, Abram [Andrei Sinyavsky]. 1960. *The Trial Begins, and On Socialist Realism*, translated by G. Dennis. Berkeley: University of California Press.

Tolts, Mark. 2007. Post-Soviet Jewish Demography, 1989–2004. In *Revolution, Repression, and Revival: The Soviet Jewish Experience*, edited by Z. Gitelman and Y. Ro'i. Lanham, MD: Rowman & Littlefield.
Tregub, S., and I. Bachelis. 1944. Schast'e Korchagina. Znamia 4:294–96.
Tsu di yidn fun gor der velt. 1942. *Eynikayt*, June 7, pp. 1–2.
Tsu Itsik Kipnises 70–yorikn iubiley. 1967. *Sovetish heymland* (3):73.
Tumarkin, Nina. 1994. *The Living and the Dead: The Rise and Fall of the Cult of World War II in Russia*. New York: Basic Books.
Ulitskaia, Liudmila. 2008. *Daniel' Shtain, perevodchik*. Moscow: Eksmo.
Vaksberg, Arkady. 1994. *Stalin Against the Jews*, translated by A. W. Bouis. New York: Knopf.
Van De Stadt, Janneke. 2007. A Question of Place: Situating Old Shloime in Isaac Babel's Oeuvre. *Russian Review* 66:36–54.
Vasil'ev, Boris 1992. Rossiia: Chetyre knigi bytiia. *Oktiabr'* 1:4–18.
Veidlinger, Jeffrey. 2000. *The Moscow State Yiddish Theater: Jewish Culture on the Soviet Stage*. Bloomington: Indiana University Press.
———. 2007. "Du lebst, mayn folk": Bergelson's Play Prints Ruveni in Historical Context (1944–1947). In *David Bergelson: From Modernism to Socialist Realism*, edited by J. Sherman and G. Estraikh. London: Legenda.
Venuti, Lawrence. 1998. *The Scandals of Translation: Towards an Ethics of Difference*. London and New York: Routledge.
Vinokur, Val. 2008. *The Trace of Judaism: Dostoevsky, Babel, Mandelshtam, Levinas*. Evanston, IL: Northwestern University Press.
Voronskii, Aleksandr. 1928. *Literaturnye portrety*. Moscow: Federatsiia.
Voskresenskaia, Ts. 1984. Na voine: iz dnevnikov i pisem rodnym 1941–1945gg. *Novyi mir* 12:163–75.
Vygodskii, David. 1920s. Novaia evreiskaia poeziia. In *D. I. Vygodskii*. St. Petersburg: Russian National Library.
———. 1934. Natsional'naia poeziia v russkikh perevodakh. *Zvezda* 11:162–69.
———. 1935. Privet evreiskim poetam. In *D. I. Vygodskii*. St. Petersburg: Russian National Library.
Wachtel, Andrew. 1999. Translation, Imperialism, and National Self-Definition in Russia. *Public Culture* 11(1):49–73.
Wallach, Amei. 1996. *Ilya Kabakov: The Man Who Never Threw Anything Away*. New York: Harry N. Abrams.
Walters, Ben. 2009. Debating Inglourious Basterds. *Film Quarterly* 63(2):19–21.
Weinberg, Robert. 1998. *Stalin's Forgotten Zion: Birobidzhan and the Making of a Soviet Jewish Homeland*. Berkeley: University of California Press.
Weiner, Amir. 1999. Nature, Nurture, and Memory in a Socialist Utopia: Delineating the Soviet Socio-Ethnic Body in the Age of Socialism. *American Historical Review* 104(4):1114–55.

———. 2001. *Making Sense of War: The Second World War and the Fate of the Bolshevik Revolution*. Princeton, NJ: Princeton University Press.

White, Hayden. 1992. Historical Emplotment and the Problem of Truth. In *Probing the Limits of Representation: Nazism and the Final Solution*, edited by S. Friedlander. Cambridge, MA: Harvard Univerity Press.

Widdis, Emma. 2003. *Visions of a New Land: Soviet Film from the Revolution to the Second World War*. New Haven, CT: Yale University Press.

Wirth-Nesher, Hannah, ed. 1994. *What Is Jewish Literature?* Philadelphia: Jewish Publication Society.

Wisse, Ruth R. 2000. *The Modern Jewish Canon: A Journey Through Language and Culture*. New York: Free Press.

Wolitz, Seth. 1995. Experiencing Visibility and Phantom Existence. In *Russian Jewish Artists in a Century of Change 1890–1990*, edited by S. T. Goodman. New York: Prestel.

Yerushalmi, Yosef Hayim. 1989. *Zakhor: Jewish History and Jewish Memory*. New York: Schocken Books.

YIVO Institute for Jewish Research. *YIVO Encyclopedia of Jews in Eastern Europe*. Available at http://www.yivoencyclopedia.org.

Young, James. 1988. *Writing and Rewriting the Holocaust*. Bloomington: Indiana University Press.

Youngblood, Denise J. 2001. A War Remembered: Soviet Films of the Great Patriotic War. *American Historical Review* 106(3):839–56.

Yurchak, Alexei. 2006. *Everything Was Forever, Until It Was No More: The Last Soviet Generation*, edited by P. Rabinow. Princeton, NJ: Princeton University Press.

Zabare, Natan. 1965. Haynt vert geboyrn a velt. *Sovetish heymland* 3:3–88.

———. 1968. *Segodnia rozhdaetsia mir*, translated by A. Semenovker. Moscow: Sovetskii pisatel'.

Zakharenko, N. G., and I. V. Khanukaeva, eds. 2000. *Russkie pisateli poety (Sovetskii period) Bibliograficheskii ukazatel'*, edited by I. V. Aleksakhina and D. A. Berman. 26 vols. Vol. 23, *Russkie pisateli poety (Sovetskii period) Bibliograficheskii ukazatel'*. St. Petersburg: Rossiiskaia natsional'naia biblioteka.

Zel'tser, Arkadii. 2006. *Evrei sovetskoi provintsii: Vitebsk i mestechki 1917–1941*. Moscow: Rosspen.

"Zey hobn opgegebn dos lebn farn heymland." 1965. *Sovetish heymland* 5(May):3.

Zhdanov, N. 1948. Buria—roman Il'i Erenburga. Izvestiia, p. 3.

Zil'pert, Boris. 1928. Pis'ma iz mestechka. *Tribuna* 11:9–12.

Zuskina-Perel'man, Alla. 2002. *Puteshestvie Veniamina*. Moscow: Gesharim.

Index

Abjection, 34, 49
Abraham, Nicholas, and Maria Torok, 25, 46, 230
Abramovitsh, Sh. Y. (Mendele Moyher Sforim), 6, 21, 254
Akhmatova, Anna, 15, 290, 294
Altman, Moshe, 5, 7, 9, 202, 207, 212, 224–26, 240–41, 244, 256, 261, 282. Works: "A mayse mit a nomen" (A story about a name), 226–27; "Bletlekh" (Pages), 227–30; "In the mirror's depths," 231; "Mayn tatn's nit opgeshikt kartl" (My father's unsent postcard), 231–32; *Medresh Pinkhes*, 225, 227; "Vos der zikorn farhit" (What memory keeps), 228–30
An-sky, S., 7, 66, 131
Arendt, Hannah, 186–87

Baal Shem Tov, 66, 92, 94, 95, 96, 269, 270, 271, 272
Babel, Isaac, 2, 3, 5, 9; approaches to, 42–43, 45; masculinity and, 48; violence in, 41. Works: "Berestechko," 42–43, 44, 47–48, 57; "Dvorets materinstva" (The palace of motherhood), 46–47; "Gedali," 45, 283; "Karl-Yankel," 16, 68, 92–95; "My First Goose," 50; *Red Cavalry*, 16, 29,33, 46, 64; "The Cemetary at Kozin," 43–44; "The Road to Brody," 46, 221–22
Babi Yar, 111, 121, 124, 150, 168
Bagritskii, Eduard, 23, 49
Bakhtin, Mikhail, 11; on carnival body, 24–25, 35, 48, 263, 281; hybridity, 287, 291; language in novels, 233

Beilis, Mendel, 21, 92, 93–95
Benjamin, Walter: and angel of history, 1, 4, 18, 58–59, 329; aura, 235; time in, 62; messianism, 63; on translation, 192–93, 300
Bergelson, David, 1, 2, 3, 5, 9, 52; time in, 58–59, 254. Works: "A zeltener sof" (A rare ending), 21–22; "An eydes" (A witness), 17, 188–93, 237; "Barg-aruf" (Uphill), 71, 73, 74, 85–91; *Baym Dnyepr* (At the Dnieper), 13–14, 52, 25–53; "Birgerkrig" (Civil war), 16, 52, 54–58; "Dray tsentern" (Three centers), 8–9; "Geven iz nakht un gevorn iz tog" (It was night and became day), 17, 142–45; "Hinter a brenendikn shtetl" (Near a burning shtetl), 54, 58; *Mides-hadin* (The harshness of the law), 52, 62–64, 250; *Prints Ruveni*, 209; Tsvishn emigrantn" (Among immigrants), 52–54, 235
Bergson, Henri, 7, 225, 228
Birobidzhan, 67, 69–71, 73, 74, 85–91, 97, 103–4, 127, 202, 325, 330–31
Black Book, The, 120, 123, 185
Blok, Aleksandr, 238–40
Body politic, 25, 31, 41, 67, 72, 107, 246, 249, 259, 264, 281, 315, 41; body politics, 56
Borenstein, Eliot, 26
Brodsky, Joseph, 295, 296, 301, 302

Caruth, Cathy, 153, 158
Cavanagh, Clare, 60–61, 29
Chagall, Marc, 23, 250, 328, 335
Chukovsky, Kornei, 7, 207
Cinema, 98, 165–66. *See also names of specific films*

Index

Circumcision, 16, 74, 68, 75, 77, 78, 80, 83, 84, 85, 86, 89, 92, 93, 94, 95, 160, 292–93, 314, 339
Clark, Katerina, 13, 34, 80, 324
Cold War, 5, 17–18, 201, 203, 232

Daniel', Iulii, 295
Der Nister, 3, 5, 8, 9, 17, 112, 115, 138, 172, 173, 194–95, 201. Works: *Di mishpokhe Mashber* (The family Mashber), 249, 258–60, 264, 266, 269; "Has" (Hatred), 142–49; "Heshl Ansheles," 138–42, 183, 278; "Vidervuks" (Offshoots), 154, 166–69
Derrida, Jacques, 157, 158, 172, 184, 293
Dimanshtein, Semen, 70–71
Dobrenko, Evgenii, 13, 44, 153; and literature of mobilization, 115, 135–36
Dodin, Lev, 324
Donskoi, Mark: *Nepokorennye* (The unvanquished), 165–66

Efros, Abram, 7, 296
Erenburg, Il'ia, 3, 14, 17, 114–15; wartime writings, 133, 135. Works: *Black Book*, 120; *Buria* (The Storm), 121–22; *Julio Jurenito*, 120; *The Thaw* (*Ottepel'*), 213–16; "Tvorchestvo cheloveka" (The deeds of a man), 120–21
Estraikh, Gennady, 2, 6, 268
Etkind, Alexander, 321–22
Eynikayt (newspaper), 113, 117, 131, 145, 147, 151, 174, 225, 237

Fadeev, Aleksandr, 16, 56, 64, 129, 294. Works: *Razgrom* (The rout), 25, 129
Fefer, Itsik, 5, 69, 71, 73, 77, 86; Birobidzhan and, 88–89, 105, 107, 201; Second World War and, 113, 131–33, 135–37, 141–43, 147, 174–75. Works: "Di shvue" (The Oath), 131–33, 174; "Di tayge vart" (The taiga waits), 88–89; "Ikh bin a yid" (I am a Jew), 113; "Nu, iz vos" (So what), 77–78
Felix, Roziner, 207, 286, 301–4
Freud, Sigmund, 7, 214, 225, 231
Frug, Semen, 7

Gekht, Semen, 3, 9, 48–49, 66, 219, 223–24. Works: "Chelovek, kotoryi zabyl svoiu zhizn'" (The Man Who Forgot His Life), 49, 51–52; *Dolgi serdtsa* (Obligations of the Heart), 207, 219–23; "Gai Makan," 49–51; *Pouchitel'naia istoriia* (An edifying story), 95–98; "Zhena podvodnika" (The submariner's wife), 165
Gender, 6, 16, 105, 107–9, 241, 244, 274, 315; history and, 108, 241, 243; revolution and, 21, 26
German, Iurii, 125–27
Gitelman, Zvi, 4, 70, 152
Gordon, Shmuel, 202, 207, 246, 247, 249, 268–74, 276, 333
Gorenshtein, Fridrikh, 3, 207, 246, 249, 260, 274. Works: "Berdichev," 260–64; *Psalom* (The psalm), 260, 320
Gorkii, Maxim, 12, 27, 66–67, 74, 120, 210
Gornfel'd, A. G., 292, 293, 366n16
Gorshman, Shire, 3, 5, 9, 16, 68, 105–6, 109. Works: *33 noveln* (33 stories), 106; "Der driter dor" (The third generation), 276–77; *Der koyekh fun lebn* (The power of life), 275; "Hoykhe shveln" (High barriers), 107; "Ikh hob lib arumforn" (I love to travel), 218–19; *Khanes shof un rinder* (Khane's sheep and cattle), 106–7, 277–78; "Mayn ershte libe" (My first love), 275; "Vilde hopn" (Wild hops), 217–18
Granitsa (The border) [film], 69, 102–3
Grossman, Vasilii, 3, 4, 9, 15, 17, 49, 112, 115, 130, 172–73, 183–84. Works: *For a Just Cause*, 174–80, 181–83, 215; *Life and Fate*, 180–81, 184–88, 321, 324; "Stary uchitel'" (The old teacher), 17, 122–24; "Ukraine Without Jews," 173; "V gorode Berdicheva" (In the city of Berdichev), 174–75

Halkin, Shmuel, 5, 115, 145–47, 149, 202, 272, 304
Happiness, 12–13, 74, 95, 133, 210, 213, 215, 223, 234, 244
Haunting, 24, 30, 43, 53, 57, 212, 234, 235, 244, 297

Hebrew, 7, 8, 22, 52, 145, 148, 155, 169, 200, 226, 232, 273, 290, 299, 307, 312, 316, 317, 321, 343
Hebrew Bible, 3, 9, 14, 35, 37, 44, 52, 103, 170, 305, 315, 321; covenant in, 68, 75, 77, 83; in Altman, 225, 228–30; in Grossman, 172–73
Hellebust, Rolf, 34, 79, 84
History, alternative, 336, 337, 338; archeology and, 334–35; doubt about progress in, 1, 45, 59, 60, 163–64, 209, 222, 245; everyday life and, 248, 250, 278, 279; gender and, 108, 241, 243; Holocaust and, 151, 165, 201; in Soviet Union, 89, 152, 210, 225, 230, 274; literary representations of, 58, 62, 87, 320; of Jews, 27, 44, 54, 87, 96–97, 194, 202, 222, 232, 246–47, 314, 320, 321, 341; Post-Soviet, 319, 321, 322; sacred, 3–4, 15, 35, 136, 194, 230, 249, 258; trauma and, 153, 279, 321. *See also* Russian Revolution
Hitler, Adolf, 5, 1, 69, 111, 113, 117, 120, 167, 174, 175, 177, 180, 201, 245, 273, 293, 321, 324
Hofshteyn, David, 5, 7–8, 21, 23, 24, 65, 201, 203, 255
Holocaust, 6, 17, 111, 121, 158, 134, 142, 152, 158, 164, 172, 200–201, 202, 226, 237–39, 249, 273, 316, 337; as term, 112, 136, 150–54, 155, 321; Yiddish terms for, 151, 222, 321–22. *See also* Nazi genocide of Jews
Holquist, Peter, 23–24

Iampol'skii, Boris, 112, 124–25, 126, 202
Identity, 4, 28, 112–13; language choice and, 8–9, 11
Incorporation, psychic, 25, 35, 40, 142, 231
Iskateli schast'ia (Seekers of happiness) [film], 69, 103–5
Iur'ev, Oleg, 319, 337–41
Iushkevich, Semen, 7

Jakobson, Roman, 163, 325, 330, 335
Jewish Anti-Fascist Committee, 113, 117, 131, 145, 151, 178, 225, 268, 294
Jewish body, 67, 68, 72, 73, 78
Jewish literature, 1, 3, 6; definitions of, 9–11

Kabakov, Ilya, 319, 333–37
Kabbala, 66, 96
Kalinovskaia, Dina, 3, 232–34, 240–44
Kanovich, Gregorii, 7, 207, 249, 264–67
Karabchievskii, Iurii, 9, 297–300, 323
Kataev, Valentin, 68
Kaverin, Veniamin, 23, 155, 291
Kazakevich, Emmanuel, 3, 17, 74, 112, 114, 126, 127. Works: *Sholem un Khava: Roman in ferzn* (Sholem and Khave: A novel in verse), 73; *Zvezda* (The star), 127–29, 130
Khait, David, 353n20
Kipnis, Itsik, 3, 5, 202, 207, 246, 248, 249, 253–55, 265, 270, 279, 283. Works: "Babi Yar," 245; "Fun mayne togbikher" (From my diaries), 8; *Khadoshim un teg* (Months and days), 253–54; *Mayn shtetele Sloveshne* (My shtetele Sloveshne), 254; "On khokhmes, on kheshboynes" (Without thinking, without calculation), 254; *Untervegns* (On the road), 254–58; "Ven-nit-ven" (No matter when), 245
Kristeva, Julia, 34
Krutikov, Mikhail, 2, 6, 260, 262
Kuniaev, Stanislav, 296
Kvitko, Leyb, 3, 5, 24, 36–38, 52, 57, 65, 106, 201, 272, 334

Lenin, Vladimir, 5, 6, 54, 64, 66, 91, 117, 200, 231, 261
Lesovaia, Inna, 3, 207, 246, 247, 250, 251, 278–83
Levman, Shmuel, 27
Lezhnev, Abram, 25–26
Libedinskii, Iurii, 16, 23, 64. Works: *Komissary* (Commissars), 25
Libkes, Dine, 108–9
Lipkin, Semen, 3, 9, 15, 49, 207, 286, 313; as translator, 304–6, 311, 317. Works: *Dekada* (The festival), 306–7; "Imenam na plitakh" (To the names on the stones), 307; "Voennaia pesnia" (War song), 211–12
Litvakov, Moshe, 8, 10, 35–36, 78
Loss, 24, 25, 32, 35, 36, 38, 40, 55, 57, 84, 138, 142, 153, 154, 173–75, 178, 181, 184, 185, 188–93; and Soviet culture, 13–14, 26, 126,

132–33, 211; of Yiddish, 9; of memory, 110. *See also* Haunting; Mourning; Nazi genocide of Jews
Luftmentsh (person of the air), 66–67, 73, 85, 92, 96, 102, 103–4, 105, 109
Lunts, Lev, 22–23
Lyotard, Jean-François, 145, 157, 158

Mandelshtam, Osip, 2, 3, 4, 5, 9, 15, 65, 67, 207, 242–43, 286, 290, 291; time split in, 59–62, 116. Works: "Fourth Prose," 60, 292–93; "On the Nature of the Word," 59; "Nashedshii podkovku" (Horseshoe finder), 61, 206; "Sumerki svobody" (The twilight of freedom), 59; "The Word and Culture, 59–60
Markish, Perets, 2, 3, 5, 7–8, 26–27; style of, 35, 42. Works: *Brider* (Brothers), 15–16, 22, 26–36; "Dem yidishn shlakhtman" (To the Jewish soldier), 113–14, 137–38, 169; "Di kupe" (The mound), 16, 27, 30, 33–34; *Eyns af eyns* (One by one), 13, 72, 78–85; *Far folk un heymland* (For my people and homeland), 113; *Milkhome* (War), 169–72; "Say di, vos kh'ker zikh op fun zeyer brokh" (Both those, from whose death I turn away), 39–41
Markish, Shimon, 2, 123, 173, 174, 180, 187, 215, 289, 304
Masculinity, 26, 31, 41, 47, 68, 105, 107
Melikhov, Alexandr, 3, 18, 319, 325–33
Memory, 13–14, 15, 17, 39, 45, 55–56, 63, 97, 110, 138, 149, 164, 168, 169, 243–44, 248, 266; destruction of, 130, 137, 152, 177, 210, 223, 230; in Altman, 227–32; in Babel, 243; in Bergelson, 189, 192, 193; in Kalinovskaia, 243–44; in Mandel'shtam, 60–62; in Nekrasov, 217; in Sel'vinskii, 162–63; in Rubin, 234–35; in Slutskii, 115–16; language and, 154, 189; places of, 202; postmemory, 151; representation of, 212
Meyerhold, Vsevolod, 79
Mikhoels, Solomon, 2, 5, 99–102, 294
Miron, Dan, 11, 248–49
Mourning, 14, 17, 21, 23, 24, 25, 29, 36, 38, 48, 52, 82, 112, 122, 132, 133, 154, 168, 212, 231; in Grossman, 172, 175, 178, 179, 183, 184

Nakhimovsky, Alice, 177, 179
Narrative, 16; approaches to, 4, 14; foundational, 6, 16
Nationalism, 35–36, 71
Nazi genocide of Jews, 17, 111, 116, 117, 124, 135, 153, 212, 271; in Altman, 225–227; in Bergelson, 188–93, 237; in Der Nister, 138–49; in Grossman, 122–24, 173, 180–81, 184–88, 321, 324; in Kanovich, 264–65; in Lesovaia, 280, 282; in Lipkin, 304; in Markish, 169–72; in Sel'vinskii, 159–64; in Slutskii, 203–6. *See also* Holocaust
Nekrasov, Victor, 216–17
Ninth of Av, 3, 44, 54, 120, 147, 168
Nusinov, Isaac, 35, 55, 62, 294

Padenie Berlina (The fall of Berlin) [film], 210–11
Pale of Settlement, 7, 1, 23, 207, 246, 248
Palestine, 22, 69
Papernyi, Vladimir, 14, 210, 225, 268
Peretz, Y.L., 6, 248, 267
Persov, Shmuel, 5
Pogroms, 23–24
Polevoi, Boris, 134, 340
Psalm 137, 136–37

Reforging (of self), 27–28, 37, 84
Roziner, Felix, 301–3
Rubin, Rivke, 202, 206, 207, 212, 213, 233–40
Rubina, Dina, 3, 207, 286, 287, 307–11, 343
Russian Civil War, 23–24
Russian-Jewish literature, 1, 2, 5, 9–10, 127, 201, 203, 206, 287. *See also names of individual authors*
Russian Revolution, 3, 14, 17, 21–28, 31–34, 38, 40, 45–48, 58, 59–60, 62, 64, 72, 78, 84, 110, 116, 210, 223, 234, 243, 261, 285, 287, 320, 336, 338

Santer, Eric, 173–74
Second World War, 2, 4, 16–17, 111–12; litera-

ture of, 129–34. *See also* names of individual authors; Holocaust; Nazi Genocide of Jews
Seekers of Happiness (film), 16, 69, 96, 103–5
Sel'vinskii, Il'ia, 3, 154–55; time split in, 61. Works: "Ia eto videl" (I saw it), 134, 155–59; "Kandava," 17, 155, 161–65, 170; "Sud v Krasnodare" (The trial in Krasnodar), 155, 159–61
Shneer, David, 2, 152, 342
Sholem Aleichem, 2, 7, 17, 49, 66, 101, 104, 202, 225, 227, 233, 248, 251, 254, 272, 288, 336
Shternshis, Anna, 2, 4, 96, 261
Shtetl, 68, 81, 97, 96, 99, 202, 207, 224, 230, 233, 240, 248, 249, 254–58, 275–78, 283, 351, 332, 343; criticized, 7, 250, 321; destruction of, 16, 24, 30, 35, 44, 54, 82, 109, 147, 178, 181, 218, 246, 247, 264; Jews in, 28–29, 49, 69, 73, 105; persistence of, 248, 250, 251, 253, 267–74, 302; transformation of, 67, 78, 95, 98, 100, 102, 106, 253, 297. *See also* names of individual authors; *Luftmentsh*
Sicher, Efraim, 2, 43
Simonov, Konstantin, 176–77, 213
Siniavsky, Andrei, 295–96
Six-Day War, 5, 247
Slezkine, Yuri, 5, 11, 71, 247, 285–86
Slutskii, Boris, 9, 15, 17, 112, 114, 127, 132–33, 142, 149, 304, 307; time split in, 61, 116. Works: "A v obshchem" (And on the whole), 115–16; "Ia osvobozhdal Ukrainu" (I liberated Ukraine), 17, 203–6; "Ia govoril ot imeni Rossii" (I spoke in the name of Russia), 116–17; "Pro evreev" (About the Jews), 118; *Zapiski o voine* (Notes on the war), 115, 118–19
Sobol, Andrei, 21–22
Socialist realism, 5, 11–14, 67, 73–74, 80
Sollors, Werner, 9–10
Solzhenitsyn, Alexandr, 320, 321, 322, 324
Sovetish heymland (journal), 8, 199, 201, 202, 211, 225, 233, 253, 268; on Second World War, 112
Soviet culture, 1, 4, 11; and minorities, 28, 70, 72–73, 306; as imperialistic, 289; "friendship of nations," 288–89, 300
Soviet Union, 1, 3, 323–25
Soviet Yiddish, 1, 5, 6, 247
Stalin, Joseph, 5, 68, 72, 73, 74, 86, 89, 91, 105, 106, 107, 121, 126, 161, 171, 174, 175, 177, 184, 185, 201–2, 210, 211, 212, 215, 243, 247, 261, 268, 294–95, 304, 306, 321, 324, 326

Testimony, 6, 120, 122, 123, 141, 145, 149, 154, 158, 192
The Return of Neitan Bekker (*Vozvrashcheniia Neitana Bekkera*) [film], 16, 69, 98–102
Time, 3; cyclical, 25–53, 250–53; socialist "bright future," 1, 14, 65, 73, 103, 200, 206, 210, 213, 216, 319, 234, 340, 341; split in, 4, 52–53; traditional Jewish approach to, 3–4, 43–44
Train, 1, 2, 32–33, 34, 58, 78, 79, 89, 100, 187, 209, 239, 245, 272, 330, 337
Translation, 2, 5, 285; hybridity and, 291; in Soviet Empire, 285–93; of Bergelson, 53; of Gordon, 269; of Sholem Aleichem, 49; theory of, 286–87
Trauma, 15, 21, 43, 153, 156, 158, 173, 174, 176, 183, 216, 231, 278, 279, 321

Ulitskaia, Liudmila, 207, 286, 311–17

Veidlinger, Jeffrey, 2
Viner, Iuliia, 343
Viner, Meir, 12, 106
Violence, 4, 31, 57; against national minorities, 71
Vygodskii, David, 207, 289–91

White, Hayden, 194

Yiddish, 1, 2, 3, 5; in Soviet Union, 70; language, 8–9; literature, 7; Soviet shutdown of, 210. *See also* names of individual authors

Zabare, Natan, 199–200
Zuskin, Veniamin, 5, 102, 103–5, 165–66